The Reformation in England

Volume One

Wycliffe's Bible, first produced 1380-84. The restoration of the Word of God to its rightful place in the Christian Church was one of the great achievements of the Reformation. See pages 89-91.

[*Frontispiece*

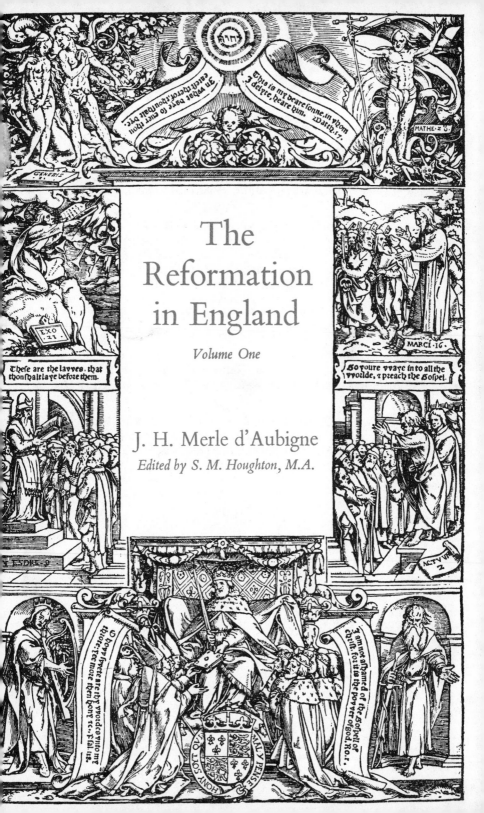

The Reformation in England

Volume One

J. H. Merle d'Aubigne

Edited by S. M. Houghton, M.A.

THE BANNER OF TRUTH TRUST
3 *Murrayfield Road, Edinburgh EH12 6EL*
P.O. Box 621, Carlisle, Pennsylvania 17013, U.S.A.

✻

First published in 1853 as Volume Five of
The History of the Reformation of the Sixteenth Century.
Translated by H. White, M.A., Ph.D.,
and carefully revised by the author.
First Banner of Truth Trust edition 1962
Reprinted 1971
Reprinted 1977

ISBN 0 85151 059 0

✻

The illustration overleaf is taken from the title page of the Coverdale
Bible, and is reproduced by courtesy of the Trustees of the British Museum

✻

This book is set in 11 on 12 point Baskerville
and printed and bound in Great Britain by
Billing & Sons Limited, Guildford, London and Worcester

Contents

BOOK ONE
England before the Reformation

CHAPTER ONE
Christ Mightier than Druid Altars and Roman Swords
(FROM 2ND TO 6TH CENTURY)

CHAPTER TWO
Iona versus Rome
(6TH & 7TH CENTURIES)

CHAPTER THREE
Rome 'Converts' Britain
(7TH CENTURY)

v

BOOK TWO
The Revival of the Church

Contents

Illustrations

Introduction

Introduction

MERLE D'AUBIGNÉ, whose work on the Reformation in England is here reprinted, was the most popular of Church historians of the nineteenth century. His *History of the Reformation* enjoyed an enormous sale. It took Protestant England by storm, and, of its kind, it must have been one of the best-sellers of the Victorian era.

Jean Henri Merle d'Aubigné was born in 1794, in the canton of Geneva, the scion of a celebrated French family. When Louis XIV revoked the Edict of Nantes (which gave protection to Protestants) in 1685, and thousands of Huguenots were driven from France, his paternal great-grandfather, Jean Louis Merle, had moved from Nîmes to Geneva. In the middle of the next century, Francis, the son of Jean Merle, married Elizabeth d'Aubigné, a descendant of the famous poet and historian, Theodore Agrippa d'Aubigné. Elizabeth's children retained her maiden name, and were all known as Merle d'Aubigné. Aime Robert, the son of Francis and Elizabeth, and the father of our historian, undertook a commercial mission to Constantinople during the troubled years following the French Revolution of 1789. Returning to Geneva by way of Vienna, he was met on the road near Zurich by a company of Russian soldiers who had recently been defeated by the French General Masséna, and cruelly murdered. At that time his second son, Jean Henri, was but five years of age. The widow survived for almost half a century longer.

Jean Henri soon displayed a liking for academic pursuits, entered the Academy of his native city (later called the University of Geneva) completed what would now be called an Arts Course, and then entered the Faculty of Theology. Unhappily the professors of the Faculty were strongly biased towards Unitarianism, and evangelical doctrine had been largely abandoned. The year was about 1816. Frédéric Monod,

3

who was a fellow student of Merle d'Aubigné, has left it on record that "Unitarianism, with all its chilling influence, and all its soul-destroying appendages, was the only doctrine taught us by our professors." "For myself," he adds, "during the four years I attended the Theological Faculty of Geneva, I did not, as part of my studies, read one single chapter of the Word of God, except a few psalms and chapters, exclusively with a view to learning Hebrew, and I did not receive one single lesson of exegesis of the Old or New Testaments."

Happily for Geneva, and, it may be added, happily too for France, there came a Scotsman to plough and sow the barren field. In 1816, as an instrument specially chosen of God for the work, there reached Geneva, without invitation from the Faculty, a theological teacher whose doctrine was identical with that of John Calvin himself. Robert Haldane, though born in London, was of Scottish descent, and in every respect a true "Scots worthy." The impact he made on the city of Geneva was so remarkable that Merle d'Aubigné in later years used to point to the apartments Haldane occupied (looking down the Lake towards Savoy and the Alps) saying, "There is the cradle of the second Genevan Reformation."

Some twenty or thirty divinity students, one of whom was d'Aubigné, responded to Haldane's invitation to meet him in his apartments, in which he had arranged chairs on both sides of a long table covered with copies of the Scriptures in French, English, German, and other modern languages, besides the Greek and Hebrew Testaments. One of the professors made it his business to pace up and down under the shady trees of the avenue at the time the students were assembling, making clear his high displeasure at their attendance, and noting their names in his pocket book.

Haldane's exposition of the Word made an ineffaceable impression on Monod, later the chief founder of the Free Churches of France, who thus records his experience: "What struck me most, and what struck us all, was Mr. Haldane's solemnity of manner. It was evident he was in earnest about our souls, and the souls of those who might be placed under our pastoral care, and such feelings were new to us. Then his meekness, the unwearying patience with which he listened to our sophisms, our ignorant objections, our attempts now and then to embarrass him by difficulties invented for the purpose, and his answers to each and all of us! But what astonished me, and made me reflect more than anything else, was his ready knowledge of the Word of God and implicit faith in its divine authority. . . . We had never seen anything like this. Even after this lapse of years, I still see presented to my mind's eye his tall and manly figure, surrounded by the students; his English Bible in his hand, wielding as his only weapon that Word which is the sword of the Spirit; satisfying every objection, removing every difficulty, answering every question by a prompt reference to various passages, by which objections, difficulties, and questions were all fairly met and conclusively answered. He never wasted his time in arguing against our so-called reasonings, but at once pointed with his finger to the Bible, adding the simple words, 'Look here—how readest thou?' 'There it stands written with the finger of God.' He was, in the full sense of the word, a living concordance. . . . He expounded to us the Epistle to the Romans which several of us had probably never read, and which none of us understood. . . . I reckon it as one of my greatest privileges to have been his interpreter . . . being almost the only one who knew English well enough to be thus honoured and employed."

Merle d'Aubigné was as deeply impressed as Monod by what he heard. "I met Robert Haldane," he said to a friend, "and heard him read from an English Bible a chapter from Romans about the natural corruption of man, a doctrine of which I had never before heard. In fact I was quite astonished to hear of man being corrupt by nature. I remember saying to Mr. Haldane, 'Now I see that doctrine in the Bible.' 'Yes,' he replied, 'but do you see it in your heart?' That was but a simple question, yet it came home to my conscience. It was the sword of the Spirit: and from that time I saw that my heart was corrupted, and knew from the Word of God that I can be saved by grace alone. So that, if Geneva gave something to Scotland at the time of the Reformation, if she communicated light to John Knox, Geneva has received something from Scotland in return in the blessed exertions of Robert Haldane."[1]

Having completed his academic course at Geneva, Merle

---

[1] The whole matter is of deep interest and should be read in Alex. Haldane's *Lives of Robert and James Haldane*, pp. 398-407.

d'Aubigné continued his studies at the Universities of Leipzig and Berlin. In the latter city he "sat at the feet" of Neander— son of a Jewish pedlar—Christian theologian and church historian, whose lectures made a deep impression on the maturing student. Unlike the historians whose interest lay chiefly in institutions, Neander's chief interest lay in persons, and he made it his aim in his study of church history to discover in it "the interpenetration of human life by the divine." It cannot be doubted that d'Aubigné's own particular genius as a historian derived from this source. The interest in persons rather than institutions which dominates the volumes of his *History* here reprinted is proof that he had been Neander's apt learner.

Even before d'Aubigné had reached Berlin, however, he had formed the project of writing the history of the Reformation. His journey from Geneva to Berlin took him through the Luther country, and he had visited Eisenach and the Castle of Wartburg, famous in the life story of the German reformer. This visit proved a life-long inspiration: and the subsequent training under Neander only confirmed the resolution to let all men know the things that God had wrought during six-teenth-century days. His study of the great reformers which now commenced did not cease until, after half a century of labour, he bequeathed to his generation and to posterity the thirteen volumes which form a major contribution to the understanding of the age of Luther, Calvin, Cranmer, and Knox.

Merle d'Aubigné's ministerial labours appropriately commenced in the Protestant Church which had been planted in Hamburg by French Huguenots fleeing from their homeland during the persecution of Louis XIV. After spending five years in the German city he was invited by William, king of the United Netherlands, to become pastor of a newly-formed French Church in Brussels. This post he held until the Revolution of 1830 which led to the separation of Belgium from Holland. Refusing an invitation to take up a tutorial post in the family of the Dutch king, and having experienced, as a friend of the king, threats against his life at the hands of irate Belgians, he felt constrained to return to Geneva where he assisted in the formation of a seminary for the training of pastors and teachers of the Word. In this he became Professor of Church History, and was shortly joined by Louis Gaussen, another member of the Haldane group of 1816, later famous as the author of an excellent treatise on the plenary inspiration of Holy Scripture. Gaussen, in 1834, became Professor of Systematic Theology. The college prospered and fulfilled a similar purpose to that in Calvin's day by sending out able, trained teachers of the Reformed Faith into a wide field of service.

Merle d'Aubigné held his post until his death in 1872. He had ample opportunity to acquaint himself not only with the main thoroughfares of Reformation history, but also with its byways. His visits to the chief libraries of Central and Western Europe led to his acquisition of a vast knowledge of the sixteenth century. Such became his fame as a historian that he was given the freedom of the city of Edinburgh and the degree of Doctor of Civil Law of the University of Oxford. He frequently visited England, being held in high honour by English evangelicals. Not a few Scotsmen would like to have secured him for a post in one of their theological colleges. On a visit to Britain in May 1862, when he was desired by Queen Victoria to preach in the Royal Chapel of St. James, he also visited the Metropolitan Tabernacle. C. H. Spurgeon purposely shortened his own discourse to allow time for d'Aubigné to speak to the vast congregation. The address was completely typical of the man, as was the story he narrated towards its close, so typical indeed that it is worthy of quotation.

"There was," he said, "in the latter part of the sixteenth century, a man in Italy who was a child of God, taught by the Spirit. His name was Aonio Paleario. He had written a book called *The Benefit of Christ's Death*. That book was destroyed in Italy, and for three centuries it was not possible to find a copy; but two or three years ago an Italian copy was found, I believe, in one of your libraries at Cambridge or Oxford, and it has been printed again. It is perhaps singular, but this man did not leave the Romish Church, as he ought to have done, but his whole heart was given to Christ. He was brought before the judge in Rome, by order of the Pope. The judge said, 'We will put to him three questions: we will ask him what is the first cause of salvation, then what is the second cause of salvation, then what is the third cause of salvation.' They thought that, in putting these three questions, he would at last be made to say something which should be to the glory of the Church of Rome. So they asked him, 'What is the first cause of salvation?' and he answered, 'CHRIST.' Then they asked him, 'What is the second cause of salvation?' and he answered, 'CHRIST.' Then they asked him, 'What is the third cause of salvation?' and he answered, 'CHRIST.' They thought he would have said, first, Christ; secondly, the Word; thirdly, the Church; but no, he said, 'CHRIST.' The first cause, Christ; the second, Christ; the third, Christ; and for that confession, which he made in Rome, he was condemned to be put to death as a martyr. My dear friends, let us think and speak like that man; let every one of us say, 'The first cause of my salvation is Christ; the second is Christ; the third is Christ. Christ and His atoning blood, Christ and His regenerating Spirit; Christ and His eternal electing grace. Christ is my only salvation. I know of nothing else."

It may be fitting to add that, some months earlier, Spurgeon had, by invitation of d'Aubigné, visited Geneva, and had preached to his great joy in Calvin's pulpit (robed in the black Genevan gown). After the service he "spent a very delightful evening with the most noted preachers of Switzerland, talking about our common Lord, and of the progress of His work in England and on the Continent." "When they bade me 'Good-bye,' " adds Spurgeon, "every one of those ministers— a hundred and fifty or perhaps two hundred of them—kissed me on both cheeks. It was rather an ordeal for me. . . ."

Merle d'Aubigné's *History of the Reformation in the Sixteenth Century* was published in Paris in five volumes between the years 1835 and 1853. This was followed by *The History of the Reformation in Europe in the time of Calvin*, a work which appeared in eight volumes between 1863 and 1878. His history of the Reformation in England is contained in various sections within these thirteen volumes. They have been extracted from the whole and are here printed together under the new title, *The Reformation in England*. Volume One of this edition[1] covers the period until the death of Cardinal Wolsey in 1530; the

[1] First published as Vol. 5 of *The History of the Reformation in the Sixteenth Century*.

second volume[1] ends with the death of Henry VIII in 1547. Unhappily the work remained incomplete on account of the author's sudden and unexpected death in 1872.

The immense popularity of Merle d'Aubigné's *History* in his own day was largely due to the fact that it was written by an expert in the field, not for fellow-experts but for the ordinary Christian public. He judged that public interest could best be stirred, not by erudite disquisitions on the intricacies of canon law and on Church institutions, but by continual stress on the personal factor in history, the emotions of the human soul, the mental strains and stresses occasioned by the impact of ancient and yet newborn truth upon minds long in bondage to Roman Catholicism, and the tortures experienced by the human spirit when the moment came for decisive action. It was this aspect of the Reformation which d'Aubigné's pen portrayed with a skill hitherto lacking in Church historians. Undue concentration on the merely legislative and political aspects of religious history leaves the human soul unmoved, whereas the graphic portrayal of souls stirred to the depths by the force of divine truth, of souls agonised by the awful tensions that can and do result from an experience of new birth in an intensely hostile ecclesiastical, not to say domestic, environment—this it was, as described by a writer able to weep with those who wept, which stirred the soul of Victorian England, and made d'Aubigné's work a potent factor in holding thousands to Protestantism and Biblical truth at a time when Rome was making a fresh effort to repair the ravages of centuries. As did Foxe the martyrologist, he wrote not so much for the scholar and the collegiate world, but for the person of scanty knowledge and non-academic bent. But his depth of scholarship enabled him to rise far above the level of a mere populariser of knowledge. A superficial reader might at times suppose that the history was itself superficial, and that, being "popular," it could not be at the same time scholarly and critical. In this, however, he would deceive himself. Normally the scholar is not the populariser, but in d'Aubigné the two roles are combined. "Art consists in concealing art" runs the ancient saying, and of this particular skill d'Aubigné was the humble master. His

[1] Taken from Vols. 4, 5 and 8 of *The History of the Reformation in Europe in the Time of Calvin.*

knowledge, based on the most extensive and prolonged research, was immense, but with it he never overloads his narrative. His terse racy style never becomes bogged in a morass of mere factual information.

That a historian should be a populariser of his theme is liable, in the eyes of the more academic type of historian, to be an unforgivable offence against all good scholarship. But it was not only in this respect that d'Aubigné departed from the generally accepted canons of historical writing. As the basis of his *History* there are two principles which are generally regarded by almost all members of the historical fraternity as forming no part of serious history, namely his conviction that the divine element in human history is essential to its true understanding and his refusal to hide from his readers his own personal faith and heart convictions. In the modern age it has become almost an axiom of the historian that he must treat his subject "scientifically," and above all impersonally, concealing to the last degree his own personal convictions, if perchance he possesses any, and writing as if possessed of neither conscience (except for the establishment of cold historical truth) nor faith. As a strictly academic exercise this method may possess its merits, but as a vehicle for the stimulation of interest in the mind of the average reader, it conspicuously fails. History, to live, must pulsate with the life of the historian. He must himself be stirred by the events on which he chooses to dilate. And it is here that d'Aubigné achieves his greatest success. He is no mere spectator from afar, dissecting, as it were, the dry bones of men of the bygone years. He lives in the age he depicts. He shares the agonies of sixteenth-century martyrs. His heart throbs and aches as he walks with confessors of the faith on the highroads of the Tudor age. He is present at their trials. He feels the heat of the flames as those who have "opened their mouths to the Lord and who cannot go back" yield themselves to fiery death. In this respect he recaptures the "living spirit" of the Tudor age, and becomes the John Foxe of the nineteenth century. "I write the history of the Reformation in its own spirit," is his claim.

The other principle likely to be held against him by secular historians is his unceasing insistence on the ever-present divine element in man's history. It might almost seem a truism to say that Reformation history cannot be understood without such insistence, but writers who fail to perceive and own the presence and work of the Spirit of God are plentiful. Sir Maurice Powicke's *Reformation in England*, first published in 1940, says, for example, that the "one definite thing which can be said about the Reformation in England is that it was an act of State." It may almost be assumed that to call it an act of God would be accounted rank historical heresy. Much historical writing is deliberately coldly factual and non-interpretative. But d'Aubigné belongs to the school of the prophets. His writing is "pregnant with celestial fire." It is his primary object to show the divine hand at work in human affairs, and this not only in respect of the spiritual movements of his period, but equally so in respect of political and ecclesiastical movements. God ruling, God overruling, God hiding His power, God openly intervening in the affairs of states and of individuals—this, to Merle d'Aubigné, is the essential stuff of history, the principal thread needful for the weaving of his tapestry. He is careful to render this point as clear as words can make it. Thus, in his preface to his first history he says, "History should be made to live with its own proper life. God is this life. God must be acknowledged—God proclaimed—in history. The history of the world should purport to be annals of the government of the supreme King. . . . Strange! this interposition of God in human affairs, which even pagans have recognised, men reared amid the grand ideas of Christianity treat as superstition. . . . The short-sighted wisdom of our boasted days is far below those heights of pagan wisdom. History has been robbed of her divine parent, and now an illegitimate child, a bold adventurer, she roams the world, not knowing whence she comes or whither she goes."

While Merle d'Aubigné laments the blindness of the secular historian, that blindness does not cause him surprise. He finds in it but the fulfilment of the apostolic word that "the natural man receiveth not the things of the Spirit of God." If the historian is but a "natural man," the spiritual interpretation of history will obviously be foolishness to him, not so much because he will not see but rather because he cannot see.

It will be well to hear d'Aubigné himself speaking on this matter, and at a time anterior to the actual beginning of his life-work as a historian. In 1832 he delivered at Geneva a

discourse on "the History of Christianity," with the history
of the Reformation particularly in view. "There are two
histories," he said; "there is what we may call 'The History
of the Church,' that is, of human institutions, forms, doctrines,
and actions; and 'The History of Christianity' which has
brought into the world, and still preserves, a new life, a life
divine, the history of the government of that King who has said,
'the words which I speak unto you are spirit and life.' . . . Most
historians have hitherto presented only the barren history of the
external church, because they themselves were only the outward
man and had scarcely even imagined the life of the spiritual
man. . . . The 'old man' sees in the field of the Church but dry
bones; the 'new man' there discerns that Spirit which blows
from the four winds, and creates for the Eternal 'an exceeding
great army.' "

The reader may expect, then, from d'Aubigné's pen a history
different in quality from that of the detached secular historian,
a history which seeks to show God as His own interpreter, and
which (to use a Lutheran phrase) aims at bringing the conscience of the reader into captivity to the Word of God. At the
same time d'Aubigné knew the potency of vivid portraiture and
picturesque narration in winning the interest and the sympathy
of the human mind, and his history acquired its reputation,
in part, because of its fine literary qualities. In this connection
the words of Principal Rainy of Edinburgh are noteworthy.
They were written in 1879: "The great quality which sustains
the popularity of d'Aubigné's history is this—that it is vivid.
It reproduces with great power the tide of human life in which
the events took shape; it sets before us the convictions, the
passions, the interests that drove men on, uttered in the
language and clothed in the colours of the time. This is not done,
as has been insidiously imputed, by efforts of idle fancy or
rhetorical amplification. It is effected by a minute study of the
physiognomy of the time, as it may be discovered in individual
men, and in specific instances; and by a sympathetic apprecia-
tion and reproduction of it, so as to bring the reader face to face
with that forgotten past. This is no cheap and vulgar way of
becoming popular. It is a great form of historical success."
And again (after speaking of the Romanism, the humanism,
and the politics of the Reformation period) "All these things

d'Aubigné conceives after the manner of a very intelligent man who has spent a thousand times more pains on the period than his readers have done, and who knows all its elements correctly and well. But one great element he knows by a perfect sympathy, an entire conviction, an unvarying attraction. He conceives it *from the inside*; it is alive for him wherever he meets it; and all his powers are spontaneously ready to reproduce it in its original truth and force."

As a historian of the Reformation, Merle d'Aubigné had the great advantage of seeing it in its full continental setting, and of having access to the multitudinous documents scattered throughout the libraries of Europe. His handling of the English story benefits from this wealth and breadth of scholarship. The *History*, as here reprinted, is not furnished with all the numerous references supplied in footnotes in the original editions. A selection has been retained, particularly those which apply to books still readily accessible—for example, the volumes of the *Parker Society* and Foxe's *Acts and Monuments*. The four chief nineteenth-century editions of Foxe's work are in eight volumes, and, very conveniently, they have the same paging, so that reference to any one edition is an easy matter. Readers who desire to track down the authority for any particular statement outside the range of the references given in the reprint should obtain access to the nineteenth-century editions of the history which contain full references.

In view of the fact that d'Aubigné makes extensive use of Foxe's *Acts and Monuments*, lest any readers should regard Foxe merely as an unreliable propagandist of Protestantism, it may be helpful here to state the present position about his degree of usefulness as a historian, and, for many of the events he narrates, a contemporary historian. Until the fourth decade of the nineteenth century, Foxe was held in high repute in all non-Romanist quarters. From 1837 onwards a school of historians, headed by S. R. Maitland, librarian at Lambeth Palace, began to pour scorn on the *Martyrology*, declaring it to be both untrustworthy and in many places plainly dishonest. In such criticisms Maitland was followed by his two "able lieutenants," J. S. Brewer and James Gairdner, and later (though in milder fashion) by Sidney Lee in the *Dictionary of National Biography*. So violent and sustained was the attack on

Foxe that not a few later historians were inclined to accept
the new school's charges as proven, and they came to regard
Foxe as a purveyor of unreliabilities. But the "debunking"
process is now over and will in all probability shortly be
forgotten. In 1940 there appeared *John Foxe and His Book* by
J. F. Mozley, which subjected the book in all its aspects to a
thorough reinvestigation. In the outcome Foxe re-emerges as a
writer of undoubted integrity and of immense value for his
own particular century; sharing, indeed, in the weaknesses of
his contemporaries as historians of earlier ages, but unrivalled
in his understanding of the Tudor scene and in his portrayal
of the Reformation story.

The testimony of C. S. Lewis, given in his *English Literature
in the Sixteenth Century* (Ox. Un. Press, 1954) runs thus: "Maitland had many successors, and the nineteenth-century tradition
represents Foxe as an unscrupulous propagandist who records
what he knows to be false, suppresses what he knows to be true,
and claims to have seen documents he has not seen. In 1940,
however, Mr. J. F. Mozley reopened the whole question and
defended Foxe's integrity, as it seems to me, with complete
success. From his examination Foxe emerges, not indeed as a
great historian, but as an honest man. For early Church history
he relies on the obvious authorities and is of very mediocre value.
For the Marian persecution his sources are usually the narratives of eyewitnesses. . . . There seems no evidence that Foxe
ever accepted what he did not himself believe or ever refused
to correct what he had written in the light of fresh evidence.
The most horrible of all his stories, the Guernsey martyr-
doms, was never refuted, though violently assailed; in some
ways the defence may be thought scarcely less damaging than
the charge. And in one respect—in his hatred of cruelty—Foxe
was impartial to a degree hardly paralleled in that age."

To what extent, the reader may ask, is the present reprint an
exact reproduction of Merle d'Aubigné's work? In answer, it
must be remarked that the work is little short of a century old,
and it would be unkind to reader and author alike to reproduce,
as originally written, any statement which has been proved by
later researchers to go beyond or fall short of truth. Historical
research has made substantial progress since d'Aubigné's day,
and this has necessitated a careful re-appraisal of all that he

wrote. Substantially, of course, the work remains unchanged, but needful amendments have been introduced wherever warranted by later findings. Footnotes inside square brackets are supplied by the reviser, and attention is occasionally drawn to books of recent days. As far as practicable, quotations have been checked against the original sources, and occasionally clarfie d. At times, the author quotes the sense rather than the exact words, and such quotations have normally been allowed to stand. In sundry places, where it was judged that a more extensive quotation from an original document than that given would enlighten the reader, this has been supplied. It is d'Aubigné's method roughly to alternate chapters of political history (to which he gives adequate attention) with chapters on the more spiritual aspects of his story. No attempt has been made to interfere with this arrangement: but one short political chapter has been omitted in its entirety, as unnecessary to the elucidation of the Reformation and as rendered somewhat obsolete by later historical writing.

It is not merely the pleasurable quality and readability of d'Aubigné's work which has led the Banner of Truth Trust to republish his account of the Reformation. Its "apologia" for so doing is that the present state of religion in England renders knowledge of the Reformation of vast spiritual importance to our people, a plain necessity for the preacher, a highly desirable acquirement for the Christian public at large. It is granted that most people can and do live quite happily without such knowledge. It is conceded, too, that knowledge of Reformation history is not for one moment to be equated with the knowledge of the Word of God itself. At the same time, however, few would dispute the claim that knowledge of more than the Word itself is good for the soul. Much of the stuff of life, spiritual as well as temporal, meets us day by day in historical garb. Controversies which still rend asunder the professing Church of Jesus Christ are only understandable in their historic setting. It was a saying of one of the most famous and respectable of ancient philosophers that "not to know what has happened in the past is always to remain a child"; and ignorance of the Reformation story tends to weaken our grasp of the spiritual verities for which the times demand unrelenting contention.

Some knowledge of history is accounted an essential part of a
c

sound education even in the secular sphere, and Scripture certainly lends strong support to the claim that certain aspects of history at least have pronounced spiritual value. Much of the divine Word is itself history, and not written merely for purposes of factual record. God's ways with men are to be vindicated. Man must be told what are the thoughts toward him of "the God of knowledge by whom actions are weighed." The Word is the critic of the thoughts and intents of the heart, and herein lies the supreme value of Bible history: it glows with divine comment. Far from being mere chronicle, it is divine judgment pronounced on the human story, so that man may be forewarned as to what will one day happen on an infinitely vaster scale at the judgment seat of God. God will judge the world in righteousness by the One whom He has ordained and raised from the dead. Of that trial and verdict Bible history is a preview and a foreshadowing.

Merle d'Aubigné, as has already been stated, was called of God to take up our national story at a period of particular spiritual importance, and to present it to view, not as a mere "act of State" but as a movement on a great scale of the Spirit of God, a work of divine initiative, a testimony of the Spirit to the truth as exemplified in the lives and deaths of many sixteenth-century men and women. Twentieth-century believers, living in days of luxury and ease, may learn in d'Aubigné's pages the story of their forerunners in the faith who loved not their lives to the death, but accounted it honour to jeopardise them, for the Son of Man's sake, in the high places of the field.

Somewhat strangely, some Christians have shown a curious unwillingness to give attention to matters historical, claiming that they possess little relevance for the Christian life. In their desire to re-establish first-century Christianity, which in itself cannot but be commended, they overleap the centuries and regard the lessons of history as unworthy of their notice. They forget that some of their choicest liberties were purchased by believers who, in the age of the Reformation, sealed their testimony with their blood: and such blood still cries to us from the ground. We are unworthy of our heritage if we turn a deaf ear to its voice.

Among our liberties is the willingness of the State to allow us to "contend earnestly for the faith once delivered to the saints," and still to claim that "the bishop of Rome hath no jurisdiction in this realm of England." Maybe we do not care to use the downright words of the Geneva Bible beloved of many Elizabethan Christians, and to assert that "the pope hath his power out of hell, and cometh thence," but we are certainly in grave danger of seeking compromise with a system which openly claims to be unchanged since days out of mind. We are prone to forget that believers of the Tudor age warned us against Romanism's "blasphemous fables and dangerous deceits." The fact is that Englishmen of today, in their easy-going attitude to all things religious, need such words to shake them out of their deep spiritual slumber and to remind them of certain things in heaven and earth which have no place in their philosophy of tolerance. That the State should not intervene in matters of religious belief, and bring no manner of pressure upon the human conscience, is a right founded on a true conception of the functions of the State; but if it is claimed, as frequently is the case, that as individuals we are to hold that one religious profession is as good as another, and that all are facets of eternal truth, no claim could be more fundamentally false. If error exists it must be opposed by truth. The two are bound to be in conflict. If masses are "dangerous deceits," the system which embodies them must be attacked by the Word of God. The sword is spiritual. If people are duped by "blasphemous fables," all right endeavours to disillusion them must be used. This is not exclusively the task of those set apart to the ministry of the Word. All true Christians are to be ministers for such a purpose. If, said Luther, a place is found to be on fire, it is not the duty of one class of citizen alone to give the alarm, but the plain responsibility of all and sundry. Thus should every Christian act according to his knowledge, opportunity, and capacity; thus should he seek to do good to his neighbour. And the aptitude of a man thus to serve the interests of the kingdom of God is augmented by his knowledge of God's acts which constitute history.

Merle d'Aubigné's stress on the content of history as something much more than "past politics" has already been mentioned. It is his glory as a historian to share with John Foxe the conviction that the rank and file of God's elect make

history just as surely as those whose names have become
household words: and with this is linked an evaluation of
events which may startle the secular historian. At times
d'Aubigné may seem to wear the mantle of the prophet, or at
least to trespass into the domain of the preacher. He would
have delighted in the pulpit saying of C. H. Spurgeon that
"when John Knox went upstairs to plead (with God) for
Scotland, it was the greatest event in Scottish history," and
would certainly have us believe that the voice of History was
the voice of God, a silver thread which might well be inter-
twined with the golden cord of the inspired Word itself.

That witness after the d'Aubigné pattern is vital today few
ardent believers will doubt. The times are out of joint. Rome
imitates in its character the unchangeableness of the Word of
God. Unrepentant, intolerant where it holds the upper hand,
it remains the chief advocate of an ancient unscriptural doctrine
in a predominantly secular and materialistic age. An archbishop pays his compliments, and a cordial visit, to its chief
representative. An ecumenical movement of considerable size,
but with very insecure doctrinal foundations, if foundations
they can be called, seeks Rome's co-operation and approval
and membership. A national church plays into Rome's hands
by the illegal reintroduction of masses, and, on the part of
those who look wistfully towards the Vatican, by secretly
believing and in some cases openly confessing that the Reformation was a tremendous mistake, the prime cause of the
divisions of Christendom. John Bunyan in his day could say of
the Pope: "He is, by reason of age, and also of the many
shrewd brushes that he met with in his younger days, grown
so crazy and stiff in his joints, that he can now do little more
than sit in his cave's mouth, grinning at pilgrims as they go by,
and biting his nails because he cannot come at them." Separated
by three hundred years from Bunyan's day, we feel that the
description is no longer valid. The Papacy is an intensely active
institution. One of its dearest ambitions is the re-conquest of
England. It pursues its aims in the language of affection. It
dangles its antiquity, its eminence, its powers, its catholicity,
in the sight of restless seeking souls. It promises soul-security
through the efficacy of its priesthood. The public press carries
its advertisements on which it lavishes considerable wealth.

Its chief functionary proclaims not only his holiness, by means of his title, but also the ancient and modern love of his church for the island kingdom. He longs to Romanize its throne. The glamour of colourful pageantry, and the claim to hold sway in this world and in the world to come, still exercise their influences on souls uninstructed in the Word and without knowledge of the past. Let the answer to "the lie" be given in the first place from Scripture and in Scriptural terms—there can be no substitute for that—but let the testimony of history too be heard. The past has a voice. History is the voice of the centuries speaking against the delusive voice of the hour. Events of the sixteenth century have lessons for us today. Reformation history is much more than a plaintive rendering of "old unhappy things and battles long ago" which have no relevance to modern life. The voices which call to us across four centuries, warning us against "blasphemous fables and dangerous deceits," and recalling us to the testimony of Scripture, are the voices of holy men of God. Let us hear their bold and faithful witness, for it has been wisely declared that "a nation which does not know its history is destined to repeat it."

The Banner of Truth Trust is confident that the present reprint deserves a wide public. It will, under God, help to stem the rising tide of Romanism, and to assist the believer to avoid the "shallows and miseries" of a Protestantism falsely so-called. It is hoped that it will be a major contribution to the religious needs of the present age, and that it will lead to the strengthening of the foundations of a wonderful God-given heritage of truth.

Rhyl, North Wales.   S. M. HOUGHTON.
15th November 1961.

BOOK ONE

England before the Reformation

CHAPTER ONE

Christ Mightier than Druid Altars and Roman Swords

(From 2nd to 6th Century)

THOSE heavenly powers which had lain dormant in the church since the first ages of Christianity, awoke from their slumber in the sixteenth century, and this awakening called the modern times into existence. The church was created anew, and from that regeneration flowed great developments of literature and science, of morality, liberty, and industry. None of these things would have existed without the Reformation. Whenever society enters upon a new era, it requires the baptism of faith. In the sixteenth century God gave to man this consecration from on high by leading him back from mere outward profession and the mechanism of works to an inward and lively faith.

This transformation was not effected without struggles—struggles which presented at first a remarkable unity. On the day of battle one and the same feeling animated every bosom: after the victory they became divided. Unity of faith indeed remained, but the difference of nationalities brought into the church a diversity of forms. Of this we are about to witness a striking example. The Reformation, which had begun its triumphal march in Germany, Switzerland, France, and several other parts of the continent, was destined to receive new strength by the conversion of a celebrated country, long known as the *Isle of Saints*. This island was to add its banner to the trophy of Protestantism, but that banner preserved its distinctive colours. When England became reformed, a puissant individualism joined its might to the great unity.

If we search for the characteristics of the British Reformation, we shall find that, beyond any other, they were social, national, and truly human. There is no people among whom the Reformation has produced to the same degree that morality and order, that liberty, public spirit, and activity, which are the very essence of a nation's greatness. Just as the papacy has degraded the Spanish peninsula, the gospel has exalted the British islands. Hence the study upon which we are entering possesses an interest peculiar to itself.

In order that this study may be useful, it should have a character of universality. To confine the history of a people within the space of a few years, or even of a century, would deprive that history of both truth and life. We might indeed have traditions, chronicles, and legends, but there would be no history. History is a wonderful organization, no part of which can be retrenched. To understand the present, we must know the past. Society, like man himself, has its infancy, youth, maturity, and old age. Ancient or Pagan society, which had spent its infancy in the East in the midst of the non-hellenic races, had its youth in the animated epoch of the Greeks, its manhood in the stern period of Roman greatness, and its old age under the decline of the empire. Modern society has passed through analogous stages: at the time of the Reformation it attained that of the full-grown man.

We shall now proceed to trace the destinies of the church in England, from the earliest times of Christianity. These long and distant preparations are one of the distinctive characteristics of its reformation. Before the sixteenth century this church had passed through two great phases.

The first was that of its formation, when Britain came within the orbit of the world-wide Gospel preaching which commenced at Jerusalem in the days of the apostles. The second phase is the story of the church's corruption and decline through its connection with Rome and the papacy. Then came the phase of the church's regeneration known to history as the Reformation.

In the second century of the Christian era vessels were frequently sailing to the savage shores of Britain from the ports of Asia Minor, Greece, Alexandria, or the Greek colonies in Gaul. Among the merchants busied in calculating the profits they could make upon the produce of the East with which their ships were laden, would occasionally be found a few pious men from the Roman province of Asia, conversing peacefully with one another about the birth, life, death, and resurrection of Jesus of Nazareth, and rejoicing at the prospect of saving by these glad tidings the pagans towards whom they were steering. It would appear that some British prisoners of war, having learnt to know Christ during their captivity, bore also to their fellow-countrymen the knowledge of this Saviour. It may be, too, that some Christian soldiers, the Corneliuses of those imperial armies whose advanced posts reached the southern parts of Scotland, desirous of more lasting conquests, may have read to the people whom they had subdued, the writings of Matthew, John, and Paul. It is of little consequence to know whether one of these first converts was, according to tradition, a prince named Lucius. It is probable that the tidings of the Son of man, crucified and raised again during the reign of the Emperor Tiberius, later spread through these islands more rapidly than the dominion of the emperors, and that before the end of the second century, Christ was worshipped by not a few beyond the wall of Hadrian. It was about A.D. 200 that Tertullian wrote thus: "Parts of Britain were inaccessible to the Romans but have yielded to Christ." In those mountains, forests, and western isles, which for centuries past the Druids had filled with their mysteries and their sacrifices, and on which the Roman eagles had never swooped, even there the Name of Christ was known and honoured.

Towards the end of the third century came the savage Diocletian persecution, which may have caused some British Christians to flee into the remote and all but inaccessible lands of the North, where, doubtless, they strengthened the hands of the few disciples already located there. The names of three of the Diocletian martyrs have survived—Alban of Verulam (St. Albans) who was executed in all probability on the hill where the abbey church of the same name now stands; Aaron, an otherwise unknown Christian; and Julius of Caerleon. We know nothing in detail about these honoured disciples of the Lord. In 305, Constantius Chlorus succeeded Diocletian in the throne of the Caesars, and shortly the persecution ended. In the fourth century, representatives of the church in Britain attended Councils on the continent, and it is more than likely that British Christians accepted as truth the creed of Athanasius which combated the heresies of the period. It is clear that the Christian faith was firmly rooted in Roman Britain before the departure of the legions early in the fifth century, but information about Christian communities beyond the Roman frontiers is scanty in the extreme.

After the extraordinary manifestations of the Holy Ghost, which had produced and distinguished the apostolic age, the church had been left to the inward power of the Word and of the Comforter. But Christians did not generally comprehend the spiritual life to which they were called. God had been pleased to give them a divine religion; and this they gradually assimilated more and more to the religions of human origin. Instead of saying, in the spirit of the gospel, the Word of God first, and through it the doctrine and the life—the doctrine and the life, and through them the forms; they said, forms first, and salvation by these forms. They began to ascribe to bishops a power which belongs only to Holy Scripture. Instead of ministers of the Word, they desired to have priests; instead of an inward sacrifice, a sacrifice offered on the altar; and costly temples instead of a living church. They began to seek in men, in ceremonies, and in holy places, what they could find only in the Word and in the lively faith of the children of God. In this manner evangelical religion gradually gave place to Catholicism, and by gradual degeneration in after-years Catholicism gave birth to Popery.

This grievous transformation took place more particularly in the East, in Africa, and in Italy. Britain was at first comparatively exempt. At the very time that the savage Picts and Scots, rushing from their heathen homes, were devastating the country, spreading terror on all sides, and reducing the people to slavery, we discover here and there some humble Christian receiving salvation not by a clerical sacramentalism, but by the work of the Holy Ghost in the heart. At the end of the fourth century we meet with an illustrious example of such conversions.

At this period, in the Christian village of Bannavern,[1] a little

---

[1] [The locality of Bannavern has been much debated. The claim that it was Kilpatrick on the Clyde is now maintained by few. Some favour the shores of the Bristol Channel. The latest conjecture, that of the Celticist Paul Grosjean, is Ravenglass in Cumberland. Professor Margaret Deanesly, in her *Pre-Conquest Church in England*, 1961, p. 37, argues that he was born in the province of Bernicia, more probably south of the Wall than in the land of the Southern Picts.]

boy, of tender heart, lively temperament, and indefatigable activity, passed the earlier days of his life. He was born about the year A.D. 385, of a British family, and was named Succat. His father was Calpurnius, deacon of the church of Bannavern, a simple-hearted pious man. Doubtless his parents endeavoured to instil into his heart the doctrines of Christianity; but Succat did not understand them. He was fond of pleasure, and delighted to be the leader of his youthful companions.

Then a terrible calamity befell him. One day as he was playing near the seashore with two of his sisters, some Irish pirates, commanded by O'Neal, carried them all three off to their boats, and sold them in Ireland to the petty chieftain of some pagan clan. Succat was sent into the fields to keep swine. It was while alone in these solitary pastures, without priest and without temple, that the young slave called to mind the Divine lessons which his pious parents had so often read to him. The faults which he had committed pressed heavily night and day upon his soul: he groaned in heart, and wept. He turned repenting towards that meek Saviour of whom his parents had so often spoken; he fell at His knees in that heathen land, and imagined he felt the arms of a father uplifting the prodigal son. Succat was then born from on high, but by an agent so spiritual and unseen that he knew not "whence it cometh or whither it goeth." The gospel was written with the finger of God on the tablets of his heart. "I was sixteen years old," said he, "and knew not the true God; but in that strange land the Lord opened my unbelieving eyes, and, although late, I called my sins to mind, and was converted with my whole heart to the Lord my God, who regarded my low estate, had pity on my youth and ignorance, and consoled me as a father consoles his children."

Such words as these from the lips of a swineherd in the green pastures of Ireland set clearly before us the Christianity which in the fourth and fifth centuries converted many souls in the British isles. In after-years, Rome established the dominion of the priest and salvation by forms, independently of the dispositions of the heart; but the primitive religion of these celebrated islands was that living Christianity whose substance is the grace of Jesus Christ, and whose power is the grace of the Holy Ghost. The herdsman from Bannavern was then undergoing those experiences which so many evangelical Christians in Britain have subsequently undergone. "The love of God increased more and more in me," said he, "with faith and the fear of His name. The Spirit urged me to such a degree that I poured forth as many as a hundred prayers in one day. And even during the night, in the forests and on the mountains where I kept my herd, the rain, and snow, and frost, and sufferings which I endured, excited me to seek after God. At that time, I felt not the indifference which now I feel: the Spirit fermented in my heart." Evangelical faith even then existed in the British islands in the person of this slave, and of some few Christians born again, like him, from on high.

Twice a captive and twice rescued, Succat, after returning to his family, felt an irresistible appeal in his heart. It was his duty to carry the gospel to those Irish pagans among whom he had found Jesus Christ. His parents and his friends endeavoured in vain to detain him; the same ardent desire pursued him in his dreams. During the silent watches of the night he fancied he heard voices calling to him from the dark forests of Erin: "Come, holy child, and walk once more among us." He awoke in tears, his breast filled with the keenest emotion. He tore himself from the arms of his parents, and rushed forth—not as heretofore with his playfellows, when he would climb the summit of some lofty hill—but with a heart full of charity in Christ. He departed: "It was not done of my own strength," said he; "it was God who overcame all."

Succat, afterwards known as Saint Patrick, and to which name, as to that of St Peter and other servants of God, many superstitions have been attached, returned to Ireland, but without visiting Rome, as an historian of the twelfth century has asserted. Ever active, prompt, and ingenious, he collected the pagan tribes in the fields by beat of drum, and then narrated to them in their own tongue the history of the Son of God. Erelong his simple recitals exercised a divine power over their rude hearts, and many souls were converted, not by external sacraments or by the worship of images, but by the preaching of the Word of God. The son of a chieftain, whom Patrick calls Benignus, learnt from him to proclaim the Gospel, and was destined to succeed him. The court bard, Dubrach Mac Valubair, no longer sang druidical hymns, but canticles addressed to Jesus Christ. Patrick was not entirely free from the errors of the time; perhaps he believed in pious miracles; but generally speaking we meet with nothing but the gospel in the earlier days of the British church.

Shortly before the evangelization of Patrick in Ireland, a Briton named Pelagius, having visited Italy, Africa, and Palestine, began to teach a strange doctrine. Desirous of making head against the moral indifference into which most of the Christians in those countries had fallen, and which would appear to have been in strong contrast with the British austerity, he denied the doctrine of original sin, extolled free-will, and maintained that, if man made use of all the powers of his nature, he would attain perfection. We do not find that he taught these opinions in his own country; but from the continent, where he disseminated them, they soon reached Britain. The British churches refused to receive this "perverse doctrine," their historian (Bede) tells us, "and to blaspheme the grace of Jesus Christ." They do not appear to have held the strict doctrine of Saint Augustine: they believed indeed that man has need of an inward change, and that this the divine power alone can effect; but they seem to have conceded something to our natural strength in the work of conversion; and Pelagius, with a good intention it would appear, went still further. However that may be, these churches, strangers to the controversy, were unacquainted with all its subtleties. Two Gaulish bishops, Germanus of Auxerre and Lupus of Troyes, came to their aid, and appear to have silenced the heretics at St Albans.

Shortly after this, events of great importance took place in Great Britain, and the light of faith disappeared in profound night. In 449, Hengist and Horsa, with their Saxon followers, being invited by the wretched inhabitants to aid them against the cruel ravages of the Picts and Scots, soon turned their swords against the people they had come to assist. Christianity was driven back with the Britons into the mountains of Wales and the wild moors of Cumberland and Cornwall. Many British families remained in the midst of the conquerors, but without exercising any religious influence over them. While the conquering races settled at Paris, Ravenna, or Toledo, gradually laid aside their paganism and savage manners, the barbarous customs of the Saxons prevailed unmoderated throughout the kingdoms of the Heptarchy, and in every quarter temples to Thor rose above the churches in which Jesus Christ had been worshipped. Gaul and the south of Europe, which still exhibited to the eyes of the barbarians the last vestiges of Roman grandeur, alone had the power of inspiring some degree of respect in the formidable invaders, and of transforming their faith. From this period, the Greeks and Latins, and even the converted Goths, looked at this island with unutterable dread. The soil, said they, is covered with serpents; the air is thick with deadly exhalations; the souls of the departed are transported thither at midnight from the shores of Gaul. Ferrymen, sons of Erebus and Night, admit these invisible shades into their boats, and listen, with a shudder, to their mysterious whisperings. England, whence light was one day to be shed over the habitable globe, was then the trysting-place of the dead. And yet the Christianity of the British isles was not to be annihilated by these barbarian invasions; it possessed a strength which rendered it capable of energetic resistance.

In one of the churches formed by Succat's preaching, there arose about two centuries after him a pious man named Columba, son of Feidlimyd, the son of Fergus. Valuing the cross of Christ more highly than the royal blood that flowed in his veins, he resolved to devote himself to the King of heaven. "I will go," said he, "and preach the Word of God in Scotland;" for the word of God and not an ecclesiastical hierarchism was then the converting agency. The grandson of Fergus communicated the zeal which animated him to the hearts of several fellow-christians. They repaired to the seashore, and cutting down the pliant branches of the osier, constructed a frail bark, which they covered with the skins of beasts. In this rude boat they embarked about the year 563, and after being driven to and fro on the ocean, the little missionary band reached the waters of the Hebrides. Columba landed near the barren rocks of Mull, to the south of the basaltic caverns of Staffa, and fixed his abode in a small island, afterwards known as Iona or Icolmkill, "the island of Columba's cell." Some Christian Culdees, driven out by the dissensions of the Picts and Scots, had already found a refuge in the same retired spot. Here the missionaries erected a chapel, whose walls, it is said, still exist among the stately ruins of a later age. Some authors have placed Columba in the first rank after the apostles. True, we do not find in him the faith of a Paul or a John; but he lived as in the sight of God; he mortified the flesh, and slept on the ground with a stone for his pillow. Amid this solemn scenery, and among customs so rude, the form of the missionary, illumined by a light from heaven, shone with love, and manifested the joy and serenity of his heart. Although subject to the same passions as ourselves, he wrestled against his weakness, and would not have one moment lost for the glory of God. He prayed and read, he wrote and taught, he preached and redeemed the time. With indefatigable activity he went from house to house, and from kingdom to kingdom. Brude, the king of the Picts, was converted, as were also many of his people; precious manuscripts were conveyed to Iona; a school of theology was founded there, in which the Word was studied; and many received through faith the salvation which is in Christ Jesus. Erelong a missionary spirit breathed over this ocean rock, so justly named "the light of the western world."

The Judaical sacerdotalism which was beginning to extend in the Christian church found no support in Iona. They had forms, but not to them did they look for life. It was the Holy Ghost, Columba maintained, that made a servant of God. When the youth of Caledonia assembled around the elders on these savage shores, or in their humble chapel, these ministers of the Lord would say to them: "The Holy Scriptures are the only rule of faith. Throw aside all merit of works, and look for salvation to the grace of God alone. Beware of a religion which consists of outward observances: it is better to keep your heart pure before God than to abstain from meats. One alone is your head, Jesus Christ. Bishops and presbyters are equal; they should be the husbands of one wife, and have their children in subjection."

The sages of Iona knew nothing of transubstantiation or of the withdrawal of the cup in the Lord's Supper, or of auricular confession, or of prayers to the dead, or tapers, or incense; they celebrated Easter on a different day from Rome; synodal assemblies regulated the affairs of the church, and the papal supremacy was unknown. The sun of the gospel shone upon these wild and distant shores. In after-years, it was the privilege

D

of Great Britain to recover with a purer lustre the same sun and the same gospel.

Iona, governed by a simple elder, had become a missionary college. It has been sometimes called a monastery, but the dwelling of the grandson of Fergus in no wise resembled the popish houses. When its youthful inmates desired to spread the knowledge of Jesus Christ, they thought not of going elsewhere in quest of episcopal ordination. Kneeling in the chapel of Icolmkill, they were set apart by the laying on of the hands of the elders: they were called *bishops*, but remained obedient to the *elder* or presbyter of Iona. They even consecrated other bishops: thus Finan laid hands upon Diuma, bishop of Middlesex. These British Christians attached great importance to the ministry; but not to one form in preference to another. Presbytery and episcopacy were with them, as with the primitive church, almost identical.[1] The religious and moral element that belongs to Christianity still predominated; the sacerdotal element, which characterizes human religions, whether among the Brahmins or elsewhere, was beginning to show itself, but in Great Britain at least it held a very subordinate station. Christianity was still a religion and not a caste. They did not require of the servant of God, as a warrant of his capacity, a long list of names succeeding one another like the beads of a rosary; they entertained serious, noble, and holy ideas of the ministry; its authority proceeded wholly from Jesus Christ its head.

The missionary fire, which Columba had kindled in a solitary island, soon spread over Great Britain. Not in Iona alone, but at Bangor (County Down) and other places, the spirit of evangelization burst out. A fondness for travelling had already become a second nature in this people. Men of God, burning with zeal, resolved to carry the evangelical torch to the continent—to the vast wilderness sprinkled here and there with barbarous and heathen tribes. They did not set forth as antagonists of Rome, for at that epoch there was no place for

[1] Somewhat later we find that neither the venerable Bede, nor Lanfranc, nor Anselm—the two last were archbishops of Canterbury—made any objection to the ordination of British bishops by plain presbyters. Bishop Munter makes this remark in his dissertation *On the Ancient British Church*, about the primitive identity of bishops and priests, and episcopal consecration. *Stud. und Krit.* an. 1833.

such antagonism; but Iona and Bangor, less illustrious than Rome in the history of nations, possessed a more lively faith than the city of the Cæsars; and that faith—unerring sign of the presence of Jesus Christ—gave those whom it inspired a right to evangelize the world, which Rome could not gainsay.

The missionary bishops of Britain accordingly set forth and traversed the Low Countries, Gaul, Switzerland, Germany, and even Italy. The free church of the Scots and Britons did more for the conversion of central Europe than the half-enslaved church of the Romans. These missionaries were not haughty and insolent like the priests of Italy; but supported themselves by the work of their hands. Columbanus (whom we must not confound with Columba) "feeling in his heart the burning of the fire which the Lord had kindled upon earth," quitted Bangor about 590 with twelve other missionaries, and carried the gospel to the Burgundians, Franks, and Swiss. He continued to preach it amidst frequent persecutions, left his disciple Gall in Helvetia, and retired to Bobbio, where he died, honouring Christian Rome, but placing the church of Jerusalem above it—exhorting it to beware of corruption, and declaring that the power would remain with it so long only as it retained the true doctrine (*recta ratio*). Thus was Britain faithful in planting the standard of Christ in the heart of Europe. We might almost imagine this unknown people to be a new Israel, and Icolmkill and Bangor to have inherited the virtues of Zion.

Yet they should have done more: they should have preached —not only to the continental heathens, to those in the north of Scotland and the distant Ireland, but also to the still pagan Saxons of England. It is true that they made several attempts; but while the Britons considered their conquerors as the enemies of God and man, and shuddered while they pronounced their name, the Saxons refused to be converted by the voice of their slaves. By neglecting this field, the Britons left room for other workmen, and thus it was that England yielded to a foreign power, beneath whose heavy yoke it long groaned in vain.

CHAPTER TWO

Iona versus Rome

(6th & 7th Centuries)

IT is matter of fact that the spiritual life had waned in Italian catholicism; and in proportion as the heavenly spirit had become weak, the lust of dominion had grown strong. The Roman metropolitans and their delegates soon became impatient to mould all Christendom to their peculiar forms.

About the end of the sixth century an eminent man filled the see of Rome. Gregory was born of senatorial family, and already on the high road to honour, when he suddenly renounced the world, and transformed the palace of his fathers into a monastery. But his ambition had only changed its object. In his view, the whole church should submit to the ecclesiastical jurisdiction of Rome. True, he rejected the title of *universal bishop* assumed by the patriarch of Constantinople; but if he desired not the name, he was not the less eager for the substance. On the borders of the West, in the island of Britain, was a Christian church independent of Rome: this must be conquered, and a favourable opportunity soon occurred.

Before his elevation to the primacy, and while he was as yet only the monk Gregory, he chanced one day to cross a market in Rome where certain foreign dealers were exposing their wares for sale. Among them he perceived some fair-haired youthful slaves, whose noble bearing attracted his attention. On drawing near them, he learned that the Anglo-Saxon nation to which they belonged had refused to receive the gospel from the Britons. When he afterwards became bishop of Rome, this crafty and energetic pontiff, "the last of the good and the first of the bad," as he has been called, determined to convert these proud conquerors, and make use of them in subduing the British church to the papacy, as he had already made use of the Frankish monarchs to reduce the Gauls. Rome has often shown herself more eager to bring Christians rather than

34

idolaters to the pope. Was it thus with Gregory? We must leave the question unanswered.

Æthelbert, king of Kent, having married a Christian princess of Frankish descent, the Roman bishop thought the conjuncture favourable for his design, and in 596 despatched a mission under the direction of one of his friends named Augustine, the prior of St Andrew's monastery at Rome. At first the missionaries recoiled from the task appointed them; but Gregory was firm. Desirous of gaining the assistance of the Frankish kings, Theodoric and Theodebert, he affected to consider them as the lords paramount of England, and commended to them the conversion of *their subjects*. Nor was this all. He claimed also the support of the powerful Brunhilda, grandmother of these two kings, and equally notorious for her treachery, her irregularities, and her crimes; and did not scruple to extol the *good works* and *godly fear* of this sixth-century Jezebel. Under such auspices the Romish mission arrived in England. The pope had made a skilful choice of his delegate. Augustine possessed even to a greater extent than Gregory himself a mixture of ambition and devotedness, of superstition and piety, of cunning and zeal. He thought that faith and holiness were less essential to the church than authority and power; and that its prerogative was not so much to save souls as to collect all the human race under the sceptre of Rome. Gregory himself was distressed at Augustine's spiritual pride, and often exhorted him to humility.

Success of that kind which popery desires soon crowned the labours of its servants. The forty-one missionaries having landed in the isle of Thanet, in the summer of 597, the king of Kent consented to receive them, but in the open air, for fear of magic. They drew up in such a manner as to produce an effect on the rude islanders. The procession was opened by a monk bearing a huge cross on which the figure of Christ was represented: his colleagues followed chanting their Latin hymns, and thus they approached the oak appointed for the place of conference. They inspired sufficient confidence in Æthelbert to gain permission to celebrate their worship in an old ruinous chapel at Durovernum (Canterbury) where British Christians had in former times adored the Saviour Christ. The king and thousands of his subjects received not long after, with certain forms, and certain Christian doctrines, the errors of the Roman pontiffs—as purgatory, for instance, which Gregory was advocating with the aid of the most absurd fables. Augustine reported the baptism of more than ten thousand pagans in one day. As yet Rome had only set her foot in Great Britain; she did not fail erelong to establish her kingdom there.

We do not wish to undervalue the religious element now placed before the Anglo-Saxons, and we can readily believe that many of the missionaries sent from Italy desired to work a Christian work. We think, too, that the Middle Ages ought to be appreciated with more equitable sentiments than have always been found in the persons who have written on that period. Man's conscience lived, spoke, and groaned during the long dominion of popery; and like a plant growing among thorns, it often succeeded in forcing a passage through the obstacles of traditionalism and hierarchy, to blossom in the quickening sun of God's grace. The Christian element is even strongly marked in some of the most eminent men of the theocracy—in Anselm for instance.

Yet as it is our task to relate the history of the struggles which took place between primitive Christianity and Roman-catholicism, we cannot forbear pointing out the superiority of the former in a religious light, while we acknowledge the superiority of the latter in a political point of view. We believe (and we shall presently have a proof of it)[1] that a visit to Iona would have taught the Anglo-Saxons much more than their frequent pilgrimages to the banks of the Tiber. Doubtless, as has been remarked, these pilgrims contemplated at Rome "the noble monuments of antiquity," but there existed at that time in the British islands—and it has been too often overlooked— a Christianity which, if not perfectly pure, was at least better than that of popery. The British church, which at the beginning of the seventh century carried faith and civilization into Burgundy, the Vosges mountains, and Switzerland, might well have spread them both over Britain. The influence of the arts, whose civilizing influence we are far from depreciating, would have come later.

But so far was the Christianity of the Britons from converting the Saxon kingdoms, that it was, alas! the Romanism of those kingdoms which was destined to conquer Britain. These

[1] In the history of Oswald, king of Northumbria.

struggles between the Roman and British churches, which fill all the seventh century, are of the highest importance to the English church, for they establish clearly its primitive liberty. They possess also great interest for the other churches of the West, as showing in the most striking characters the usurping acts by which the papacy eventually reduced them beneath its yoke.

Augustine, appointed archbishop not only of the Saxons, but of the free Britons, was settled by papal ordinance at Canterbury although it was probably intended to transfer his seat to London at the first suitable opportunity. Being at the head of a hierarchy composed of twelve bishops, he soon attempted to bring all the Christians of Britain under the Roman jurisdiction. At that time there existed at Bangor Iscoed, in North Wales about twenty-five miles south of Chester, a large Christian society, amounting to nearly three thousand individuals, collected together to work with their own hands, to study, and to pray, and from whose bosom numerous missionaries had from time to time gone forth. The president of this church was Dionoth, a faithful teacher, ready to serve all men in charity, yet firmly convinced that no one should have supremacy in the Lord's vineyard. Although one of the most influential men in the British church, he was somewhat timid and hesitating; he would yield to a certain point for the love of peace; but would never flinch from his duty. He was another apostle John, full of mildness, and yet condemning the Diotrephes, *who love to have pre-eminence among the brethren.* Augustine thus addressed him: "Acknowledge the authority of the Bishop of Rome." These are the first words of the papacy to the ancient Christians of Britain. "We desire to love all men," meekly replied the venerable Briton; "and what we do for you, we will do for him also whom you call the pope. But he is not entitled to call himself the *father of fathers*, and the only submission we can render him is that which we owe to every Christian." This was not what Augustine asked.

He was not discouraged by this first check. Proud of the pallium which Rome had sent him, and relying on the swords of the Anglo-Saxons, he convoked in 601 a general assembly of British and Saxon bishops. The meeting took place in the open air, beneath a venerable oak, near Wigornia (Worcester, or

perhaps Hereford) and here occurred the second Romish
aggression. Dionoth resisted with firmness the extravagant
pretensions of Augustine, who again summoned him to
recognize the authority of Rome. Another Briton protested
against the presumption of the Romans, who ascribed to their
consecration a virtue which they refused to that of Iona or of
the Eastern churches. The Britons, exclaimed a third, "cannot
submit either to the haughtiness of the Romans or the tyranny
of the Saxons." To no purpose did the archbishop lavish his
arguments, prayers, censures, and miracles even; the Britons
were firm. Some of them who had eaten with the Saxons while
they were as yet heathens, refused to do so now that they had
submitted to the pope. The Scots were particularly inflexible;
for one of their number, by name Dagam, would not only
take no food at the same table with the Romans, but not
even under the same roof. Thus did Augustine fail a second
time, and the independence of the British church appeared
secure.

And yet the formidable power of the popes, aided by the
sword of the conquerors, alarmed the Britons. They imagined
they saw a mysterious decree once more yoking the nations of
the earth to the triumphal car of Rome, and many left Wigornia
uneasy and sad at heart. How is it possible to save a cause,
when even its defenders begin to despair? It was not long
before they were summoned to a new council. "What is to be
done?" they explained with sorrowful forebodings. Popery was
not yet thoroughly known: it was hardly formed. The half-
enlightened consciences of these believers were a prey to the
most violent agitation. They asked themselves whether, in
rejecting this new power, they might not be rejecting God
himself. A pious Christian, who led a solitary life, had acquired
a great reputation in the surrounding district. Some of the
Britons visited him, and inquired whether they should resist
Augustine or follow him. "If he is a man of God, follow him,"
replied the hermit.—"And how shall we know that?"—"If he is
meek and humble of heart, he bears Christ's yoke; but if he is
violent and proud, he is not of God."—"What sign shall we
have of his humility?"—"If he rises from his seat when you
enter the room." Thus spoke the oracle of Britain: it would
have been better to have consulted the Holy Scriptures.

But humility is not a virtue that flourishes among Romish pontiffs and legates: they love to remain seated while others court and worship them. The British bishops entered the council-hall, and the archbishop, desirous of indicating his superiority, proudly kept his seat. Astonished at this sight, the Britons would hear no more of the authority of Rome. For the third time they said No—they knew *no other master but Christ*. Augustine, who expected to see these bishops prostrate their churches at his feet, was surprised and indignant. He had reckoned on the immediate submission of Britain, and the pope had now to learn that his missionary had deceived him. Animated by that insolent spirit which is found too often in the ministers of the Romish church, Augustine exclaimed: "If you will not receive brethren who bring you peace, you shall receive enemies who will bring you war. If you will not unite with us in showing the Saxons the way of life, you shall receive from them the stroke of death." Having thus spoken, the haughty archbishop withdrew, and occupied his last days in preparing the accomplishment of his ill-omened prophecy. Argument had failed: now for the sword!

Shortly after the death of Augustine, Æthelfrith, one of the Anglo-Saxon kings, and who was still a heathen, made war against Solomon, son of Cynan, King of Powys, the country between the Upper Severn and the Dee, and advanced towards Bangor Iscoed, the centre of British Christianity. The magnitude of the danger seemed to recall the Britons to their pristine piety: not to men, but to the Lord Himself will they turn their thoughts. Twelve hundred and fifty servants of the living God, calling to mind what are the arms of Christian warfare, after preparing themselves by fasting, met together in a retired spot to send up their prayers to God. A British chief, named Brocmail, moved by tender compassion, stationed himself near them with a few soldiers; but the cruel Æthelfrith, observing from a distance this band of kneeling Christians, demanded: "Who are these people, and what are they doing?" On being informed, he added: "They are fighting then against us, although unarmed;" and immediately he ordered his soldiers to fall upon the prostrate crowd. Almost all of them were slain. They prayed and they died. The Saxons forthwith proceeded to Bangor, the chief seat of Christian learning, and razed it to

the ground. Romanism was triumphant in England. The news
of these massacres filled the country *with weeping and great
mourning*; but the priests of Romish consecration (and the
venerable Bede, who narrates the massacre, shared their
sentiments) beheld in this cruel slaughter the accomplishment
of the prophecy of "the *holy pontiff* Augustine;"[1] and a national
tradition among the Welsh for many ages pointed to him as
the instigator of this cowardly butchery.

But while the Saxon sword appeared to have swept everything
from before the papacy, the ground trembled under its feet,
and seemed about to swallow it up. The hierarchical rather than
Christian conversions effected by the priests of Rome were so
unreal that a vast number of the new converts suddenly
returned to the worship of their idols. Eadbald, king of Kent,
was himself among them. Such reversions to paganism are not
infrequent in the history of the Romish missions. The bishops
fled into Gaul: Mellitus of London and Justus of Rochester
had already reached the continent in safety, and Laurentius,
Augustine's successor, was about to follow them. While lying in
the church where he had desired to pass the night before leaving
England, he groaned in spirit as he saw the work founded by
Augustine perishing in his hands. He saved it, says Bede, by a
miracle. The next morning he presented himself before the
king with his clothes all disordered and his body covered with
wounds. "Saint Peter," he said, "appeared to me during the
night and scourged me severely because I was about to forsake
his flock." The *scourge* was a means of moral persuasion which
Peter had forgotten in his epistles. Did Laurentius cause these
blows to be inflicted by others—or did he inflict them himself—
or is the whole account an idle dream? We should prefer
adopting the last hypothesis. The superstitious prince, excited
at the news of this supernatural intervention, eagerly acknowledged the authority of the pope, the vicar of an apostle who
so mercilessly scourged those who had the misfortune to
displease him. If the dominion of Rome had then disappeared
from England, it is probable that the Britons, regaining their
courage, and favoured in other respects by the wants which
would have been felt by the Saxons, would have recovered
from their defeat, and would have imparted their free

[1] *Bede's Ecclesiastical History of England*, Book II, Chapter 2.

Christianity to their conquerors. Now, however, the Roman bishop seemed to remain master of England, and the faith of the Britons to be crushed for ever. But it was not so. A young man, sprung from the energetic race of the Anglo-Saxon conquerors, was about to become the champion of truth and liberty, and to cause almost the whole island to be freed from the Roman yoke.

Oswald, King of Northumbria, son of the heathen and cruel Æthelfrith, had been compelled by family reverses to take refuge in Scotland, when very young, accompanied by his brother Oswiu and several other youthful chiefs. He acquired the language of the country, was instructed in the truths of Holy Writ, converted by the grace of God, and baptized into the Scottish church. He loved to sit at the feet of the elders of Iona and listen to their words. They showed him Jesus Christ going from place to place doing good, and he desired to do likewise; they told him that Christ was the only head of the church, and he promised never to acknowledge any other. Being a single-hearted, generous man, he was especially animated with tender compassion towards the poor, and would take off his own cloak to cover the nakedness of one of his brethren. Often, while mingling in the quiet assemblies of the Scottish Christians, he had desired to go as a missionary to the Anglo-Saxons. It was not long before he conceived the bold design of leading the people of Northumbria to the Saviour; but being a prince as well as a Christian, he determined to begin by reconquering the throne of his fathers. There was in this young Englishman the love of a disciple and the courage of a hero. At the head of an army, small indeed, but strong by faith in Christ, he entered Northumbria, knelt with his troops in prayer on the field of battle, and gained a signal victory over Cadwallon, King of Gwynedd, A.D. 633.

To recover the kingdom of his ancestors was only a part of his task. Oswald desired to give his people the benefits of the true faith. The Christianity taught in 625 to King Edwin and the Northumbrians by preachers from York had disappeared amidst the ravages of pagan armies. Oswald requested a missionary from the Scots who had given him asylum, and they accordingly sent one of the brethren named Corman, a pious but uncultivated and austere man. He soon returned dispirited to Iona: "The people to whom you sent me," he told the elders of that island, "are so obstinate that we must renounce all idea of changing their manners." As Aidan, one of their number, listened to this report, he said to himself: "If Thy love had been preached to this people, oh, my Saviour, many hearts would have been touched! . . . I will go and make Thee known— Thee who breakest not the bruised reed!" Then, turning to the missionary with a look of mild reproach, he added: "Brother, you have been too severe towards hearers so dull of heart. You should have given them spiritual milk to drink until they were able to receive more solid food." All eyes were fixed on the man who spoke so wisely. "Aidan is worthy of the episcopate," exclaimed the brethren of Iona; and, like Timothy, he was consecrated by the laying on of the hands of the company of elders.

Oswald received Aidan as an angel from heaven and, as the missionary was ignorant of the Saxon language, the king accompanied him everywhere, standing by his side, and interpreting his gentle discourses. The people crowded joyfully around Oswald, Aidan, and other missionaries from Scotland and Ireland, listening eagerly to the *Word of God*. The king preached by his works still more than by his words. One day during Easter, as he was about to take his seat at table, he was informed that a crowd of his subjects, driven by hunger, had collected before his palace gates. Instantly he ordered the food prepared for himself to be carried out and distributed among them; and taking the silver vessels which stood before him, he broke them in pieces and commanded his servants to divide them among the poor. He also introduced the knowledge of the Saviour to the people of Wessex, whither as overlord of all the English Kingdoms south of the Humber, he had gone to marry the king's daughter. After a reign of nine years, he died at the head of his army while repelling an invasion of the idolatrous Mercians, headed by the cruel Penda (5th August, A.D. 642). As he fell he exclaimed: "Lord, have mercy on the souls of my people!" This youthful prince has left a name dear to the churches of Great Britain.

His death did not interrupt the labours of the missionaries. Their meekness and the recollection of Oswald endeared them to all. As soon as the villagers caught sight of one on the high-road, they would throng round him, begging him to teach them the *Word of life*. The faith which the terrible Æthelfrith thought he had washed away in the blood of the worshippers of God, was re-appearing in every direction; and Rome, which once already in the days of Honorius, in the first part of the fifth century, had been forced to leave Britain, might be perhaps a second time compelled to flee to its ships from before the face of a people who asserted their liberty.

Rome 'Converts' Britain

(7th Century)

THEN uprose the papacy. If victory remained with the Britons, their church, becoming entirely free, might even in these early times head a strong opposition against the papal dominion. If, on the contrary, the last champions of liberty were defeated, centuries of slavery awaited the Christian church. We shall have to witness the struggle that took place erelong in the very palace of the Northumbrian kings.

Oswald was succeeded in Bernicia (the northern section of Northumbria) by his brother Oswiu, a prince instructed in the free doctrine of the Britons, but whose religion was all external. His heart overflowed with ambition, and he shrank from no crime that might increase his power. The throne of Deira (the southern section of Northumbria) was filled by his relation, Oswine, an amiable king, much beloved by his people. Oswiu, conceiving a deadly jealousy towards him, marched against him at the head of an army, and Oswine, desirous of avoiding bloodshed, took shelter with a chief whom he had loaded with favours. But the latter offered to lead Oswiu's soldiers to his hiding-place; and at dead of night the fugitive king was basely assassinated, one only of his servants fighting in his defence. The gentle Aidan died of sorrow at his cruel fate. Such was the first exploit of that monarch who surrendered England to the papacy. Various circumstances tended to draw Oswiu nearer Rome. He looked upon the Christian religion as a means of combining the Christian princes against the heathen Penda, and such a religion, in which expediency predominated, was not very unlike popery. And further, Oswiu's wife, Eanfled, was of the Romish communion. The private chaplain of this princess was a priest named Romanus, a man worthy of the name. He zealously maintained the rites of the Latin church, and accordingly the festival of Easter was celebrated at court twice in the year; for while the king, following the eastern rule, was joyfully commemorating the resurrection of our Lord, the queen, who adopted the Roman ritual, was keeping Palm Sunday with fasting and humiliation. Eanfled and Romanus would often converse together on the means of winning over Northumbria to the papacy. But the first step was to increase the number of its partisans, and the opportunity soon occurred.

A young Northumbrian, named Wilfrid, was one day admitted to an audience of the queen. He was a comely man, of extensive knowledge, keen wit, and enterprising character, of indefatigable activity, and insatiable ambition. In this interview he remarked to Eanfled: "The way which the Scots teach us is not perfect; I will go to Rome and learn in the very temples of the apostles." She approved of his project, and with her assistance and directions he set out for Italy. Alas! he was destined at no very distant day to chain the whole British church to the Roman see. After a stay of three years at Lyons, where the bishop, delighted at his talents, would have desired to keep him, he arrived at Rome, and immediately became on the most friendly footing with archdeacon Boniface, the pope's favourite councillor. He soon discovered that the priests of France and Italy possessed more power both in ecclesiastical and secular matters than the humble missionaries of Iona; and his thirst for honours was inflamed at the court of the pontiffs. If he should succeed in making England submit to the papacy, there was no dignity to which he might not aspire. Henceforward this was his only thought, and he had hardly returned to Northumbria before Eanfled eagerly summoned him to court. A fanatical queen, from whom he might hope everything; a king with no religious convictions, and enslaved by political interests; a pious and zealous prince, Alfred, the king's son, who was desirous of imitating his noble uncle Oswald and converting the pagans, but who had neither the discernment nor the piety of the illustrious disciple of Iona—such were the materials Wilfrid had to work upon. He saw clearly that if Rome had gained her first victory by the sword of Æthelfrith, she could only expect to gain a second by craft and management. He came to an understanding on the subject with the queen and Romanus, and having been placed about the person of the young prince, by adroit flattery he soon gained over

Alfred's mind. Then finding himself secure of two members of the royal family, he turned all his attention to Oswiu.

The elders of Iona could not shut their eyes to the dangers which threatened Northumbria. They had sent Finan to supply Aidan's place, and this bishop, consecrated by the presbyters of Iona, had witnessed the progress of popery at the court; at first humble and inoffensive, and then increasing year by year in ambition and audacity. He had openly opposed the pontiff's agents, and his frequent contests had confirmed him in the truth. He was dead, and the presbyters of the Western Isles, seeing more clearly than ever the wants of Northumbria, had sent thither bishop Colman, a simple-minded but stout-hearted man, one determined to oppose a front of adamant to the wiles of the seducers.

Yet Eanfled, Wilfrid, and Romanus were skilfully digging the mine that was to destroy the apostolic church of Britain. At first Wilfrid prepared his attack by adroit insinuations; and next declared himself openly in the king's presence. If Oswiu withdrew into his domestic circle, he there found the bigoted Eanfled, who zealously continued the work of the Roman missionary. No opportunities were neglected: in the midst of the diversions of the court, at table, and even during the chase, discussions were perpetually raised on the controverted doctrines. Men's minds became excited: the Romanists already assumed the air of conquerors; and the Britons often withdrew full of anxiety and fear. The king, placed between his wife and his faith, and wearied by these disputes, inclined first to one side, and then to the other, as if he would soon fall altogether.

The papacy had more powerful motives than ever for coveting Northumbria. Oswiu had not only usurped the throne of Deira, but after the death of the cruel Penda, who fell in battle near Leeds in 654, he had conquered his states with the exception of a portion governed by his son-in-law Peada, the son of Penda. But Peada himself having fallen in a conspiracy said to have been made by his wife, the daughter of Oswiu, the latter completed the conquest of Mercia, and thus united most of England under his sceptre. Kent alone at that time acknowledged the jurisdiction of Rome: in every other province, free ministers, protected by the kings of Northumbria, preached the gospel. This wonderfully simplified the question. If Rome gained over

Oswiu, she would gain England: if she failed, she must sooner or later leave that island altogether.

This was not all. The blood of Oswine, the premature death of Aidan, and other things besides, troubled the king's breast. He desired to appease the Deity he had offended and, not knowing that *Christ is the door*, as Holy Scripture tells us, he sought among men for a *doorkeeper* who would open to him the kingdom of heaven. He was far from being the last of those kings whom the necessity of expiating their crimes impelled towards Romish practices. The crafty Wilfrid, keeping alive both the hopes and fears of the prince, often spoke to him of Rome, and of the grace to be found there. He thought that the fruit was ripe, and that now he had only to shake the tree. "We must have a public disputation, in which the question may be settled once for all," said the queen and her advisers; "but Rome must take her part in it with as much pomp as her adversaries. Let us oppose bishop to bishop." A Saxon bishop named Agilbert, a friend of Wilfrid's, who had won the affection of the young prince Alfred, was invited by Eanfled to the conference and he duly arrived in Northumbria. Alas! poor British church, the earthen vessel is about to be dashed against the vase of iron. Britain must yield before the invading march of Rome.

On the coast of Yorkshire, at the farther extremity of a quiet bay, was situated the monastery of Streanæshalch, or Whitby, of which Hilda, a descendant of the Northumbrian royal line, was abbess. She, too, was desirous of seeing a termination of the violent disputes which had agitated the church since Wilfrid's return. On the shores of the North Sea the struggle was to be decided between Britain and Rome, between the East and the West, or, as they said then, between Saint John and Saint Peter. It was not a mere question about Easter, or certain rules of discipline, but of the great doctrine of the freedom of the church under Jesus Christ, or its enslavement under the papacy. Rome, ever domineering, desired for the second time to hold England in its grasp, not by means of the sword, but by her dogmas. With her usual cunning she concealed her enormous pretensions under secondary questions, and many superficial thinkers were deceived by this manœuvre.

The meeting took place in the monastery of Whitby. The king and his son entered first; then, on the one side, Colman,

E

with the bishops and elders of the Britons; and, on the other, bishop Agilbert, Agatho, Wilfrid, Romanus, a deacon named James, and several other priests of the Latin confession. Last of all came Hilda with her attendants, among whom was an English bishop named Cedda, one of the most active missionaries of the age. He had at first preached the Gospel in the midland districts, whence he turned his footsteps towards the Anglo-Saxons of the East and, after converting a great number of these pagans, he had returned to Finan, and, although an Englishman, had received Episcopal consecration from a bishop, who had been himself ordained by the elders of Iona. An indefatigable evangelist, he founded churches and appointed elders and deacons wherever he went. By birth an Englishman, by ordination a Scotsman, everywhere treated with respect and consideration, he appeared to be set apart as mediator in this solemn conference. His intervention could not, however, retard the victory of Rome. Alas! the primitive evangelism had gradually given way to an ecclesiasticism, coarse and rude in one place, subtle and insinuating in another. Whenever the priests were called upon to justify certain doctrines or ceremonies, instead of referring solely to the Word of God as the fountain of all light, they maintained that thus St James did at Jerusalem, St Mark at Alexandria, St John at Ephesus, or St Peter at Rome. They gave the name of *apostolical canons* to rules which the apostles had never known. They went even further than this: at Rome and in the East, ecclesiasticism represented itself to be a law of God. Some marks of this error were already beginning to appear in the Christianity of the Britons.

King Oswiu was the first to speak: "As servants of one and the same God, we hope all to enjoy the same inheritance in heaven; why then should we not have the same rule of life here below? Let us inquire which is the true one, and follow it."

"Those who sent me hither as bishop," said Colman, "and who gave me the rule which I observe, are the beloved of God. Let us beware how we despise their teaching, for it is the teaching of Columba, of the blessed evangelist John, and of the churches over which that apostle presided."

"As for us," boldly rejoined Wilfrid, for to him as to the most skilful had bishop Agilbert intrusted the defence of their cause, "our custom is that of Rome, where the holy apostles Peter and

Paul taught; we find it in Italy and Gaul, nay, it is spread over every nation. Shall the Picts and Britons, cast on these two islands on the very confines of the ocean, dare to contend against the whole world? However holy your Columba may have been, will you prefer him to the prince of the apostles, to whom Christ said, *Thou art Peter, and I will give unto thee the keys of the kingdom of heaven?*"

Wilfrid spoke with animation, and his words being skilfully adapted to his audience, began to make them waver. He had artfully substituted Columba for the apostle John, from whom the British church claimed descent, and opposed to Saint Peter a plain elder of Iona. Oswiu, whose idol was power, could not hesitate between paltry bishops and that pope of Rome who commanded the whole world. Already imagining he saw Peter at the gates of paradise, with the keys in his hand, he exclaimed with emotion: "Is it true, Colman, that these words were addressed by our Lord to Saint Peter?"—"It is true." "Can you prove that similar powers were given to your Columba?" —The bishop replied, "We cannot;" but he might have told the king: "John, whose doctrine we follow, and indeed every disciple, has received in the same sense as St Peter the power to remit sins, to bind and to loose on earth and in heaven."[1] But the knowledge of the Holy Scriptures was fading away in Iona, and the unsuspecting Colman had not observed Wilfrid's stratagem in substituting Columba for Saint John. Upon this Oswiu, delighted to yield to the continual solicitations of the queen and, above all, to find some one who would admit him into the kingdom of heaven, exclaimed: "Peter is the door-keeper, I will obey him, lest when I appear at the gate there should be no one to open it to me." The spectators, carried away by this royal confession, hastened to give in their submission to the vicar of St Peter.

Thus did Rome triumph at the Whitby conference. Oswiu forgot that the Lord had said: *I am he that openeth, and no man shutteth; and shutteth, and no man openeth.*[2] It was by ascribing to Peter the servant what belongs to Jesus Christ the master, that the papacy reduced Britain. Oswiu stretched out his hands, Rome riveted the chains, and the liberty which Oswald had given his church seemed at the last gasp.

[1] John xx. 23; Matth. xviii. 18.   [2] John x. 9; Rev. iii. 7.

Colman saw with grief and consternation Oswiu and his subjects bending their knees before the foreign priests. He did not,
however, despair of the ultimate triumph of the truth. The
apostolic faith could still find shelter in the old sanctuaries of
the British church in Scotland and Ireland. Immovable in the
doctrine he had received, and resolute to uphold Christian
liberty, Colman withdrew with those who would not bend beneath the yoke of Rome, and returned to Scotland. Thirty
Anglo-Saxons, and a great number of Britons, shook off the
dust of their feet against the tents of the Romish priests. The
hatred of popery became intensified among the remainder of
the Britons. Determined to repel its erroneous dogmas and its
illegitimate dominion, they maintained their communion with
the Eastern Church, which was more ancient than that of
Rome. They ascribed their misfortunes to a horrible conspiracy
planned by the iniquitous ambition of the foreign monks, and
the bards in their chants cursed the negligent ministers who defended not the flock of the Lord against the wolves of Rome.
But vain were their lamentations!

The Romish priests, aided by the queen, lost no time.
Wilfrid, whom Oswiu desired to reward for his triumph, was
named bishop of Northumbria, and he immediately visited
Gaul to receive episcopal consecration, at Compiègne, in due
form. He soon returned, and proceeded with singular activity
to establish the Romish doctrine in all the churches. Bishop of
a diocese extending from Edinburgh to Northampton, enriched with the goods which had belonged to divers monasteries, surrounded by a numerous train, served upon gold and
silver plate, Wilfrid congratulated himself on having espoused
the cause of the papacy; he offended every one who approached
him by his insolence, and taught England how wide was the
difference between the humble ministers of Iona and a Romish
priest. At the same time Oswiu, coming to an understanding
with the king of Kent, sent another priest named Wighard to
Rome to learn the pope's intentions respecting the church in
England, and to receive consecration as archbishop of Canterbury. There was no episcopal ordination in England worthy of
a priest! In the meanwhile Oswiu, with all the zeal of a new
convert, ceased not to repeat that "the Roman Church was the
catholic and apostolic church," and thought night and day on

the means of converting his subjects, hoping thus (says a pope) to redeem his own soul.

The arrival of this news at Rome created a great sensation. Vitalian, who then filled the papal chair, and was as insolent to his bishops as he was fawning and servile to the emperor, exclaimed with transport: "Who would not be overjoyed! a king converted to the true apostolic faith, a people that believes at last in Christ the Almighty God!" For many long years this people had believed in Christ, but they were now beginning to believe in the pope, and the pope will soon make them forget Jesus the Saviour. Vitalian wrote to Oswiu, and sent him—not copies of the Holy Scriptures (which were already becoming scarce at Rome) but—relics of the Saints Peter, John, Laurentius, Gregory, and Pancratius; and being in an especial manner desirous of rewarding Queen Eanfled, to whom with Wilfrid belonged the glory of this work, he offered her a cross, made, as he assured her, out of the chains of St Peter and St Paul. "Delay not," said the pope in conclusion, "to reduce all your island under Jesus Christ,"—or in other words, under the bishop of Rome.

The essential thing, however, was to send an archbishop from Rome to Britain; but Wighard was dead, and no one seemed willing to undertake so long a journey. There was not much zeal in the city of the pontiffs: and the pope was compelled to look out for a stranger. There happened at that time to be in Rome a man of great reputation for learning, who had come from the east, and adopted the rites and doctrines of the Latins in exchange for the knowledge he had brought them. He was pointed out to Vitalian as well qualified to be the metropolitan of England. Theodore, for such was his name, belonging by birth to the churches of Asia Minor, would be listened to by the Britons in preference to any other, when he solicited them to abandon their eastern customs. The Roman pontiff, however, fearful perhaps that he might yet entertain some leaven of his former Greek doctrines, gave him as companion, or rather as overseer, a zealous African monk named Hadrian.

Theodore began the great crusade against British Christianity, and endeavouring to show the sincerity of his conversion by his zeal, he traversed all England in company with Hadrian, everywhere imposing on the people the ecclesiastical supremacy of Rome. The superiority of character which distinguished Saint Peter, Theodore transformed into a superiority of office. For the jurisdiction of Christ and His Word, he substituted that of the bishop of Rome and of his decrees. He insisted on the necessity of ordination by bishops who, in an unbroken chain, could trace back their authority to the apostles themselves. The British still maintained the validity of their consecration; but the number was small of those who understood that pretended successors of the apostles, who sometimes carry Satan in their hearts, are not true ministers of Christ. It was forgotten that the one thing needful for the church is the Word of God and the presence of the Holy Spirit, and that just as the apostles themselves had been members only by faith in Christ, so must their successors manifest the same faith and possess the same divine Comforter.

The grand defection now began: the best were sometimes the first to yield. When Theodore met Cedda, who had been consecrated by a bishop who had himself received ordination from the elders of Iona, he said to him: "You have not been regularly ordained." Cedda, instead of standing up boldly for the truth, gave way in a carnal modesty, and replied: "I never thought myself worthy of the episcopate, and am ready to lay it down."—"No," said Theodore, "you shall remain a bishop, but I will consecrate you anew according to the catholic ritual." The British minister submitted. Rome triumphant felt herself strong enough to deny the imposition of hands of the elders of Iona, which she had hitherto recognized. The most steadfast believers took refuge in Scotland.

In this manner a church in some respects deficient, but still a church in which the spiritual element held the foremost place, was succeeded by another in which the clerical element predominated. This was soon apparent: questions of authority and precedence, hitherto unknown among the British Christians, were now of daily occurrence. Wilfrid, who had fixed his residence at York, thought that no one deserved better than he to be primate of all England; and Theodore on his part was irritated at the haughty tone assumed by this bishop. During the life of Oswiu, peace was maintained, for Wilfrid was his favourite; but erelong that prince fell ill; and, terrified by the near approach of death, he vowed that if he recovered he would make a pilgrimage to Rome and there end his days. "If you will be my guide to the city of the apostles," he said to Wiltrid, "I will give you a large sum of money." But his vow was of no avail: Oswiu died in the spring of the year 670, and his youngest brother Ecgfrith was raised to the throne. The new monarch, who had often been offended by Wilfrid's insolence, denounced this haughty prelate to the archbishop. Nothing could be more agreeable to Theodore. He assembled a council at Hertford in September, 672, before which the chief of his converts were first summoned and, presenting to them not the Holy Scripture but the *canons of the Romish church*, he received their solemn oaths: such was the religion then taught in England. But this was not all. "The diocese of our brother Wilfrid is so extensive," said the primate, "that there is room in it for four bishops." They were appointed accordingly. Wilfrid indignantly appealed from the primate and the king to the pope. "Who converted England, who, if not I? . . . and it is thus I am rewarded!" . . . Not allowing himself to be checked by the difficulties of the journey, he set out for Rome, attended by a few monks and, Pope Agatho assembling a council (679), the Englishman presented his complaint, and the pontiff declared the destitution to be illegal. Wilfrid immediately returned to England, and haughtily presented the pope's decree to the king. But Ecgfrith, who was not of a disposition to tolerate these transalpine manners, far from restoring the see, cast the prelate into prison, and did not release him until the end of the year, and then only on condition that he would immediately quit Northumbria.

Wilfrid—for we must follow even to the end of his life that remarkable man, who exercised so great an influence over the destinies of the English church—was determined to be a bishop at any cost. The kingdom of Sussex was still pagan; and the deposed prelate, whose indefatigable activity we cannot but acknowledge, formed the resolution of winning a bishopric, as other men plan the conquest of a kingdom. He arrived in Sussex during a period of famine, and having brought with him a number of nets, he taught the people the art of fishing, and thus gained their affections. Their king Æthelwalh was baptized, his subjects followed his example, and Wilfrid was placed at the head of the church.

In 685 King Ecgfrith died, and was succeeded by his brother Alfred, whom Wilfrid had brought up, a prince fond of learning and religion, and ambitious to serve his people. The ambitious Wilfrid now hastened to claim his see of York, by acquiescing in the partition imposed by the Council of Hertford; it was restored to him, and he forthwith began to plunder others to enrich himself. A council begged him to submit to the decrees of the church of England; he refused and, having lost the esteem of the king, his former pupil, he undertook, notwithstanding his advanced years, a third journey to Rome. Knowing how popes are won, he threw himself at the pontiff's feet, exclaiming that "the suppliant bishop Wilfrid, the humble slave of the servant of God, implored the favour of our most blessed lord, the pope universal." But Wilfrid was not restored to his see and spent the short remainder of his life in the midst of the riches his cupidity had so unworthily accumulated.[1]

Yet he had accomplished the task of his life: all England was subservient to the papacy. The names of *Oswiu* and of *Wilfrid* should be inscribed in letters of mourning in the annals of Great Britain. Posterity has erred in permitting them to sink into oblivion; for they were two of the most influential and energetic men that ever flourished in England. Still this very forgetfulness is not wanting in generosity. The grave in which the liberty of the church lay buried for nine centuries is the only monument—a mournful one indeed—that should perpetuate their memory.

But Scotland was still free and, to secure the definitive triumph of Rome, it was necessary to invade that virgin soil, over which the standard of the faith had floated for so many years.

Adamnan (known in Ireland as St Eunan) was then at the head of the church of Iona, the first elder of that religious house. He was virtuous and learned, but weak and somewhat vain, and his religion had little spirituality. To gain him was in the eyes of Rome to gain Scotland. A singular circumstance favoured the plans of those who desired to draw him into the papal communion. One day during a violent tempest, a ship

---

[1] [The course of events that followed Wilfrid's last visit to the pope is far from clear. Ultimately he was restored to church office in the Ripon and Hexham areas, about four years before he died in the Mercian monastery of Oundle.]

coming from the Holy Land, and on board of which was a Gaulish bishop named Arculf, was wrecked in the neighbourhood of Iona. Arculf sought asylum among the pious inhabitants of that island. Adamnan never grew tired of hearing the stranger's descriptions of Bethlehem, Jerusalem, and Golgotha, of the sun-burnt plains over which our Lord had wandered, and the cleft stone which still lay before the door of the sepulchre. The elder of Iona, who prided himself on his learning, noted down Arculf's conversation, and from it composed a description of the Holy Land. As soon as his book was completed, the desire of making these wondrous things more widely known, combined with a little vanity, and perhaps other motives, urged him to visit the court of Northumbria, where he presented his work to the pious King Alfred, who, being fond of learning and of the Christian traditions, caused a number of copies of it to be made.

Nor was this all: the Romish clergy perceived the advantage they might derive from this imprudent journey. They crowded round the elder; they showed him all the pomp of their worship, and said to him: "Will you and your friends, who live at the very extremity of the world, set yourselves in opposition to the observances of the universal church?" The nobles of the court flattered the author's self-love, and invited him to their festivities, while the king loaded him with presents. The free presbyter of Britain became a priest of Rome, and Adamnan returned to Iona to betray his church to his new masters. But it was all to no purpose: Iona would not give way. He then went to hide his shame in Ireland, where having brought a few individuals to the Romish uniformity, he took courage and revisited Scotland. But that country, still inflexible, repelled him with indignation.

When Rome found herself unable to conquer by the priest, she had recourse to the prince, and her eyes were turned to Naitam, king of the Picts. "How much more glorious it would be for you," urged the Latin priests, "to belong to the powerful church of the universal pontiff of Rome, than to a congregation superintended by miserable elders! The Romish church is a monarchy, and ought to be the church of every monarch. The Roman ceremonial accords with the pomp of royalty, and its temples are palaces." The prince was convinced by the last argument. He despatched messengers to Abbot Ceolfrith of Wearmouth, begging him to send him *architects* capable of building a church *after the Roman pattern*—of stone and not of wood. Architects, majestic porches, lofty columns, vaulted roofs, gilded altars, have often proved the most influential of Rome's missionaries. The builder's art, though in its earliest and simplest days, was more powerful than the Bible. Naitam, who, by submitting to the pope, thought himself the equal of Clovis and Clotaire, kings of the Franks, assembled the nobles of his court and the pastors of his church, and thus addressed them: "I recommend all the clergy of my kingdom to receive the tonsure of Saint Peter." Then without delay (as Bede informs us) this important revolution was accomplished by royal authority. He sent agents and letters into every province, and caused all the ministers and monks to receive the circular tonsure according to the Roman fashion. It was the mark that popery stamped, not on the forehead, but on the crown. A royal proclamation and a few clips of the scissors placed the Scots, like a flock of sheep, beneath the crook of the shepherd of the Tiber.

Iona still held out. The orders of the Pictish king, the example of his subjects, the sight of that Italian power which was devouring the earth, had shaken some few minds; but the Church still resisted the innovation. Iona was the last citadel of liberty in the western world, and popery was filled with anger at that miserable band which in its remote corner refused to bend before it. Human means appeared insufficient to conquer this rock: something more was needed, visions and miracles for example; and these Rome always finds when she wants them. One day towards the end of the seventh century, an English monk named Egbert, arriving from Ireland, appeared before the elders of Iona, who received him with their accustomed hospitality. He was a man in whom enthusiastic devotion was combined with great gentleness of heart, and he soon captured the minds of these simple believers. He spoke to them of an external unity, urging that a universality manifested under different forms was unsuited to the church of Christ. He advocated the special form of Rome and, for the truly catholic element which the Christians of Iona had thus far possessed, substituted a sectarian element. He attacked the traditions of the British church, and lavishly distributing the rich presents confided to him by the lords of Ireland and of England, he soon had reason to acknowledge the truth of the saying of the wise man: *A gift is as a precious stone in the eyes of him that hath it: whithersoever it turneth it prospereth.*

Some pious souls, however, still held out in Iona. The enthusiast Egbert—for such he appears to have been rather than an impostor—had recourse to other means. He represented himself to be a messenger from heaven: the saints themselves, said he, have commissioned me to convert Iona; and then he told the following history to the elders who stood round him. "About thirty years ago I entered the monastery of Rathmelfig in Ireland, when a terrible pestilence fell upon it, and of all the brethren the monk Eelhun and myself were left alone. Attacked by the plague, and fearing my last hour was come, I rose from my bed and crept into the chapel. There my whole body trembled at the recollection of my sins, and my face was bathed with tears. 'O God,' I exclaimed, 'suffer me not to die until I have redeemed my debt to thee by an abundance of good works.' I returned staggering to the infirmary, got into bed, and fell asleep. When I awoke, I saw Eelhun with his eyes fixed on mine. 'Brother Egbert,' said he, 'it has been revealed to me in a vision that thou shalt receive what thou hast asked.' On the following night Eelhun died and I recovered.

"Many years passed away: my repentance and my vigils did not satisfy me and, wishing to pay my debt, I resolved to go with a company of monks and preach the blessings of the gospel to the heathens of Germany. But during the night a blessed saint from heaven appeared to one of the brethren and said: 'Tell Egbert that he must go to the monasteries of Columba, for their ploughs do not plough straight, and he must put them into the right furrow.' I forbade this brother to speak of his vision, and went on board a ship bound for Germany. We were waiting for a favourable wind, when, of a sudden, in the middle of the night, a frightful tempest burst upon the vessel, and drove us on the shoals. 'For my sake this tempest is upon us,' I exclaimed in terror; 'God speaks to me as He did to Jonah;' and I ran to take refuge in my cell. At last I determined to obey the command which the holy man had brought me. I left Ireland, and came among you, in order to pay my debt by converting you. And now," continued Egbert, "make answer to the voice of heaven, and submit to Rome."

A ship thrown on shore by a storm was a frequent occurrence on those coasts, and the dream of a monk, absorbed in the plans of his brother, was nothing very unnatural. But in those times of darkness, everything appeared miraculous; phantoms and apparitions had more weight than the Word of God. Instead of detecting the emptiness of these visions by the falseness of the religion they were brought to support, the elders of Iona listened seriously to Egbert's narrative. The primitive faith planted on the rock of Icolmkill was now like a pine-tree tossed by the winds: but one gust, and it would be uprooted and blown into the sea. Egbert, perceiving the elders to be shaken, redoubled his prayers, and even had recourse to threats. "All the west," said he, "bends the knee to Rome: alone against all, what can you do?" The Scots still resisted: obscure and unknown, the last British Christians contended in behalf of expiring liberty. At length bewildered—they stumbled and fell. The scissors were brought; they received the Latin tonsure—they were the pope's.

Thus fell Scotland. Yet there still remained some sparks of grace, and the mountains of Caledonia long concealed the hidden fire which after many ages burst forth with such power and might. Here and there a few independent spirits were to be found who testified against the tyranny of Rome. In the time of Bede they might be seen "halting in their paths" (to use the words of the Romish historian) refusing to join in the holidays of the pontifical adherents and pushing away the hands that were eager to shave their crowns. But the leaders of the state and of the church had laid down their arms. The contest was over, after lasting more than a century. British Christianity had in some degree prepared its own fall, by substituting too often the form for the faith. The foreign superstition took advantage of this weakness, and triumphed in these islands by means of royal decrees, church ornaments, monkish phantoms, and conventual apparitions. At the beginning of the eighth century the British Church became the serf of Rome; but an internal struggle was commencing, which did not cease until the period of the Reformation.

CHAPTER FOUR

The Conflict with Papal Supremacy

(7th to 11th Century)

THE independent Christians of Scotland, who subordinated
the authority of man to that of God, were filled with
sorrow as they beheld these backslidings: and it was this
no doubt which induced many to leave their homes and fight
in the very heart of Europe in behalf of that Christian liberty
which had just expired among themselves.

At the commencement of the eighth century a great idea
took possession of a pious doctor of the Scottish church named
Clement. The *work of God* is the very essence of Christianity,
thought he, and this work must be defended against all the
encroachments of man. To human traditionalism he opposed
the sole authority of the Word of God; to clerical materialism,
a church which is the assembly of the saints; and to Pelagianism, the sovereignty of grace. He was a man of decided
character and firm faith, but without fanaticism; his heart was
open to the holiest emotions of our nature; he was a husband
and a father. He quitted Scotland and travelled among the
Franks, everywhere scattering the seeds of the faith. It happened
unfortunately that a man of kindred energy, Winifrid or
Boniface of Wessex (680-754), was planting the pontifical
Christianity in the same regions. This great missionary, who
possessed in an essential degree the faculty of organization,
aimed at external unity above all things and, when he had
taken the oath of fidelity to Gregory II, he had received from
that pope a collection of the Roman laws. Boniface, henceforth
a docile disciple or rather a fanatical champion of Rome,
supported on the one hand by the pontiff, and on the other
by Charles Martel, ruler of the Franks, had preached to the
people of Germany, among some undoubted Christian truths,
the doctrine of tithes and of papal supremacy. The Englishman
and the Scotsman, representatives of two great systems, were
about to engage in deadly combat in the heart of Europe

—in a combat whose consequences might be incalculable.

Alarmed at the progress made by Clement's evangelical doctrines, Boniface, archbishop of the German churches, undertook to oppose them. At first he confronted the Scotsman with the laws of the Roman church; but the latter denied the authority of these ecclesiastical canons, and refuted their contents. Boniface then put forward the decisions of various councils; but Clement replied that if the decisions of the councils were contrary to Holy Scripture, they had no authority over Christians. The archbishop, astonished at such audacity, next had recourse to the writings of the most illustrious fathers of the Latin church, quoting Jerome, Augustine, and Gregory; but the Scotsman told him that, instead of submitting to the word of men, he would obey the Word of God alone. Boniface with indignation now introduced the Catholic church which, by its priests and bishops, all united to the pope, formed an invincible unity; but to his great surprise his opponent maintained that there only, where the Holy Spirit dwells, can be found the spouse of Jesus Christ. Vainly did the archbishop express his horror; Clement was not to be turned aside from his great idea, either by the clamours of the followers of Rome, or by the imprudent attacks made on the papacy by other Christian ministers.

Rome had, indeed, other adversaries. A Gallic bishop named Adalbert, with whom Boniface affected to associate Clement, one day saw the archbishop complacently exhibiting to the people some relics of St Peter which he had brought from Rome; and being desirous of showing the ridiculous character of these Romish practices, he distributed among the bystanders his own hair and nails, praying them to pay these the same honours as Boniface claimed for the relics of the papacy. Clement smiled, like many others, at Adalbert's singular argument; but it was not with such arms that he was wont to fight. Gifted with profound discernment, he had remarked that the authority of man substituted for the authority of God was the source of all the errors of Romanism. At the same time he maintained on predestination what the archbishop called "horrible doctrines, contrary to the Catholic faith." Clement's character inclines us to believe that he was favourable to the doctrine of predestination. A century later the pious Gottschalk

was persecuted by one of Boniface's successors for holding this
very doctrine of Augustine's. Thus then did a Scotsman, the
representative of the ancient faith of his country, withstand
almost unaided in the centre of Europe the invasion of the
Romans. But he was not long alone: the nobility especially,
more enlightened than the common people, thronged around
him. If Clement had succeeded, a Christian church would have
been founded on the continent independent of the papacy.

Boniface was confounded. He wished to do in central Europe
what his fellow-countryman Wilfrid had done in England;
and, at the very moment he fancied he was advancing from
triumph to triumph, victory escaped from his hands. He turned
against this new enemy and, applying to Charles Martel's sons,
Pepin and Carloman, he obtained their consent to the assembling of a council before which he summoned Clement to appear.

The bishops, counts, and other notabilities having met at
Soissons on the 2nd March 744, Boniface accused the Scotsman of despising the laws of Rome, the councils, and the
fathers; attacked his marriage, which he called an adulterous
union, and called in question some secondary points of doctrine.
Clement was accordingly excommunicated by Boniface, at
once his adversary, accuser, and judge, and thrown into prison,
with the approbation of the pope and the king of the Franks.

The Scotsman's cause was everywhere taken up; accusa-
tions were brought against the German primate, his persecuting
spirit was severely condemned, and his exertions for the
triumph of the papacy were resisted. Carloman yielded to this
unanimous movement. The prison doors were opened, and
Clement had hardly crossed the threshold before he began to
protest boldly against human authority in matters of faith: the
Word of God is the only rule. Upon this Boniface applied to
Rome for the heretic's condemnation, and accompanied his
request by a silver cup and a garment of delicate texture. The
pope decided in synod that if Clement did not retract his
errors, he should be delivered up to everlasting damnation, and
then requested Boniface to send him to Rome under a sure
guard. We here lose all traces of the Scotsman, but it is easy
to conjecture what must have been his fate.

Clement was not the only Briton who became distinguished
in this contest. Two fellow-countrymen, Sampson and Virgil,

who preached in central Europe, were in like manner persecuted by the Church of Rome. Virgil, one of the most learned
men of his age, anticipating Galileo, and believing in the
existence of the antipodes, dared maintain that there were other
men and another world beneath our feet. He was denounced by
Boniface for this *heresy*, and condemned by the pope, as were
other Britons for the apostolical simplicity of their lives. In
813, certain Scotsmen who called themselves bishops, says a
canon, having appeared before a council of the Roman church
at Châlons, were rejected by the French prelates, because, like
St Paul, *they worked with their own hands*. Those enlightened and
faithful men were superior to their time: Boniface and his
ecclesiastical materialism were better fitted for an age in which
clerical forms were regarded as the substance of religion!

Even Britain, although its light was not so pure, was not
altogether plunged in darkness. The Anglo-Saxons imprinted
on their church certain characteristics which distinguished it
from that of Rome; several books of the Bible were translated
into their tongue, and daring spirits on the one hand, with some
pious souls on the other, laboured in a direction hostile to popery.

At first we see the dawning of that philosophic rationalism,
which gives out a certain degree of brightness, but which can
neither conquer error nor still less establish truth. In the ninth
century there was a learned scholar in Ireland, who afterwards
settled at the court of Charles the Bald. He was a strange
mysterious man, of profound thought, and as much raised
above the doctors of his age by the boldness of his ideas, as
Charlemagne above the princes of his day by the force of his
will. John Scot Erigena—that is, 'born in the Isle of Saints'
(Ireland)—was a meteor in the theological heavens. With a
great philosophic genius he combined a cheerful jesting
disposition. One day, while seated at table opposite to Charles
the Bald, the latter archly inquired of him: "What is the
distance between a *Scot* and a *sot*?" "The width of the table,"
was his ready answer, which drew a smile from the king.
While the doctrine of Bede, Boniface, and even Alcuin was
traditional, servile, and, in one word, Romanist, that of Scot
was mystical, philosophic, free, and daring. He sought for the
truth not in the Word or in the Church, but in himself:—"The
knowledge of ourselves is the true source of religious wisdom.

Every creature is a theophany—a manifestation of God; since revelation presupposes the existence of truth, it is this truth, which is above revelation, with which man must set himself in immediate relation, leaving him at liberty to show afterwards its harmony with Scripture and the other theophanies. We must first employ reason, and then authority. Authority proceeds from reason, and not reason from authority." Yet this bold thinker, when on his knees, could give way to aspirations full of piety: "O Lord Jesus," exclaimed he, "I ask no other happiness of Thee, but to understand, unmixed with deceitful theories, the word that Thou hast inspired by Thy Holy Spirit! Show Thyself to those who ask for Thee alone!" But while Scot rejected on the one hand certain traditional errors, and in particular the doctrine of transubstantiation which was creeping into the church, he was near falling as regards God and the world into other errors savouring of pantheism. The philosophic rationalism of this contemporary of Charles the Bald—the strange product of one of the obscurest periods of history (850)—was destined after the lapse of many centuries to be taught once more in Britain as a modern invention of the most enlightened age.

While Scot was thus plumbing the depths of philosophy, others were examining their Bibles; and if thick darkness had not spread over these first glimpses of the dawn, perhaps the Church of Britain might even then have begun to labour for the regeneration of Christendom. A youthful prince, thirsting for intellectual enjoyments, for domestic happiness, and for the Word of God, and who sought, by frequent prayer, for deliverance from the bondage of sin, had ascended the throne of Wessex, in the year 871. Alfred being convinced that Christianity alone could rightly mould a nation, assembled round him the most learned men from all parts of Europe, and was anxious that the English, like the Hebrews, Greeks, and Latins, should possess the Holy Scripture in their own language. He is the real patron of the biblical work, which indeed constitutes one of his chief titles to fame. After having fought numerous campaigns and battles by land and sea, he died while translating the Psalms of David for his subjects.[1]

[1] [An Anglo-Saxon version of the first fifty psalms has been attributed to Alfred. There is no absolute proof that the work is his but the ascription is reasonably certain.]

F

After this gleam of light thick darkness once more settled upon Britain. Nine Anglo-Saxon kings ended their days in monasteries; there was a seminary in Rome from which every year fresh scholars bore to England the new forms of popery; the celibacy of priests, that cement of the Romish hierarchy, was re-affirmed by a bull about the close of the tenth century; convents were multiplied, considerable possessions were bestowed on the Church, and the tax of *Peter's pence*, laid at the pontiff's feet, proclaimed the triumph of the papal system. But a reaction took place: England collected her forces for a war against the papacy—a war at one time secular and at another spiritual. William of Normandy, Edward III, Wycliffe, and the Reformation, are the four ascending steps of protestantism in England.

William of Normandy, a proud, enterprising, and far-sighted prince, the illegitimate son of a peasant girl of Falaise and Robert the Devil, duke of Normandy, began a contest with the papacy which lasted until the Reformation. After defeating the Saxons at Hastings in A.D. 1066, he took possession of England, under the benediction of the Roman pontiff. But the conquered country was destined to conquer its master. William, who had invaded England in the pope's name, had no sooner touched the soil of his new kingdom, than he learned to resist Rome, as if the ancient liberty of the British Church had revived in him. Being firmly resolved to allow no foreign prince or prelate to possess in his dominions a jurisdiction independent of his own, he made preparations for a conquest far more difficult than that of the Anglo-Saxon kingdom. The papacy itself furnished him with weapons. The Roman legates prevailed on the king to dispossess the English episcopacy in a mass, and this was exactly what he wished. To resist the papacy, William desired to be sure of the submission of the priests of England. Stigand, archbishop of Canterbury, was removed, and Lanfranc of Pavia, who had been summoned from Bec in Normandy to fill his place, was commissioned by the Conqueror to bend the clergy to obedience. This prelate, who was regular in his life, abundant in almsgiving, a learned disputant, a prudent politician, and a skilful mediator, finding that he had to choose between his master King William and his friend the pontiff Hildebrand, gave the prince the preference.

He refused to go to Rome, notwithstanding the threats of the pope, and applied himself resolutely to the work the king had intrusted to him. The Saxons sometimes resisted the Normans, as the Britons had resisted the Saxons; but the second struggle was less glorious than the first. A synod at which the king was present having met in the abbey of Westminster, William commanded Wulfstan, bishop of Worcester, to give up his crosier to him. The old man rose and animatedly cried: "O king, from a better man than you I received it, and to him only will I return it." Unhappily this "better man" was not Jesus Christ. Then, approaching the tomb of Edward the Confessor, and addressing the deceased monarch, he continued: "O my master, it was you who compelled me to assume this office; but now behold a new king and a new primate who promulgate new laws. Not unto them, O master, but unto you, do I resign my crosier and the care of my flock." With these words Wulfstan laid his pastoral staff on Edward's tomb. On the sepulchre of the Confessor perished the liberty of the Anglo-Saxon hierarchy. The deprived Saxon bishops were consigned to fortresses or shut up in monasteries.

The Conqueror, being thus assured of the obedience of the bishops, put forward the supremacy of the sword in opposition to that of the pope. He nominated directly to all vacant ecclesiastical offices, filled his treasury with the riches of the churches, required that all priests should make oath to him, forbade them to excommunicate his officers without his consent, not even for incest, and declared that all synodal decisions must be countersigned by him. "I claim," said he to the archbishop one day, raising his arm towards heaven, "I claim to hold in this hand all the pastoral staffs in my kingdom." Lanfranc was astonished at this daring speech, but prudently kept silent, for a time at least. Episcopacy connived at the royal pretensions.

Would Hildebrand (Gregory VII) the most inflexible of popes, bend before William? The king was earnest in his desire to enslave the Church to the State; the pope to enslave the State to the Church: the collision of these two mighty champions threatened to be terrible. But the haughtiest of pontiffs was seen to yield as soon as he felt the mail-clad hand of the Conqueror, and to shrink unresistingly before it. The pope filled all Christendom with confusion, that he might deprive princes of the right of investiture to ecclesiastical dignities: William would not permit him to interfere with that question in England, and Hildebrand submitted. The king went even farther: the pope, wishing to enslave the clergy, deprived the priests of their lawful wives; William got a decree passed by the council of Winchester in 1076 to the effect that the married priests living in castles and towns should not be compelled to put away their wives. This was too much: Hildebrand summoned Lanfranc to Rome, but William forbade him to go. "Never did king, not even a pagan," exclaimed Gregory, "attempt against the holy see what this man does not fear to carry out!" To console himself, he demanded payment of the *Peter's pence*, and an oath of fidelity. William sent the money, but refused the homage; and when Hildebrand saw the tribute which the king had paid, he said bitterly: "What value can I set on money which is contributed with so little honour!" William forbade his clergy to recognize a pope, or to publish a bull without the royal approbation, which did not prevent Hildebrand from styling him "the pearl of princes." "It is true," said he to his legate, "that the English king does not behave in certain matters so religiously as we could desire. . . . Yet beware of exasperating him. . . . We shall win him over to God and St Peter more surely by mildness and reason than by strictness or severity." In this manner the pope acted like the archbishop—*siluit*: he was silent. It is for feeble governments that Rome reserves her energies.

The Norman kings, desirous of strengthening their work, constructed Gothic cathedrals in the room of wooden churches, in which they installed their soldier-bishops, as if they were strong fortresses. Instead of the moral power and the humble crook of the shepherd, they gave them secular power and a staff. The religious episcopate was succeeded by a political one. William Rufus went to even greater lengths than his father. Taking advantage of the schism which divided the papacy, he did without a pope for ten years, leaving abbeys, bishoprics, and even Canterbury vacant, and scandalously squandering their revenues. Cæsaropapia (which transforms a king into a pope) having thus attained its greatest excess, a sacerdotal reaction could not fail to take place.

CHAPTER FIVE

The Iron Age of Spiritual Slavery

(11th to 13th Century)

W E are now entering upon a new phase of history. Romanism was on the point of triumphing by the exertions of learned men, energetic prelates, and princes in whom extreme imprudence was joined with extreme servility. This was the era of the dominion of popery, and we shall see it unscrupulously employing the despotism by which it is characterized.

A malady having occasioned some degree of remorse in William Rufus, he consented to fill up the vacancy in the archiepiscopal see. And now Anselm first appears in England. He was born in an Alpine valley, at the town of Aosta in Piedmont. Imbibing the instructions of his pious mother Ermenberga, and believing that God's throne was placed on the summit of the gigantic mountains, he saw rising around him, the child Anselm climbed them in his dreams, and received the bread of heaven from the hands of the Lord. Unhappily in after-years he recognized another throne in the church of Christ, and bowed his head before the chair of St Peter. In 1078 he became Abbot of Bec in Normandy. This was the man whom William II summoned in 1093 to fill the primacy of Canterbury. Anselm, who was then sixty years old, refused at first: the character of Rufus terrified him. "The church of England," said he, "is a plough that ought to be drawn by two oxen of equal strength. How can you yoke together an old and timid sheep like me and that wild bull?" At length he accepted and, concealing a mind of great power under an appearance of humility, he had hardly arrived in England before he recognized Pope Urban II (against the Imperial anti-Pope Wibert whom the king supported), demanded the estates of his see which the treasury had seized upon, refused to pay the king the sums he demanded, contested the right of investiture against Henry I, forbade all ecclesiastics to take the feudal oath, and determined that the priests should forthwith put away their wives. Scholasticism,[1] of which Anselm was one of the earlier representatives, freed the church from the yoke of royalty, but only to chain it to the papal chair. The fetters were about to be riveted by a still more energetic hand; and what this great theologian had begun, a great worldling was to carry on.

At the hunting parties of Henry II a man attracted the attention of his sovereign by his air of frankness, agreeable manners, witty conversation, and exuberant vivacity. This was Thomas Becket, born in 1118 of middle-class Norman parents. Being both priest and soldier, he was appointed at the same time by the king prebend of Hastings and governor of the Tower. When nominated chancellor of England in 1155, he showed himself no less expert than Wilfrid in misappropriating the wealth of the minors in his charge, and of the abbeys and bishoprics, and indulged in the most extravagant luxury. Henry, the first of the Plantagenets, a young inexperienced king of twenty-two, having noticed Becket's zeal in upholding the prerogatives of the crown, in 1162 appointed him archbishop of Canterbury. "Now, sire," remarked the primate, with a smile, "when I shall have to choose between God's favour and yours, remember it is yours that I shall sacrifice."

Becket, who, as keeper of the seals, had been the most magnificent of courtiers, affected as archbishop to be the most venerable of saints. He resigned the chancellorship, assumed the robe of a monk, wore sackcloth filled with vermin, lived on the plainest food, every day knelt down to wash the feet of the poor, paced the cloisters of his cathedral with tearful eyes, and spent hours in prayer before the altar. As champion of the priests, even in their crimes, he took under his protection one who to the crime of seduction had added the murder of his victim's father.

The judges having represented to Henry that during the first eight years of his reign a hundred murders had been committed by ecclesiastics, the king in 1164 summoned a council at Clarendon, in which certain regulations or *Con-*

[[Scholasticism, a form of Mediaevalism, was a method of systematizing and expounding religious doctrines according to the rules of logic laid down by Aristotle.]

stitutions were drawn up, with the object of preventing the encroachments of the hierarchy. Becket at first refused to sign them, but at length consented, and then withdrew into solitary retirement to mourn over his fault. Pope Alexander III released him from his oath of consent; and then began a fierce and long struggle between the king and the primate. Finally, four knights of the court, catching up a hasty expression of their master's, barbarously murdered the archbishop at the foot of the altar in his own cathedral church in the afternoon of 27 December, 1170. The people looked upon Becket as a saint: immense crowds came to pray at his tomb, at which it was said that many miracles were worked. "Even from his grave," said Becket's partisans, "he renders his testimony in behalf of the papacy."

Henry now passed from one extreme to the other. He entered Canterbury barefooted, and prostrated himself before the martyr's tomb: the bishops, priests, and monks, to the number of eighty, passed before him, each bearing a scourge, and struck three or five blows according to their rank on the naked shoulders of the king. In former ages, so the priestly fable ran, Saint Peter had scourged an archbishop of Canterbury: now Rome in sober reality scourges the back of royalty, and nothing can henceforward check her victorious career. A Plantagenet surrendered England to the pope, and the pope gave him authority to subdue Ireland.

Rome, who had set her foot on the neck of a king, was destined under one of the sons of Henry II to set it on the neck of England. King John being unwilling to acknowledge an archbishop of Canterbury illegally nominated by Pope Innocent III, the latter, more daring than Hildebrand, laid the kingdom under an interdict (1208). Many of the higher clergy fled from England to escape the king's wrath. Five years later, as John still remained obdurate, the Pope moved Philip Augustus, King of France, to invade and rule England. John thereupon decided to submit. On the 15th May, 1213, he laid his crown at the papal legate's feet, declared that he surrendered his kingdom of England to the pope, and made oath to him as to his lord paramount.

Shortly a national protest boldly claimed the ancient liberties of the people. Forty-five mounted barons, armed in complete mail, and accompanied by some two thousand knights, besides a large number of men-at-arms and infantry, met at Brackley during the festival of Easter in 1215, and sent a deputation to the king. "Here," they said, "is the charter which consecrates the liberties confirmed by Henry I, and which you also have solemnly sworn to observe.". . . "Why do they not demand my crown also?" said the king in a furious passion, and then with an oath, he added: "I will not grant them liberties which will make me a slave." But the nation was firmer still in its resolve to avoid enslavement. The barons occupied London, and on the 15th June, 1215, the king signed the famous *Magna Carta* at Runnymede. The political protestantism of the thirteenth century would have done but little, however, for the greatness of the nation, without the religious protestantism of the sixteenth.

This was the first time that the papacy came into collision with modern liberty. It shuddered in alarm, and the shock was violent. Innocent swore (as was his custom) and then declared the Great Charter null and void, forbade the king underpain of anathema to respect the liberties which he had confirmed, ascribed the conduct of the barons to the instigation of Satan, and ordered them to make apology to the king, and to send a deputation to Rome to learn from the mouth of the pope himself what should be the government of England. This was the way in which the papacy welcomed the first manifestations of liberty among the nations, and made known the model system under which it claimed to govern the whole world.

The priests of England supported the anathemas pronounced by their chief. They indulged in a thousand jeers and sarcasms against John about the charter he had accepted:—"This is the twenty-fifth king of England—not a king, not even a kingling—but the disgrace of kings—a king without a kingdom —the fifth wheel of a waggon—the last of kings, and the disgrace of his people!—I would not give a straw for him. . .. *Fuisti rex, nunc fex* (once a king, but now a clown)." John, unable to support his disgrace, groaned and gnashed his teeth and rolled his eyes, tore sticks from the hedges and gnawed them like a maniac, or dashed them into fragments on the ground.

The barons, unmoved alike by the insolence of the pope and the despair of the king, replied that they would maintain the charter. Innocent excommunicated them. "Is it the pope's business to regulate temporal matters?" asked they. "By what right do vile usurers and foul simoniacs domineer over our country and excommunicate the whole world?"

The pope soon triumphed throughout England. His vassal John having hired some bands of adventurers from the continent, traversed at their head the whole country from the Channel to the Forth. These mercenaries carried desolation in their track: they extorted money, made prisoners, burnt the barons' castles, laid waste their parks, and dishonoured their wives and daughters. The king would sleep in a house, and the next morning set fire to it. Blood-stained assassins scoured the country during the night, the sword in one hand and the torch in the other, marking their progress by murder and conflagration. Such was the enthronement of popery in England. At this sight the barons, overcome by emotion, denounced both the king and the pope: "Alas! poor country!" they exclaimed. "Wretched England! . . . And thou, O pope, a curse light upon thee!"

The curse was not long delayed. As the king was returning from some more than usually successful foray, and as the royal waggons were crossing the sands of the Wash, the tide rose and all sank in the abyss. This accident filled John with terror: it seemed to him that the earth was about to open and swallow him up. Stricken with dysentery which, finally, was aggravated by a surfeit of peaches and new cider, John reached Newark and died.

Such was the end of the pope's vassal—of his armed missionary in Britain. Never had so vile a prince been the involuntary occasion to his people of such great benefits. From his reign England may date her enthusiasm for liberty and her dread of popery.

During this time a great transformation had been accomplished. Magnificent churches and the marvels of religious art, with ceremonies and a multitude of prayers and chantings dazzled the eyes, charmed the ears, and captivated the senses; but testified also to the absence of every strong moral and Christian disposition, and the predominance of worldliness in the church. At the same time the adoration of images and relics, saints, angels, and Mary the mother of God, the worships of *latria*, *doulia*, and *hyperdoulia*,[1] at once indicated and kept up among the people that ignorance of truth and absence of grace which characterize popery. All these errors tended to bring about a reaction: and in fact the march of the Reformation may now be said to begin.

England had been brought low by the papacy: it rose up again by resisting Rome. Grosseteste, Bradwardine, and Edward III prepared the way for Wycliffe, and Wycliffe for the Reformation.

[1] The Romish church distinguishes three kinds of worship: *latria*, that paid to God; *doulia*, to saints; and *hyperdoulia*, to the Virgin Mary.

CHAPTER SIX

Grosseteste and Bradwardine

(13th & 14th Centuries)

IN the reign of Henry III, son of John, while the king was conniving at the usurpations of Rome, and the pope ridiculing the complaints of the barons, a pious and energetic man, of comprehensive understanding, was occupied in the study of the Holy Scriptures in their original languages, and bowing to their sovereign authority. Robert Grosseteste was born of poor parents at Stradbroke in Suffolk, and being raised to the see of Lincoln in 1235, when he was about sixty years of age, he boldly undertook to reform his diocese, one of the largest in England. Nor was this all. At the very time when the Roman pontiff, who had hitherto been content to be called the vicar of St Peter, proclaimed himself the vicar of God, and was ordering the English bishops to find benefices for *three hundred Romans*, Grosseteste was declaring that "to follow a pope who rebels against the will of Christ, is to separate from Christ and his body; and if ever the time should come when all men follow an erring pontiff, then will be the great apostasy. Then will true Christians refuse to obey, and Rome will be the cause of an unprecedented schism." Thus did he predict the Reformation. Disgusted at the avarice of the monks and priests, he visited Rome to demand a reform. "Brother," said Innocent IV to him with some irritation, "*Is thine eye evil, because I am good?*" The English bishop exclaimed with a sigh: "O money, money! how great is thy power—especially in this court of Rome!"

A year had scarcely elapsed before Innocent commanded the bishop to give a canonry in Lincoln cathedral to his infant nephew. Grosseteste replied: "After the sin of Lucifer there is none more opposed to the gospel than that which ruins souls by giving them a faithless minister. Bad pastors are the cause of unbelief, heresy, and disorder. Those who introduce them into the church are little better than antichrists, and their culpability is in proportion to their dignity. Although the chief of the angels should order me to commit such a sin, I would refuse. My obedience forbids me to obey; and therefore I rebel."

Such was the bishop's response to the papal requirement: his obedience to the Word of God forbade him to obey the pope. This was the principle of the Reformation. "Who is this old driveller that in his dotage dares to judge of my conduct?" exclaimed Innocent, whose wrath was appeased by the intervention of certain cardinals. Grosseteste on his dying bed— he died in 1253—professed still more clearly the principles of the reformers; he declared that a heresy was "an opinion conceived by carnal motives, *contrary to Scripture*, openly taught and obstinately defended," thus asserting the authority of Scripture instead of the authority of the church. He died in peace, and the public voice proclaimed him "a searcher of the Scriptures, an adversary of the pope, and despiser of the Romans." Innocent, desiring to take vengeance on his bones, meditated the exhumation of his body, when one night (says the Mediaeval chronicler, Matthew of Paris) the bishop appeared before him. Drawing near the pontiff's bed, he struck him with his crosier, and thus addressed him with terrible voice and threatening look: "Wretch! the Lord doth not permit thee to have any power over me. Woe be to thee!" The vision disappeared, and the pope, uttering a cry as if he had been struck by some sharp weapon, lay senseless on his couch. Never after did he pass a quiet night, and pursued by the phantoms of his troubled imagination, the year after Grosseteste's death he also expired while the palace re-echoed with his lamentable groans.

Grosseteste was not alone in his opposition to the pope. Sewal, archbishop of York, did the same, and "the more the pope cursed him, the more the people blessed him."—"Moderate your tyranny," said the archbishop to the pontiff, "for the Lord said to Peter, *Feed* my sheep, and not *shear them, flay them*, or *devour them*." The pope smiled and let the bishop speak, because the king allowed the pope to act. The power of England, which was constantly increasing, was soon able to give more force to these protests.

The nation was indeed growing in greatness. The madness

of John, which had caused the English people to lose their continental possessions, had given them more unity and power. The Angevin kings, being compelled to renounce entirely the country which had been their cradle, had at length made up their minds to look upon England as their home. The two races, so long hostile, melted one into the other. Free institutions were formed; the laws were studied; and colleges were founded. The language began to assume a regular form, and the ships of England were already formidable at sea. For more than a century the most brilliant victories attended the British armies. A king of France was brought captive to London: an English king was crowned at Paris. Even Spain and Italy felt the valour of these proud islanders. The English people took their station in the foremost rank. Now the character of a nation is never raised by halves. When the mighty ones of the earth were seen to fall before her, England could no longer crawl at the feet of an Italian priest.

At no period did her laws attack the papacy with so much energy. At the beginning of the fourteenth century an Englishman having brought to London one of the pope's bulls—a bull of an entirely spiritual character, it was an excommunication—was prosecuted as a traitor to the crown, and would have been hanged, had not the sentence, at the chancellor's intercession, been changed to perpetual banishment. The *common law* was the weapon the government then opposed to the papal bulls. Shortly afterwards, in 1307, King Edward ordered the sheriffs to resist the arrogant pretensions of the Romish agents. But it is to two great men in the fourteenth century, equally illustrious, the one in the state, and the other in the church, that England is indebted for the development of the protestant element in England.

In 1346, an English army, about 15,000 strong, met face to face at Crécy a French army of much greater size. Two individuals of very different characters were in the English host. One of them was King Edward III, a brave and ambitious prince, who, being resolved to recover for the royal authority all its power, and for England all her glory, had undertaken the conquest of France. The other was his chaplain Thomas Bradwardine, a native of Chichester, a man of so humble a character that his meekness was often taken for stupidity. And thus it was that on his receiving the pallium at Avignon from the hands of the pope on his elevation to the see of Canterbury, a jester mounted on an ass rode into the hall and petitioned the pontiff to make him *primate* instead of that imbecile priest.

Bradwardine was one of the most pious men of the age, and to his prayers his sovereign's victories were ascribed. He was also one of the greatest geniuses of his time, and occupied the first rank among astronomers, philosophers, and mathematicians. The pride of science had at first alienated him from the doctrine of the cross. But one day while in the house of God and listening to the reading of the Holy Scriptures, these words struck his ear: *It is not of him that willeth, nor of him that runneth, but of God that showeth mercy.* His ungrateful heart, he tells us, at first rejected this humiliating doctrine with aversion. Yet the Word of God had laid its powerful hold upon him; he was converted to the truths he had despised, and immediately began to set forth the doctrines of eternal grace at Merton College, Oxford. He drank so deep at the fountain of Scripture that the traditions of men concerned him but little, and he was so absorbed in adoration in spirit and in truth, that he remarked not outward superstitions. His lectures were eagerly listened to and circulated through all Europe. The grace of God was their very essence, as it was of the Reformation. With sorrow Bradwardine beheld Pelagianism everywhere substituting a mere religion of externals for inward Christianity, and on his knees he struggled for the salvation of the church. "As in the times of old four hundred and fifty prophets of Baal strove against a single prophet of God; so now, O Lord," he exclaimed, "the number of those who strive with Pelagius against thy free grace cannot be counted. They pretend not to receive grace freely, but to buy it. The will of men (they say) should precede, and thine should follow: theirs is the mistress, and thine the servant. . . . Alas! nearly the whole world is walking in error in the steps of Pelagius. Arise, O Lord, and judge thy cause."[1] And the Lord did arise, but not until after the death of this pious archbishop—in the days of Wycliffe, who matriculated at Oxford probably shortly after Bradwardine's departure—and especially in the days of Luther and of

[1] *Concerning the cause of God against Pelagius*, Book 3, ed. H. Savile (London, 1618).

Calvin. His contemporaries gave him the name of the *profound doctor*.

If Bradwardine walked truthfully in the path of faith, his illustrious patron Edward III advanced triumphantly in the field of policy. Pope Clement IV having decreed that the first two vacancies in the Anglican church should be conferred on two of his cardinals: "France is becoming *English*," said the courtiers to the king; "and by way of compensation, England is becoming *Italian*." Edward, desirous of guaranteeing the religious liberties of England, passed with the consent of parliament in 1350 the Statute of *Provisors*, which made void every ecclesiastical appointment contrary to the rights of the king, the chapters, or the patrons. Thus the privileges of the chapters and the liberty of the English Catholics, as well as the independence of the crown, were protected against the invasion of foreigners; and imprisonment or banishment for life was denounced upon all offenders against the law.

This bold step alarmed the pontiff. Accordingly, three years after, the king having nominated one of his secretaries to the see of Durham—a man without any of the qualities becoming a bishop—the pope readily confirmed the appointment. When someone expressed his astonishment at this, the pope made answer: "If the king of England had nominated *an ass*, I would have accepted him." Thus the pope withdrew his pretensions. "Empires have their term," observes the quaint Thomas Fuller in his *Church History of Britain*, at this place; "when once they have reached it, they halt, they go back, they fall."

The term seemed to be drawing nearer every day. In the reign of Edward III, between 1343 and 1353, again in 1364, and finally under Richard II in 1393, those stringent laws were passed which interdicted all appeal to the court of Rome, all bulls from the Roman bishop, all excommunications, in a word, every act infringing on the rights of the crown; and declared that whoever should bring such documents into England, or receive, publish, or execute them, should be put out of the king's protection, deprived of their property, arrested, and brought before the king in council to undergo their trial according to the terms of the act. Such was the Statute of *Præmunire*.

Great was the indignation of the Romans at the news of

this law: "If the Statute of *Mortmain* put the pope into a sweat,"
says Fuller, "this of *præmunire* gave him a fit of fever." One pope
called it an "execrable statute"—"a horrible crime." Such
are the terms applied by the pontiffs to all that thwarts their
ambitions.

Of the two wars carried on by Edward—the one against the
King of France, and the other against popery—the latter was
the more righteous and important. The benefits which this
prince had hoped to derive from his brilliant victories at Crécy
and Poitiers dwindled away almost entirely before his death;
while his struggles with the papacy, founded as they were on
truth, have exerted even to our own days an indisputable
influence on the destinies of Great Britain. Yet the prayers and
the conquests of Bradwardine, who proclaimed in that fallen
age the doctrine of grace, produced effects still greater, not
only for the salvation of many souls, but for the liberty, moral
force, and greatness of England.

CHAPTER SEVEN

Light Streams from Lutterworth

(c. 1329–80)

THUS in the first half of the fourteenth century, nearly two hundred years before the Reformation, England appeared weary of the yoke of Rome. Bradwardine died in 1349; but a greater than he was about to succeed him, and without attaining to the highest functions, to exhibit in his person the past and future tendencies of the church of Christ in Britain. The English Reformation did not begin with Henry VIII: the revival of the sixteenth century is but a link in the chain commencing with the apostles and reaching to us.

The resistance of Edward III to the papacy *without* had not suppressed the papacy *within*. The mendicant friars, and particularly the Franciscans, those fanatical soldiers of the pope, were endeavouring by pious frauds to monopolize the wealth of the country. "Every year," said they, "Saint Francis descends from heaven to purgatory, and delivers the souls of all those who were buried in the dress of his order." These friars were said to kidnap children from their parents and shut them up in monasteries. They affected to be poor and, with a wallet on their back, begged with a piteous air from both high and low; but at the same time they dwelt in palaces, heaped up treasures, dressed in costly garments and wasted their time in luxurious entertainments.[1] The least of them looked upon themselves as *lords*, and those who wore the doctor's cap considered themselves *kings*. While they diverted themselves, eating and drinking at their well-spread tables, they used to send ignorant uneducated persons in their place to preach fables and legends to amuse and plunder the people. If any rich man talked of giving alms to the poor and not to the

---

[1] "When they have overmuch riches, both in great waste houses and precious clothes, in great feasts and many jewels and treasures." Wycliffe's *Tracts and Treatises*, edited by the Wycliffe Society, p. 224.

G

church, they exclaimed loudly against such impiety, and declared with threatening voice: "If you do so we will lea᷈᷈᷈᷈᷈᷈᷈ the country, and return accompanied by a legion of glittering helmets." Public indignation was at its height. "The monks and priests of Rome," was the cry, "are eating us away like a cancer. God must deliver us or the people will perish. . . . Woe be to them! the cup of wrath will run over. Men of holy church shall be despised as carrion, as dogs shall they be cast out in open places."[1]

The arrogance of Rome made the cup run over. Pope Urban V, heedless of the laurels won by the conqueror at Crécy and Poitiers, summoned Edward III to recognize him as legitimate sovereign of England, and to pay as feudal tribute the annual sum of one thousand marks. In case of refusal the king was to appear before him at Rome. For thirty-three years the popes had never mentioned the tribute accorded by John to Innocent III, and which had always been paid very irregularly. The conqueror of the Valois was irritated by this insolence on the part of an Italian bishop, and called on God to avenge England. From Oxford came forth the avenger.

John Wycliffe, born about 1329 near Richmond, in Yorkshire, probably arrived in Oxford as a student shortly after the departure of the pious Bradwardine from Merton College. He quickly acquired a great reputation for learning and came to bekn own as "flos Oxonie" (the flower, or pride, of Oxford). In 1348, a terrible pestilence, which is said to have carried off half the human race, appeared in England after successively devastating Asia and the continent of Europe. This visitation of the Almighty sounded like the trumpet of the judgment-day in the heart of Wycliffe. Alarmed at the thoughts of eternity, the young man—for he was then a mere youth—passed days and nights in his cell groaning and sighing, and calling upon God to show him the path he ought to follow. He found it in the Holy Scriptures, and resolved to make it known to others. He commenced with prudence; but being elected in 1360 Master of Balliol, and about 1365 Warden of Canterbury Hall (later incorporated in Christ Church) he began to set forth the doctrine of faith in a more energetic manner. His biblical and philosophical studies, his knowledge of theology, his

---

[1] Wycliffe, *The Last Age of the Church.*

penetrating mind, the purity of his manners, and his unbending courage, rendered him the object of general admiration. A profound teacher, like Bradwardine, and an eloquent preacher, he demonstrated to the learned during the course of the week what he intended to preach, and on Sunday he preached to the people what he had previously demonstrated. His disputations gave strength to his sermons, and his sermons shed light upon his disputations. He accused the clergy of having banished the Holy Scriptures, and required that the authority of the Word of God should be re-established in the church. Loud acclamations crowned these discussions, and the crowd of vulgar minds trembled with indignation when they heard these shouts of applause.

Wycliffe was in middle life when the papal arrogance stirred England to its depths. Being at once an able politician and a fervent Christian, he vigorously defended the rights of the crown against the Romish aggression, and by his arguments not only enlightened his fellow-countrymen generally, but stirred up the zeal of several members of both Houses of Parliament.

The parliament assembled, and never perhaps had it been summoned on a question which excited to so high a degree the emotions of England, and indeed of Christendom. The debates in the House of Lords were especially remarkable: all the arguments of Wycliffe were reproduced. "Feudal *tribute* is due," said one, "only to him who can grant feudal *protection* in return. Now how can the pope wage war to protect his fiefs?"—"Is it as vassal of the crown or as feudal superior," asked another, "that the pope demands part of our property? Urban V will not accept the first of these titles. . . . Well and good! but the English people will not acknowledge the second." —"Why," said a third, "was this tribute originally granted? To pay the pope for absolving John. . . . His demand, then, is mere simony, a kind of clerical swindling, which the lords spiritual and temporal should indignantly oppose."—"No," said another speaker, "England belongs not to the pope. The pope is but a man, subject to sin; but Christ is the Lord of lords, and this kingdom is held directly and solely of Christ alone." Thus spoke the lords inspired by Wycliffe. Parliament decided unanimously that no prince had the right to alienate the sovereignty of the kingdom without the consent of the other two estates, and that if the pontiff should attempt to proceed against the king of England as his vassal, the nation should rise in a body to maintain the independence of the crown.

To no purpose did this generous resolution excite the wrath of the partisans of Rome; to no purpose did they assert that, by the canon law, the king ought to be deprived of his fief, and that England now belonged to the pope: "No," replied Wycliffe, "the canon law has no force when it is opposed to the Word of God." Edward III made Wycliffe one of his chaplains, and the papacy has ceased from that hour to lay claim—in explicit terms at least—to the sovereignty of England.

When the pope gave up his temporal, he was desirous, at the very least, of keeping up his ecclesiastical pretensions, and to procure the repeal of the statutes of *Præmunire* and *Provisors*. It was accordingly resolved to hold a conference at Bruges to treat of this question, and Wycliffe, who had been created doctor of divinity two years before, proceeded thither with the other commissioners in July 1374, although he only remained with them two or three months. The decision of the conference was that the king should bind himself to repeal the penalties denounced against the pontifical agents, and that the pope should confirm the king's ecclesiastical presentations. But the nation was not pleased with this compromise. "The clerks sent from Rome," said the Commons, "are more dangerous for the kingdom than Jews or Saracens: every papal agent resident in England, and every Englishman living at the court of Rome, should be punished with death." Such was the language of the *Good Parliament* (1376). In the fourteenth century the English nation called a parliament *good* which did not yield to the papacy.

Wycliffe, immediately prior to his visit to Bruges, had been presented by the king to the rectory of Lutterworth, and from that time a practical activity was added to his academic influence. At Oxford he spoke as a master to the young theologians; in his parish he addressed the people as a preacher and as a pastor. "The Gospel," said he, "is the only source of religion. The Roman pontiff is a mere cut-purse, and, far from having the right to reprimand the whole world, he may be lawfully reproved by his inferiors, and even by laymen."

The papacy grew alarmed. Courtenay, fourth son of the Earl
of Devon, an imperious but grave priest, and full of zeal for
what he believed to be the truth, had recently been appointed
to the see of London. In parliament he had resisted Wycliffe's
patron, John of Gaunt, duke of Lancaster, third son of
Edward III, and head of the house of that name. The bishop,
observing that the doctrines of the reformer were spreading
among the people, both high and low, charged him with
heresy, and summoned him to appear before the convocation
assembled in St Paul's Cathedral.

On the 19th February, 1377, an immense crowd, heated
with fanaticism, thronged the approaches to the church and
filled its aisles, while the citizens favourable to the reform
remained concealed in their houses. Wycliffe moved forward,
preceded by Lord Percy, marshal of England, and supported
by the Duke of Lancaster, who defended him from purely
political motives. He was followed by four doctors of divinity,
his counsel, and passed through the hostile multitude who looked
upon Lancaster as the enemy of their liberties, and upon himself as the enemy of the church. "Let not the sight of these
bishops make you shrink a hair's-breadth in your profession of
faith," said the prince to the doctor. "They are unlearned; and
as for this concourse of people, fear nothing, we are here to
defend you." When the reformer had crossed the threshold of
the cathedral, the crowd within appeared like a solid wall;
and, notwithstanding the efforts of the earl-marshal, Wycliffe
and Lancaster could not advance. The people swayed to and
fro, hands were raised in violence, and loud hootings re-echoed
through the building. At length Percy made an opening in the
dense multitude, and Wycliffe passed on.

The haughty Courtenay, who had been commissioned by
the archbishop to preside over the assembly, watched these
strange movements with anxiety, and beheld with displeasure
the learned doctor accompanied by the two most powerful men
in England. He said nothing to the Duke of Lancaster, who
at that time administered the kingdom, but turning towards
Percy observed sharply: "If I had known, my lord, that you
claimed to be master in this church, I would have taken
measures to prevent your entrance." Lancaster coldly rejoined:
"He shall keep such mastery here, though you say nay."

Percy now turned to Wycliffe, who had remained standing, and said: "Sit down and rest yourself." At this Courtenay gave way to his anger, and exclaimed in a loud tone: "It is unreasonable that one, cited to appear before a bishop, should sit down during his answer. He must and shall stand." Lancaster, indignant that a learned doctor of England should be refused a favour to which his age alone entitled him (for he was approaching fifty years) made answer to the bishop: "My lord, you are very arrogant; take care . . . or I may bring down your pride, and not yours only, but that of all the prelacy in England."—"Do your worst, sir," was Courtenay's reply. The prince rejoined with some emotion: "You are insolent, my lord. You think, no doubt, you can trust on your family . . . but your relations will have trouble enough to protect themselves." To this the bishop nobly replied: "My confidence is not in my parents nor in any man; but only in God, in whom I trust, and by whose assistance I will be bold to speak the truth." Lancaster, who saw hypocrisy only in these words, turned to one of his attendants, and whispered in his ear, but so loud as to be heard by the bystanders: "I would rather pluck the bishop by the hair of his head out of the church, than take this at his hands." Every impartial reader must confess that the prelate spoke with greater dignity than the prince. Lancaster had hardly uttered these imprudent words before the bishop's partisans fell upon him and Percy, and even upon Wycliffe, who alone had remained calm. The two noblemen resisted, their friends and servants defended them, the uproar became extreme, and there was no hope of restoring tranquillity. The two lords escaped with difficulty, taking Wycliffe with them, and the assembly broke up in great confusion.

On the following day the earl-marshal having called upon parliament to apprehend the disturbers of the public peace, the clerical party uniting with the enemies of Lancaster filled the streets with their clamour; and while the Duke and the Earl escaped by the Thames, the mob collected before Percy's house, broke down the doors, searched every chamber, and thrust their swords into every dark corner. When they found that he had escaped, the rioters, imagining that he was concealed in Lancaster's palace, rushed to the Savoy, at that time the most magnificent building in the kingdom. They killed a priest who endeavoured to stay them, tore down the ducal arms, and hung them up reversed, in Cheapside, like those of a traitor. They would have gone still farther if the bishop had not very opportunely reminded them that they were *in Lent.* As for Wycliffe, he was dismissed with an injunction against preaching his doctrines.

But this decision of the priests was not ratified by the people of England. Public opinion declared in favour of Wycliffe. "If he is guilty," said they, "why is he not punished? If he is innocent, why is he ordered to be silent? If he is the weakest in power, he is the strongest in truth!" And so indeed he was, and never had he spoken with such energy. He openly attacked the pretended apostolical chair, and declared that the *two* antipopes who sat at Rome and Avignon—for this was the period when there were rival popes, each imprecating curses on the other—together made *one* antichrist. Being now in opposition to the pope, Wycliffe was soon to confess that Christ alone was king of the church; and that it is not possible for a man to be excommunicated, unless first and principally he be excommunicated by himself.

Rome could not close her ears. Wycliffe's enemies sent thither nineteen propositions which they ascribed to him, and in the month of June 1377, just as Richard II, son of the Black Prince, a child ten years old, was ascending the throne, three letters from Gregory XI, addressed to the king, the archbishop of Canterbury, and the university of Oxford, denounced Wycliffe as a heretic, and called upon them to proceed against him as against a common thief. The archbishop issued the citation: the crown and the university were silent.

On the appointed day, Wycliffe, unaccompanied by either Lancaster or Percy, proceeded to the archiepiscopal chapel at Lambeth. "Men expected he should be devoured," says an historian, "being brought into the lion's den." But the burgesses had taken the prince's place. The assault of Rome had aroused the friends of liberty and truth in England. "The pope's briefs," said they, "ought to have no effect in the realm without the king's consent. Every man is master in his own house."

The archbishop had scarcely opened the sitting, when Sir Louis Clifford entered the chapel, and forbade the court, on the part of the widowed Princess of Wales (the mother of

Richard II) to proceed against the reformer. The bishops were struck with a panic-fear: "they bent their heads," says a Roman-catholic historian, "like a reed before the wind." Wycliffe retired after handing in a protest. "In the first place," said he, "I resolve with my whole heart, and by the grace of God, to be a sincere Christian; and, while my life shall last, to profess and defend the law of Christ so far as I have power." Wycliffe's enemies attacked this protest, and one of them eagerly maintained that whatever the pope ordered should be looked upon as right. "What!" answered the reformer; "the pope may then exclude from the canon of the Scriptures any book that displeases him, and alter the Bible at pleasure?" Wycliffe thought that Rome, unsettling the grounds of infallibility, had transferred it from the Scriptures to the pope. He was desirous of restoring it to its true place, and re-establishing authority in the church on a truly divine foundation.

A great change was now taking place in the reformer. Busying himself less about the kingdom of England, he occupied himself more about the kingdom of Christ. In him the political phase was followed by the religious. To carry the glad tidings of the gospel into the remotest hamlets, was now the great idea which possessed Wycliffe. If begging friars (said he) stroll over the country, preaching the legends of saints and the history of the Trojan war, we must do for God's glory what they do to fill their wallets, and form a vast itinerant evangelization to convert souls to Jesus Christ. Turning to the most pious of his disciples, he said to them: "Go and preach, it is the sublimest work; but imitate not the priests whom we see after the sermon sitting in the ale-houses, or at the gaming-table, or wasting their time in hunting. After your sermon is ended, do you visit the sick, the aged, the poor, the blind, and the lame, and succour them according to your ability." Such was the new practical theology which Wycliffe inaugurated—it was that of Christ Himself.

The "poor priests," as they were called, set off barefoot, a staff in their hands, clothed in a coarse robe, living on alms, and satisfied with the plainest food. They stopped in the fields near some village, in the churchyards, in the market-places of the towns, and sometimes in the churches themselves. The people, among whom they were favourites, thronged around them, as the men of Northumbria had done at Aidan's preaching.

They spoke with a popular eloquence that entirely won over those who listened to them. Of these missionaries none was more beloved than John Aston, a Fellow of Merton College, Oxford. He might be seen wandering over the country in every direction, or seated at some cottage hearth, or alone in some retired crossway, preaching to an attentive crowd. Missions of this kind have constantly revived in England at the great epochs of the church.

The "poor priests" were not content with mere disputings against Rome: they preached the great mystery of godliness. "An angel could have made no propitiation for man," one day exclaimed their master Wycliffe, "for the nature which has sinned is not that of the angels. The mediator must needs be a man; but every man being indebted to God for every thing that he is able to do, this man must needs have infinite merit, and be at the same time God."

The clergy became alarmed, and a law was passed commanding every king's officer to commit the preachers and their followers to prison. In consequence of this, as soon as the humble missionary began to preach, the monks set themselves in motion. They watched him from the windows of their cells, at the street-corners, or from behind a hedge, and then hastened off to procure assistance. But when the constables approached, a body of stout bold men stood forth, with arms in their hands, who surrounded the preacher, and zealously protected him against the attacks of the clergy. Carnal weapons were thus mingled with the preachings of the word of peace. The poor priests returned to their master: Wycliffe comforted them, advised them, and then they departed once more. Every day this evangelization reached some new spot, and the light was thus penetrating into every quarter of England, when the reformer was suddenly stopped in his work.

Wycliffe was at Oxford in the year 1379, busied in the discharge of his duties as professor of divinity, when he fell dangerously ill. His was not a strong constitution; and work, age, and above all persecution had weakened him. Great was the joy in the monasteries; but for that joy to be complete, the *heretic* must recant. Every effort was made to bring this about in his last moments.

Representatives of the four religious orders, accompanied by four aldermen, hastened to the bedside of the dying man, hoping to frighten him by threatening him with the vengeance of Heaven. They found him calm and serene. "You have death on your lips," said they; "be touched by your faults, and retract in our presence all that you have said to our injury." Wycliffe remained silent, and the visitors flattered themselves with an easy victory. But the nearer the reformer approached eternity, the greater was his horror of their evil doctrine. The consolation he had found in Jesus Christ had given him fresh energy. He begged his servant to raise him on his couch. Then feeble and pale, and scarcely able to support himself, he turned towards the friars, who were waiting for his recantation and, opening his livid lips, and fixing on them a piercing look, he said with emphasis: "I shall not die but live, and again declare the evil deeds of the friars." We might almost picture to ourselves the spirit of Elijah threatening the priests of Baal. The visitors looked at one another with astonishment. They left the room in confusion, and the reformer recovered to put the finishing touch to the most important of his works against false religion and against the pope.

CHAPTER EIGHT

The Morning Star of the Reformation

(1380–84)

WYCLIFFE's ministry had followed a progressive course. At first he had attacked the papacy; next he preached the gospel to the poor; he could take one more step and put the people in permanent possession of the Word of God. This was the third phase of his activity.

Scholasticism had banished the Scriptures into a mysterious obscurity. It is true that Bede had translated the Gospel of St John; that the learned men at Alfred's court had translated the four evangelists; that Ælfric in the reign of Ethelred II had translated some books of the Old Testament; that an Anglo-Norman priest had paraphrased the Gospels and the Acts; that Richard Rolle, "the hermit of Hampole" (near Doncaster), and some pious clerks in the fourteenth century, had produced a version of the Psalms, the Gospels, and Epistles—but these rare volumes were hidden, like theological curiosities, in the libraries of a few monasteries. It was then a maxim that the reading of the Bible was injurious to the laity; and accordingly the priests forbade it, just as the Brahmins forbid the Shastras to the Hindus. Oral tradition alone preserved among the people the histories of the Holy Scriptures, mingled with legends of the saints. The time appeared ripe for the publication of a Bible. The increase of population, the attention the English were beginning to devote to their own language, the development which the system of representative government had received, the awakening of the human mind—all these circumstances favoured the reformer's design.

Wycliffe was ignorant indeed of Greek and Hebrew; but was it nothing to shake off the dust which for ages had covered the Latin Bible, and to translate it into English? He was a good Latin scholar, of sound understanding and great penetration; but above all he loved the Bible, he understood it, and desired to communicate this treasure to others. Let us imagine him in his quiet study: on his table is the Vulgate text, corrected after the best manuscripts; and lying open around him are the commentaries of the doctors of the church, especially those of St Jerome and Nicholas of Lyra. Between ten and fifteen years he steadily prosecuted his task; learned men aided him with their advice, and one of them, Nicholas of Hereford, a Fellow of Queen's College, Oxford, appears to have translated a few chapters for him.[1] At last, some time between 1380 and 1384, it was completed. This was a great event in the religious history of England; outstripping the nations on the continent, she took her station in the foremost rank in the great work of disseminating the Scriptures.

As soon as the translation was finished, the labour of the copyists began, and the Bible was erelong widely circulated either wholly or in portions. The reception of the work surpassed all expectations. The Holy Scriptures exercised a reviving influence over men's hearts; minds were enlightened; souls were converted; the voices of the "poor priests" had done little in comparison with this voice; something new had entered into the world. Citizens, soldiers, and the lower classes welcomed this new era with acclamations; the high-born curiously examined the unknown book; and even Anne of Bohemia, wife of Richard II, prompted perhaps by the popular interest, began to read the Gospels diligently. She did more than this: she made them known to Thomas Arundel, archbishop of York and chancellor, and afterwards a persecutor, but who now, struck by the sight of a foreign lady—of a queen, humbly devoting her leisure to the study of "such virtuous books," commenced reading them himself, and rebuked the prelates who neglected this holy pursuit. "You could not meet two persons on the highway," says a contemporary writer, "but one of them was Wycliffe's disciple."

Yet all in England did not equally rejoice: the lower clergy opposed this enthusiasm with complaints and maledictions.

---

[1] [Since these words were written the whole question has been several times investigated. Some modern scholars are inclined to doubt whether Wycliffe was himself the author of the translation which bears his name. F. F. Bruce discusses the matter in *The English Bible* (1961), pp. 13–20. It may at least be claimed that the traditional view, though called in question, has not been satisfactorily disproved.]

"Master John Wycliffe, by translating the gospel into English," said the monks, "has rendered it more acceptable and more intelligible to laymen and even to women, than it has hitherto been to learned and intelligent clerks! . . . The gospel pearl is everywhere cast out and trodden under foot of swine." New contests arose for the reformer. Wherever he bent his steps, he was violently attacked. "It is heresy," cried the monks, "to speak of Holy Scripture in English."—"Since the church has approved of the four Gospels, she would have been just as able to reject them and admit others! The church sanctions and condemns what she pleases. . . . Learn to believe in the church rather than in the gospel." These clamours did not alarm Wycliffe. "Many nations have had the Bible in their own language. The Bible is the faith of the church. Though the pope and all his clerks should disappear from the face of the earth," said he, "our faith would not fail, for it is founded on Jesus alone, our Master and our God." But Wycliffe did not stand alone: in the palace as in the cottage, and even in parliament, the rights of Holy Scripture found defenders. A motion having been made in the Upper House (1390) to seize all the copies of the Bible, the Duke of Lancaster exclaimed: "Are we then the very dregs of humanity, that we cannot possess the laws of our religion in our own tongue?"

Having given his fellow-countrymen the Bible, Wycliffe began to reflect on its contents. This was a new step in his onward path. There comes a moment when the Christian, saved by a lively faith, feels the need of giving an account to himself of this faith, and this originates the science of theology. This is a natural movement: if the child, who at first possesses sensations and affections only, feels the want, as he grows up, of reflection and knowledge, why should it not be the same with the Christian? Politics—home missions—Holy Scripture— had engaged Wycliffe in succession; theology had its turn, and this was the fourth phase of his life.

It is clear that up to the year 1378 Wycliffe was a firm believer in the doctrine of transubstantiation, which stands at the very centre of the Roman Catholic system, the belief that when at the mass, the "words of consecration" are pronounced by the "priest," the bread and wine are miraculously changed into the very body and blood of the Lord. It is equally clear,

however—it might even be claimed that it is clearer still—
that three years later Wycliffe denied this doctrine with
tremendous energy. Indeed he was now asserting that there
never had been a heresy more cunningly smuggled into the
church than transubstantiation. The reasons for his complete
change of front are clear: he denounced it as contrary to
Scripture (both Gospels and Epistles), as unsupported by early
church tradition,[1] as plainly opposed to the testimony of the
senses, and as based upon false reasoning.[2] He proclaimed
furthermore, with immense vigour, that the doctrine was
essentially idolatrous, and productive of arrogant priestly
claims without warrant in Scripture. In sum, the doctrine of
the mass was to Wycliffe in the closing years of his life a
"blasphemous deceit," or, to use his exact language, "a
veritable abomination of desolation in the holy place."

When Wycliffe's enemies heard these propositions, they
appeared horror-stricken, and yet in secret they were delighted
at the prospect of destroying him. They met together, examined
twelve theses he had published, and pronounced against him
suspension from all teaching, imprisonment, and the greater
excommunication.[3] At the same time his friends became
alarmed, their zeal cooled, and many of them forsook him.
The Duke of Lancaster, in particular, could not follow him
into this new sphere. That prince had no objection to an
ecclesiastical opposition which might aid the political power,
and for that purpose he had tried to enlist the reformer's
talents and courage; but he feared a dogmatic opposition that
might compromise him. The sky was heavy with clouds;
Wycliffe was alone.

The storm soon burst upon him. One day, while he was seated

---

[1] [Nor had the Anglo-Saxon church professed this doctrine. "The host is
the body of Christ, not bodily but spiritually," said Aelfric in the tenth
century in a letter addressed to the archbishop of York. Berengar of Tours
in the eleventh century had written a treatise denying the possibility of
material change in the elements, and refuting Lanfranc, archbishop of
Canterbury, who had taught England that at the word of a priest God quitted
heaven and descended on the altar.]

[2] [Lechler's *Wycliffe and his English precursors*, pp. 340–51, should be
consulted on all these points.]

[3] [The "greater" excommunication, as distinguished from the "less"
deprived a man of the right to administer or receive the sacraments, and
of all intercourse, public or private, with his fellow-christians.]

in his doctoral chair in Oxford, and calmly explaining the nature of the Lord's Supper, an officer entered the hall, and read the sentence of condemnation. It was the design of his enemies to humble the professor in the eyes of his disciples. Lancaster immediately became alarmed and, hastening to his old friend, begged him—ordered him even—to trouble himself no more about this matter. Attacked on every side, Wycliffe for a time remained silent. Shall he sacrifice the truth to save his reputation—his repose—perhaps his life? Shall expediency get the better of faith? Shall Lancaster prevail over Wycliffe? No: his courage was invincible. "Since the year of our Lord 1000," said he, "all the doctors have been in error about the sacrament of the altar—except, perhaps, it may be Berengar of Tours. How canst thou, O priest, who art but a man, make thy Maker? What! the thing that groweth in the fields—that ear which thou pluckest to-day, shall be God to-morrow! . . . As you cannot make the works which He made, how shall ye make Him who made the works? Woe to the adulterous generation that believeth the testimony of Innocent rather than of the Gospel." Wycliffe called upon his adversaries to refute the opinions they had condemned and, finding that they threatened him with a civil penalty (imprisonment), he appealed to the king.

The time was not favourable for such an appeal. A fatal circumstance increased Wycliffe's danger. Wat Tyler and a dissolute priest named Ball, taking advantage of the ill-will excited by the rapacity and brutality of the royal tax-gatherers, had occupied London with a tremendous company of supporters. John Ball kept up the spirits of the insurgents, not by expositions of the gospel, like Wycliffe's *poor priests*, but by fiery comments on the distich they had chosen for their device—

> When Adam delved and Eve span,
> Who was then the gentleman?

There were many who felt no scruple in ascribing these disorders to the reformer, who was quite innocent of them; and Courtenay, bishop of London, having been translated to the see of Canterbury, lost no time in convoking a synod to pronounce on this matter. They met in the middle of May, about two o'clock in the afternoon, and were proceeding to pronounce sentence on Wycliffe when a severe earthquake shook the city of London and so alarmed the members of the council that they unanimously demanded the adjournment of a decision which appeared so manifestly rebuked by God. But the archbishop skilfully turned this strange phenomenon to his own purposes: "Know you not," said he, "that the noxious vapours which catch fire in the bosom of the earth, and give rise to these phenomena which alarm you, lose all their force when they burst forth? Well, in like manner, by rejecting the wicked from our community, we shall put an end to the convulsions of the church." The bishops regained their courage; and one of the primate's officers read ten propositions, said to be Wycliffe's, but ascribing to him certain errors of which he was quite innocent. The following most excited the anger of the priests: "God must obey the devil. . . . After Urban VI we must receive no one as pope, but live according to the manner of the Greeks." The ten propositions were condemned as heretical, and the archbishop enjoined all persons to shun, as they would a venomous serpent, all who should preach the aforesaid errors. "If we permit this heretic to appeal continually to the passions of the people," said the primate to the king, "our destruction is inevitable. We must silence these *lollards*— these psalm-singers."[1] The king gave authority "to confine in the prisons of the state any who should maintain the condemned propositions."

Day by day the circle contracted around Wycliffe. Some of his chief supporters, the prudent Philip Repingdon, the learned Nicholas of Hereford, and even the eloquent John Aston, the firmest of the three, departed from him. The veteran champion of the truth which had once gathered a whole nation round it, had reached the days when "strong men shall bow themselves," and now, when harassed by persecution, he found himself alone. But boldly he uplifted his hoary head and exclaimed: "The doctrine of the gospel shall never perish; and if the earth once quaked, it was because they condemned Jesus Christ."

He did not stop here. In proportion as his physical strength decreased, his moral strength increased. Instead of parrying

[1] [The origin of the term "lollards" is uncertain. Some derive it from the old Dutch "lollen," to sing or to chant; others from the Latin "lolium," tares (mingled with the Catholic wheat).]

the blows aimed at him, he resolved on dealing more terrible ones still. He knew that if the king and the nobility were for the priests, the lower house and the citizens were for liberty and truth. He therefore presented a bold petition to the Commons in the month of November 1382. "Since Jesus Christ shed his blood to free his church, I demand its freedom. I demand that every one may leave those gloomy walls (the monasteries) within which a tyrannical law prevails, and embrace a simple and peaceful life under the open vault of heaven. I demand that the poor inhabitants of our towns and villages be not constrained to furnish a worldly priest, often a vicious man and a heretic, with the means of satisfying his ostentation, his gluttony, and his licentiousness—of buying a showy horse, costly saddles, bridles with tinkling bells, rich garments, and soft furs, while they see their wives, children, and neighbours, dying of hunger."[1] The House of Commons, recollecting that they had not given their consent to the persecuting statute drawn up by the clergy and approved by the king and the lords, demanded its repeal. Was the Reformation about to begin by the will of the people?

Courtenay, indignant at this intervention of the Commons, and ever stimulated by a zeal for his church, which would have been better directed towards the Word of God, visited Oxford in November 1382, and having gathered round him a number of bishops, doctors, priests, students, and laymen, summoned Wycliffe before him. A generation ago the reformer had come up to the university: Oxford had become his home . . . and now it was turning against him! Weakened by labours, by trials, by that ardent soul which preyed upon his feeble body, he might have refused to appear. But Wycliffe, who never feared the face of man, came before them with a good conscience. We may conjecture that there were among the crowd some disciples who felt their hearts burn at the sight of their master; but no outward sign indicated their emotion. The solemn silence of a court of justice had succeeded the shouts of enthusiastic youths. Yet Wycliffe did not despair: he raised his venerable head, and turned to Courtenay with that confident look which had in earlier days made his opponents shrink away. Growing

[1] A complaint of John Wycliffe. *Tracts and Treatises* edited by the Wycliffe Society, p. 268.

H

wroth against the *priests of Baal*, he reproached them with disseminating error in order to sell their masses. Then he stopped, and uttered these simple and energetic words: "The truth shall prevail!" Having thus spoken he prepared to leave the court: his enemies dared not say a word; and, like his divine master at Nazareth, he passed through the midst of them, and no man ventured to stop him. He then withdrew to his parish of Lutterworth.

He had not yet reached the harbour. He was living peacefully among his books and his parishioners, and the priests seemed inclined to leave him alone, when another blow was aimed at him. A papal brief summoned him to Rome, to appear before that tribunal which had so often shed the blood of its adversaries. His bodily infirmities convinced him that he could not obey this summons. But if Wycliffe refused to hear Urban, Urban could not choose but hear Wycliffe. The church was at that time divided between two chiefs: France, Scotland, Savoy, Lorraine, Castile, and Aragon acknowledged Clement VII; while Italy, England, Germany, Sweden, Poland, and Hungary acknowledged Urban VI. Wycliffe shall tell us who is the true head of the church universal. And while the two popes were excommunicating and abusing each other, and selling heaven and earth for their own gain, the reformer was confessing that incorruptible Word, which establishes real unity in the church. "I believe," said he, "that the gospel of Christ is the whole body of God's law. I believe that Christ, who gave it to us, is very God and very man, and by this it passes all other laws. I believe that the bishop of Rome is bound more than all other men to submit to it, for greatness among Christ's disciples did not consist in worldly dignity or honours, but in the exact following of Christ in his life and manners. No faithful man ought to follow the pope, but in such points as he hath followed Jesus Christ. The pope ought to leave unto the secular power all temporal dominion and rule; and thereunto effectually more and more exhort his whole clergy. . . . If I could labour according to my desire in mine own person, I would surely present myself before the bishop of Rome, but the Lord hath otherwise visited me to the contrary, and hath taught me rather to obey God than men."

Urban, who at that moment chanced to be very busied in

his contest with Clement, did not think it prudent to begin another with Wycliffe and so let the matter rest there. From this time the doctor passed the remainder of his days in peace in the company of three personages, two of whom were his particular friends and the third his constant adversary: these were *Aletheia, Phronesis,* and *Pseudes. Aletheia* (truth) proposed questions; *Pseudes* (falsehood) urged objections; and *Phronesis* (understanding) laid down the sound doctrine. These three characters carried on a conversation (*trialogue*) in which great truths were boldly professed. The opposition between the pope and Christ—between the canons of Romanism and the Bible— was painted in striking colours. This is one of the primary truths which the church must never forget. "The church has fallen," said one of the interlocutors in the work in question, "because she has abandoned the gospel, and preferred the laws of the pope. Although there should be a hundred popes in the world at once, and all the friars living should be transformed into cardinals, we must withhold our confidence from them in the matter of faith except so far as their teachings are those of the Scriptures."

These words were the last flicker of the torch. Wycliffe looked upon his end as near, and entertained no idea that it would come in peace. A dungeon on one of the seven hills, or a burning pile in London, was all he expected. "Why do you talk of seeking the crown of martyrdom afar?" asked he. "Preach the gospel of Christ to haughty prelates, and martyrdom will not fail you. What! I should live and be silent? . . . never! Let the blow fall, I await its coming."

The stroke was spared him. The war between two wicked priests, Urban and Clement, left the disciples of our Lord in peace. And besides, was it worth while cutting short a life that was drawing to a close? Wycliffe, therefore, continued tranquilly to preach Jesus Christ; and on the 29th December 1384, as he was in his church at Lutterworth, in the midst of his flock, he was suddenly stricken with paralysis. He was carried to his house by the affectionate friends around him, and, after lingering forty-eight hours, resigned his soul to God on the last day of the year.

Thus was removed from the church one of the boldest witnesses to the truth. The seriousness of his language, the

holiness of his life, and the energy of his faith, had intimidated
the popedom. Travellers relate that if a lion is met in the desert,
it is sufficient to look steadily at him, and the beast turns away
roaring from the eye of man. Wycliffe had fixed the eye of a
Christian on the papacy, and the affrighted papacy had left
him in peace. Hunted down unceasingly while living, he died
in quiet, in life and death a faithful witness to the truth of the
Word of God. A glorious end to a glorious life.

The Reformation of England had begun.

Wycliffe is the greatest of English reformers: he was in truth
the first reformer of Christendom, and to him, under God,
Britain is indebted for the honour of being the foremost in
the attack upon the theocratic system of Gregory VII. The work
of the Waldenses, excellent as it was, cannot be compared to
his. If Luther and Calvin are the fathers of the Reformation,
Wycliffe is its grandfather.

Wycliffe, like most great men, possessed qualities which are
not generally found together. While his understanding was emin-
ently speculative—his treatise entitled *De universalibus realibus*
(*on the Reality of universal Ideas*) made a sensation in philosophy
—he possessed that practical and active mind which characterizes the Anglo-Saxon race. As a divine, he was at once
scriptural and spiritual, soundly orthodox, and possessed of an
inward and lively faith. With a boldness that impelled him to
rush into the midst of danger, he combined a logical and con-
sistent mind, which constantly led him forward in knowledge,
and caused him to maintain with perseverance the truths he had
once proclaimed. First of all, as a Christian, he had devoted
his strength to the cause of the church; but he was at the same
time a citizen, and the realm, his nation, and his king, had also
a great share in his unwearied activity. He was a man complete.

If the man is admirable, his teaching is no less so. Scripture,
which is the rule of truth, should be (according to his views)
the rule of Reformation, and we must reject every doctrine
and every precept which does not rest on that foundation. He
declared that to believe in the power of man in the work of
regeneration is the great heresy of Rome, and from that error
has come the ruin of the church. Conversion proceeds from
the grace of God alone, and the system which ascribes it partly
to man and partly to God is worse than Pelagianism. Christ

is everything in Christianity; whosoever abandons that fountain which is ever ready to impart life, and turns to muddy and stagnant waters, is a madman. Faith is a gift of God; it puts aside all merit, and should banish all fear from the mind. The one thing needful in the Christian life and in the Lord's Supper is not a vain formalism and superstitious rites, but communion with Christ according to the power of the spiritual life. Let Christians submit not to the word of a priest but to the Word of God. In the primitive church there were but two orders, the deacon and the presbyter: the presbyter and the bishop were one. The sublimest calling which man can attain on earth is that of preaching the Word of God. The true church is the assembly of the righteous for whom Christ shed his blood. So long as Christ is in heaven, in Him the church possesses the best pope. It is possible for a pope to be condemned at the last day because of his sins. Should men compel us to recognize as our head "a devil of hell?" Such were the essential points of Wycliffe's doctrine. It was the echo of the doctrine of the apostles—the prelude to that of the reformers.[1]

[1] [Professor Gotthard Lechler's *John Wycliffe and his English Precursors* (described by Prof. Lorimer, who translated it from the German, as "a preliminary history of the Reformation") should be consulted by all who desire to reach an understanding of Wycliffe's doctrine. Discussing Wycliffe's doctrine of the church, he writes as follows: "There is one peculiar feature of his fundamental idea of the Church. Not that this peculiarity was anything new, or belonged only to Wycliffe (he has it, as he was well aware, in common with Augustine) but it is one of very great importance, and runs like a scarlet thread through the whole system of Wycliffe's thinking—we mean the thought that the Church is nothing else than *the whole number of the elect*. . . . According to Wycliffe, the eternal ground or basis of the Church lies in the *divine election* . . . he places himself in deliberate opposition to the idea of the Church which prevailed in his time . . . according to which men took the Church to mean the *visible* Catholic Church—the organized communion of the hierarchy. Wycliffe, on the contrary, seeks the Church's centre of gravity in the past eternity, in the invisible world above. . . . A soul is incorporated with Christ, or betrothed to Christ, not by any act of man, not by any earthly means and visible signs, but by the decree of God, according to His eternal election and fore-ordination. The Church, therefore, has in the visible world only its manifestation, its temporary pilgrimage; it has its home and its origin, as also its end, in the invisible world, in eternity. Every individual devout Christian owes all that he possesses in his inner life to the regeneration which is the fruit of election. It is only by virtue of the gracious election of God that the individual belongs to the number of the saved. . . . Further, as Wycliffe carries back conversion, salvation, and membership of the Church to the election of grace, *i.e.* to the eternal and free decree of God in Christ, he, at the same

In many respects Wycliffe is the Luther of England; but the times of revival had not yet come, and the English reformer could not gain such striking victories over Rome as the German reformer. While Luther was surrounded by an ever-increasing number of scholars and princes, who confessed the same faith as himself, Wycliffe shone almost alone in the firmament of the church. The boldness with which he substituted a living spirituality for a superstitious formalism, caused those to shrink back in affright who had gone with him against friars, priests, and popes. Erelong the Roman pontiff ordered him to be thrown into prison, and the monks threatened his life; but God protected him, and he remained calm amidst the machinations of his adversaries. "Antichrist," said he, "can only kill the body." Having one foot in the grave already, he foretold that, from the very bosom of monkery, would some day proceed the regeneration of the church. "If the friars, whom God condescends to teach, shall be converted to the primitive religion of Christ," said he, "we shall see them abandoning their unbelief, returning freely, with or without the permission of Antichrist, to the primitive religion of the Lord, and building up the church, as did St Paul."

Thus did Wycliffe's piercing glance discover, at the distance of nearly a century and a half, the young monk Luther in the Augustine convent at Erfurt, converted by the Epistle to the Romans, and returning to the spirit of St Paul and the religion of Jesus Christ. Time was hastening on to the fulfilment of this prophecy. "The morning star of the Reformation," for so has Wycliffe been called, had appeared above the horizon, and its beams were no more to be extinguished. In vain will thick clouds veil it at times; the distant hilltops of Central Europe will soon reflect its rays;[1] and its piercing light, increasing in brightness, will pour over all the world, at the hour of the church's renovation, floods of knowledge and of life.

time, is far removed from the assumption, which up to that time was universal, that participation in salvation and the hope of heaven were conditioned exclusively by a man's connection with the official Church, and were dependent entirely upon the mediation of the priesthood. There is thus included in Wycliffe's idea of the Church the recognition of the free and immediate access of believers to the grace of God in Christ; in other words, of the general priesthood of believers." (R.T.S. edition, revised by Lorimer, pp. 288–90.)]

[1] John Huss in Bohemia.

CHAPTER NINE

The Lollard Burnings

(15th Century)

YCLIFFE's death manifested the power of his teaching. The master being removed, his disciples set their hands to the plough, and England was almost won over to the reformer's doctrines. The Wycliffites recognized a ministry independent of Rome, and deriving authority from the Word of God alone. "Every minister," said they, "can administer the sacraments and attend to the cure of souls as well as the pope." To the licentious wealth of the clergy they opposed a Christian poverty, and to the degenerate asceticism of the mendicant orders, a spiritual and free life. The townsfolk crowded around these humble preachers; the soldiers listened to them, armed with sword and buckler to defend them; the nobility took down the images from their baronial chapels; and even the royal family was partly won over to the Reformation. England was like a tree cut down to the ground, from whose roots fresh buds were shooting out on every side, erelong to cover all the earth beneath their shade.

This augmented the courage of Wycliffe's disciples, and in many places the people took the initiative in the reform. The walls of St Paul's and other cathedrals were hung with placards aimed at the priests and friars, and the abuses of which they were the defenders; and in 1395 the friends of the Gospel petitioned parliament for a general reform. "The essence of the worship which comes from Rome," said they, "consists in signs and ceremonies, and not in the effectual ministry of the Holy Ghost: and therefore it is not that which Christ has ordained. Temporal things are distinct from spiritual things: a king and a bishop ought not to be one and the same person." And then, from not clearly understanding the principle of the separation of the functions which they proclaimed, they called upon parliament to "abolish celibacy, transubstantiation, prayers for the dead, offerings to images, auricular confession, war, the arts unnecessary to life, the practice of blessing oil, salt, wax, incense, stones, mitres, and pilgrims' staffs. All these pertain to necromancy and not to theology." Emboldened by the absence of the king in Ireland, they fixed their *Twelve Conclusions* on the gates of St Paul's and Westminster Abbey. This became the signal for persecution.

As soon as Arundel, archbishop of York, and Braybrooke, bishop of London, had read these propositions, they hastily crossed St George's Channel, and conjured the king to return to England. He did so. Richard, during childhood and youth, had been committed in succession to the charge of several guardians, and like children (says an historian) whose nurses have been often changed, he thrived none the better for it. He did good or evil, according to the influence of those around him, and, after the death of his pious wife, Anne of Bohemia, in 1394, he had no decided inclinations except for ostentation and licentiousness. The clergy were not mistaken in calculating on such a prince. On his return to London he forbade the parliament to take the Wycliffite petition into consideration; and having summoned before him the most distinguished of its supporters, such as Story, Clifford, Latimer, and Montacute, he threatened them with death if they continued to defend their abominable opinions. Thus was the work of the reformer about to be destroyed.

But Richard had hardly withdrawn his hand from the gospel, when God (says Foxe the annalist) withdrew his hand from him. His cousin, Henry Bolingbroke, son of the famous Duke of Lancaster, and who had been banished from England, suddenly sailed from the continent, landed in Yorkshire, gathered all the malcontents around him, and was acknowledged king. The unhappy Richard, after being formally deposed, was confined in Pontefract castle, where his earthly career was soon terminated.

The son of Wycliffe's old defender was now king with the title of Henry IV: a reform of the church seemed imminent; but the primate Arundel had foreseen the danger. This cunning priest and skilful politician had observed which way the wind blew, and deserted Richard in good time. Taking Lancaster by the hand, he put the crown on his head, saying to him: "To consolidate your throne, conciliate the clergy, and

sacrifice the Lollards."—"I will be the protector of the church,"
replied Henry IV, and from that hour the power of the priests
was greater than the power of the nobility. Rome has ever
been adroit in profiting by revolutions.

Henry ascended the throne in the late summer of 1399. In
1401 the famous Act for the burning of heretics, *De Haeretico
Comburendo*, was passed by Parliament. The church claimed
that the Act was in accord with a well-established principle,
and to provide evidence that this was so, they hurried through
the burning of a Lollard martyr in March, 1401. The Act was
passed some eight days later.

Protestantism's proto-martyr was a pious priest named
William Sawtre who had presumed to say: "Instead of
adoring the cross on which Christ suffered, I adore Christ who
suffered on it." He was dragged to St Paul's; his hair was
shaved off; a layman's cap was placed on his head; and the
primate handed him over to the *mercy* of the earl-marshal of
England. This *mercy* was shown him—he was burnt alive at
Smithfield, the first of a "noble army" in England who loved
not their lives unto the death.

Encouraged by this act of faith—this *auto da fé*—the clergy
drew up the articles known as the "Constitutions of Arundel,"
which forbade the translation and reading of the Bible without
the permission of the Ordinary (*i.e.* a bishop or similar high
officer of the church) and styled the pope, "not a mere man,
but a true God." The Lollards' tower, in the archiepiscopal
palace of Lambeth, was soon filled with pretended heretics,
many of whom carved on the walls of their dungeons the
expression of their sorrow and their hopes: *Jesus amor meus*,
(Jesus is my love) wrote one of them. The words are still to
be read in the tower.

To crush the lowly was not enough: the gospel must be
driven from the more exalted stations. The priests, who were
sincere in their belief, regarded those noblemen as misleaders,
who set the Word of God above the laws of Rome; and accordingly they girded themselves for the work. A few miles from
Rochester stood Cowling Castle, in the midst of the fertile
pastures watered by the Medway,

> The fair Medwaya that with wanton pride
> Forms silver mazes with her crooked tide.

In the beginning of the fifteenth century it was inhabited by Sir John Oldcastle, who became by his marriage, Lord Cobham, a man in high favour with the king.[1] The "poor priests" thronged to Cowling in quest of Wycliffe's writings, of which Cobham had caused numerous copies to be made, and whence they were circulated through the dioceses of Canterbury, Rochester, London, and Hertford. Cobham attended their preaching and, if any enemies ventured to interrupt them, he threatened them with his sword. "I would sooner risk my life," said he, "than submit to such unjust decrees as dishonour the everlasting Testament." The king would not permit the clergy to lay hands on his favourite.

But Henry V having succeeded his father in 1413, and passed from the houses of ill-fame he had hitherto frequented to the foot of the altars and the head of the armies, the archbishop immediately denounced Cobham to him, and he was summoned to appear before the king. Sir John had understood Wycliffe's doctrine, and experienced in his own person the might of the divine Word. "As touching the pope and his spirituality," he said to the king, "I owe them neither suit nor service, forasmuch as I know him by the Scriptures to be the great antichrist." Henry thrust aside Cobham's hand as he presented his confession of faith: "I will not receive this paper; lay it before your judges." When he saw his profession refused, Cobham had recourse to the only arm which he knew of out of the gospel. The differences which we now settle by pamphlets were then very commonly settled by the sword—"I offer in defence of my faith to fight for life or death with any man living, Christian or pagan, always excepting your majesty." Cobham was led to the Tower.

On the 23rd September, 1413, he was taken before the ecclesiastical tribunal then sitting at St Paul's. "We must believe," said the primate to him, "what the holy church of Rome teaches, without demanding Christ's authority."— "Believe!" shouted the priests, "believe!"—"I am willing to believe all that God desires," said Sir John; "but that the pope should have authority to teach what is contrary to Scripture—

---

[1] [It is highly probable that he had been the close friend and companion of the youthful Henry V in the days of that prince's "riotous living." As such he is said to have been the basis of Shakespeare's Falstaff.]

that I can never believe." He was led back to the Tower. The Word of God was to have its martyr.

On Monday, 25th September, a crowd of priests, canons, friars, clerks, and indulgence-sellers, thronged the large hall of the Dominican convent, and attacked Lord Cobham with abusive language. These insults, the importance of the moment for the Reformation of England, the catastrophe that must needs close the scene: all agitated his soul to its very depths. When the archbishop called upon him to confess his offence, he fell on his knees and, lifting up his hands to heaven, exclaimed: "I confess to Thee, O God! and acknowledge that in my frail youth I seriously offended Thee by my pride, anger, intemperance, and impurity: for these offences I implore Thy mercy!" Then standing up, his face still wet with tears, he said: "I ask not your absolution: it is God's only that I need." The clergy did not despair, however, of reducing this high-spirited gentleman: they knew that spiritual strength is not always conjoined with bodily vigour, and they hoped to vanquish by priestly sophisms the man who dared challenge the papal champions to single combat. "Sir John," said the primate at last, "you have said some very strange things; we have spent much time in endeavours to convince you, but all to no effect. The day passeth away: you must either submit yourself to the ordinance of the most holy church or . . ." "I will none otherwise believe than what I have told you. Do with me what you will."— "Well then, we must needs do the law," the archbishop made answer.

Arundel stood up; all the priests and people rose with him and uncovered their heads. Then holding the sentence of death in his hand, he read it with a loud clear voice. "It is well," said Sir John; "though you condemn my body, you can do no harm to my soul, by the grace of my eternal God." He was again led back to the Tower, and given forty days in which to recant. But one night before that period ended Lord Cobham escaped, and took refuge in Wales. He was retaken in December 1417, carried to London, dragged on a hurdle to Saint Giles's fields, and there suspended by chains over a slow fire, and cruelly burned to death. Thus died a Christian, illustrious after the fashion of his age—a champion of the Word of God. Shortly the London prisons were filled with Wycliffites, and it was decreed that they should be hanged on the king's account, and burnt for God's.

The intimidated Lollards were compelled to hide themselves in the humblest ranks of the people, and to hold their meetings in secret. The work of redemption was proceeding noiselessly among the elect of God. Of these Lollards, there were many who were doubtless true disciples of Jesus Christ; but in general they knew not, to the same extent as the evangelical Christians of the sixteenth century, the quickening and justifying power of faith. They were plain, meek, and often timid folks, attracted by the Word of God, affected at the condemnation it pronounces against the errors of Rome, and desirous of living according to its commandments. God had assigned them a part—and an important part too—in the great transformation of Christianity. Their humble piety, their passive resistance, the shameful treatment which they bore with resignation, the penitent's robes with which they were covered, the tapers they were compelled to hold at the church door—all these things betrayed the pride of the priests, and filled the most generous minds with doubts and vague desires. By a baptism of suffering, God was then preparing the way to a glorious reformation.

CHAPTER TEN

The New Learning and the New Dynasty

(c. 1485–1512)

THIS reformation was to be the result of two distinct forces—
the revival of learning and the resurrection of the Word of
God. The latter was the principal cause, but the former was
necessary as a means. Without it the living waters of the gospel
would probably have traversed the age, like summer streams
which soon dry up, such as those which had burst forth here
and there during the middle ages; it would not have become
that majestic river, which, by its inundations, fertilized all the
earth. It was necessary to discover and examine the original
fountains, and for this end the study of Greek and Hebrew was
indispensable. Lollardism and humanism (the study of the
classics) were the two laboratories of the reform. Having seen
the preparations of the one, we must now trace the commencement of the other; and as we have discovered the light in the
lowly valleys, we shall discern it also on the lofty mountain tops.

About the end of the fifteenth century, several young
Englishmen chanced to be at Florence, attracted thither by the
literary glory which environed the city of the Medici. Cosmo
had collected together a great number of works of antiquity,
and his palace was thronged with learned men. William
Sellyng, a young English ecclesiastic, afterwards distinguished
at Canterbury by his zeal in collecting valuable manuscripts;
his fellow-countrymen, William Grocyn, William Lilly, and
William Latimer "more bashful than a maiden;" and, above
all, Thomas Linacre, whom Erasmus ranked before all the
scholars of Italy—used to meet in the delightful villa of the
Medici with Politian, Chalcondyles, and other men of learning;
and there, in the calm evenings of summer, under that glorious
Tuscan sky, they dreamt romantic visions of the Platonic
philosophy. When they returned to England, these learned
men laid before the youth of Oxford the marvellous treasures

of the Greek language. Some Italians even, attracted by the desire to enlighten the barbarians, and a little, it may be, by the brilliant offers made them, quitted their beloved country for the distant Britain. Cornelio Vitelli taught at Oxford, and Caius Amberino at Cambridge. Caxton imported the art of printing from Germany, and the nation hailed with enthusiasm the brilliant dawn which was breaking at last in their cloudy sky.

While learning was reviving in England, a new dynasty succeeded to the throne, bringing with it that energy of character which of itself is able to effect great revolutions; the Tudors succeeded the Plantagenets. That inflexible intrepidity by which the reformers of Germany, Switzerland, France, and Scotland were distinguished, did not exist so generally in those of England; but it was found in the character of her kings, who often stretched it even to violence. It may be that to this preponderance of energy in its rulers, the church owes the preponderance of the state in its affairs.

Henry Tudor, the Louis XI of England, was a clever prince, of decided but suspicious character, avaricious and narrow-minded. Being descended from a Welsh family, he belonged to that ancient race of Celts, who had so long contended against the papacy. Henry extinguished faction at home, and taught foreign nations to respect his power. A good genius seemed to exercise a salutary influence over his court as well as over himself: this was his mother, the Countess of Richmond. From her chamber, where she consecrated the first five hours of the day to reading, meditation, and prayer, she moved to another part of the palace to dress the wounds of some of the lowest mendicants; thence she passed into the gay saloons, where she would converse with the scholars, whom she encouraged by her munificence. This noble lady's passion for study, of which her son inherited but little, was not without its influence in her family. Arthur and Henry, the king's sons, trembled in their father's presence; but, captivated by the affection of their pious grandmother, they began to find a pleasure in the society of learned men. An important circumstance gave a new impulse to one of them.

Among the countess's friends was William Blount, Lord Mountjoy, who had known Erasmus at Paris, and heard his cutting sarcasms upon the schoolmen and friars. He invited the illustrious Dutchman to England, and Erasmus, who was fearful of catching the plague, gladly accepted the invitation, and set out for what he believed to be the kingdom of darkness. But he had not been long in England before he discovered unexpected light.

Shortly after his arrival, happening to dine with the lord-mayor of London, Erasmus noticed on the other side of the table a young man of nineteen, slender, fresh-coloured, with blue eyes, coarse hands, and the right shoulder somewhat higher than the other. His features indicated affability and gaiety, and pleasant jests were continually dropping from his lips. If he could not find a joke in English, he would in French, and even in Latin or Greek. A literary contest soon ensued between Erasmus and the English youth. The former, astonished at meeting with any one that could hold his own against him, exclaimed: *Aut tu es Morus aut nullus!* (you are either More or nobody); and his companion, who had not learnt the stranger's name, quickly replied: *Aut tu es Erasmus aut diabolus!* (you are either the devil or Erasmus). More flung himself into the arms of Erasmus, and they became inseparable friends. More was continually joking, even with women, teasing the sprightly, and making fun of the dull, though without any tinge of ill-nature in his jests. But under this sportive exterior he concealed a deep understanding. He was at that time lecturing on Augustine's *City of God* before a numerous audience composed of priests and aged men. The thought of eternity had seized him; and being ignorant of that internal discipline of the Holy Ghost, which is the only true discipline, he had recourse to the scourge every Friday. Thomas More is the ideal of the catholicism of this period. He had, like the Romish system, two poles—worldliness and asceticism; which, although contrary, often meet together. In fact, asceticism makes a sacrifice of *self*, only to preserve it; just as a traveller attacked by robbers will readily give up a portion of his treasures to save the rest. This was the case with More, if we rightly understand his character. He sacrificed the accessories of his fallen nature to save that same nature. He submitted to fasts and vigils, wore a shirt of hair-cloth, mortified his body by small chains next his skin—in a word, he immolated everything in order to preserve that *self* which a real regeneration alone can sacrifice.

From London Erasmus went to Oxford, where he met with John Colet, a friend of More's, but older, and of very dissimilar character. Colet, the scion of an ancient family, was a very portly man, of imposing aspect, great fortune, and elegance of manners, to which Erasmus had not been accustomed. Order, cleanliness, and decorum prevailed in his person and in his house. He kept an excellent table, which was open to all the friends of learning, and at which the Dutchman, no great admirer of the colleges of Paris with their sour wine and stale eggs, was glad to take a seat. He there met also most of the classical scholars of England, especially Grocyn, Linacre, Thomas Wolsey, bursar of Magdalen College, Halsey, and some others. "I cannot tell you how I am delighted with your England," he wrote to Lord Mountjoy from Oxford. "With such men I could willingly live in the farthest coasts of Scythia."

But if Erasmus on the banks of the Thames found a Mæcenas in Lord Mountjoy, a Labeo and perhaps a Virgil in More, he nowhere found an Augustus. One day as he was expressing his regrets and his fears to More, the latter said: "Come, let us go to Eltham, perhaps we shall find there what you are looking for." They set out, More jesting all the way, inwardly resolving to expiate his gaiety by a severe scourging at night. On their arrival they were heartily welcomed by Lord and Lady Mountjoy, the governor and governess of the king's children. As the two friends entered the hall, a pleasing and unexpected sight greeted Erasmus. The whole of the family were assembled, and they found themselves surrounded not only by some of the royal household, but by the domestics of Lord Mountjoy also. On the right stood the Princess Margaret, a girl of eleven years, whose great-grandson under the name of Stuart was to continue the Tudor line in England; on the left was Mary, a child four years of age; Edmund was in his nurse's arms; and in the middle of the circle, between his two sisters, stood a boy, at that time only nine years old, whose handsome features, royal carriage, intelligent eye, and exquisite courtesy, had an extraordinary charm for Erasmus. That boy was Henry, Duke of York, the king's second son, born on the 28th June 1491. More, advancing towards the young prince, presented to him some piece of his own writing; and from that hour Erasmus kept up a friendly intercourse with Henry, which in all probability exercised a certain influence over the destinies of England. The scholar of Rotterdam was delighted to see the prince excel in all the manly sports of the day. He sat his horse with perfect grace and rare intrepidity, could hurl a javelin farther than any of his companions, and having an excellent taste for music, he was already a performer on several instruments. The king took care that he should receive a learned education—it may have been the case that he destined him to fill the see of Canterbury—and the illustrious Erasmus, noticing his aptitude for every thing he undertook, did his best to cut and polish this English diamond that it might glitter with the greater brilliancy. "He will begin nothing that he will not finish," said the scholar. And it is but too true that this prince always attained his end, even if it were necessary to tread on the bleeding bodies of those he had loved. Flattered by the attentions of the young Henry, attracted by his winning grace, charmed by his wit, Erasmus on his return to the continent everywhere proclaimed that England at last had found its Octavius.

As for Henry VII he thought of everything but Virgil or Augustus. Avarice and ambition were his predominant tastes, which he gratified by the marriage of his eldest son Arthur in 1501. Burgundy, Artois, Provence, and Brittany having been recently united to France, the European powers felt the necessity of combining against that encroaching state. It was in consequence of this that Ferdinand of Aragon had given his daughter Joanna to Philip of Austria, and that Henry VII asked the hand of his daughter Catherine, then in her sixteenth year and the richest princess in Europe, for Arthur, prince of Wales, a youth about ten months younger. The catholic king attached one condition to the marriage of his daughter. Warwick, the last of the Plantagenets and a pretender to the crown, was confined in the Tower. Ferdinand, to secure the certainty that Catherine would really ascend the English throne, required that the unhappy prince should be put to death. Nor did this alone satisfy the king of Spain. Henry VII, who was not a cruel man, might conceal Warwick, and say that he was no more. Ferdinand demanded that the chancellor of Castile should be

I

present at the execution. The blood of Warwick was shed; his head rolled duly on the scaffold; the Castilian chancellor verified and registered the murder, and on the 14th November the marriage was solemnized at St Paul's. At midnight the prince and princess were conducted with great pomp to the bridal-chamber. These were ill-omened nuptials—fated to set the kings and nations of Christendom in battle against one another, and to serve as a pretext for the external and political discussions of the English Reformation. The marriage of Catherine the Catholic was a marriage of blood.

In the early part of 1502 Prince Arthur fell ill, and on the 2nd of April he died. The necessary time was taken to be sure that Catherine had no hope of becoming a mother, after which the friend of Erasmus, the youthful Henry, was declared heir to the crown, to the great joy of all the learned. This prince did not forsake his studies: he spoke and wrote in French, German, and Spanish with the facility of a native; and England hoped to behold one day the most learned of Christian kings upon the throne of Alfred the Great.

A very different question, however, filled the mind of the covetous Henry VII. Must he restore to Spain the one hundred thousand crowns which formed the half of Catherine's dowry already paid, and forfeit his claims to the half as yet unpaid? Should this rich heiress be permitted to marry some rival of England? To prevent so great a misfortune the king conceived the project of uniting Henry to Arthur's widow. The most serious objections were urged against it. "It is not only inconsistent with propriety," said Warham, the primate, "but the will of God himself is against it. It is declared in His law that *if a man shall take his brother's wife, it is an unclean thing* (Lev. xx. 21); and in the Gospel John Baptist says to Herod: *It is not lawful for thee to have thy brother's wife*" (Mark vi. 18). Fox, bishop of Winchester, suggested that a dispensation might be procured from the pope, and in December 1503 Julius II granted a bull[1] declaring that for the sake of preserving union between the catholic princes he authorized Catherine's marriage with the

---

[1] [The Papal Bull dated 26th December 1503 is extant, but it seems that Henry VII did not receive it at that time, for months later he was in correspondence with the pope complaining that it had not been received in England.]

brother of her first husband, *accedente forsan copula carnali*. These four words, it is said, were inserted in the bull at the express desire of the princess. All these details will be of importance in the course of our history. The two parties were betrothed, but not married in consideration of the youth of the prince of Wales.

The second marriage projected by Henry VII was ushered in with auspices still less promising than the first. The king having fallen sick and lost his queen, looked upon these visitations as a divine judgment. The nation murmured, and demanded whether it was in the pope's power to permit what God had forbidden. The young prince, being informed of his father's scruples and of the people's discontent, declared, on the eve of his fourteenth birthday (27th June 1505) in the presence of the bishop of Winchester and several royal counsellors, that he protested against the engagement entered into during his minority, and that he would never make Catherine his wife.

His father's death, which made him free, made him also recall this virtuous decision. In 1509, the hopes of the learned seemed about to be realized. On the 9th of May, a hearse decorated with regal pomp, bearing on a rich pall of cloth of gold the mortal remains of Henry VII, with his sceptre and his crown, entered London from Richmond, followed by a long procession. The great officers of state, assembled round the coffin, broke their staves and cast them into the vault, and the heralds cried with a loud voice: "God send the noble King Henry VIII long life." Such a cry perhaps had never on any previous occasion been so joyfully repeated by the people. The young king gratified the wishes of the nation by ordering the arrest of Empson and Dudley, who were charged with extortion; and he conformed to the enlightened counsels of his grandmother, by choosing the most able ministers, and placing the archbishop of Canterbury as lord-chancellor at their head. Warham was a man of great capacity. The day was not too short for him to hear mass, receive ambassadors, consult with the king in the royal chamber, entertain as many as two hundred guests at his table, take his seat on the woolsack, and find time for his private devotions. The joy of the learned surpassed that of the people. The old king wanted none of their praises or congratulations, for fear he should have to pay for them; but now they could give free course to their enthusiasm.

Mountjoy pronounced the young king "divine;" the Venetian ambassador likened his bearing to Apollo's, and his noble chest to the torso of Mars; he was lauded both in Greek and Latin; he was hailed as the founder of a new era, and Henry seemed desirous of meriting these eulogiums. Far from permitting himself to be intoxicated by so much adulation, he said to Mountjoy: "Ah! how I should like to be a scholar!"—"Sire," replied the courtier, "it is enough that you show your regard for those who possess the learning you desire for yourself."— "How can I do otherwise," he replied with earnestness; "without them we hardly exist!" Mountjoy immediately communicated this to Erasmus.

Erasmus!—Erasmus!—the walls of Eltham, Oxford, and London resounded with the name. The king could not live without the learned; nor the learned without Erasmus. This scholar, who was an enthusiast for the young king, was not long in answering to the call. When Richard Pace, the king's secretary, and one of the most accomplished men of that age, met the learned Dutchman at Ferrara, the latter took from his pocket a little box which he always carried with him: "You do not know," he said, "what a treasure you have in England: I will just show you;" and he took from the box a letter of Henry's expressing in Latin of considerable purity the tenderest regard for his correspondent. Immediately after the coronation Mountjoy wrote to Erasmus: "Our Henry *Octavus*, or rather *Octavius*, is on the throne. Come and behold the new star. The heavens smile, the earth leaps for joy, and all is flowing with milk, nectar, and honey. Avarice has fled away, liberality has descended, scattering on every side with gracious hand her bounteous largesses. Our king desires not gold or precious stones, but virtue, glory, and immortality."

In such glowing terms was the young king described by a man who had seen him closely. Erasmus could resist no longer: he bade the pope farewell, and hastened to London, where he met with a hearty welcome from Henry. Knowledge and power embraced each other: England was about to have its Medici; and the friends of learning no longer doubted of the regeneration of Britain.

Julius II, who had permitted Erasmus to exchange the white frock of the monks for the black dress of the seculars, allowed him to depart without much regret. This pontiff had little taste for letters, but was fond of war, hunting, and the pleasures of the table. The English sent him a dish to his taste in exchange for the scholar. Sometime after Erasmus had left, as the pope was one day reposing from the fatigues of the chase, he heard voices near him singing a strange song. He asked with surprise what it meant. "It is some Englishmen," was the answer, and three foreigners entered the room, each bearing a closely-covered jar, which the youngest presented on his knees. This was Thomas Cromwell, who appears here for the first time on the historic scene. He was the son of a blacksmith of Putney; but he possessed a mind so penetrating, a judgment so sound, a heart so bold, ability so consummate, such easy elocution, such an accurate memory, such great activity, and so able a pen, that the most brilliant career awaited him. At about eighteen years of age he left England, being desirous to see the world, and after a period in Italy he began life as a trader in the English factory at Antwerp. Shortly after this two fellow-countrymen from Boston came to him in their embarrassment. "What do you want?" he asked them. "Our townsmen have sent us to the pope," they told him, "to get the renewal of the *greater* and *lesser pardons*, whose term is nearly run, and which are necessary for the repair of our harbour. But we do not know how to appear before him." Cromwell, prompt to undertake everything, and knowing a little Italian, replied, "I will go with you." Then slapping his forehead he muttered to himself: "What fish can I throw out as a bait to these greedy cormorants?" A friend informed him that the pope was very fond of dainties. Cromwell immediately ordered some exquisite jelly to be prepared, after the English fashion, and set out for Italy with his provisions and his two companions.

This was the man who appeared before Julius after his return from the chase. "Kings and princes alone eat of this preserve in England," said Cromwell to the pope. One cardinal, who was a greedier "cormorant" than his master, eagerly tasted the delicacy. "Try it," he exclaimed, and the pope, relishing this new confectionery, immediately signed the pardons, on condition however that the recipe for the jelly should be left with him. "And thus were the *jelly-pardons* obtained," says the annalist. It was Cromwell's first exploit, and the man who began his busy career by presenting jars of confectionery to the pope was also the man destined to separate England from Rome.

The court of the pontiff was not the only one in Europe devoted to gaiety. Hunting parties were as common in London as at Rome. The young king and his companions were at that time absorbed in balls, banquets, and the other festivities inseparable from a new reign. He recollected however that he must give a queen to his people: Catherine of Aragon was still in England, and the council recommended her for his wife. He admired her piety without caring to imitate it; he was pleased with her love for literature, and even felt some inclination towards her. His advisers represented to him that "Catherine, daughter of the illustrious Isabella of Castile, was the image of her mother; that, like her, she possessed that wisdom and greatness of mind which win the respect of nations; and that if she carried to any of his rivals her marriage-portion and the Spanish alliance, the long-contested crown of England would soon fall from his head. . . . We have the pope's dispensation: will you be more scrupulous than he is?" The archbishop of Canterbury opposed in vain: Henry gave way, and on the eleventh of June, about seven weeks after his father's death, the nuptials were privately celebrated at Greenwich. On the twenty-third the king and queen went in state through the city, the bride wearing a white satin dress with her hair hanging down her back nearly to her feet. On the next day they were crowned at Westminster with great magnificence.

Then followed a series of expensive entertainments. The treasures which the nobility had long concealed from fear of the old king, were now brought out; the ladies glittered with gold and diamonds; and the king and queen, whom the people never grew tired of admiring, amused themselves like children with the splendour of their royal robes. Henry VIII was the forerunner of Louis XIV. Naturally inclined to pomp and pleasure, the idol of his people, a devoted admirer of female beauty, and the husband of almost as many wives as Louis had adulterous mistresses, he made the court of England what the son of Anne of Austria made the court of France—one constant scene of amusements. He thought he could never get to the end of the riches amassed by his prudent father. His youth—for he was only eighteen—the gaiety of his disposition, the grace he displayed in all bodily exercises, the tales of chivalry in which he delighted, and which even the clergy recommended to their high-born hearers, the flattery of his courtiers—all these combined to set his young imagination in a ferment. Wherever he appeared, all were filled with admiration of his handsome countenance and graceful figure: such is the portrait bequeathed to us by the Jesuit, Nicholas Sander, his greatest enemy. "His brow was made to wear the crown, and his majestic port the kingly mantle," adds Noryson.

Henry resolved to realize without delay the chivalrous combats and fabulous splendours of the heroes of the Round Table, as if to prepare himself for those more real struggles which he would one day have to maintain against the papacy. At the sound of the trumpet the youthful monarch would enter the lists, clad in costly armour, and wearing a plume that fell gracefully down to the saddle of his vigorous courser; "like an untamed bull," says an historian, "which breaks away from its yoke and rushes into the arena." On one occasion, at the celebration of the queen's churching, Catherine with her ladies was seated in a tent of purple and gold, in the midst of an artificial forest, strewn with rocks and variegated with flowers. On a sudden a monk stepped forward, wearing a long brown robe, and kneeling before her, begged permission to run a course. It was granted, and rising up he threw aside his coarse frock, and appeared gorgeously armed for the tourney. He was Charles Brandon, afterwards Duke of Suffolk, one of the handsomest and strongest men in the kingdom, and the first after Henry in military exercises. He was followed by a number of others dressed in black velvet, with wide-brimmed hats on their heads, staffs in their hands, and scarfs across their shoulders ornamented with cockle shells, like pilgrims from St James of Compostella. These also threw off their disguise, and stood forth in complete armour. At their head was Sir Thomas Boleyn, whose daughter was destined to surpass in beauty, greatness, and misfortune, all the women of England. The tournament began. Henry, who has been compared to Amadis in boldness, to the lion-hearted Richard in courage, and to Edward III in courtesy, did not always escape danger in these chivalrous contests. One day the king had forgotten to lower his vizor, and Brandon, his opponent, setting off at full gallop, the spectators noticed the oversight, and cried out in alarm. But nothing could stop their horses: the two cavaliers met. Suffolk's lance was shivered against Henry, and the fragments struck him in the face. Everyone thought the king was dead, and some were running to arrest Brandon, when Henry, recovering from the blow whch had fallen on his helmet, recommenced the combat, and ran six new courses amid the admiring cries of his subjects. This intrepid courage changed, as he grew older, into unsparing cruelty; and it was this young tiger, whose movements were then so graceful, that at no distant day tore with his blood-red fangs the mother of his children.

CHAPTER ELEVEN

War, Marriage, and Preaching

(1513–15)

A MESSAGE from the pope stopped Henry in the midst of these amusements. In Scotland, Spain, France, and Italy, the young king had nothing but friends; a harmony which the papacy was intent on disturbing. One day, immediately after high-mass had been celebrated, the archbishop of Canterbury, on behalf of Julius II laid at his feet a golden rose, which had been blessed by the pope, anointed with holy oil, and perfumed with musk. It was accompanied by a letter saluting him as head of the Italian league. The warlike pontiff having reduced the Venetians, desired to humble France, and to employ Henry as the instrument of his vengeance. Henry, only a short time before, had renewed his alliance with Louis XII; but the pope was not to be baffled by such a trifle as that, and the young king soon began to dream of rivalling the glories of Crécy, Poitiers, and Agincourt. To no purpose did his wisest councillors represent to him that England, in the most favourable times, had never been able to hold her ground in France, and that the sea was the true field open to her conquests. Julius, knowing his vanity, had promised to deprive Louis of the title of Most Christian King, and confer it upon him. "His Holiness hopes that your Grace will utterly exterminate the king of France," wrote the king's agent. Henry saw nothing objectionable in this very unapostolic mission, and decided on substituting the terrible game of war for the gentler sports of peace.

After some unsuccessful attempts by his generals, Henry determined to invade France in person. He was in the midst of his preparations when the festival of Easter arrived. Dean Colet had been appointed to preach before Henry on Good Friday, and in the course of his sermon he showed more courage than could have been expected in a scholar, for a spark of the

Christian spirit was glowing in his bosom. He chose for the subject of his discourse Christ's victory over death and the grave. "Whoever takes up arms from ambition," said he, "fights not under the standard of Christ, but of Satan. If you desire to contend against your enemies, follow Jesus Christ as your prince and captain, rather than Cæsar or Alexander." His hearers looked at each other with astonishment; the friends of polite literature became alarmed; and the priests, who were getting uneasy at the uprising of the human mind, hoped to profit by this opportunity of inflicting a deadly blow on their antagonists. There were among them men whose opinions we must condemn, while we cannot forbear respecting the zeal for what they believed to be the truth: of this number were Bricot, Fitzjames, and above all Standish. Their zeal, however, went a little too far on this occasion: they even talked of *burning* the dean.[1] After the sermon, Colet was informed that the king requested his attendance in the garden of the Franciscan monastery, and immediately the priests and monks crowded round the gate, hoping to see their adversary led forth as a criminal. "Let us be alone," said Henry; "put on your cap, Mr Dean, and we will take a walk. Cheer up," he continued, "you have nothing to fear. You have spoken admirably of Christian charity, and have almost reconciled me to the king of France; yet, as the contest is not one of choice, but of necessity, I must beg of you in some future sermon to explain this to my people. Unless you do so, I fear my soldiers may misunderstand your meaning." Colet was not a John Baptist, and, affected by the king's condescension, he gave the required explanation. The king was satisfied, and exclaimed: "Let every man have his doctor as he pleases; this man is my doctor, and I will drink his health!" Henry was then young: very different was the fashion with which in after-years he treated those who opposed him.

At heart the king cared little more about the victories of Alexander than of Jesus Christ. Having fitted out his army, he embarked at the end of June, 1513, accompanied by his almoner, Wolsey, who was rising into favour, and set out for the war as if for a tournament. Shortly after this, he went, all

---

[1] Dr Colet was in trouble and should have been burnt, if God had not turned the King's heart to the contrary. *Latimer's Sermons.* (Parker Society, p. 440.)

glittering with jewels, to meet the Emperor Maximilian, who received him in a plain doublet and cloak of black serge. After his victory at the battle of the Spurs, Henry, instead of pressing forward to the conquest of France, returned to the siege of Thérouanne, wasted his time in jousts and entertainments, conferred on Wolsey the bishopric of Tournai which he had just captured, and then returned to England, delighted at having made so pleasant an excursion.

Louis XII was a widower in his 53rd year, and bowed down by the infirmities of a premature old age; but being desirous of preventing, at any cost, the renewal of the war, he sought the hand of Henry's sister, the Princess Mary, then in her 18th year. Her affections were already fixed on Charles Brandon, and for him she would have sacrificed the splendour of a throne. But reasons of state opposed their union. "The princess," remarked Wolsey, "will soon return to England a widow with a royal dowry." This decided the question. The disconsolate Mary, who was an object of universal pity, embarked at Dover with a numerous train, and from Boulogne, where she was received by the duke of Angoulême, she was conducted to the king, who was elated at the idea of marrying the hand-somest princess in Europe.

Among Mary's attendants was the youthful Anne Boleyn. Her father, Sir Thomas Boleyn, had been charged by Henry, conjointly with the bishop of Ely, with the diplomatic negotiations preliminary to this marriage. Anne had passed her childhood at Hever Castle, Kent, surrounded by all that could heat the imagination. Her maternal grandfather, the earl of Surrey, whose eldest son had married the sister of Henry the Seventh's queen, had filled, as did his sons also, the most important offices of state. When summoned by her father to court, she wrote him the following letter in French, which appears to refer to her departure for France:

"SIR—I find by your letter that you wish me to appear at court in a manner becoming a respectable female, and likewise that the queen will condescend to enter into conversation with me; at this I rejoice, as I do to think that conversing with so sensible and elegant a princess will make me even more desirous of continuing to speak and to write good French; the more as it is by your earnest advice, which (I acquaint you by this present writing) I shall follow to the best of my ability. . . . As to myself, rest assured that I shall not ungratefully look upon this fatherly office as one that might be dispensed with; nor will it tend to diminish my affection, quest [wish], and deliberation to lead as holy a life as you may please to desire of me; indeed my love for you is founded on so firm a basis that it can never be impaired. I put an end to this my lucubration after having very humbly craved your good will and affection. Written at Hever, by

Your very humble and obedient daughter,

ANNA DE BOULLAN."

Such were the feelings under which this young and interesting lady, so calumniated by papistical writers, appeared at court.

The marriage which took place by proxy in London, on the 18th August, 1514, was formally proclaimed and celebrated at Abbeville on the 9th of October, and, after a sumptuous banquet, the king of France distributed his royal largesses among the English lords, who were charmed by his courtesy. But the morrow was a day of trial to the young queen. Louis XII had dismissed the numerous train which had accompanied her, and even Lady Guildford, to whom Henry had specially confided her. Three only were left—of whom the youthful Anne Boleyn was one. At this separation, Mary gave way to the keenest sorrow. To cheer her spirits, Louis proclaimed a grand tournament. Brandon hastened to France at its first announcement, and carried off all the prizes, while the king, languidly reclining on a couch, could with difficulty look upon the brilliant spectacle over which his queen presided, sick at heart yet radiant with youth and beauty. Mary was unable to conceal her emotion, and Louisa of Savoy, who was watching her, divined her secret. But Louis, if he experienced the tortures of jealousy, did not feel them long, for his death took place on the 1st January, 1515.

Even before her husband's funeral was over, Mary's heart beat high with hope. The new French monarch, Francis I, impatient to see her wedded to some unimportant political personage, encouraged her love for Brandon. The latter, who

had been commissioned by Henry to convey to her his letters
of condolence, feared his master's anger if he should dare aspire
to the hand of the princess. But the widowed queen, who was
resolved to brave everything, told her lover: "Either you
marry me in four days or you see me no more." The choice
the king had made of his ambassador announced that he would
not behave very harshly. The marriage was celebrated in the
abbey of Clugny, and Henry pardoned them, but only on the
payment of a heavy fine by both parties.

While Mary returned to England, as Wolsey had predicted,
Anne Boleyn remained in France. Her father, desiring his
daughter to become an accomplished woman, intrusted her to
the care of the virtuous Claude of France, *the good queen*, at
whose court the daughters of the first families of the kingdom
were trained. Margaret, duchess of Alençon, the sister of
Francis, and afterwards queen of Navarre, often charmed the
queen's circle by her lively conversation. She soon became deeply
attached to the young Englishwoman, and on the death of
Claude took her into her own family. Anne Boleyn was destined
at no very remote period to be at the court of London a reflection of the graceful Margaret, and her relations with that
princess were not without influence on the English Reformation.

And indeed the literary movement which had passed from
Italy into France appeared at that time as if it would cross
from France into Britain. Oxford exercises over England as
great an influence as the metropolis; and it is almost always
within its walls that a movement commences whether for
good or evil. At this period of our history, enthusiastic youth
hailed with joy the first beams of the new sun, and attacked
with their sarcasms the idleness of the monks, the immorality
of the clergy, and the superstition of the people. Disgusted with
the priestcraft of the middle ages, and captivated by the writers
of antiquity and the purity of the Gospel, Oxford boldly called
for a reform which should burst the bonds of clerical domination and emancipate the human mind. Men of letters thought
for a while that they had found in the most powerful man in
England, Thomas Wolsey, the ally that would give them the
victory. He possessed little taste for learning, but seeing the
wind of public favour blow in that direction, he readily spread
his sails before it. He got the reputation of a profound divine,

by quoting a few words of Thomas Aquinas, and the fame of a Mæcenas and a Ptolemy, by inviting the learned to his gorgeous entertainments. "O happy cardinal," exclaimed Erasmus, "who can surround his table with such torches!"

At that time the king felt the same ambition as his minister, and, having tasted in turn the pleasures of war and diplomacy, he now bent his mind to literature. He desired Wolsey to present Sir Thomas More to him.—"What shall I do at court?" replied the latter. "I shall be as awkward as a man that never rode sitteth in a saddle." Happy in his family circle, where his father, mother, and children, gathering round the same table, formed a pleasing group, which the pencil of Holbein has transmitted to us, More had no desire to leave it. But Henry was not a man to put up with a refusal; he employed force almost to draw More from his retirement, and in a short time he could not live without the society of the man of letters. On calm and starlight nights they would walk together upon the leads at the top of the palace, discoursing on the motions of the heavenly bodies. If More did not appear at court, Henry would go to Chelsea and share the frugal dinner of the family with some of their simple neighbours. "Where," asked Erasmus, "where is the Athens, the Porch, or the Academy, that can be compared with the court of England? . . . It is a seat of the muses rather than a palace. . . . The golden age is reviving, and I congratulate the world."

But the friends of classical learning were not content with the cardinal's banquets or the king's favours. They wanted victories, and their keenest darts were aimed at the cloisters, those strong fortresses of the hierarchy and of uncleanness. The abbot of Saint Albans, having taken a married woman for his concubine, and placed her at the head of a nunnery, his monks had followed his example, and indulged in the most scandalous debauchery. Public indignation was so far aroused, that Wolsey himself—Wolsey, the father of several illegitimate children, and who was suffering the penalty of his irregularities —was carried away by the spirit of the age, and demanded of the pope a general reform of manners. When they heard of this request, the priests and friars were loud in their outcries. "What are you about?" said they to Wolsey. "You are giving the victory to the enemies of the church, and your only reward will be the hatred of the whole world." As this was not the cardinal's game, he abandoned his project, and conceived one more easily executed. Wishing to deserve the name of "Ptolemy" conferred on him by Erasmus, he undertook to build two large colleges, one at Ipswich, his native town, the other at Oxford, and found it convenient to take the money necessary for their endowment, not from his own purse, but from the purses of the monks. He pointed out to the pope twenty-two monasteries in which (he said) vice and impiety had taken up their abode. The pope granted their secularization, and Wolsey having thus procured a revenue of £2000 sterling, laid the foundations of his college, traced out various courts, and constructed spacious kitchens. He fell into disgrace before he had completed his work, which led Gualter to say with a sneer: "He began a college and built a cook's shop." But a great example had been set: the monasteries had been attacked, and the first breach made in them by a cardinal. Cromwell, Wolsey's secretary, took note how his master had set about his work, and in after-years profited by the lesson.

It was fortunate for learning that it had sincerer friends in London than Wolsey. Of these were Colet, dean of St Paul's, whose house was the centre of the literary movement which preceded the Reformation, and his friend and guest Erasmus. The latter was the hardy pioneer who opened the road of antiquity to modern Europe. One day he would entertain Colet's guests with the account of a new manuscript; on another, with a discussion on the forms of ancient literature; and at other times he would attack the schoolmen and monks, when Colet would take the same side. The only antagonist who dared measure his strength with him was Sir Thomas More, who, although a layman, stoutly defended the ordinances of the church.

But mere table-talk could not satisfy the dean: a numerous audience attended his sermons at St Paul's. The spirituality of Christ's words, the authority which characterizes them, their admirable simplicity and mysterious depth had deeply charmed him: "I admire the writings of the apostles," he would say, "but I forget them almost, when I contemplate the wonderful majesty of Jesus Christ." Setting aside the texts prescribed by the church, he explained, like Zwingli, the Gospel of St Matthew. Nor did he stop here. Taking advantage of the Convocation, he delivered a sermon on *conformation* and *reformation*, which was one of the numerous forerunners of the great reform of the sixteenth century. "We see strange and heretical ideas appear in our days, and no wonder," said he. "But you must know there is no heresy more dangerous to the church than the vicious lives of its priests. A reformation is needed; and that reformation must begin with the bishops and be extended to the priests. The clergy once reformed, we shall proceed to the reformation of the people." Thus spoke Colet, while the citizens of London listened to him with rapture, and called him a new Saint Paul.

Such discourses could not be allowed to pass unpunished. Richard Fitzjames, bishop of London, was a superstitious obstinate old man of eighty, fond of money, excessively irritable, a poor theologian, and a slave to Duns Scotus, the *subtle doctor*. Calling to his aid two other bishops as zealous as himself for the preservation of abuses, namely, Bricot and Standish, he denounced the dean of St Paul's to Warham. The archbishop having inquired what he had done: "What has he done?" rejoined the bishop of London. "He teaches that we must not worship images; he translates the Lord's Prayer into English; he pretends that the text *Feed my sheep*, does not include the temporal supplies the clergy draw from their flock. And besides all this," he continued with some embarrassment, "he has spoken against those who carry their manuscripts into the pulpit and read their sermons!" As this was the bishop's practice, the primate could not refrain from smiling; and since Colet refused to justify himself, Warham did so for him.

From that time Colet laboured with fresh zeal to scatter the darkness. He devoted the larger portion of his fortune to found the celebrated school of St Paul, of which the learned William Lilly was the first master. Two parties, the *Greeks* and the *Trojans*, entered the lists, not to contend with sword and spear, as in the ancient epic, but with the tongue, the pen, and sometimes the fist. If the *Trojans* (the obscurants) were defeated in the public disputations, they had their revenge in the secret of the confessional. *Cave a Græcis ne fias hereticus* (Beware of the Greeks, lest you should become a heretic) was the watchword of the priests—their daily lesson to the youths under their care. They looked on the school founded by Colet as the monstrous horse of the perjured Sinon, and announced that from its bosom would inevitably issue the destruction of the people. Colet and Erasmus replied to the monks by inflicting fresh blows. Linacre, a thorough literary enthusiast—Grocyn, a man of sarcastic humour but generous heart—and many others, reinforced the *Grecian* phalanx. Henry himself used to take one of them with him during his journeys, and if any hostile *Trojan* ventured in his presence to attack the tongue of Plato and of Saint Paul, the young king would set his Hellenian on him. Not more numerous were the contests witnessed in times of yore on the classic banks of Xanthus and Simois.

K

CHAPTER TWELVE

Wolsey's Rise to Power

(1507–18)

JUST as everything seemed tending to a reformation, a powerful priest rendered the way more difficult.

One of the most striking personages of the age was then making his appearance on the stage of the world. It was the destiny of that man, in the reign of Henry VIII, to combine extreme ability with notorious immorality; and to be a new and striking example of the wholesome truth that immorality is more effectual to destroy a man than ability to save him. Wolsey was the last high-priest of Rome in England, and when his fall startled the nation, it was the signal of a still more striking fall—the fall of popery.

Thomas Wolsey, the son of a wealthy butcher and inn-keeper of Ipswich, according to the common story, which is sanctioned by high authority, had attained under Henry VII the post of a royal chaplain, at the recommendation of Sir Richard Nanfan, deputy lieutenant of Calais and an old patron of his. But Wolsey was not at all desirous of passing his life in saying mass. As soon as he had discharged the regular duties of his office, instead of spending the rest of the day in idleness, as his colleagues did, he strove to win the good graces of the persons round the king.

Fox, bishop of Winchester, keeper of the privy-seal under Henry VII, uneasy at the growing powers of the Earl of Surrey, looked about for a man to counterbalance them. He thought he had found such a one in Wolsey. It was doubtless to oppose the Surreys, the grandfather and uncles of Anne Boleyn, that the son of the Ipswich butcher was drawn from his obscurity. Fox began to praise Wolsey in the king's hearing, and at the same time he encouraged him to give himself to public affairs. The latter was not deaf to the call, and soon found an opportunity of winning his sovereign's favour.

The king, having business of importance with the Emperor Maximilian, who was then in Flanders, sent for Wolsey, explained his wishes, and ordered him to prepare to set out. The chaplain determined to show Henry VII how capable he was of serving him. It was about noon when he took leave of the king at Richmond—by four o'clock he was in London, by seven at Gravesend. By travelling all night he reached Dover just as a boat carrying passengers was about to sail. After a passage of three hours he reached Calais, whence he travelled post, and the same evening appeared before Maximilian. Having obtained what he desired, he set off again by night, and on the next day but one reached Richmond, three days and some few hours after his departure. The king, catching sight of him just as he was going to mass, sharply inquired why he had not set out. "Sire, I am just returned," answered Wolsey, placing the Emperor's letters in his master's hands. Henry was delighted, and Wolsey saw that his fortune was made.[1] Shortly Henry VII died and his only surviving son ascended the throne.

The courtiers hoped at first that Wolsey, like an inexperienced pilot, would run his vessel on some hidden rock; but never did helmsman manage his ship with more skill. Although twenty years older than Henry VIII, the almoner (for such he had now been appointed) danced, and sang, and laughed with the prince's companions, and amused his new master with tales of scandal and quotations from Thomas Aquinas; and while Henry's councillors were entreating him to leave his pleasures and attend to business, Wolsey was continually reminding him that he ought to devote his youth to learning and amusement, and leave the toils of government to others. Wolsey was created bishop of Tournai during Henry's campaign in Flanders, and on his return to England, was raised to the sees of Lincoln and of York. Three mitres had been placed on his head in one year. He found at last the vein he so ardently sought for.

And yet he was not satisfied. The archbishop of Canterbury had insisted, as primate, that the cross of York should be lowered to his. Wolsey was not of a disposition to concede this,

[1] [The story of the speedy journey is narrated in *The life of Wolsey* by George Cavendish, Wolsey's gentleman-usher. Some modern historians give it little credence, but there are no sound reasons for rejecting it.]

and, when he found that Warham was not content with being
his equal, he resolved to make him his inferior. He wrote to
Paris and to Rome. Francis I, who desired to conciliate
England, demanded the purple for Wolsey, and the archbishop
of York received the title of Cardinal St Cecilia beyond the
Tiber. In November 1515, the red hat was brought by the
envoy of the pope: "It would have been better to have given
him a Tyburn tippet," said some indignant Englishmen; "these
Romish hats never brought good into England"[1]—a saying that
has become proverbial.

This was not enough for Wolsey: he desired secular greatness
above all things. Warham, tired of contending with so arrogant
a rival, resigned the seals of the lord-chancellorship, and the
king immediately transferred them to the cardinal. At length
a bull appointed him legate *a latere* of the holy see, and placed
under his jurisdiction all the colleges, monasteries, spiritual
courts, and bishops (1518). Over the primate himself Wolsey
now believed himself to have precedence.[2] From that time, as
lord-chancellor of England and papal legate, Wolsey administered almost everything in church and state. He filled his
coffers with money procured both at home and from abroad,
and yielded without restraint to his dominant vices, ostentation
and pride. Whenever he appeared in public, two priests, the
tallest and comeliest that could be found, carried before him
two huge silver crosses, one to mark his dignity as archbishop,
the other as papal legate. Chamberlains, gentlemen, pages,
sergeants, chaplains, choristers, clerks, cupbearers, cooks, and
other domestics, to the number of more than 500, among whom
were nine or ten lords and the stateliest yeomen of the country,
filled his palace. He generally wore a dress of scarlet velvet and
silk, with hat and gloves of the same colour. His shoes were
embroidered with gold and silver, inlaid with pearls and
precious stones. A kind of papacy was thus forming in England;
for wherever pride flourishes there popery is developed.

One thing occupied Wolsey more than all the pomp with
which he was surrounded—his desire to captivate the king.
For this purpose, says Tyndale, he cast Henry's nativity, and

---

[1] *Latimer's Sermons* (Parker Society), p. 119.
[2] Warham out-lived Wolsey by two years and retained the office of
primate to the end. Hence Wolsey never became archbishop of Canterbury.

procured an amulet which he wore constantly, in order to charm his master by its magic properties.[1] Then having recourse to a still more effectual form of bewitchment, he selected from among the licentious companions of the young monarch those of the keenest discernment and most ambitious character; and after binding them to him by a solemn oath, he placed them at court to be as eyes and ears to him. Accordingly not a word was said in the presence of the monarch, particularly against Wolsey, of which he was not informed an hour afterwards. If the culprit was not in favour, he was expelled without mercy; in the contrary case, the minister sent him on some distant mission. The queen's ladies, the king's chaplains, and even their confessors, were the cardinal's spies. He pretended to omnipresence, as the pope to infallibility.

Wolsey was not devoid of certain showy virtues, for he was liberal to the poor even to affectation. As chancellor he was inexorable to every kind of irregularity, and strove particularly to make the rich and high-born bend beneath his power. Men of learning alone obtained from him some little attention, and hence Erasmus calls him "the Achates of a new Æneas." But the nation was not to be carried away by the eulogies of a few scholars. Wolsey—a man of more than suspected morals, double-hearted, faithless to his promises, ostentatious to the last degree, and exceedingly arrogant—Wolsey soon became hated by the people of England.

The elevation of a prince of the Roman church could not be favourable to the Reformation. The priests, encouraged by it, determined to make a stand against the triple attack of the learned, the reformers, and the state; and they soon had an opportunity of trying their strength. Holy orders had become during the middle ages a warrant for every sort of crime. Parliament, desirous of correcting this abuse and checking the encroachments of the church, declared in the year 1513 that any ecclesiastic, accused of theft or murder, should be tried before the secular tribunals. Exceptions, however, were made in favour of bishops, priests, and deacons—that is to say, nearly all the clergy. Notwithstanding this timid precaution,

---

[1] "He calked [calculated] the king's nativity . . . he made by craft of necromancy graven imagery to bear upon him, wherewith he bewitched the king's mind". Tyndale's *Expositions* (Parker Society), p. 308.

Richard Kidderminster, an insolent clerk, the abbot of Wynchcombe, began the battle by exclaiming in a sermon at St Paul's: "*Touch not mine anointed,* said the Lord." At the same time Wolsey, accompanied by a long train of priests and prelates, had an audience of the king, at which he said with hands upraised to heaven: "Sire, to try a clerk is a violation of God's laws." This time, however, Henry did not give way. "By God's will, we are king of England," he replied, "and the kings of England in times past had never any superior but God only. Therefore know you well that we will maintain the right of our crown." He saw distinctly that to put the clergy above the laws was to put them above the throne. The priests were defeated, but not disheartened: perseverance is a characteristic feature of every hierarchical order. Not walking by faith, they walk all the more by sight; and skilful combinations supply the place of the holy aspirations of the Christian. Humble disciples of the gospel were soon to experience this, for the clergy by a few isolated attacks were about to flesh their swords for the great struggles of the Reformation.

CHAPTER THIRTEEN

The Need for Reformation

(1514–17)

IT is occasionally necessary to soften down the somewhat exaggerated colours in which contemporary writers describe the Romish clergy; but there are certain appellations which history is bound to accept. The *wolves*, for so the priests were called, by attacking the Lords and Commons had attempted a work beyond their reach. They turned their wrath on others. There were many shepherds endeavouring to gather together the sheep of the Lord beside the peaceful waters: these must be frightened, and the sheep driven into the howling wilderness. "The wolves" determined to fall upon the Lollards.

There lived in London a prosperous merchant-tailor of good reputation named Richard Hunne, one of those witnesses of the truth who, sincere though unenlightened, have been often found in the bosom of Catholicism. It was his practice to retire to his chamber and spend a portion of each day in the study of the Bible. At the death of one of his children, the priest required of him an exorbitant mortuary fee, which Hunne refused to pay, and for which he was summoned before the legate's court. He felt indignant that an Englishman should be cited before a foreign tribunal, and laid an information against the priest and his counsel under the act of *præmunire*. Such boldness—most extraordinary at that time—exasperated the clergy beyond all bounds. "If these proud citizens are allowed to have their way," exclaimed the clerics, "every layman will dare to resist a priest."

Exertions were accordingly made to snare the pretended rebel in the trap of heresy; he was thrown into the Lollards' Tower at St Paul's, and an iron collar was fastened round his neck, attached to which was a chain so heavy that neither man nor beast (says Foxe) would have been able to bear it long. When taken before his judges, they could not convict him of heresy, and it was observed with astonishment "that he had his beads in prison with him." They would have set him at liberty, after inflicting on him perhaps some trifling penance—but then, what a bad example it would be, and who could stop the reformers, if it was so easy to resist the papacy? Unable to triumph by justice, certain fanatics resolved to triumph by crime.

At midnight on the 2nd December—the day of his examination—three men stealthily ascended the stairs of the Lollards' Tower: the bellringer went first carrying a torch; the jailer, Charles Joseph, followed, and last came the bishop's chancellor, Dr. Horsey. Having entered the cell, they went up to the bed on which Hunne was lying and, finding that he was asleep, the chancellor said: "Lay hands on the thief." Charles Joseph and the bellringer fell upon the prisoner, who, awaking with a start, saw at a glance what this midnight visit meant. He resisted the assassins at first, but was soon overpowered and strangled. Charles Joseph then fixed the dead man's belt round his neck, the bellringer helped to raise his lifeless body, and the chancellor slipped the other end of the belt through a ring fixed in the wall. They then placed his cap on his head, and hastily quitted the cell. Immediately after, the conscience-stricken Charles Joseph got on horseback and rode from the city; the bellringer left the cathedral and hid himself: the crime dispersed the criminals. The chancellor alone kept his ground, and he was at prayers when the news was brought him that the turnkey had found Hunne hanging. "He must have killed himself in despair," said the hypocrite. But everyone knew poor Hunne's Christian feelings. "It is the priests who have murdered him," was the general cry in London, and an inquest was ordered to be held on his body.

On Tuesday, the 5th of December, Thomas Barnwell the city coroner, the two sheriffs, and twenty-four jurymen proceeded to the Lollards' Tower. They remarked that the belt was so short that the head could not be got out of it, and that consequently it had never been placed in it voluntarily, and hence the jury concluded that the suspension was an afterthought of some other persons. Moreover they found that the ring was too high for the poor victim to reach it—that the body bore marks of violence—and that traces of blood were to be seen in the cell: "Wherefore all we find by God and all our consciences (runs the verdict) that Richard Hunne was murdered. Also we acquit the said Richard Hunne of his own death."

It was but too true, and the criminals themselves confessed it. The miserable Charles Joseph having returned home on the evening of the 6th December, said to his maid-servant: "If you will swear to keep my secret, I will tell you all."—"Yes, master," she replied, "if it is neither felony nor treason."— Joseph took a book, swore the girl on it, and then said to her: "I have killed Richard Hunne!"—"O master! how? he was called a worthy man."—"I would lever [rather] than a hundred pounds it were not done," he made answer; "but what is done cannot be undone." He then rushed out of the house.

The clergy foresaw what a serious blow this unhappy affair would be to them, and to justify themselves they examined Hunne's Bible (it was Wycliffe's version) and, having read in the preface that "poor men and idiots [simple folks] have the truth of the holy Scriptures more than a thousand prelates and religious men and clerks of the school," and further, that "the pope ought to be called Antichrist," the bishop of London, assisted by the bishops of Durham and Lincoln, declared Hunne guilty of heresy, and on the 20th December his dead body was burnt at Smithfield. "Hunne's bones have been burnt, and therefore he was a heretic," said the priests; "he was a heretic, and therefore he committed suicide."

The triumph of the clergy was of short duration; for almost at the same time William Horsey, the bishop's chancellor, Charles Joseph, and John Spalding the bellringer, were convicted of the murder. Strenuous ecclesiastical pressure led to the dropping of the charge against Horsey, but he only escaped justice by paying a fine of £600 and suffering exile from London. By royal letter, the confiscated property of Hunne was restored to his children.[1]—"If the clerical theocracy should gain the mastery of the state," was the general remark in London, "it would not only be a very great lie, but the most frightful tyranny!" England has never gone back since that time, and a theocratic rule has always inspired the sound portion

---

[1] [Foxe in his *Book of Martyrs* produces extremely strong evidence to prove that Hunne was murdered. Thomas More in his *Dialogue concerning Heresies* attempts an unconvincing defence of Horsey which is clearly "special pleading."]

of the nation with a just and insurmountable antipathy. Such were the events taking place in England shortly before the Reformation. This was not all.

The clergy had not been fortunate in Hunne's affair, but they were not for that reason unwilling to attempt a new one.

In the spring of 1517—the year in which Luther posted up his *theses*—a priest, whose manners announced a man swollen with pride, happened to be on board the passage-boat from London to Gravesend with an intelligent and pious Christian of Ashford, by name John Browne. The passengers, as they floated down the stream, were amusing themselves by watching the banks glide away from them, when the priest, turning towards Browne, said to him insolently: "You are too near me, you are sitting on my clothes, get farther off. Do you know who I am?"—"No, sir," answered Browne.—"Well then, you must know that I am a priest."—"Indeed, sir; are you a parson, or vicar, or a lady's chaplain?"—"No; I am a *soul-priest*," he haughtily replied; "I sing mass to save souls."—"Do you, sir," replied Browne somewhat ironically, "that is well done; and can you tell me where you find the soul when you begin the mass?"—"I cannot," said the priest.—"And where you leave it when the mass is ended?"—"I do not know."—"What!" continued Browne with marks of astonishment, "you do not know where you find the soul or where you leave it . . . and yet you say that you save it!"—"Go thy ways," said the priest angrily, "thou art a heretic, and I will be even with thee." Thenceforward the priest and his neighbour conversed no more together. At last they reached Gravesend and the boat anchored.

As soon as the priest had landed, he hastened to two of his friends, Walter and William More, and all three mounting their horses set off for Canterbury, and denounced Browne to the archbishop.

In the meantime John Browne had reached home. Three days later, his wife, Elizabeth, who had just left her chamber, went to church, dressed all in white, to return thanks to God for delivering her in the perils of childbirth. Her husband, assisted by her daughter Alice and the maid-servant, were preparing for their friends the feast usual on such occasions, and they had all of them taken their seats at table, joy beaming on every face, when the street-door was abruptly opened, and

Chilton, the constable, a cruel and savage man, accompanied by several of the archbishop's servants, seized upon the worthy townsman. All sprang from their seats in alarm; Elizabeth and Alice uttered the most heartrending cries; but the primate's officers, without showing any emotion, pulled Browne out of the house, and placed him on horseback, tying his feet under the animal's belly. It is a serious matter to jest with a priest. The cavalcade rode off quickly, and Browne was thrown into prison, and there left forty days.

At the end of this time, the archbishop of Canterbury and the bishop of Rochester called before them the impudent fellow who doubted whether a priest's mass could save souls, and required him to retract this "blasphemy." But Browne, if he did not believe in the mass, believed in the Gospel: "Christ was once offered," he said, "to take away the sins of many. It is by this sacrifice we are saved, and not by the repetitions of the priests." At this reply the archbishop made a sign to the executioners, one of whom took off the shoes and stockings of this pious Christian, while the other brought in a pan of burning coals, upon which they set the martyr's feet. The English laws in truth forbade torture to be inflicted on any subject of the crown, but the clergy thought themselves above the laws. "Confess the efficacy of the mass," cried the two bishops to Browne. "If I deny my Lord upon earth," he replied, "He will deny me before His Father in heaven." The flesh was burnt off the soles of the feet even to the bones, and still John Browne remained unshaken. The bishops therefore ordered him to be given over to the secular arm that he might be burnt alive.

On the Saturday preceding the festival of Pentecost, in the year 1517, the martyr was led back to Ashford, where he arrived just as the day was drawing to a close. A number of idle persons were collected in the street, and among them was Browne's maid-servant, who ran off crying to the house, and told her mistress: "I have seen him! . . . He was bound, and they were taking him to prison." Elizabeth hastened to her husband and found him sitting with his feet in the stocks, his features changed by suffering, and expecting to be burnt alive on the morrow. The poor woman sat down beside him, weeping most bitterly, while he, being hindered by his chains, could not so much as bend towards her. "I cannot set my feet to the ground," said he, "for bishops have burnt them to the bones; but they could not burn my tongue and prevent my confessing the Lord. . . . O Elizabeth! . . . continue to love Him for He is good; and bring up our children in His fear."

On the following morning—it was Whitsunday—the brutal Chilton and his assistants led Browne to the place of execution, and fastened him to the stake. Elizabeth and Alice, with his other children and his friends, desirous of receiving his last sigh, surrounded the pile, uttering cries of anguish. The faggots were set on fire, while Browne, calm and collected, and full of confidence in the blood of the Saviour, clasped his hands, and repeated this hymn, which Foxe has preserved:[1]

> O Lord, I yield me to thy grace,
> Grant me mercy for my trespass;
> Let never the fiend my soul chase.
> Lord, I will bow, and thou shalt beat,
> Let never my soul come in hell-heat.

The martyr was silent: the flames had consumed their victim. Then redoubled cries of anguish rent the air. His wife and daughter seemed as if they would lose their senses. The bystanders showed them the tenderest compassion, and turned with a movement of indignation towards the executioners. The brutal Chilton perceiving this, cried out:—"Come along; let us toss the heretic's children into the flames, lest they should one day spring from their father's ashes."[2] He rushed towards Alice, and was about to lay hold of her, when the maiden shrank back screaming with horror. To the end of her life, she recollected the fearful moment, and to her we are indebted for the particulars. The fury of the monster was checked. Such were the scenes passing in England shortly before the Reformation.

The priests were not yet satisfied, for the scholars still remained in England: if they could not be burnt, they could at least be banished. They set to work accordingly. Standish, bishop of St Asaph, a sincere man, as it would seem, but fanatical, was inveterate in his hatred of Erasmus, who had

---

[1] Foxe, *Acts and Monuments*, edited by Josiah Pratt, iv. p. 132 (London, 1838).
[2] Bade cast in his children also, for they would spring of his ashes. Ibid.

irritated him by an idle sarcasm. When speaking of *St Asaph's* it was very common to abbreviate it into *St As's*; and as Standish was a theologian of no great learning, Erasmus, in his jesting way, would sometimes call him *Episcopus a Sancto Asino*. As the bishop could not destroy Colet, the disciple, he flattered himself that he should triumph over the master.

Erasmus knew Standish's intentions. Should he commence in England that struggle with the papacy which Luther was about to begin in Germany? It was no longer possible to steer a middle course: he must either fight or leave. The Dutchman was faithful to his nature—we may even say, to his vocation: he left the country.

Erasmus was, in his time, the head of the great literary community. By means of his connections and his correspondence, which extended over all Europe, he established between those countries where learning was reviving, an interchange of ideas and manuscripts. The pioneer of antiquity, an eminent critic, a witty satirist, the advocate of correct taste, and a restorer of literature, one only glory was wanting: he had not the creative spirit, the heroic soul of a Luther. He calculated with no little skill, could detect the smile on the lips or the knitting of the brows; but he had not that self-abandonment, that enthusiasm for the truth, that firm confidence in God, without which nothing great can be done in the world, and least of all in the church. "Erasmus *had* much, but *was* little," said one of his biographers.

In the year 1517 a crisis had arrived: the period of the revival was over, that of the Reformation was beginning. The restoration of letters was succeeded by the regeneration of religion: the days of criticism and neutrality by those of courage and action. Erasmus was then only about fifty years old; but he had finished his career. From being first, he must now be second: the monk of Wittenberg dethroned him. He looked around himself in vain: placed in a new country, he had lost his road. A hero was needed to inaugurate the greatest movement of modern times: Erasmus was a mere man of letters.

When attacked by Standish in 1516, the literary king determined to quit the court of England, and take refuge in a printing-office. But before laying down his sceptre at the foot of a Saxon monk, he signalized the end of his reign by the most brilliant of his publications. The epoch of 1516–17, memorable for the theses of Luther, was destined to be equally remarkable by a work which was to imprint on the new times their essential character. What distinguishes the Reformation from all anterior revivals is the union of learning with piety, and a faith more profound, more enlightened, and based on the Word of God. Christians were then emancipated from the tutelage of the schools and the popes, and their charter of enfranchisement was the Bible. The sixteenth century did more than its predecessors: it went straight to the fountain (the Holy Scriptures), cleared it of weeds and brambles, plumbed its depths, and caused its abundant streams to pour forth on all around. The Reformation age studied the Greek Testament, which the clerical age had almost forgotten—and this is its greatest glory. One of the first explorers of this divine source was Erasmus. When attacked by the hierarchy, the leader of the schools withdrew from the splendid halls of Henry VIII. It seemed to him that the new era which he had announced to the world was rudely inter-rupted: he could do nothing more by his conversation for the country of the Tudors. But he carried with him those precious leaves, the fruit of his labours—a book which would do more than he desired. He hastened to Basle, and took up his quarters in Johann Froben's printing-office, where he not only laboured himself, but made others labour. England was soon to receive the seed of the new life, and the Reformation was about to begin.

BOOK TWO

The Revival of the Church

CHAPTER ONE

The Origin of the English Reformation

(1516–19)

IT was within the province of four powers in the sixteenth
century to effect a reformation of the church: these were
the papacy, the episcopate, the monarchy, and Holy
Scripture. The Reformation in England was essentially the
work of Scripture.

The only true reformation is that which emanates from the
Word of God. The Holy Scriptures, by bearing witness to the
incarnation, death, and resurrection of the Son of God, create
in man by the Holy Ghost a faith which justifies him. That faith
which produces in him a new life, unites him to Christ, without
his requiring a chain of bishops or a Roman mediator, who
would separate him from the Saviour instead of drawing him
nearer. This reformation *by the Word* restores that spiritual
Christianity which the outward and hierarchical religion destroys; and from the regeneration of individuals naturally
results the regeneration of the church.

The Reformation of England, perhaps to a greater extent
than that of the continent, was effected by the Word of God.
This statement may appear paradoxical, but it is not the less
true. Those great personages we meet with in Germany,
Switzerland, and France—men like Luther, Zwingli, and
Calvin—do not appear in England; but Holy Scripture is
widely circulated. What brought light into the British isles
subsequent to the year 1517, and on a more extended scale
after the year 1526, was the Word—the invisible power of the
invisible God. The religion of the Anglo-Saxon race—a race
called more than any other to circulate the oracles of God
throughout the world—is particularly distinguished by its
biblical character.

The Reformation of England could not be papal. No reform
can be expected from that which ought to be not only reformed

but abolished; and besides, no monarch dethrones himself. We may even affirm that the popedom has always felt a peculiar affection for its conquests in Britain, and that they would ha· ·e been the last it would have renounced. A Carthusian prior had declared in the middle of the fifteenth century: "A reform is neither in the will nor in the power of the popes."

The Reformation of England was not episcopal. Roman hierarchism will never be abolished by Roman bishops. An episcopal assembly may perhaps, as at Constance, depose three competing popes, but then it will be to save the papacy. And if the bishops could not abolish the papacy, still less could they reform themselves. The then-existing episcopal power being at enmity with the Word of God, and the slave of its own abuses, was incapable of renovating the church. On the contrary, it exerted all its influence to prevent such a renovation.

The Reformation in England was not royal. Samuel, David, and Josiah were able to do something for the raising up of the church, when God again turned His face towards it; but a king cannot rob his people of their religion, and still less can he give them one. It has often been repeated that "the English Reformation derives its origin from the monarch;" but the assertion is incorrect. The work of God, here as elsewhere, cannot be put in comparison with the work of the king; and if the latter was infinitely surpassed in importance, it was also preceded in time by many years. The monarch was still keeping up a vigorous resistance behind his entrenchments, when God had already decided the victory along the whole line of operations.

Shall we be told that a reform effected by any other principle than the established authorities, both in *church* and *state*, would have been a revolution? But has God, the lawful sovereign of the church, forbidden all revolution in a sinful world? A *revolution* is not a revolt. The fall of the first man was a great revolution: the restoration of man by Jesus Christ was a counter-revolution. The corruption occasioned by popery was allied to the fall: the reformation accomplished in the sixteenth century was connected therefore with the restoration. There will no doubt be other interventions of the Deity, which will be revolutions in the same direction as the Reformation. When God creates a new heaven and a new earth, will not that be one of the most glorious of revolutions? The Reformation by the Word alone gives truth, alone gives unity; but more than that, it alone bears the marks of true *legitimacy*; for the church belongs not unto men, even though they be priests. God alone is its lawful sovereign.

And yet the human elements which we have enumerated were not wholly foreign to the work that was accomplishing in England. Besides the Word of God, other principles were in operation, and although less radical and less primitive, they still retain the sympathy of eminent men of that nation.

And in the first place, the intervention of the king's authority was necessary to a certain point. Since the supremacy of Rome had been established in England by several usages which had the force of law, the intervention of the temporal power was necessary to break the bonds which it had previously sanctioned. But it was requisite for the monarchy, while adopting a negative and political action, to leave the positive, doctrinal, and creative action to the Word of God.

Besides the Reformation *in the name of the Scriptures*, there was then in England another *in the name of the king*. The Word of God began, the kingly power followed; and ever since, these two forces have sometimes gone together against the authority of the Roman pontiffs—sometimes in opposition to each other, like those troops which march side by side in the same army, against the same enemy, and which have occasionally been seen, even on the field of battle, to turn their swords against each other.

Finally, the episcopate, which had begun by opposing the Reformation, was compelled to accept it in despite of its convictions. The majority of the bishops were opposed to it; but the better portion were found to incline, some to the side of outward reform, of which separation from the papacy was the very essence, and others to the side of internal reform, whose mainspring was union with Jesus Christ. At last, the episcopate took up its ground on its own account, and soon two great parties alone existed in England: the scriptural party and the clerical party.

These two parties have survived even to our days, and their colours are still distinguishable in the river of the church, like the muddy River Arve and the limpid Rhone after their confluence. The royal supremacy, from which many Christians, preferring the paths of independence, have withdrawn since the end of the 16th century, is recognized by both parties in t̄e Establishment, with some few exceptions. But whilst the High Church is essentially hierarchical, the Low Church is essentially biblical. In the one, the Church is above and the Word below; in the other, the Church is below and the Word above. These two principles, evangelicalism and hierarchism, are found in the Christianity of the first centuries, but with a signal difference. Hierarchism then almost entirely effaced evangelicalism; in the age of Protestantism, on the contrary, evangelicalism continued to exist by the side of hierarchism, and it has remained *de jure*, if not always *de facto*, the only legitimate opinion of the church.

Thus there is in England a complication of influences and contests, which render the work more difficult to describe; but it is on that very account more worthy the attention of the philosopher and the Christian.

Great events had just occurred in Europe. Francis I had crossed the Alps, gained a signal victory at Marignano, and conquered the north of Italy. The affrighted Maximilian knew of none who could save him but Henry VIII. "I will adopt you; you shall be my successor in the Empire," he intimated to him in May 1516. "Your army shall invade France; and then we will march together to Rome, where the sovereign pontiff shall crown you king of the Romans." The king of France, anxious to effect a diversion, had formed a league with Denmark and Scotland, and had made preparations for invading England to place on the throne the "white rose;" at least he had offered the pretender Richard Pole, heir to the claims of the house of York, the services of 12,000 German mercenaries for that purpose. Henry now showed his prudence; he declined Maximilian's offer, and turned his whole attention to the security of his kingdom. But while he refused to bear arms in France and Italy, a war of quite another kind broke out in England.

The great work of the 16th century was about to begin. A volume fresh from the presses of Basle had just crossed the Channel. Being transmitted to London, Oxford, and Cambridge, this book, the fruit of Erasmus' vigils, soon found its way wherever there were friends of learning. It was the *New Testament* of our Lord Jesus Christ, published for the first time in Greek with a new Latin translation—an event more important for the world than would have been the landing of the Yorkist pretender in England, or the appearance of the chief of the Tudors in Italy. This book, in which God has deposited for man's salvation the seeds of life, was about to effect alone, without patrons and without interpreters, the most astonishing revolution which had ever taken place in Britain.

When Erasmus published this work, at the dawn, so to say, of modern times, he did not see all its scope. Had he foreseen it, he would perhaps have recoiled in alarm. He saw indeed that there was a great work to be done, but he believed that all good men would unite to do it with common accord. "A spiritual temple must be raised in desolated Christendom," said he. "The mighty of this world will contribute towards it their marble, their ivory, and their gold; I who am poor and humble offer the foundation-stone," and he laid down before the world his edition of the Greek Testament. Then glancing disdainfully at the traditions of men, he said: "It is not from human reservoirs, fetid with stagnant waters, that we should draw the doctrine of salvation; but from the pure and abundant streams that flow from the heart of God." And when some of his suspicious friends spoke to him of the difficulties of the times, he replied: "If the ship of the church is to be saved from being swallowed up by the tempest, there is only one anchor that can save it: it is the heavenly word, which, issuing from the bosom of the Father, lives, speaks, and works still in the gospel." These noble sentiments served as an introduction to those blessed pages which were to reform England. Erasmus, like Caiaphas, prophesied without being aware of it.

The New Testament in Greek and Latin had hardly appeared when it was received by all men of upright mind with unprecedented enthusiasm. Never had any book produced such a sensation. It was in every hand: men struggled to procure it, read it eagerly, and would even kiss it. The words it contained enlightened every heart. But a reaction soon took place. Traditional catholicism uttered a cry from the depths of its noisome pools (to use Erasmus' figure). Franciscans and Dominicans, priests and bishops, not daring to attack the educated and well-born, went among the ignorant populace, and endeavoured by their tales and clamours to stir up susceptible women and credulous men. "Here are horrible heresies," they exclaimed, "here are frightful antichrists! If this book be tolerated it will be the death of the papacy!"—"We must drive this man from the university," said one. "We must turn him out of the church," added another. "The public places re-echoed with their howlings," said Erasmus. The firebrands tossed by their furious hands were raising fires in every quarter; and the flames kindled in a few obscure monasteries threatened to spread over the whole country.

This irritation was not without a cause. The book, indeed, contained nothing but Latin and Greek; but this first step seemed to augur another—the translation of the Bible into the vulgar tongue. Erasmus loudly called for it. "Perhaps it may be necessary to conceal the secrets of kings," he remarked, "but we must publish the mysteries of Christ. The Holy Scriptures, translated into all languages, should be read not only by the Scotish and Irish, but even by Turks and Saracens. The husbandman should sing them as he holds the handle of his plough, the weaver repeat them as he plies his shuttle, and the wearied traveller, halting on his journey, refresh himself under some shady tree by these godly narratives." These words prefigured a golden age after the iron age of popery. A number of Christian families in Britain and on the continent were soon to realize these evangelical forebodings, and England after three centuries was to endeavour to carry them out for the benefit of all the nations on the face of the earth.

The priests saw the danger and, by a skilful manœuvre, instead of finding fault with the Greek Testament, attacked the Latin translation and the translator. "He has corrected the Vulgate," they said, "and puts himself in the place of Saint Jerome. He sets aside a work authorized by the consent of ages and inspired by the Holy Ghost. What audacity!" And then, turning over the pages, they pointed out the most odious passages: "Look here! this book calls upon men to *repent*, instead of requiring them, as the Vulgate does, *to do penance*!" (Matt. iv. 17.) The priests thundered against him from their pulpits: "This man has committed the unpardonable sin," they asserted, "for he maintains that there is nothing in common between the Holy Ghost and the monks—that they are logs rather than men!" These simple remarks were received with a general laugh; but the priests, in no wise disconcerted, cried out all the louder: "He's a heretic, an heresiarch, a forger! he's a goose . . . what do I say? he's a very antichrist!"

It was not sufficient for the papal janissaries to make war in the plain, they must carry it to the higher ground. Was not the king a friend of Erasmus? If he should declare himself a patron of the Greek and Latin Testament, what an awful calamity! . . . After having agitated the cloisters, towns, and universities, they resolved to protest against it boldly, even in Henry's presence. They thought: "If he is won, all is won." It happened one day that a certain theologian (whose name is unknown) having to preach in his turn before the king, he declaimed violently against the *Greek* language and its new interpreters. Pace, the king's secretary, was present, and turning his eyes on Henry, observed him smiling good-humouredly. On leaving the church every one began to exclaim against the preacher. "Bring the priest to me," said the king; and then turning to Thomas More, he added: "You shall defend the Greek cause against him, and I will listen to the disputation." The literary tribunal was soon formed, but the sovereign's order had taken away all the priest's courage. He came forward trembling, fell on his knees, and with clasped hands exclaimed: "I know not what spirit impelled me."—"A spirit of madness," said the king, "and not the spirit of Jesus Christ." He then added: "Have you ever read Erasmus?"—"No, Sire."—"Away with you then, you are a blockhead."—"And yet," said the preacher in confusion, "I remember to have read something about *Moria*" (Erasmus' treatise on *Folly*).—"A subject, your majesty, that ought to be very familiar to him," wickedly interrupted Pace. The *obscurant* could say nothing in his justification. "I am not altogether opposed to the Greek," he added at last, "seeing that it is derived from the Hebrew." This was greeted with a general laugh, and the king impatiently ordered the monk to leave the room, and never appear before him again.

Erasmus was astonished at these discussions. He had imagined the season to be most favourable. "Every thing looks peaceful," he had said to himself; "now is the time to launch my Greek Testament into the learned world." As well might the sun rise upon the earth, and no one see it! At that very hour God was raising up a monk at Wittenberg who would lift the trumpet to his lips, and proclaim the new day. "Wretch that I am!" exclaimed the timid scholar, beating his breast, "who could have foreseen this horrible tempest!"

Nothing was more important at the dawn of the Reformation than the publication of the Testament of Jesus Christ in the original language. Never had Erasmus worked so carefully. "If I told what sweat it cost me, no one would believe me." He had collated the Greek manuscripts of the New Testament then available to him, and was surrounded by all the commentaries and translations, by the writings of Origen, Cyprian, Ambrose, Basil, Chrysostom, Cyril, Jerome, and Augustine. *Hic sum in campo meo!* (Here I am in my field of action) he exclaimed as he sat in the midst of his books. He had investigated the texts according to the principles of sacred criticism. When a knowledge of Hebrew was necessary, he had consulted Capito and more particularly Œcolampadius. *Nothing without Theseus*, said he of the latter, making use of a Greek proverb. He had corrected the ambiguities, obscurities, hebraisms, and barbarisms of the Vulgate; and had caused a list to be printed of the errors in that version.

"We must restore the pure text of the Word of God," he had said; and when he heard the maledictions of the priests, he had exclaimed: "I call God to witness I thought I was doing a work acceptable to the Lord and necessary to the cause of Christ." Nor in this was he deceived.

At the head of his adversaries was Edward Lee, successively king's almoner, archdeacon of Colchester, and archbishop of York. Lee, at that time but little known, was a man of talent and activity, but also vain and loquacious, and determined to make his way at any cost. Even when a schoolboy he looked down on all his companions. As child, youth, man, and in mature years, he was always the same, Erasmus tells us; that is to say, vain, envious, jealous, boastful, passionate, and revengeful. We must bear in mind, however, that when Erasmus describes the character of his opponents, he is far from being an impartial judge. In the bosom of Roman-catholicism, there have always existed well-meaning, though ill-informed men, who, not knowing the inward power of the Word of God, have thought that if its authority were substituted for that of the Romish church, the only foundation of truth and of Christian society would be shaken. Yet while we judge Lee less severely than Erasmus does, we cannot close our eyes to his faults. His memory was richly furnished, but his heart was a stranger to divine truth: he was a schoolman and not a believer. He wanted the people to obey the church and not trouble themselves about the Scriptures. He was the Doctor Eck of England, but with more of outward appearance and morality than Luther's adversary. Yet he was by no means a rigid moralist. On one occasion, when preaching at the palace, he introduced ballads into his sermon, one of which began thus: "Pass time with good company." And the other: "I love unloved." We are indebted to Secretary Pace for this characteristic trait.[1]

During Erasmus' stay in England, Lee, observing his influence, had sought his friendship, and Erasmus, with his usual courtesy, had solicited his advice upon his work. But Lee, jealous of his great reputation, only waited for an opportunity to injure it, which he seized upon as soon as it occurred. The New Testament had not been long published, when Lee turned round abruptly, and from being Erasmus' friend became his implacable adversary. "If we do not stop this leak," said he, when he heard of the New Testament, "it will sink the ship." Nothing terrifies the defenders of human traditions so much as the Word of God.

Lee immediately leagued himself with all those in England who abhorred the study of Scripture, says Erasmus. Although exceedingly conceited, he showed himself the most amiable of men, in order to accomplish his designs. He invited Englishmen to his house, welcomed strangers, and gained many recruits by the excellence of his dinners. While seated at table among his guests, he hinted perfidious charges against Erasmus, and his company left him (so Erasmus claims in his letters) "loaded with lies."—"In this New Testament," said he, "there are three hundred dangerous, frightful passages . . . three hundred did I say? . . . there are more than a thousand!" Not satisfied with using his tongue, Lee wrote scores of letters, and employed several secretaries. Was there any monastery in the odour of sanctity, he "forwarded to it instantly wine, choice viands, and

[1] State Papers, Henry VIII, etc. i. p. 10, edition of 1830.

other presents." To each one he assigned his part, and over all England they were rehearsing what Erasmus calls *Lee's tragedy*. In this manner they were preparing the catastrophe: a prison for Erasmus, the fire for the Holy Scriptures.

When all was arranged, Lee issued his manifesto. Although a poor Greek scholar, he drew up some *Annotations* on Erasmus' book, which the latter called "mere abuse and blasphemy;" but which the members of the league regarded as *oracles*. They passed them secretly from hand to hand, and these obscure sheets, by many indirect channels, found their way into every part of England, and met with numerous readers. There was to be no publication—such was the watchword; Lee was too much afraid. "Why did you not publish your work," asked Erasmus, with cutting irony. "Who knows whether the holy father, appointing you the Aristarchus of letters, might not have sent you a birch to keep the whole world in order!"

The *Annotations* having triumphed in the monasteries, the *conspiracy* took a new flight. In every place of public resort, at fairs and markets, at the dinner-table and in the council-chamber, in shops, and taverns, and houses of ill-fame, in churches and in the universities, in cottages and in palaces, the league prated against Erasmus and the Greek Testament. Carmelites, Dominicans, and Sophists, invoked heaven and conjured hell. What need was there of Scripture? Had they not the apostolical succession of the clergy? No hostile landing in England could, in their eyes, be more fatal than that of the New Testament. The whole nation must rise to repel this impudent invasion. There is, perhaps, no country in Europe where the Reformation encountered so unexpected a storm.

[The author, in this section of his work, frequently quotes from the letters of Erasmus. A complete collection of these letters has been edited by P.S. Allen, 1906-47.]

CHAPTER TWO

The Greek Testament Awakens the Dead

(1516–21)

WHILE this rude blast was rushing over England, and roaring in the long galleries of its monasteries, the still small voice of the Word was making its way into the peaceful homes of praying men and into the ancient halls of Oxford and Cambridge. In private chambers, in the lecture-rooms and refectories, students, and even masters of arts, were to be seen reading the Greek and Latin Testament. Animated groups were discussing the principles of the Reformation. When Christ came on earth (said some) He gave the Word, and when He ascended up into heaven He gave the Holy Spirit. These are the two forces which created the church, and these are the forces that must regenerate it.—No (replied the partisans of Rome) it was the teaching of the apostles at first, and it is the teaching of the priests now.—The apostles (rejoined the friends of the Testament of Erasmus)—yes, it is true—the apostles were during their ministry a living scripture; but their oral teaching would most certainly have been altered by passing from mouth to mouth. God willed, therefore, that these precious lessons should be preserved to us in their writings, and thus become the ever-undefiled source of truth and salvation. To set the Scriptures in the foremost place, as your pretended reformers are doing (replied the schoolmen of Oxford and Cambridge) is to propagate heresy! And what are the reformers doing (asked their defenders) but what Christ did before them? The sayings of the prophets existed in the time of Jesus only as *Scripture*, and it was to this written Word that our Lord appealed when He founded His kingdom.[1] And now in like manner the teaching of the apostles exists only as Scripture, and it is to this written Word that we appeal in order to re-establish the king-

[1] Matth. xxii. 29; xxvi. 24, 54; Mark, xiv. 49; Luke, xviii. 31; xxiv. 27, 44, 45; John, v. 39, 46; x. 35; xvii. 12, etc.

153

dom of our Lord in its primitive condition. The night is far spent, the day is at hand; all is in motion—in the lofty halls of our colleges, in the mansions of the rich and noble, and in the lowly dwellings of the poor. If we want to scatter the darkness, must we light the shrivelled wick of some old lamp? Ought we not rather to open the doors and shutters and admit freely into the house the great light which God has placed in the heavens?

There was in Trinity Hall, Cambridge, a young student of the canon law, of serious turn of mind and bashful disposition, and whose tender conscience strove, although ineffectually, to fulfil the commandments of God. Anxious about his salvation, Thomas Bilney applied to the priests, whom he looked upon as physicians of the soul. Kneeling before his confessor, with humble look and pale face, he told him all his sins, and even those of which he doubted. The priest prescribed at one time fasting, at another prolonged vigils, and then masses and indulgences which cost him dearly. Bilney went through all these practices with great devotion, but found no consolation in them. Being weak and slender, his body wasted away by degrees; his understanding grew weaker, his imagination faded, and his purse became empty. "Alas!" said he with anguish, "my last state is worse than the first." From time to time an idea crossed his mind: "May not the priests be seeking their own gain, and not the salvation of my soul?" But immediately rejecting the rash doubt, he fell back under the iron hand of the clergy.

One day Bilney heard his friends talking about a new book: it was the Greek Testament printed with a translation which was highly praised for its elegant Latinity. Attracted by the beauty of the style rather than by the divinity of the subject, he stretched out his hand; but just as he was going to take the volume, fear came upon him and he withdrew it hastily. In fact the confessors strictly prohibited Greek and Hebrew books, "the sources of all heresies;" and Erasmus' Testament was particularly forbidden. Yet Bilney regretted so great a sacrifice; was it not the Testament of Jesus Christ? Might not God have placed therein some word which perhaps might heal his soul? He stepped forward, and then again shrank back. . . . At last he took courage. Urged, said he, by the hand of God, he walked out of the college, slipped into the house where the volume was sold in secret, bought it with fear and trembling, and then hastened back and shut himself up in his room.

He opened it—his eyes caught these words: *This is a faithful saying, and worthy of all acceptation, that Christ Jesus came into the world to save sinners; of whom I am chief.*[1] He laid down the book, and meditated on the astonishing declaration. "What! St Paul the chief of sinners, and yet St Paul is sure of being saved!" He read the verse again and again. "O assertion of St Paul, how sweet art thou to my soul!" he exclaimed. This declaration continually haunted him, and in this manner God instructed him in the secret of his heart. He could not tell what had happened to him; it seemed as if a refreshing wind were blowing over his soul, or as if a rich treasure had been placed in his hands. The Holy Spirit took what was Christ's, and announced it to him. "I also am like Paul," exclaimed he with emotion, "and more than Paul, the greatest of sinners! . . . But Christ saves sinners. At last I have heard of Jesus."

His doubts were ended—he was saved. Then took place in him a wonderful transformation. An unknown joy pervaded him; his conscience until then sore with the wounds of sin was healed; instead of despair he felt an inward peace passing all understanding. "Jesus Christ," exclaimed he. "Yes, Jesus Christ saves!" . . . Such is the character of the Reformation: it is Jesus Christ who saves and not the church. "I see it all," said Bilney; "my vigils, my fasts, my pilgrimages, my purchase of masses and indulgences were destroying instead of saving me. All these efforts were, as St Augustine says, a hasty running out of the right way."

Bilney never grew tired of reading his New Testament. He no longer lent an attentive ear to the teaching of the schoolmen; he heard Jesus at Capernaum, Peter in the temple, Paul on Mars' hill, and felt within himself that Christ possesses the words of eternal life. A witness to Jesus Christ had just been born by the same power which had transformed Paul, Apollos, and Timothy. The Reformation in England was beginning. Bilney was united to the Son of God, not by a remote succession, but by an immediate generation. Leaving to the disciples of the pope the entangled chain of their imaginary succession, whose links it is impossible to disengage, he found himself closely

[1] 1 Tim. i. 15.

attached to Christ. The word of the first century gave birth to the work of reformation in the sixteenth. Protestantism does not descend from the gospel in the fiftieth generation like the Romish church of the Council of Trent: it is the direct legitimate son—the son of the Master.

God's action was not limited to one spot. The first rays of the sun from on high gilded with their fires at once the gothic colleges of Oxford and the ancient schools of Cambridge.

Along the banks of the Severn extends a picturesque country, bounded by the forest of Dean, and sprinkled with villages, steeples, and ancient castles. In the sixteenth century it was particularly admired by priests and friars, and a familiar oath among them was: "As sure as God's in Glo'ster!" The papal birds of prey had swooped upon it. For the fifty years commencing in 1484, four Italian bishops, placed in succession over the diocese, had surrendered it to the pope, to the monks, and to immorality.[1] Thieves in particular were the objects of the tenderest favours of the hierarchy. John de Giglis, collector of the apostolical chamber, had received from the sovereign pontiff authority to pardon murder and theft, on condition that the criminal shared his profits with the pontifical commissioners.

It was in this county of Gloucester, and probably between the years 1490 and 1494, William Tyndale was born. Whether his childhood was passed amid the "breezy beauties" of the Western Cotswolds or beside the "rushy-fringed banks" of the Lower Severn, it cannot certainly be said, but it is on record that "Tyndale was brought up from a child in the University of Oxford," a pointer to the child's linguistic skill which was shortly dedicated to the service of the Word of God. In the university city he learnt grammar and philosophy in Magdalen Hall, adjoining the college of that name. He made rapid progress, particularly in languages, under the finest classical scholars in England—Grocyn, William Latimer, and Linacre—and took his degrees. A more excellent master than these doctors—the Holy Spirit speaking in Scripture—was soon to teach him a science which is not in the power of man to impart.

---

[1] [After 1512 and until the appointment of Hugh Latimer in 1535 there was no resident bishop of Worcester].

Oxford, where Erasmus had so many friends, was the city in which his New Testament met with the warmest welcome. The young Gloucestershire student, inwardly impelled towards the study of sacred literature, read the celebrated book which was then attracting the attention of Christendom. At first he regarded it only as a work of learning, or at most as a manual of piety, whose beauties were calculated to excite religious feelings; but erelong he found it to be something more. The more he read it, the more was he struck by the truth and energy of the Word. This strange book spoke to him of God, of Christ, and of regeneration, with a simplicity and authority which completely subdued him. William had found a master whom he had not sought at Oxford—this was God Himself. The pages he held in his hand were the divine revelation so long mislaid. Possessing a noble soul, a bold spirit, and indefatigable activity, he did not keep this treasure to himself. He uttered that cry, more suited to a Christian than to Archimedes: εὕρηκα, *I have found it!* It was not long before several of the younger members of the university, attracted by the purity of his life and the charm of his conversation, gathered round him, and read with him the Greek and Latin gospels of Erasmus. "A certain well-informed young man," wrote Erasmus in a letter wherein he speaks of the publication of his New Testament, "began to lecture with success on Greek literature at Oxford." He was probably speaking of Tyndale.

The monks took the alarm. "*A barbarian,*" continues Erasmus, "entered the pulpit and violently abused the Greek language." —"These folk," said Tyndale, "wished to extinguish the light which exposed their trickery, and they have been laying their plans these dozen years."[1] This observation was made in 1531, and refers doubtless to the proceedings of 1517. Germany and England were beginning the struggle at nearly the same time, and Oxford perhaps before Wittenberg. Tyndale, bearing in mind the injunction: "When they persecute you in one city, flee ye into another," left Oxford and proceeded to Cambridge. It must needs be that souls whom God has brought to His knowledge should meet and enlighten one another: live coals, when separated, go out; when gathered together, they brighten up, so as even to purify silver and gold. The Romish hierarchy,

[1] Tyndale's *Expositions* (Parker Society), p. 225.

not knowing what they did, were collecting the scattered brands of the Reformation.

Bilney had not been inactive at Cambridge. Not long had the "sublime lesson of Jesus Christ" filled him with joy, before he fell on his knees and exclaimed: "O Thou who art the truth, give me strength that I may teach it; and convert the ungodly by means of one who has been ungodly himself." After this prayer his eyes gleamed with new fire; he had assembled his friends and, opening Erasmus' Testament, had placed his finger on the words that had reached his soul, and these words had touched many. The arrival of Tyndale gave him fresh courage, and the light burnt brighter in Cambridge.

John Fryth, a young man of eighteen, the son of an innkeeper of Westerham in Kent, was distinguished among the students of King's College, by the promptitude of his understanding and the integrity of his life. He was as deeply read in mathematics as Tyndale in the classics, and Bilney in canon law. Although of an exact turn of mind, yet his soul was elevated, and he recognized in Holy Scripture a learning of a new kind. "These things are not demonstrated like a proposition of Euclid," he said; "mere study is sufficient to impress the theories of mathematics on our minds; but this science of God meets with a resistance in man that necessitates the intervention of a divine power. Christianity is a regeneration." "Through Tyndale's instructions," says John Foxe, "he first received with his heart the seed of the Gospel and sincere godliness."

These three young scholars set to work with enthusiasm. They declared that neither priestly absolution nor any other religious rite could give remission of sins; that the assurance of pardon is obtained by faith alone; and that faith purifies the heart. Then they addressed to all men that saying of Christ's at which the monks were so greatly offended: *Repent and be converted!*

Ideas so new produced a great clamour. A famous orator undertook one day at Cambridge to show that it was useless to preach conversion to the sinner. "Thou, who, for sixty years past," said he, "hast wallowed in thy lusts, like a sow in her mire, dost thou think that thou canst in one year take as many steps towards heaven, and that in thine age, as thou hast done towards hell?" Bilney left the church with indignation. "Is

Lindisfarne Abbey, built on ground given to Aidan by King Oswald of Northumbria in 635 as a base for his mission to pagan England. See page 42.

[*To face p.* 128

The New Learning in England. The painting by F. C. Cowper, A.R.A., in the House of Lords. Thomas More kneels before the future Henry VIII with Erasmus standing behind him, at Greenwich, 1499. These men were destined to play important roles in the Reformation. See pages 110-111.

that preaching repentance in the name of Jesus?" he asked. "Does not this priest tell us: Christ will not save thee. Alas! for so many years that this deadly doctrine has been taught in Christendom, not one man has dared open his mouth against it!" Many of the Cambridge fellows were scandalized at Bilney's language: was not the preacher whose teaching he condemned duly *ordained* by the bishop? He replied: "What would be the use of being a hundred times consecrated, were it even by a thousand papal bulls, if the inward calling is wanting?[1] To no purpose hath the bishop breathed on our heads if we have never felt the breath of the Holy Ghost in our hearts?" Thus, at the very beginning of the Reformation, England, rejecting the Romish superstitions, discerned with extreme nicety what constitutes the essence of consecration to the service of the Lord.

After pronouncing these noble words, Bilney, who longed for an outpouring of the Holy Ghost, shut himself up in his room, fell on his knees, and called upon God to come to the assistance of his church. Then rising up, he exclaimed, as if animated by a prophetic spirit: "A new time is beginning. The Christian assembly is about to be renewed. . . . Some one is coming unto us, I see him, I hear him—it is Jesus Christ. . . . He is the king, and it is He who will call the true ministers commissioned to evangelize His people."

Tyndale, full of the same hopes as Bilney, left Cambridge, probably at the close of 1521.

Thus the English Reformation began independently of those of Luther and Zwingli—deriving its origin from God alone. In every province of Christendom there was a simultaneous action of the divine Word. The principle of the Reformation at Oxford, Cambridge, and London was the *Greek New Testament*, published by Erasmus. England in course of time learnt to be proud of this origin of its Reformation.

[1] Without this inward calling it helpeth nothing before God to be a hundred times elect and consecrated. Foxe, *Acts*, iv. 638.

M

CHAPTER THREE

Persecution and Intrigue

(1518–20)

THE divine work of revival caused great alarm throughout the Roman hierarchy. Content with the baptism they administered, they feared the baptism of the Holy Ghost perfected by faith in the Word of God. Some of the clergy, who were full of zeal, but of zeal without knowledge, prepared for the struggle, and the cries raised by the prelates were repeated by all the inferior orders.

The first blows did not fall on the members of the universities, but on those humble Christians, the relics of Wycliffe's ministry, to whom the reform movement among the learned had imparted a new life. The awakening of the fourteenth century was about to be succeeded by that of the sixteenth, and the last gleams of the closing day were almost lost in the first rays of that which was commencing. The young scholars of Oxford and Cambridge aroused the attention of the agitated hierarchy, and attracted their eyes to the humble disciples of the Lord, who here and there still recalled the days of Wycliffe.

An artisan named Thomas Man sometimes called Doctor Man, from his knowledge of Holy Scripture, and his bold testimony to the truth as it is in Jesus, had been imprisoned for his faith in the monastery of Osney, near Oxford (A.D. 1511) Tormented by the remembrance of a recantation which had been extorted from him, he had escaped from Oxford and fled into the eastern parts of England, where he had preached the Word, supplying his daily wants by the labour of his hands. This "champion of God" afterwards drew near the capital, and assisted by his wife, the new Priscilla of this new Aquila, he proclaimed the doctrine of Christ to the crowd collected around him in some "upper chamber" of London, or in some lonely meadow watered by the Thames, or under the aged oaks of Windsor Forest. He thought with Chrysostom of old, that "all priests are not saints, but all saints are priests."[1] "He that receiveth the Word of God," said he, "receiveth God Himself: that is the true *real presence*. The vendors of masses are not the high-priests of this mystery; but the men whom God hath *anointed with His Spirit* to be kings and priests." From six to seven hundred persons were converted by his preaching.

The monks who dared not as yet attack the universities, resolved to fall upon those preachers who made their temple on the banks of the Thames, or in some remote corner of the city. Man was seized, condemned, and burnt alive on the 29th March 1518, at Smithfield.

And this was not all. There lived at Coventry a little band of serious Christians—four shoemakers, a glover, a hosier, and a widow named Smith—who gave their children a pious education. The Franciscans were annoyed that *laymen*, and even a *woman*, should dare meddle with religious instruction. On Ash Wednesday (1519) Simon Mourton, the bishop's summoner, apprehended them all, men, women, and children. On the following Friday, the parents were taken to the abbey of Mackstock, about six miles from Coventry, and the children to the Grey Friars' convent. "Let us see what heresies you have been taught?" said Friar Stafford to the intimidated little ones. The poor children confessed they had been taught in English the Lord's prayer, the apostles' creed, and the ten commandments. On hearing this, Stafford told them angrily: "I forbid you (unless you wish to be burnt as your parents will be) to have anything to do with the *Pater*, the *credo*, or the ten commandments *in English*."

Five weeks after this, the men were condemned to be burnt alive, but the judges had compassion on the widow, because of her young family (for she was their only support) and let her go. It was night: Mourton offered to see Dame Smith home; he took her arm, and they threaded the dark and narrow streets of Coventry. "Eh, eh!" said the summoner on a sudden, "what have we here?" He heard in fact the rattling of a scroll within her sleeve. "What have you got there?" he continued, putting his hand up her sleeve, from which he drew out a parchment. Approaching a window whence issued the faint rays of a lamp, he examined the mysterious scroll, and found it to contain the

[1] Chrysostom, 43 Homily on Matth.

Lord's prayer, certain articles of faith, and the ten commandments *in English.* "Oh, oh! sirrah!" said he; "come along. As
good now as another time!" Then seizing the poor widow by
the arm, he dragged her before the bishop. Sentence of death
was immediately pronounced on her, and on the 4th of April,
Dame Smith, Robert Hatchets, Archer, Hawkins, Thomas
Bond, Wrigsham, and Landsdale, were burnt alive at Coventry
in the Little Park, for the crime of teaching their children the
Lord's prayer, the apostles' creed, and the commandments of
God.

But what availed it to silence these obscure lips, so long as
the Testament of Erasmus could speak? Lee's conspiracy must
be revived. Henry Standish, bishop of St Asaph, was a narrow-
minded man, rather fanatical, but probably sincere, of great
courage, and not without some degree of piety. This prelate,
being determined to preach a crusade against the New Testament, began at London, in St Paul's Cathedral, before the
mayor and corporation. "Away with these new translations," he
said, "or else the religion of Jesus Christ is threatened with
utter ruin." But Standish was deficient in tact, and instead of
confining himself to general statements, like most of his party,
he endeavoured to show how far Erasmus had corrupted the
gospel, and continued thus: "Must I who for so many years
have been a doctor of the Holy Scriptures, and who have always
read in my Bible: *In principio erat* VERBUM—must I now be
obliged to read: *In principio erat* SERMO," for thus had Erasmus
translated the opening words of St John's Gospel. "Let us
restrain our laughter," whispered one to another, when they
heard this puerile charge. "My lord," proceeded the bishop,
turning to the mayor, "magistrates of the city, and citizens all,
fly to the succour of religion!" Standish continued his pathetic
appeals, but his oratory was all in vain; some stood unmoved,
others shrugged their shoulders, and others grew impatient.
The citizens of London seemed determined to support liberty
and the Bible.

Seeing the failure of his attack in the city, Standish sighed
and groaned and prayed, and repeated mass against the so
much dreaded book. But he also made up his mind to do more.
One day, during the rejoicings at court for the betrothal of the
Princess Mary, then two years old, with a French prince who

was an infant in arms, St Asaph, eaten up with zeal, decided upon a bold step. Suddenly he made his way through the crowd, and threw himself at the feet of the king and queen. All were thunderstruck, and asked one another what the old bishop could mean. "Great king," said he, "your ancestors who have reigned over this island—and yours, O great queen, who have governed Aragon, were always distinguished by their zeal for the church. Show yourselves worthy of your forefathers. Times full of danger are come upon us; a book has just appeared, and been published too, by Erasmus! It is such a book that, if you close not your kingdom against it, it is all over with the religion of Christ among us."

The bishop ceased, and a dead silence ensued. The devout Standish, fearing lest Henry's well-known love of learning should cause his prayer to be rejected, raised his eyes and his hands toward heaven and, kneeling in the midst of the courtly assembly, exclaimed in a sorrowful tone: "O Christ! O Son of God! save Thy spouse! . . . for no man cometh to her help."

Having thus spoken, the prelate, whose courage was worthy of a better cause, rose up and waited. Every one strove to guess at the king's thoughts. Sir Thomas More was present, and he could not forsake his friend Erasmus. "What are the heresies this book is likely to engender?" he inquired. After the sublime came the ridiculous. With the forefinger of his right hand, touching successively the fingers of his left, Standish replied: "First, this book destroys *the resurrection*; secondly, it annuls the *sacrament of marriage*; thirdly, it abolishes *the mass*." Then uplifting his thumb and two fingers, he showed them to the assembly with a look of triumph. The bigoted Catherine shuddered as she saw these unusual signs of the three heresies of Erasmus; and Henry himself, an admirer of Aquinas, was embarrassed. It was a critical moment: the Greek Testament was on the point of being banished from England. "The proof, the proof?" exclaimed the friends of literature.—"I will give it," rejoined the impetuous Standish, and then once more touching his left thumb: "Firstly," he said . . . But he brought forward such foolish reasons that even the women and the unlearned were ashamed of them. The more he endeavoured to justify his assertions, the more confused he became: he affirmed among other things that the Epistles of St Paul were written in *Hebrew*.

"There is not a schoolboy that does not know that Paul's epistles were written in *Greek*," said a doctor of divinity kneeling before the king. Henry, blushing for the bishop, turned the conversation, and Standish, ashamed at having made a Greek write to the Greeks in Hebrew, would have withdrawn unobserved. "The beetle must not attack the eagle," was whispered in his ear. Thus did the book of God remain in England the standard of a faithful band, who found in its pages the motto which the church of Rome had usurped: *The truth is in me alone.*

A more formidable adversary than Standish aspired to combat the Reformation, not only in England, but in all the West. One of those ambitious designs, which easily germinate in the human heart, developed itself in the soul of the chief minister of Henry VIII; and if this project succeeded, it promised to secure for ever the empire of the papacy on the banks of the Thames, and perhaps in the whole of Christendom.

Wolsey, as chancellor and legate, governed both in state and in church, and could, without an untruth, utter his famous *Ego et rex meus.* Having reached so great a height, he desired to soar still higher. The favourite of Henry VIII, almost his master, treated as a brother by the Emperor, by the king of France, and by other crowned heads, invested occasionally with the title of Majesty, the peculiar property of sovereigns, the cardinal, sincere in his faith in the popedom, aspired to fill the throne of the pontiffs, and thus become *Deus in terris.* He thought that if God permitted a Luther to appear in the world, it was because He had a Wolsey to oppose to him.

It would be difficult to fix the precise moment when this immoderate desire entered his mind: it was about the end of 1518 that it began to show itself. The bishop of Ely, ambassador at the court of Francis I, being in conference with that prince on the 18th of December in that year, said to him mysteriously: "The cardinal has an idea in his mind . . . on which he can unbosom himself to nobody . . . except it be to your majesty." Francis understood him.

An event occurred to facilitate the cardinal's plans. If Wolsey desired to be the first priest, Henry desired to be the first king. The imperial crown, vacant by the death of Maximilian in 1519, was sought by two princes—by Charles of Spain, a cold and calculating man, caring little about the pleasures and even the pomp of power, but forming great designs, and knowing how to pursue them with energy; and by Francis I of France, a man of less penetrating glance and less indefatigable activity, but more daring and impetuous. At the same time, Henry VIII, several years older than these continental kings, passionate, capricious, and selfish, thought himself strong enough to contend with them and secretly strove to win "the monarchy of all Christendom." Wolsey flattered himself that, hidden under the cloak of his master's ambition, he might satisfy his own. If he procured the crown of the Cæsars for Henry, he might easily obtain the tiara of the popes for himself; if he failed, the least that could be done to compensate England for the loss of the Empire, would be to give the sovereignty of the church to her prime minister.

Henry first sounded the king of France. Sir Thomas Boleyn appeared one day before Francis I just as the latter was returning from mass. The king, desirous to anticipate a confidence that might be embarrassing, took the ambassador aside to the window and whispered to him: "Some of the electors have offered me the Empire; I hope your master will be favourable to me." Sir Thomas, in confusion, made some vague reply, and the chivalrous king, following up his idea, took the ambassador firmly by one hand and, laying the other on his breast, exclaimed: "By my faith, if I become Emperor, in three years I shall be in Constantinople, or I shall die on the road!" This was not what Henry wanted; but, dissembling his wishes, he took care to inform Francis that he would support his candidature. Upon hearing this Francis raised his hat and exclaimed: "I desire to see the king of England; I will see him, I tell you, even if I go to London with only one page and one lackey."

Francis was well aware that if he threatened the king's ambition, he must flatter the minister's and, recollecting the hint given by the bishop of Ely, he said one day to Boleyn: "It seems to me that my brother of England and I could do, indeed ought to do . . . something for the cardinal. He was prepared by God for the good of Christendom . . . one of the greatest men in the church . . . and on the word of a king, if he consents, I will do it." A few minutes after he continued: "Write and tell the cardinal that if he aspires to be the head of the church and, if anything should happen to the reigning pope, I will promise him fourteen cardinals on my part. Let us only act in concert, your master and me, and I promise you, Mr Ambassador, that neither pope nor emperor shall be created in Europe without our consent."

But Henry did not act in concert with the king of France. At Wolsey's instigation he supported three candidates at once: at Paris he was for Francis I; at Madrid for Charles V; and at Frankfort for himself. The kings of France and England failed, and on the 10th August, Dr Pace, Henry's envoy at Frankfort, having returned to England, desired to console the king by mentioning the sums of money which Charles had spent, totalling, so Pace reckoned, no less than 1,500,000 gold florins. Henry congratulated himself on not having obtained the crown at so dear a rate.

Charles had scarcely ascended the imperial throne, in despite of the king of France, when these two princes swore eternal hatred of each other, and each was anxious to win over Henry VIII. At one time Charles, under the pretence of seeing his uncle and aunt, visited England; at another, Francis had an interview with the king in the neighbourhood of Calais. Cardinal Wolsey shared in the flattering attentions of the two monarchs. "It is easy for the king of Spain, who has become the head of the Empire, to raise whomsoever he pleases to the supreme pontificate," said the young Emperor to him; and at these words the ambitious cardinal surrendered himself to Maximilian's successor. But erelong Francis I flattered him in his turn, and Wolsey replied also to his advances. The king of France gave Henry tournaments and banquets of Asiatic luxury; and Wolsey, whose countenance yet bore the marks of the graceful smile with which he had taken leave of Charles, smiled also on Francis, and sang mass in his honour. He engaged the hand of the Princess Mary to the Dauphin of France and to Charles V, leaving the care of unravelling the matter to futurity. Then proud of his skilful practices he returned to London full of hope. By walking in falsehood he hoped to attain the tiara: and if it was yet too far above him, there were certain *gospellers* in England who might serve as a ladder to reach it. Murder might serve as the complement to fraud.

CHAPTER FOUR

A Storm at Sodbury Hall

(1522–23)

WHILST the ambitious prelate was thinking of nothing but his own glory and the means necessary to acquire the Roman pontificate, a great desire, but of a very different nature, was springing up in the heart of one of the humble "gospellers" of England. If Wolsey had his eyes fixed on the throne of the popedom in order to seat himself there, Tyndale thought of raising up the true throne of the church by re-establishing the legitimate sovereignty of the Word of God. The Greek Testament of Erasmus had been one step; and it now became necessary to place before the simple what the king of the schools had given to the learned. This idea, which pursued the young Oxford scholar everywhere, was to be the mighty mainspring of the English Reformation.

On a south-western slope of the Cotswolds there stood a plain but large mansion, the manor-house of Little Sodbury, commanding an extensive view over the beautiful vale of the Severn where Tyndale was born. It was inhabited by a family of gentle birth: Sir John Walsh had shone in the tournaments of the court, and by this means conciliated the favour of his prince. He kept open table; and gentlemen, deans, abbots, archdeacons, doctors of divinity, and rectors, charmed by Sir John's cordial welcome and by his good table, were ever at his house. The former brother-at-arms of Henry VIII felt an interest in the questions then discussing throughout Christendom. Lady Walsh herself, a sensible and generous woman, lost not a word of the animated conversation of her guests, and discreetly tried to incline the balance to the side of truth.

Tyndale after leaving Oxford and Cambridge had returned to the home of his fathers. Sir John had requested him to educate his children, and he had accepted the trust. Then in the prime of life (he was about thirty) and well instructed in

Scripture, Tyndale was full of desire to show forth the light which God had given him. Opportunities were not wanting. Seated at table with all the clerics welcomed by Sir John, Tyndale entered into conversation with them. They talked of the learned men of the day—of Erasmus much, and sometimes of Luther, who was beginning to astonish England. They discussed questions touching the Holy Scriptures, and sundry points of theology. Tyndale expressed his convictions with admirable clearness, supported them with great learning, and kept his ground against all with unbending courage. These animated conversations in the vale of the Severn are one of the essential features of the picture presented by the Reformation in this country. The historians of antiquity invented the speeches which they have put into the mouths of their heroes. In our times history, without such inventions, should make us acquainted with the sentiments of the persons of whom it treats. It is sufficient to read Tyndale's works to form some idea of these conversations. It is from his writings that the following discussion has been drawn.

In the dining-room of the old hall a varied group was assembled round the hospitable table. There were Sir John and Lady Walsh, a few gentlemen of the neighbourhood, with several abbots, deans, monks, and doctors, in their respective costumes. Tyndale occupied the humblest place, and kept Erasmus' New Testament within reach in order to prove what he advanced.[1] Numerous domestics were moving about engaged in waiting on the guests. At length the conversation, after wandering a little, took a more precise direction. The priests grew impatient when they saw the terrible volume appear. "Your Scriptures only serve to make heretics," they exclaimed. "On the contrary," replied Tyndale, "the source of all heresies is *pride*; now the Word of God strips man of everything, and leaves him as bare as Job."—"*The Word of God!* why even *we* don't understand it; how then can the common people understand it?"—"You do not understand it," rejoined Tyndale, "because you look into it only for foolish questions, as you would into *our Lady's Matins* or *Merlin's Prophecies*.[2] Now

---

[1] When they at any time did vary from Tyndale in opinions and judgment, he would show them in the book. Foxe, *Acts*, v, p. 115.

[2] Tyndale, *Expositions*, p. 141.

the Scriptures are a clue which we must follow, without turning aside, until we arrive at Christ; for Christ is the end."—"And I tell you," shouted out a priest, "that the Scriptures are a Dædalian labyrinth, rather than Ariadne's clue—a conjuring book wherein everybody finds what he wants."—"Alas!" replied Tyndale; "you read them without Jesus Christ; that is why they are an obscure book to you, a thicket of thorns where you only escape from the briers to be caught by the brambles."[1] "No!" exclaimed another clerk, heedless of contradicting his colleague, "nothing is obscure to us; it is we who give the Scriptures, and we who explain them to you."—"You would lose both your time and your trouble," said Tyndale; "do you know who taught the eagles to spy out their prey? Well, that same God teaches His hungry children to spy out their Father in His Word. Christ's elect spy out their Lord, and trace out the paths of His feet, and follow; yea, though He go upon the plain and liquid water, which will receive no step, yet there they find out His foot. His elect know Him, but the world knows Him not.[2] And as for you, far from having given us the Scriptures, it is you who have hidden them from us; it is you who burn those who teach them and, if you could, you would burn the Scriptures themselves."

Tyndale was not satisfied with merely laying down the great principles of faith: he always sought after what he calls "the sweet marrow within;" but to the divine unction he added no little humour, and unmercifully ridiculed the superstitions of his adversaries. "You set candles before images," he said to them; "and since you give them *light*, why don't you give them *food*. Why don't you make their bellies hollow, and put victuals and drink inside. To serve God by such mummeries is treating Him like a spoilt child, whom you pacify with a toy or with a horse made of a stick."

But Tyndale soon returned to more serious thoughts; and when his adversaries extolled the papacy as the power that would save the church in the tempest, he replied: "Let us only take on board our ship the anchor of faith in Christ's blood; let us secure it by the cable of love; and when the storm bursts

[1] A grave of briers; if thou loose thyself in one place thou art caught in another. Tyndale, *Expositions*, p. 5.
[2] Ibid. *Answer to More* (Parker Society), p. 49.

upon us, let us boldly cast the anchor into the sea; then you may be sure the ship will remain safe on the great waters." And, in fine, if his opponents rejected any doctrine of the truth, Tyndale (says the chronicler) opening his Testament would set his finger on the verse which refuted the Romish error, and exclaim: "Look and read."

The beginnings of the English Reformation are not to be found, as we have seen, in a material ecclesiasticism, which has been decorated with the name of *English Catholicism*: they are essentially spiritual. The Divine Word, the Creator of the new life in the individual, is also the Founder and Reformer of the church. The reformed churches, and particularly the reformed churches of Great Britain, are the fruit of the word of the Gospel.

The contemplation of God's works refreshed Tyndale after the discussions he had to maintain at his patron's table. He would often ramble to the top of Sodbury hill, where Queen Margaret of Anjou halted during the war of the Roses; and here too rested Edward IV, who pursued her, before the fatal battle of Tewkesbury, which caused this princess to fall into the hands of the Yorkists. But Tyndale meditated upon other battles, which were to restore liberty and truth to Christendom, battles not against flesh and blood but against the rulers of the darkness of the world, and against spiritual wickedness in high places.

Behind the mansion stood a little church, overshadowed by two large yew trees, and dedicated to Saint Adeline. On Sundays Tyndale used to preach there, Sir John and Lady Walsh, with the older children, occupying the manorial pew. This humble sanctuary was filled by their household and tenantry, listening attentively to the words of their teacher, which fell from his lips like *the waters of Shiloah that go softly*. Tyndale was very lively in conversation; but he explained the Scriptures with so much unction, says the chronicler, "that his hearers thought they heard St John himself." If he resembled John in the mildness of his language, he resembled Paul in the strength of his doctrine. The pope, he said, "turneth the roots of the trees upward. He makes the goodness of God the branches and our goodness the roots. We must be first good, says he, and move God to be good to us for our goodness' sake: so must God's goodness spring out of our goodness. Nay verily; God's goodness is the root of all goodness; and our goodness, if we have any, springs out of His goodness."[1] . . . "As the husband marrieth the wife, before he can have any lawful children by her; even so faith justifieth us to make us fruitful in good works.[2] But neither the one nor the other should remain barren. Faith is the holy candle wherewith you must bless yourselves at the last hour; without it, you will go astray in the valley of the shadow of death, though you had a thousand tapers about you, a hundred tons of holy water, a shipful of pardons, a cloth-sack full of friars' coats, and all the ceremonies of the world, and all the good works, deservings, and merits of all the men in the world, be they, or were they, never so holy. God's Word only lasteth for ever; and that which He hath sworn doth abide when all other things perish."[3]

The priests, irritated at such observations, determined to ruin Tyndale, and some of them invited Sir John and his lady to an entertainment, at which he was not present. During dinner, they so abused the young scholar and his New Testament that his patrons retired greatly annoyed that their tutor should have made so many enemies. They told him all they had heard, and Tyndale successfully refuted his adversaries' arguments. "What!" exclaimed Lady Walsh, "there are some of these doctors worth one hundred, some two hundred, and some three hundred pounds . . . and were it reason, think you, Master William, that we should believe you before them?" Tyndale thought it wise to give her no answer at the time, but as weeks passed by, she and her husband were alike convinced that their children's tutor was imparting to them nothing less than the plain truth of the Gospel of God.

Before long the manor-house and St Adeline's church became too narrow for Tyndale's zeal. He preached every Sunday, sometimes in a village, sometimes in a town. The inhabitants of Bristol assembled to hear him in a large meadow, called St Austin's Green. But no sooner had he preached in any place than the priests hastened thither, tore up what he had planted, called him a heretic, and threatened to expel from the church

---

[1] Antichrist turneth the roots of the trees upward. Tyndale, *Doctrinal Treatises* (Parker Society), p. 295.
[2] Tyndale, *Parable of the Wicked Mammon.* Ibid., p. 126.
[3] Ibid., p. 48.

every one who dared listen to him. When Tyndale returned he found the field laid waste by the enemy; and looking sadly upon it, as the husbandman who sees his corn beaten down by the hail, and his rich furrows turned into a barren waste, he exclaimed: "What is to be done? While I am sowing in one place, the enemy ravages the field I have just left. I cannot be everywhere. Oh! if Christians possessed the Holy Scriptures in their own tongue, they could of themselves withstand these sophists. Without the Bible it is impossible to establish the laity in the truth."

Then a great idea sprang up in Tyndale's heart: "It was in the language of Israel," said he, "that the Psalms were sung in the temple of Jehovah; and shall not the gospel speak the language of England among us? . . . Ought the church to have less light at noonday than at the dawn? . . . Christians must read the New Testament in their mother-tongue." Tyndale believed that this idea proceeded from God. The new sun would lead to the discovery of a new world, and the infallible rule would make all human diversities give way to a divine unity. "One holdeth this doctor, another that," said Tyndale, "one followeth Duns Scotus, another St Thomas Aquinas, another Bonaventure, Alexander of Hales, Raymond de Pennaforti, Nicholas de Lyra, Hugh de Sancto Victore, and so many others besides. . . . Now, each of these authors contradicts the other. How then can we distinguish him who says right from him who says wrong? . . . How? . . . Verily, by God's Word. Nay, say they, the Scripture is so hard that we could not understand it but by the help of the doctors. But that is to measure the measuring rod by the cloth. Here be twenty cloths of divers lengths and of divers breadths: how shall I be sure of the length of the meteyard by them? I suppose, rather, I must be first sure of the length of the meteyard, and thereby measure and judge of the cloths. If I must first believe the doctor, then is the doctor first true and the truth of the Scripture is dependent on his truth: and so the truth of God springs out of the truth of man. Thus Antichrist turns the roots of the trees upward."[1] Tyndale hesitated no longer. While Wolsey sought to win the papal tiara, the humble tutor of Sodbury undertook to place the torch of heaven in the midst of his fellow-country-

[1] Tyndale, *Doctrinal Treatises*, pp. 149–54.

men. The translation of the Bible must be the chief work of his life.

The first triumph of the Word was a revolution in the manor-house. In proportion as Sir John and Lady Walsh acquired a taste for the gospel, they became disgusted with the priests. The clergy were not so often invited to Sodbury, nor did they meet with the same welcome. "Neither," says Foxe, "had they the cheer and countenance when they came, as before they had." They soon discontinued their visits, and thought of nothing but how they could drive Tyndale from the mansion and from the diocese.

Unwilling to compromise themselves in this warfare, they sent forward some of those light troops which the church has always at her disposal. Mendicant friars and poor curates, who could hardly understand their missal, and the most learned of whom made *Albertus de secretis mulierum*[1] their habitual study, fell upon Tyndale like a pack of hungry hounds. They trooped to the alehouses and, calling for a jug of beer, took their seats, one at one table, another at another. They invited the peasantry to drink with them and, entering into conversation with them, poured forth a thousand curses upon the daring reformer: "He's a hypocrite," said one; "he's a heretic," said another. The most skilful among them would mount upon a stool and, turning the tavern into a temple, deliver, for the first time in his life, an extemporaneous discourse. They reported words that Tyndale had never uttered, and actions that he had never committed. Rushing upon the poor tutor (he himself informs us) "like unclean swine that follow their carnal lusts," they tore his good name to very tatters, and shared the spoil among them; while the audience, excited by their calumnies and heated by the beer, departed overflowing with rage and hatred against the heretic of Sodbury.

After the friars came the dignitaries. The deans and abbots, Sir John's former guests, accused Tyndale to the chancellor of the diocese, and the storm which had begun in the tavern burst forth in the episcopal palace.

The titular bishop of Worcester (an appanage of the Italian prelates) was Julio de Medici, a learned man, great politician, and crafty priest, who already governed the popedom without

[1] Treatise *On the secrets of wives*, by Albertus Magnus.

being pope, and who later, as Pope Clement VII, was appealed
to in the question of the divorce of Henry VIII. Wolsey, who
administered the diocese for his absent colleague, had appointed
Dr Thomas Parker chancellor, a man devoted to the Roman
church. It was to him the churchmen made their complaint.
A judicial inquiry had its difficulties; the king's companion-
at-arms was the employer and patron of the pretended heretic,
and Sir Anthony Poyntz, Lady Walsh's brother, was sheriff of
the county. The chancellor was therefore content to convoke a
general conference of the clergy. Tyndale obeyed the summons,
but foreseeing what awaited him, he cried heartily to God, as
he pursued his way up the banks of the Severn, "to give him
strength to stand fast in the truth of His Word."

When they were assembled, the abbots and deans, and other
ecclesiastics of the diocese, with haughty heads and threatening
looks, crowded round the humble but unbending Tyndale.
When his turn arrived, he stood forward, and the chancellor
administered him a severe reprimand, to which he made a
calm reply. This so exasperated the chancellor, that, giving
way to his passion, he treated Tyndale as if he had been a dog.[1]
"Where are your witnesses?" demanded the latter. "Let them
come forward, and I will answer them." Not one of them dared
support the charge—they looked another way. The chancellor
waited, one witness at least he must have, but he could not get
that. Annoyed at this desertion of the priests, the representative
of the Medici became more equitable, and let the accusation
drop. Tyndale quietly returned to Sodbury, blessing God who
had saved him from the cruel hands of his adversaries,[2] and
entertaining nothing but the tenderest charity towards them.
"Take away my goods," he said to them one day, "take away
my good name! yet so long as Christ dwelleth in my heart, so
long shall I love you not a whit the less."[3] Here indeed is the
Saint John to whom Tyndale has been compared.

In this violent warfare, however, he could not fail to receive
some heavy blows; and where could he find consolation? Fryth
and Bilney were far from him. Tyndale recollected an *aged*

[1] He threatened me grievously and reviled me, and rated me as though
I had been a dog. Tyndale, *Doctrinal Treatises*, p. 395.
[2] Escaping out of their hands. Foxe, *Acts*, v., p. 116.
[3] Tyndale, *Doctrinal Treatises*, p. 298.

The quadrangle of Christ Church, Oxford, first called Cardinal College in honour of Wolsey, who founded it in 1525. This centre of the Reformation in Oxford saw several young men consigned to its cellars and consequent death for reading and distributing the English New Testament. See page 260.

Little Sodbury Manor, Gloucestershire, the scene of Tyndale's labours in 1522–23 before he accepted exile as the price of

doctor, formerly chancellor to a bishop, who lived near Sodbury and who had shown him great affection. He went to see him, and opened his heart to him. The old man looked at him for a while as if he hesitated to disclose some great mystery. "Do you not know," said he, lowering his voice "that *the pope is very Antichrist* whom the Scripture speaketh of? . . . But beware what you say. . . . That knowledge may cost you your life." This doctrine of Antichrist, which Luther was at that moment enunciating so boldly, struck Tyndale. Strengthened by it, as was the Saxon reformer, he felt fresh energy in his heart, and the aged doctor was to him what the aged friar had been to Luther.

When the priests saw that their plot had failed, they commissioned a celebrated divine to undertake his conversion. The reformer replied with his Greek Testament to the schoolman's arguments. The theologian was speechless: at last he exclaimed: "Well then! it were better to be without God's laws than the pope's." Tyndale, who did not expect so plain and blasphemous a confession, made answer: "I defy the pope and all his laws!" and then, as if unable to keep his secret, he added: "If God spares my life, ere many years I will take care that a ploughboy shall know more of the Scriptures than you do."

All his thoughts were now directed to the means of carrying out his plans; and desirous of avoiding conversations that might compromise them, he thenceforth passed the greater portion of his time in the library. He prayed, he read, he began his translation of the Bible, and in all probability communicated portions of it to Sir John and Lady Walsh.

All his precautions were useless: the scholastic divine had betrayed him, and the priests had sworn to stop him in his translation of the Bible. One day he fell in with a troop of monks and curates, who abused him in the grossest manner. "It's the favour of the gentry of the county that makes you so proud," said they; "but notwithstanding your patrons, there will be a talk about you before long, and in a pretty fashion too! . . . You shall not always live in a manor-house!"—"Banish me to the obscurest corner of England," replied Tyndale; "provided you will permit me to teach children and preach the gospel, and give me ten pounds a year for my support. . . . I shall be satisfied!" The priests left him, but with the intention of preparing him a very different fate.

N

Tyndale indulged in his pleasant dreams no longer. He saw that he was on the point of being arrested, condemned, and interrupted in his great work. He must seek a retreat where he could discharge in peace the task God had allotted him. "You cannot save me from the hands of the priests," said he to Sir John, "and God knows to what troubles you would expose yourself by keeping me in your family. Permit me to leave you." Having said this, he gathered up his papers, took his Testament, pressed the hands of his benefactors, kissed the children, and then descending the hill, bade farewell to the smiling banks of the Severn, and departed alone—alone with his faith. What shall he do? What will become of him? Where shall he go? He went forth like Abraham, one thing alone engrossing his mind—the Scriptures must be translated into the language of the people, and deposited as the oracles of God in the midst of his countrymen.[1]

[1] [An excellent biography of Tyndale was produced by R. Demaus in 1872, and subsequently republished as revised by Richard Lovett. A more recent biography by J. F. Mozley, supplementing but not superseding that by Demaus, was published by the S.P.C.K. in 1937.]

CHAPTER FIVE

The Onslaught on Luther

(1517–21)

WHILST a plain minister was commencing the Reformation in a tranquil valley in the west of England, powerful reinforcements were landing on the shores of Kent. The writings and actions of Luther excited a lively sensation in Great Britain. His appearance before the Diet of Worms was a common subject of conversation. Ships from the harbours of the Low Countries brought his books to London, and the German printers had made answer to the nuncio Aleander, who was prohibiting the Lutheran works in the Empire: "Very well! we shall send them *to England!*" One might almost say that England was destined to be the asylum of truth. And in fact, the *Theses* of 1517, the *Explanation of the Lord's Prayer*, the books *against Emser, against the papacy of Rome, against the bull of Antichrist, the Commentary on the Epistle to the Galatians,* the *Appeal to the German nobility,* and above all, the *Babylonish Captivity of the Church*—all crossed the sea, were translated, and circulated throughout the kingdom. The German and English nations, having a common origin, and being sufficiently alike at that time in character and civilization, the works intended for one might be read by the other with advantage. The monk in his cell, the country gentleman in his hall, the doctor in his college, the tradesman in his shop, and even the bishop in his palace, studied these extraordinary writings. The laity in particular, who had been prepared by Wycliffe and disgusted by the avarice and disorderly lives of the priests, read with enthusiasm the eloquent pages of the Saxon monk. They strengthened all hearts.

The papacy was not inactive in presence of all these efforts. The times of Gregory VII and of Innocent III, it is true, had passed; and weakness and irresolution had succeeded to the former energy and activity of the Roman pontificate. The spiritual power had resigned the dominion of Europe to the secular powers, and it was doubtful whether faith in the papacy could be found in the papacy itself. Yet a German (Dr Eck) by the most indefatigable exertions had extorted a bull from the profane Leo X, and this bull had just reached England. The pope himself sent it to Henry, calling upon him to extirpate the Lutheran heresy. The king handed it to Wolsey, and the latter transmitted it to the bishops, who, after reading *the heretic's* books, met together to discuss the matter. There was more Romish faith in London than in the Vatican. "This false friar," exclaimed Wolsey, "attacks submission to the clergy —that fountain of all virtues." The humanist prelates were the most annoyed; the road they had taken ended in an abyss, and they shrank back in alarm. Tunstall, the friend of Erasmus, afterwards bishop of London, and who had just returned from his embassy to Germany where Luther had been painted to him in the darkest colours, was particularly violent: "This monk is a *Proteus*. . . . I mean an *atheist*. If you allow the heresies to grow up which he is scattering with both hands, they will choke the faith and the church will perish. Have we not enough of the Wycliffites—here are new legions of the same kind! . . . To-day Luther calls for the abolition of the mass; to-morrow he will ask for the abolition of Jesus Christ. He rejects everything, and puts nothing in its place. What? if barbarians plunder our frontiers, we punish them . . . and shall we bear with heretics who plunder our altars? . . . No! by the mortal agony that Christ endured, I entreat you. . . . What am I saying? the whole church conjures you to combat against this devouring *dragon* . . . to punish this *hell-dog*, to silence his sinister howlings, and to drive him shamefully back into his den." Thus spoke the eloquent Tunstall. Nor was Wolsey far behind him. The only attachment at all respectable in this man was that which he entertained for the church; it may perhaps be called respectable, for it was the only one that did not exclusively regard himself. On the 14th May 1521, this English pope, in imitation of the Italian pope, issued his bull against Luther.

It was read (probably on the first Sunday in June) in all the churches during high mass, when the congregation was most numerous. A priest exclaimed: "For every book of Martin

Luther's found in your possession within fifteen days after this injunction, you will incur the greater excommunication." Then a public notary, holding the pope's bull in his hand, with a description of Luther's *perverse opinions*, proceeded towards the principal door of the church and fastened up the document. The people gathered round it; the most competent person read it aloud, while the rest listened. The following are some of the Lutheran "heresies" which, by the pope's order, resounded in the porches of all the cathedral, conventual, collegiate, and parish churches of every county in England, and were the subjects of papal condemnation:

"11. Sins are not pardoned to any, unless, the priest remitting them, he believe they are remitted to him.

"13. If by reason of some impossibility, the *contrite* be not confessed, or the priest absolve him, not in earnest, but in jest; yet if he believe that he is absolved, he is most truly absolved.

"14. In the sacrament of *penance* and the remission of a fault, the pope or bishop doth not more than the lowest priest; yea, where there is not a priest, then any Christian will do; yea, if it were a woman or a child.

"26. The pope, the successor of Peter, is not Christ's vicar.

"28. It is not at all in the hand of the church or the pope to decree articles of faith, no, nor to decree the laws of manners or of good works."

The cardinal-legate, accompanied by the nuncio, by the ambassador of Charles V, and by several bishops, proceeded in great pomp to St Paul's, where the bishop of Rochester preached, and Wolsey burnt Luther's books. But they were hardly reduced to ashes, before sarcasms and jests were heard in every direction. "*Fire* is not a theological argument," said one. "The papists, who accuse Martin Luther of slaying and murdering Christians," added another, "are like the pickpocket, who began to cry *stop thief*, as soon as he saw himself in danger being caught."—"The bishop of Rochester," said a third, "concludes that because Luther has thrown the pope's decretals into the fire, he would throw in the pope himself. . . . We may hence deduce another syllogism, quite as sound: Rochester and his brethren have burnt the New Testament, an evident sign, verily, that they would have burnt Christ Himself also, if they had had Him!"[1] These sayings were rapidly circulated from mouth to mouth. It was not enough that Luther's writings were in England, they must needs be known, and the priests took upon themselves to advertise them. The Reformation was advancing, and Rome herself pushed behind the car.

The cardinal saw that something more was required than these paper *autos-da-fé*, and the activity he displayed may indicate what he would have done in Europe, if ever he had reached the pontifical chair. "The spirit of Satan left him no repose," says the papist Sanders. Some action out of the ordinary course is needful, thought Wolsey. Kings have hitherto been the enemies of the popes: a king shall now undertake their defence. Princes are not very anxious about learning, a prince shall publish a book! . . . "Sire," said he to the king, to get Henry in the vein, "you ought to write to the princes of Germany on the subject of this heresy." He did so. Writing to the Archduke Palatine, he said: "This fire, which has been kindled by Luther, and fanned by the arts of the devil, is raging everywhere. If Luther does not repent, deliver him and his audacious treatises to the flames. I offer you my royal co-operation, and even, if necessary, my life."[2] This was the first time Henry showed that cruel thirst, which was in after-days to be quenched in the blood of his wives and friends.

The king having taken the first step, it was not difficult for Wolsey to induce him to take another. To defend the honour of Thomas Aquinas, to stand forward as the champion of the church, and to obtain from the pope a title equivalent to that of *Christianissimus*, Most Christian King, were more than sufficient motives to induce Henry to break a lance with Luther. "I will combat with the pen this Cerberus, sprung from the depths of hell," said he, "and if he refuses to retract, the fire shall consume the heretic and his heresies together."

The king shut himself up in his library: all the scholastic tastes with which his youth had been imbued were revived; he

---

[1] They would have burnt Christ himself. Tyndale, *Doctrinal Treatises*, p. 221.

[2] [An excellent recent work on Henry's letters against Luther is, Erwin Doernberg, *Henry VIII and Luther* (Barrie and Rockliff).]

worked as if he were archbishop of Canterbury, and not king of England; with the pope's permission he read Luther's writings; he ransacked Thomas Aquinas; forged, with infinite labour, the arrows with which he hoped to pierce the heretic; called several learned men to his aid; and at last published his book. His first words were a cry of alarm. "Beware of the track of this serpent," said he to his Christian readers; "walk on tiptoe; fear the thickets and caves in which he lies concealed, and whence he will dart his poison on you. If he licks you, be careful! the cunning viper caresses only that he may bite!" After that Henry sounded a charge: "Be of good cheer! Filled with the same valour that you would display against Turks, Saracens, and other infidels, march now against this *little friar*— a fellow apparently weak, but more formidable through the spirit that animates him than all infidels, Saracens, and Turks put together." Thus did Henry VIII, the *Peter the Hermit* of the sixteenth century, preach a crusade against Luther, in order to save the papacy.

He had skilfully chosen the ground on which he gave battle: sacramentalism and tradition are in fact the two essential features of the papal religion; just as a lively faith and Holy Scripture are of the religion of the gospel. Henry did a service to the Reformation, by pointing out the principles it would mainly have to combat; and by furnishing Luther with an opportunity of establishing the authority of the Bible, he made him take a most important step in the path of reform. "If a teaching is opposed to Scripture," said the Reformer, "whatever be its origin—traditions, custom, kings, Thomists, sophists, Satan, or even an angel from heaven—all from whom it proceeds must be accursed. *Nothing can exist contrary to Scripture,* and everything must exist for it."

Henry's book having been finished by the aid of the bishop of Rochester, the king showed it to Sir Thomas More, who begged him to pronounce less decidedly in favour of the papal supremacy. "I will not change a word," replied the king, full of servile devotion to the popedom. "Besides, I have my reasons," and he whispered them in More's ear.

Doctor Clarke, ambassador from England at the court of Rome, was commissioned to present the pope with a magnificently bound copy of the king's work. "The glory of England,"

said he, "is to be in the foremost rank among the nations in
obedience to the papacy." Happily Britain was erelong to know
a glory of a very different kind. The ambassador added that
his master, after having refuted Luther's errors with the *pen*,
was ready to combat his adherents with the *sword*. The pope,
touched with this offer, gave him his foot, and then his cheek
to kiss, and said to him: "I will do for your master's book as
much as the church has done for the works of St Jerome and
St Augustine."

The enfeebled papacy had neither the power of intelligence
nor even of fanaticism. It still maintained its pretensions and
its pomp, but it resembled the corpses of the mighty ones of the
earth that lie in state, clad in their most magnificent robes:
splendour above, death and corruption below. The thunderbolts
of a Hildebrand ceasing to produce their effect, Rome gratefully
accepted the defence of laymen, such as Henry VIII and Sir
Thomas More, without disdaining their judicial sentences and
their scaffolds. "We must honour those noble champions," said
the pope to his cardinals, "who show themselves prepared to
cut off with the sword the rotten members of Jesus Christ.
What title shall we give to the virtuous king of England?"—
Protector of the Roman church, suggested one; *Apostolic king*, said
another; and finally, but not without some opposition, Henry
VIII was proclaimed *Defender of the Faith*. At the same time the
pope promised ten years' indulgence to all readers of the king's
book. This was a lure after the fashion of the middle ages, and
which never failed in its effect. The clergy compared its author
to the wisest of kings; and the book, of which many thousand
copies were printed, filled the Christian world (Cochlæus tells
us) with admiration and delight.

Nothing could equal Henry's joy. "His majesty," said the
vicar of Croydon, "would not exchange that name for all
London and twenty miles round." According to a tradition
preserved by Thomas Fuller, the king's fool, entering the room
just as his master had received the title, asked him the cause of
his transports. "The pope has just named me *Defender of the
Faith!*"—"Ho! ho! good Harry," replied the fool, "let you and
me defend one another; but . . . take my word for it . . . *let the
faith alone to defend itself.*" In the midst of the general intoxication,
the fool was the only sensible person. But Henry could listen

to nothing. Seated on an elevated throne, with the cardinal at his right hand, he caused the pope's letter to be read in public. The trumpets sounded: Wolsey said mass; the king and his court took their seats around a sumptuous table, and the heralds at arms proclaimed: *Henricus Dei gratia Rex Angliæ et Franciæ, Defensor Fidei et Dominus Hiberniæ!*[1]

Thus did it appear that the pope of Rome and the king of England were united firmly in their resolve to maintain the doctrine of the Romish church. Henry VIII had, as it were, thrown down the gauntlet. He aimed at warning all English followers of the German reformer that in his kingdom they might expect to encounter the utmost opposition of the law (which was little more than the expression of the royal will) and the use of that material sword in which the papacy so much delighted.

[1] [Henry by the grace of God King of England and France, Defender of the Faith, and Lord of Ireland. It may seem strange that, long after the Middle Ages, kings of England should still lay claim to the title of King of France. Such was the case, however, until 1802, when George III relinquished it. The title is retained in the Address to James I, often printed with the Authorised Version of 1611.]

CHAPTER SIX

Early Martyrs in Lincolnshire

(1521–22)

HENRY had now to justify the title conferred on him by the pope; Wolsey desired to gain the popedom; and both could satisfy their desires by hunting down heretics. Thus it was not long before persecution again broke out against the disciples of the Word of God.

In the county of Lincoln on the shores of the North Sea, along the fertile banks of the Humber, Trent, and Witham, and on the slopes of the smiling hills, dwelt many peaceful Christians—labourers, artificers, and shepherds—who spent their days in toil, in keeping their flocks, in doing good, and in reading (says Foxe) "a few English books such as they could get in corners." The more the gospel-light increased in England, the greater was the increase in the number of these children of peace. These "just men," as they were called, were possessed of little human knowledge, but they thirsted for the knowledge of God. Thinking they were alone the true disciples of the Lord, they married only among themselves. They appeared occasionally at church; but instead of repeating their prayers like the rest, they sat, said their enemies, "mum like beasts," and especially so when the elevation of the host took place. On Sundays and holidays, they assembled in each other's houses, and sometimes passed a whole night in reading a portion of Scripture. If there chanced to be few books among them, one of the brethren, who had learnt by heart the Epistle of St James, the beginning of St Luke's Gospel, the Sermon on the Mount, or an Epistle of St Paul's, would recite a few verses in a loud and calm voice; then all would piously converse about the holy truths of the faith, and exhort one another to put them in practice. But if any person joined their meetings who did not belong to their body, they would all keep silent. Speaking much among each other, they were speechless before those from without: fear of the priests and of the faggot made them dumb. There was no family rejoicing without the Scriptures. At the marriage of a daughter of the aged Durdant, one of their patriarchs, the wedding party met secretly in a barn, and read the whole of one of St Paul's epistles. Marriages are rarely celebrated with such pastimes as this!

Although they were dumb before enemies or suspected persons, these poor people did not keep silence in the presence of the humble: a glowing proselytism characterized them all. "Come to my house," said the pious Agnes Ashford to James Morden, "and I will teach you some verses of Scripture." Agnes was an educated woman; she could read; Morden came, and the poor woman's chamber was transformed into a school of theology. Agnes began: "We be the salt of the earth," and then recited the following verses. "If it be putrefied and vanished away, it is nothing worth. A city set upon a hill may not be hid. Teen ye not a candle, and put it under a bushel but set it on a candlestick that it may give a light to all in the house. So shine your light before men, as they may see your works, and glorify the Father that is in heaven. No tittle nor letter of the law shall pass over till all things be done." Five times did Morden return to Agnes before he had well learned his lesson. "We are spread like salt over the various parts of the kingdom," said this Christian woman to the neophyte, "in order that we may check the progress of superstition by our doctrine and our life. But," added she in alarm, "keep this secret in your heart, as a man would keep a thief in prison."[1] Then again, Agnes taught him to say this lesson: "Blessed be the poor men in spirit, for the kingdom of heaven is theirs. Blessed be mild men for they shall weld the earth." Twice he came to her to learn these words.

As books were rare these pious Christians had established a kind of itinerant library, and one John Scrivener was continually engaged in carrying the precious volumes from one to another. But at times, as he was proceeding along the banks of

---

[1] [Foxe records that when apprehended and questioned, "Agnes was bid to recite before six bishops who straightway enjoined and commanded her that she should teach these lessons no more to any man, and specially not to her children."]

the river or through the forest glades, he observed that he was
followed. He would quicken his pace and run into some barn
where the friendly peasants promptly hid him beneath the
straw, or, like the spies of Israel, under the stalks of flax. The
bloodhounds arrived, sought and found nothing; and more
than once those who so generously harboured these evangelists
cruelly expiated the crime of charity.

The disappointed officers had scarcely retired from the
neighbourhood when these friends of the Word of God came
out of their hiding-place, and profited by the moment of liberty
to assemble the brethren. The persecutions they suffered
irritated them against the priests. They worshipped God, read,
and sang with a low voice; but when the conversation became
general, they gave free course to their indignation. "Would
you know the use of the pope's pardons?" said one of them;
"they are to blind the eyes and empty the purse."—"True
pilgrimages," said the tailor Geoffrey of Uxbridge, "consist in
visiting the poor, the weak and the sick—barefoot, if so it
please you—for these are the little ones that are God's true
image."—"Money spent in pilgrimages," added a third, "serves
only to maintain thieves and harlots." The women were often
the most animated in the controversy. "What need is there to
go to the *feet*," said Agnes Ward, who disbelieved in saints,
"when we may go to the *head*?"—"The clergy of the good old
times," said the wife of David Lewis, "used to lead the people
as a hen leadeth her chickens; but now if our priests lead their
flocks anywhere, it is to the devil assuredly."

Erelong there was a general panic throughout this district.
The king's confessor, John Longland, was bishop of Lincoln.
This fanatic priest, Wolsey's creature, took advantage of his
position to petition Henry for a severe persecution: this was the
ordinary use in England, France, and elsewhere, of the confessors of princes. It was unfortunate that among these pious
disciples of the Word, men of a cynical turn were now and then
met with, whose biting sarcasms went beyond all bounds.
Wolsey and Longland knew how to employ these expressions
in arousing the king's anger. "As one of these fellows," they
said, "was busy beating out his corn in his barn, a man chanced
to pass by. 'Good morrow, neighbour,' (said the latter) 'you
are hard at it!'—'Yes,' replied the old heretic, thinking of

transubstantiation, 'I am thrashing the corn out of which the priests make God Almighty.' " Henry hesitated no longer.

On the 20th October 1521, nine days after the bull on the *Defender of the Faith* had been signed at Rome, the king, who was at Windsor, summoned his secretary, and dictated an order commanding all his subjects to assist the bishop of Lincoln against the heretics. "You disobey it at the peril of your lives," added he. The order was transmitted to Longland, and the bishop immediately issued his warrants, and his officers spread terror far and wide. When they beheld them, these peaceful but timid Christians were troubled. Isabella Bartlet, hearing them approach her cottage, cried out to her husband: "You are a lost man! and I am a dead woman!" This cry was re-echoed in many of the cottages of Lincolnshire. The bishop, on his judgment-seat, skilfully played upon the fears of these poor unhappy beings to make them accuse one another. Alas! according to the ancient prophecy: "the brother delivered up the brother to death." Robert Bartlet deposed against his brother Richard and his own wife; Jane Bernard accused her own father, and Thomas Tredway his mother, who had taught him that he should not worship the images of saints. It was not until after the most cruel anguish that these poor creatures were driven to such frightful extremities; but the bishop and the threat of death terrified them: a small number alone remained firm. As regards heroism, Wycliffe's Reformation brought but a feeble aid to the Reformation of the sixteenth century; still, if it did not furnish many heroes, it prepared the English people to love God's Word above all things. Of these humble people, some were condemned to do penance in different monasteries; others to carry a faggot on their shoulders thrice round the market-place, and then to stand some time exposed to the jeers of the populace; others were fastened to a post while an official branded them on the cheek with a red-hot iron. They also had their martyrs. Wycliffe's revival had never been without them. Four of these brethren were chosen to be put to death, and among them the pious evangelical *colporteur* John Scrivener. By burning him to ashes, the clergy desired to make sure that he would no longer circulate the Word of God; and by a horrible refinement of cruelty his children were compelled to set fire to the pile that was to consume their father, "the example of which cruelty," says Foxe, "as it is contrary both to God and nature, so it hath not been seen or heard of in the memory of the heathen." But it is easier to burn the limbs of Christians than to quench the Spirit of Heaven. These cruel fires could not destroy among the Lincolnshire peasantry that love of the Bible which in all ages has been England's strength, far more than the wisdom of her senators or the bravery of her generals.

Having by these exploits gained indisputable claims to the papal tiara, Wolsey turned his efforts towards Rome. Leo X died on the first day of December, 1521. The cardinal sent Dr Pace to Rome, instructing him to "Represent to the cardinals that by choosing a partisan of Charles or Francis, they will incur the enmity of one or the other of these princes, and that if they elect some feeble Italian priest, the apostolical see must become the prey of the strongest. Luther's revolt and the Emperor's ambition endanger the papacy. There is only one means of preventing the threatening dangers. . . . It is to choose me. . . . Now go and exert yourself." The conclave opened at Rome on the 27th December, and Wolsey was proposed; but the cardinals were not generally favourable to his election. "He is too young," said one.—"Too firm," said another.—"He will fix the seat of the papacy in England and not in Rome," urged many. He received insufficient votes; as few as seven, says one account, nineteen says another. "The cardinals," wrote the English ambassador, "snarled and quarrelled with each other; and their bad faith and hatred increased every day." Finally, to enable the cardinals to reach a decision, their food supplies were drastically restricted; and then in despair they chose Adrian, who had been tutor to the Emperor, and the cry was raised: *Papam habemus!* (we have a pope.)

During all this time Wolsey was in London, consumed by ambition, and counting the days and hours. At length a despatch from Ghent, dated the 22nd January, reached him with these words: "On the 9th of January, the cardinal of Tortosa was elected!" . . . Wolsey was almost distracted. To gain Charles, he had sacrificed the alliance of Francis I; there was no stratagem that he had not employed, and yet Charles, in spite of his engagements, had procured the election of his tutor! . . . The Emperor knew what must be the cardinal's anger, and endeavoured to appease it: "The new pope," he wrote, "is old and sickly; he cannot hold his office long. . . . Beg the cardinal of York for my sake to *take great care of his health.*"

Charles did more than this: he visited London in person, under pretence of his betrothal with Mary of England, and, on the 19th June, 1522, in the treaty then drawn up, he consented to the insertion of an article by virtue of which Henry VIII and the mighty Emperor bound themselves, if either should infringe the treaty, to appear before Wolsey and to submit to his decisions. The cardinal, gratified by such condescension, grew calm; and at the same time he was soothed with the most flattering hopes. "Charles' imbecile preceptor," they told him, "has arrived at the Vatican, attended only by his female cook; you shall soon make your entrance there surrounded by all your grandeur." To be certain of his game, Wolsey made secret approaches to Francis I, and then waited for the death of the pope.

CHAPTER SEVEN

All England Closed to Tyndale

(1523–24)

WHILE the cardinal was intriguing to attain his selfish ends, Tyndale was humbly carrying out the great idea of giving the Scriptures of God to England.

After bidding a sad farewell to the manor-house of Sodbury, the learned tutor had departed for London. This probably occurred during the summer of 1523. He had left the university —he had forsaken the house of his protector; his wandering career was about to commence, but a thick veil hid from him all its sorrows. Tyndale, a man simple in his habits, sober, daring and generous, fearing neither fatigue nor danger, inflexible in his duty, anointed with the Spirit of God, overflowing with love for his brethren, emancipated from human traditions, the servant of God alone, and loving nought but Jesus Christ, imaginative, quick at repartee, and of touching eloquence—such a man might have shone in the foremost ranks; but he preferred a retired life in some poor corner, provided he could give his countrymen the Scriptures of God. Where could he find this calm retreat? Such was the question he doubtless put to himself as he was making his solitary way to London. The metropolitan see was then filled by Cuthbert Tunstall, who was more of a statesman and a scholar than of a churchman, "the first of Englishmen in Greek and Latin literature," said Erasmus. This eulogy pronounced by the learned Dutchman occurred to Tyndale's memory. It was the Greek Testament of Erasmus that led me to Christ, said he to himself; why should not the house of Erasmus' friend offer me a shelter that I may translate it. . . . At last he reached London, and, a stranger in that crowded city, he wandered along the streets, a prey by turns to hope and fear.

Being recommended by Sir John Walsh to Sir Harry Guildford, Controller of the Royal Household, and by him to several priests, Tyndale began to preach almost immediately, especially at St Dunstan's-in-the-west, and bore into the heart of the capital the truth which had been banished from the banks of the Severn. The *Word* of God was with him the basis of salvation, and the *grace* of God its essence. His inventive mind presented the truths he proclaimed in a striking manner. He said on one occasion: "It is the blood of Christ that opens the gates of heaven, and not thy works. I am wrong. . . . Yes, if thou wilt have it so, by thy good works shalt thou be saved. Yet, understand me well, not by those which thou hast done, but by those which Christ has done for thee. Christ is in thee and thou in Him, knit together inseparably. Thou canst not be damned, except Christ be damned with thee; neither can Christ be saved except thou be saved with Him." This lucid view of justification by faith places Tyndale among the reformers. He did not take his seat on a bishop's throne, or wear a silken cope; but he mounted the scaffold, and was clothed with a garment of flames. In the service of a crucified Saviour this latter distinction is higher than the former.

Yet the translation was his chief business; he spoke to his acquaintances about it, and some of them opposed his project. "The teachings of the doctors," said some of the city tradesmen, "can alone make us understand Scripture." To this Tyndale replied: "Whatsoever opinions every man findeth with his doctor, that is his gospel, and that only is true with him: and that holdeth he all his life long. And every man, to maintain his doctor withal, corrupteth the Scripture and fashioneth it after his own imagination, as a potter doth his clay. Of what text thou provest hell will another prove purgatory, and another limbo . . . and of what text the grey friar proveth our lady was without original sin, of the same will the black friar prove that she was conceived in original sin . . . and all this with false similitudes and likenesses, and with arguments and persuasions of man's wisdom. . . . Happy are they which search the testimonies of the Lord."

Desirous of carrying out his project, Tyndale aspired to become the bishop's chaplain; his ambition was more modest than Wolsey's. The hellenist possessed qualities which could not fail to please the most learned of Englishmen in Greek literature: Tunstall and Tyndale both liked and read the same authors.

o

The ex-tutor determined to plead his cause through the elegant and harmonious disciple of Radicus and Gorgias: "Here is one of Isocrates' orations that I have translated into Latin," said he to Sir Harry Guildford; "I should be pleased to become chaplain to his lordship the bishop of London; will you beg him to accept this trifle. Isocrates ought to be an excellent recommendation to a scholar; will you be good enough to add yours?" Guildford spoke to the bishop, placed the translation in his hands, and Tunstall replied with that benevolence which he showed to every one. "Your business is in a fair way," said the controller to Tyndale; "write a letter to his lordship, and deliver it yourself."

Tyndale's hopes now began to be raised. He wrote his letter in the best style, and then, commending himself to God, proceeded to the episcopal palace. He fortunately knew one of the bishop's officers, William Hebilthwayte, to whom he gave the letter. Hebilthwayte carried it to his lordship, while Tyndale waited. His heart throbbed with anxiety: would he find at last the long-hoped-for asylum? The bishop's answer might decide the whole course of his life. If the door were to be opened, if the translator of the Scriptures should be settled in the episcopal palace, why should not his London patron receive the truth like his patron at Sodbury? and, in that case, what a future for the church and for the kingdom! . . . The Reformation was knocking at the door of the hierarchy of England, and the latter was about to utter its yea or its nay. After a few moments' absence Hebilthwayte returned: "I am going to conduct you to his lordship." Tyndale fancied himself that he had attained his wishes.

The bishop was too courteous to refuse an audience to a man who called upon him with the triple recommendation of Isocrates, of the controller, and of the king's old companion-in-arms. He received Tyndale with cool politeness, as if he were a man whose acquaintanceship might compromise him. Tyndale having made known his wishes, the bishop hastened to reply: "Alas! my house is full; I have now more people than I can employ."[1] Tyndale was discomfited by this answer. The bishop of London was a learned man, but wanting in courage and consistency; he gave his right hand to the friends of letters and of the gospel, and his left hand to the friends of the priests;

------

[1] Tyndale, *Doctrinal Treatises,* p. 395.

and then endeavoured to walk with both. But when he had to choose between the two parties, clerical interests prevailed. There was no lack of bishops, priests, and laymen about him, who intimidated him by their clamours. After taking a few steps forward, he suddenly recoiled. Still Tyndale ventured to hazard a word; but the prelate was cold as before. The humanists, who laughed at the ignorance of the monks, hesitated to touch an ecclesiastical system which lavished on them such rich sinecures. They accepted the new ideas in theory, but not in practice. They were very willing to discuss them at table, but not to proclaim them from the pulpit; and covering the Greek Testament with applause, they tore it in pieces when rendered into the vulgar tongue. "If you will look well about London," said Tunstall coldly to the poor priest; "you will not fail to meet with some suitable employment." This was all Tyndale could obtain. He departed from the bishop's presence sad and desponding.

His expectations were disappointed. Driven from the banks of the Severn, without a home in the capital, what would become of the translation of the Scriptures? "Alas!" he said; "I was deceived . . . there is nothing to be looked for from the bishops . . . Christ was smitten on the cheek before the bishop, Paul was buffeted before the bishop . . . and a bishop has just turned me away." His dejection did not last long: there was an elastic principle in his soul. "I hunger for the Word of God," said he, "I will translate it, whatever they may say or do. God will not suffer me to perish. He never made a mouth but He made food for it, nor a body, but He made raiment also."

This trustfulness was not misplaced. It was the privilege of a layman to give what the bishop refused. Among Tyndale's hearers at St Dunstan's was a wealthy cloth-merchant named Humphrey Monmouth, who had visited Jerusalem and Rome, and to whom (as well as to his companions) the pope had been so kind as to give certain Roman curiosities, such as indulgences, *a culpâ et a pœnâ*. Ships laden with his manufactures every year quitted London for foreign countries. He had formerly attended Colet's preaching at St Paul's, and from the year 1515 he had known the word of God.[1] He was one of the gentlest and most

---

[1] The rich man began to be a Scripture man. Latimer's *Sermons*, p. 440 (Parker Society).

obliging men in England; he kept open house for the friends of learning and of the Gospel, and his library contained the newest publications. In putting on Jesus Christ, Monmouth had particularly striven to put on His character; he helped generously with his purse both priests and men of letters; he gave forty pounds sterling to the chaplain of the bishop of London, the same to the king's, to the provincial of the Augustines, and to others besides. Hugh Latimer, who sometimes dined with him, once related in the pulpit an anecdote characteristic of the friends of the Reformation in England. Among the regular guests at Monmouth's table was one of his poorest neighbours, a zealous Romanist, to whom his generous host often used to lend money. One day when the pious merchant was extolling Scripture and blaming popery, his neighbour turned pale, rose from the table, and left the room. "I will never set foot in his house again," he said to his friends, "and I will never borrow another shilling of him." He next went to the bishop and laid an information against his benefactor. Monmouth forgave him, and tried to bring him back; but the neighbour constantly turned out of his way. Once, however, they met in a street so narrow that he could not escape. "I will pass by without looking at him," said the Romanist turning away his head. But Monmouth went straight to him, took him by the hand, and said affectionately: "Neighbour, what wrong have I done you?" and he continued to speak to him with so much love, that the poor man fell on his knees, burst into tears, and begged his forgiveness. Such was the spirit which, at the very outset, animated the work of the Reformation in England: it was acceptable to God, and found favour with the people.

Monmouth, being edified by Tyndale's sermons, inquired into his means of living. "I have none," replied he, "but I hope to enter into the bishop's service." This was before his visit to Tunstall. When Tyndale saw all his hopes frustrated, he went to Monmouth and told him everything. "Come and live with me," said the wealthy merchant, "and there labour." God did to Tyndale according to his faith. Simple, frugal, devoted to work, he studied night and day; and wishing to guard his mind against "being overcharged with surfeiting," he refused the delicacies of his patron's table, and would take nothing but sodden meat and small beer. It would even seem

that he carried simplicity in dress almost too far. By his conversation and his works, he shed over the house of his patron
the mild light of the Christian virtues, so that Monmouth's
love for him steadily increased.

Tyndale was advancing in his work when John Fryth, the
mathematician of King's College, Cambridge, arrived in
London. It is probable that Tyndale, feeling the want of an
associate, had invited him. United like Luther and Melanchthon,
the two friends held many precious conversations together. "I
will consecrate my life wholly to the church of Jesus Christ,"
said Fryth. "To be a good man, you must give a great part of
yourself to your parents, a greater part to your country; but
the greatest part of all to the church of the Lord."—"The
people should know the Word of God," they unitedly said.
"The interpretation of the gospel, without the intervention of
councils or popes, is sufficient to create a saving faith in the
heart." They shut themselves up in the little room in Monmouth's house, and translated chapter after chapter from the
Greek into plain English. The bishop of London knew nothing
of the work going on a few yards from him, and everything
was succeeding to Tyndale's wishes when it was interrupted by
an unforeseen circumstance.

Bishop Longland, the persecutor of the Lincolnshire
Christians, did not confine his activity within the limits of his
diocese; he besieged the king, the cardinal, and the queen with
his cruel importunities, using Wolsey's influence with Henry,
and Henry's with Wolsey. "His majesty," he wrote to the
cardinal, "shows in this holy dispute as much goodness as
zeal ... yet, be pleased to urge him to overthrow God's enemies."
And then turning to the king, the confessor said, to spur him
on: "The cardinal is about to fulminate the greater excommunication against all who possess Luther's works or hold his
opinions, and to make the booksellers sign a bond before the
magistrates, not to sell *heretical* books." "Wonderful!" replied
Henry with a sneer, "they will fear the *magisterial* bond, I think,
more than the *clerical* excommunication." And yet the consequences of the "clerical" excommunication were to be very
positive; whosoever persevered in his offence was to be pursued
by the law *ad ignem*, even to the fire. At last the confessor
applied to the queen: "We cannot be sure of restraining the

press," he said to her. "These wretched books come to us from Germany, France, and the Low Countries; and are even printed in the very midst of us. Madam, we must train and prepare skilful men, such as are able to discuss the controverted points, so that the laity, struck on the one hand by well developed arguments, and frightened by the fear of punishment on the other, may be kept in obedience." In the bishop's system, "fire" was to be the complement of Roman learning. The essential idea of Jesuitism is already visible in this conception of Henry the Eighth's confessor. That system is the natural development of Romanism.

Tunstall, urged forward by Longland, and desirous of showing himself as holy a churchman as he had once been a skilful statesman and elegant scholar—Tunstall, the friend of Erasmus, began to persecute. Like Longland, he would have feared to shed blood; but there are measures which torture the mind and not the body, and which the most moderate men fear not to make use of. John Higgins, Henry Chambers, Thomas Eglestone, a priest named Edmund Spilman, and some other Christians in London, used to meet and read portions of the Bible in English; they even asserted publicly that "Luther had more learning in his little finger than all the doctors in England in their whole bodies." The bishop ordered these rebels to be arrested: he flattered and alarmed them, threatening them with a cruel death (which he would hardly have inflicted on them) and by these skilful practices reduced them to silence.

Tyndale, who witnessed this persecution, feared lest the stake should interrupt his labour. If those who read a few fragments of Scripture were threatened with death, what would he not have to endure who was translating the whole? His friends entreated him to withdraw from the bishop's pursuit. "Alas!" he exclaimed, "is there then no place where I can translate the Bible? . . . It is not the bishop's house alone that is closed against me, but all England."[1]

He then made a great sacrifice. Since there is no place in his own country where he can translate the Word of God, he will go and seek one among the nations of the continent. It is true the people are unknown to him; he is without resources;

---

[1] But also that there was no place to do it in all England. Tyndale, *Doctrinal Treatises*, p. 396.

perhaps persecution and even death await him there. . . .
It matters not! Some time must elapse before it is known what
he is doing, and perhaps he will have been able to translate the
Bible. He turned his eyes towards Germany. "God does not
destine us to a quiet life here below," he said.[1] "If he calls us
to peace on the part of Jesus Christ, he calls us to war on the
part of the world."

There lay at that moment in the river Thames a vessel
loading for Hamburg. Monmouth gave Tyndale ten pounds
sterling for his voyage, and other friends contributed a like
amount. He left the half of this sum in the hands of his benefactor
to provide for his future wants, and prepared to quit London,
where he had spent a year. Rejected by his fellow-countrymen,
persecuted by the clergy, and carrying with him only his New
Testament and his ten pounds, he went on board the ship,
shaking off the dust of his feet, according to his Master's
precept, and that dust fell back on the priests of England. He
was indignant (says the chronicler) against those coarse monks,
covetous priests, and pompous prelates, who were waging an
impious war against God. "What a trade is that of the priests!"
he said in one of his later writings; "they want money for
every thing: money for baptism, money for churchings, for
weddings, for buryings, for images, brotherhoods, penances,
soul-masses, bells, organs, chalices, copes, surplices, ewers,
censers, and all manner of ornaments. Poor sheep! The parson
shears, the vicar shaves, the parish priest polls, the friar scrapes,
the indulgence seller pares . . . we lack but a butcher to pull
off the skin. He will not leave you long. Why are the prelates
dressed in red? To signify that they are ready every hour to
suffer martyrdom for the testimony of God's Word. But what
a false sign is this, when because of them no man dares once
open his mouth to ask a question concerning God's Word; if
he does so they are ready to burn him." Scourge of states,
devastators of kingdoms, the priests take away not only Holy
Scripture, but also prosperity and peace; but of their councils
is no layman; reigning over all, they obey nobody; and making
all concur to their own greatness, they conspire against every
kingdom."

No kingdom was to be more familiar than England with the

[1] We be not called to a soft living. Ibid., ii, p. 249.

conspiracies of the papacy of which Tyndale spoke; and yet none was to free itself more irrevocably from the power of Rome.

Yet Tyndale was leaving the shores of his native land, and as he turned his eyes towards the new countries, hope revived in his heart. He was going to be free, and he would use his liberty to deliver the Word of God, so long held captive. "The priests," he said one day, "when they had slain Christ, set poleaxes[1] to keep him in his sepulchre, that he should not rise again; even so have our priests buried the testament of God, and all their study is to keep it down, that it rise not again. But the hour of the Lord is come, and nothing can hinder the Word of God, as nothing could hinder Jesus Christ of old from issuing from the tomb."

And so Tyndale left England and sailed for Germany. A poor man in material things, he was soon to send back to his countrymen, even from the banks of the Elbe, the book which was to lead many of them to become "rich in faith and heirs of the kingdom which God has promised to them that love Him." With what greater boon can a man bless his native land?

The lines which appear beneath Tyndale's portrait preserved in Hertford College, Oxford, aptly describe the reformer's courage and purpose:

> Hac ut luce tuas dispergam Roma tenebras
> Sponte ex terris ero sponte sacrificium.
> (That light o'er all thy darkness, Rome,
> In triumph might arise,
> An exile freely I become,
> Freely a sacrifice.)

[1] [An allusion to the poleaxes which were carried before papal legates *a latere*.]

CHAPTER EIGHT

Bluff Hugh Latimer

(1485–1524)

THIS ship did not bear away all the hopes of England. A society of Christians had been formed at Cambridge, of which Bilney was the centre. He now knew no other canon law than Scripture, and had found a new master, "the Holy Spirit of Christ," says an historian. Although he was naturally timid, and often suffered from the exhaustion brought on by his fasts and vigils, there was in his language a life, liberty, and strength, strikingly in contrast with his sickly appearance. He desired to draw to the knowledge of God, all who came nigh him; and by degrees, the rays of the gospel sun, which was then rising in the firmament of Christendom, pierced the ancient windows of the colleges, and illuminated the solitary chambers of certain of the masters and fellows. Master Thomas Arthur, Master Thistle of Pembroke Hall, and Master Stafford, were among the first to join Bilney. George Stafford, professor of divinity, was a man of deep learning and holy life, clear and precise in his teaching. He was admired by everyone in Cambridge, so that his conversion, like that of his friends, spread alarm among the partisans of the schoolmen. But a conversion still more striking than this was destined to give the English Reformation a champion more illustrious than either Stafford or Bilney.

There was in Cambridge, at that time, a priest notorious for his ardent fanaticism. In the processions, amidst the pomp, prayers, and chanting of the train, none could fail to notice a master of arts, about thirty years of age, who, with erect head, carried proudly the university cross. Hugh Latimer, for such was his name, combined a biting humour with an impetuous disposition and indefatigable zeal, and was very quick in ridiculing the faults of his adversaries. There was more wit and raillery in his fanaticism than can often be found in such characters. He followed the friends of the Word of God into the colleges and houses where they used to meet, debated with them, and pressed them to abandon their faith. He was a second Saul, and was soon to resemble the apostle of the Gentiles in another respect.

He first saw light about the year 1485, at Thurcaston in the county of Leicester. Hugh's father was an honest yeoman; and, accompanied by one of his six sisters, the little boy had often tended in the pastures the five score sheep belonging to the farm, or driven home to his mother the thirty cows it was her business to milk.[1] In 1497, the Cornish rebels, under Lord Audley, having encamped at Blackheath, our farmer had donned his rusty armour, and, mounting his horse, responded to the summons of the crown. Hugh was present at his departure, and, as if he had wished to take his little part in the battle, he had buckled the straps of his father's armour.[2] Fifty-two years afterwards he recalled this circumstance to mind in a sermon preached before king Edward VI. His father's house was always open to the neighbours; and no poor man ever turned away from the door without having received alms. The old man brought up his family in the love of men and in the fear of God and, having remarked with joy the precocious under-standing of his son, he had him educated in the country schools, and then sent to Cambridge. This was in 1506, shortly after Luther entered the Augustine monastery of Erfurt.

The son of the Leicestershire yeoman was lively, fond of pleasure, and of cheerful conversation, and mingled frequently in the amusements of his fellow-students. One day, as they were dining together, one of the party exclaimed: *Nil melius quam lætari et facere bene!*—"There is nothing better than to be merry and to do well."[3]—"A vengeance on that *bene!*" replied a monk of impudent mien; "I wish it were beyond the sea;[4] it mars all the rest. I like to be merry, and I like to do, but I love not to do well." Young Latimer was much surprised at the remark: "I understand it now," said he; "that will be a heavy *bene* to these monks when they have to render God an account of their lives."

Latimer, having become more serious, threw himself heart

[1] Latimer's *Sermons* (Parker Society), p. 101.
[2] I can remember that I buckled his harness. Ibid.
[3] Eccles. iii. 12.   [4] Latimer's *Sermons*, p. 153.

and soul into the practices of superstition, and a very bigoted old cousin undertook to instruct him in them. One day, when one of their relations lay dead, she said to him: "Now we must drive out the devil. Take this holy taper, my child, and pass it over the body, first longways and then athwart, so as always to make the sign of the cross."

But the scholar performing this exorcism very awkwardly, his aged cousin snatched the candle from his hand, exclaiming angrily: "It's a great pity your father spends so much money on your studies: he will never make anything of you."

This prophecy was not fulfilled. While still an undergraduate he became Fellow of Clare Hall in 1510, and took his master's degree in 1514. His classical studies being ended, he began to study divinity. Duns Scotus, Aquinas, and Hugo de Sancto Victore were his favourite authors. The practical side of things, however, engaged him more than the speculative; and he was more distinguished in Cambridge for his asceticism and enthusiasm than for his learning. He attached importance to the merest trifles. As the missal directs that water should be mingled with the sacramental wine, often while saying mass he would be troubled in his conscience for fear he had not put in sufficient water. This remorse never left him a moment's tranquillity during the service. In him, as in many others, attachment to puerile ordinances occupied in his heart the place of faith in the great truths. With him, the cause of the church was the cause of God, and he respected Thomas Becket at least as much as St Paul. "I was then," said he, "as obstinate a papist as any in England." Luther said a similar thing of himself.

The fervent Latimer soon observed that everybody around him was not equally zealous with himself for the ceremonies of the church. He watched with surprise certain young members of the university who, forsaking the doctors of the School, met daily to read and search into the Holy Scriptures. People sneered at them in Cambridge: "It is only the *sophists*," was the cry; but raillery was not enough for Latimer. One day he entered the room where these *sophists* were assembled, and begged them to cease studying the Bible. All his entreaties were useless. Can we be astonished at it? said Latimer to himself. Don't we see even the tutors setting an example to these

stray sheep? There is Master Stafford, the most illustrious
professor in English universities, devoting his time *ad Biblia*, like
Luther at Wittenberg, and explaining the Scriptures according
to the Hebrew and Greek texts! while the delighted students
celebrate in bad verse the doctor,

Qui Paulum explicuit rite et evangelium.[1]

That young people should occupy themselves with these new
doctrines was conceivable, but that a doctor of divinity should
do so—what a disgrace! Latimer therefore determined to
attack Stafford. He insulted him;[2] he entreated the youth of
Cambridge to abandon the professor and his heretical teaching; he attended the hall in which the doctor taught, made
signs of impatience during the lesson, and cavilled at it after
leaving the school. He even preached in public against the
learned doctor. But it seemed to him that Cambridge and
England were struck blind: true, the clergy approved of
Latimer's proceedings—nay, praised them; and yet they did
nothing. To console him, however, he was named cross-bearer
to the university, and we have already seen him discharging
this duty.

Latimer desired to show himself worthy of such an honour.
He had left the students to attack Stafford; and he now left
Stafford for a more illustrious adversary. But this attack led
him to someone *that was stronger than he*. In 1524 on the occasion
of receiving the degree of bachelor of theology he had to deliver
a Latin discourse in the presence of the university; Latimer
chose for his subject *Philip Melanchthon and his doctrines*. Had not
this daring heretic presumed to say quite recently that the
fathers of the church have altered the sense of Scripture? Had
he not asserted that, like those rocks whose various colours are
imparted to the polypus which clings to them, so the doctors
of the church give each their own opinion in the passages they
explain? And finally had he not discovered a new *touchstone*
(it is thus he styles the Holy Scripture) by which we must test
the sentences even of St Thomas Aquinas?

Latimer's discourse made a great impression. At last (said
his hearers) England, nay Cambridge, will furnish a champion

[1] Who has explained to us the true sense of St Paul and of the gospel.
Strype's *Eccles. Memorials*, I, p. 74.
[2] Most spitefully railing against him. Foxe, *Acts*, viii, p. 437.

for the church that will confront the Wittenberg doctors, and save the vessel of our Lord. But very different was to be the result. There was among the hearers one man almost hidden through his small stature: it was Bilney. For some time he had been watching Latimer's movements, and his zeal interested him, though it was a zeal without knowledge. Bilney's energy was not great, but he possessed a delicate tact, a skilful discernment of character which enabled him to distinguish error, and to select the fittest method for combating it. Accordingly, a chronicler styles him "a trier out of Satan's subtleties, called of God to detect the bad money that the enemy was circulating through the church."[1] Bilney easily detected Latimer's sophisms, but at the same time loved his person, and conceived the design of winning him to the gospel. But how to manage it? The prejudiced Latimer would not even listen to the evangelical Bilney. The latter reflected, prayed, and at last planned a very candid and very strange plot, which led to one of the most astonishing conversions recorded in history.

He went to the college where Latimer resided. "For the love of God," he said to him, "be pleased to hear my confession."[2] The *heretic* prayed to make confession to the *catholic*: what a singular fact! My discourse against Melanchthon has no doubt converted him, said Latimer to himself. Was he not once among the number of the most pious zealots? His pale face, his wasted frame, and his humble look are clear signs that he ought to belong to the ascetics of catholicism. If he turns back, all will turn back with him, and the reaction will be complete at Cambridge. The ardent Latimer eagerly yielded to Bilney's request, and the latter, kneeling before the cross-bearer, related to him with touching simplicity the anguish he had once felt in his soul, the efforts he had made to remove it; their unprofitableness so long as he determined to follow the precepts of the church and, lastly, the peace he had felt when he believed that Jesus Christ is *the Lamb of God that taketh away the sin of the world*. He described to Latimer the spirit of adoption he had received, and the happiness he experienced in being able now to call God his Father. . . . Latimer, who expected to receive a confession, listened without mistrust. His heart was opened,

[1] Foxe, *Acts*, vii, p. 438.
[2] Latimer's *Sermons* (Parker Society), p. 334.

and the voice of the pious Bilney penetrated it without obstacle. From time to time the confessor would have chased away the new thoughts which came crowding into his bosom; but the penitent continued. His language, at once so simple and so lively, entered like a two-edged sword. Bilney was not without assistance in his work. A new, a strange witness—the Holy Ghost[1]—was speaking in Latimer's soul. He learned from God to know God: he received a new heart. At length grace prevailed: the penitent rose up, but Latimer remained seated, absorbed in thought. The strong cross-bearer contended in vain against the words of the feeble Bilney. Like Saul on the way to Damascus, he was conquered, and his conversion, like the apostle's, was instantaneous. He stammered out a few words; Bilney drew near him with love, and God scattered the darkness which still obscured his mind. He saw Jesus Christ as the only Saviour given to man: he contemplated and adored Him. "I learnt more by this confession," he said afterwards, "than in many years before. From that time forward I began to smell the word of God, and forsook the doctors of the schools and such fooleries."[2] It was not the penitent but the confessor who received absolution. Latimer viewed with horror the obstinate war he had waged against God; he wept bitterly; but Bilney consoled him. "Brother," said he, "though your sins be as scarlet, they shall be white as snow." These two young men, then locked in their solitary chamber at Cambridge, were one day to mount the scaffold for that divine Master whose spirit was teaching them. But one of them before going to the stake was first to sit on an episcopal throne.

Latimer was changed. The energy of his character was tempered by a divine unction. Becoming a believer, he ceased to be superstitious. Instead of persecuting Jesus Christ, he became a zealous seeker after Him.[3] Instead of cavilling and railing, he showed himself meek and gentle;[4] instead of frequenting company, he sought solitude, studying the Scriptures and advancing in true theology. He threw off the old man and

[1] He was through the good Spirit of God so touched. Foxe, *Acts,* viii, p. 438.
[2] Latimer's *Sermons,* p. 334–5.
[3] Whereas before he was an enemy and almost a persecutor of Christ, he was now a zealous seeker after him. Foxe, *Acts,* vii, p. 438.
[4] Ibid.

put on the new. He waited upon Stafford, begged forgiveness for the insult he had offered him, and then regularly attended his lectures, being subjugated more by this doctor's angelic conversation[1] than by his learning. But it was Bilney's society Latimer cultivated most. They conversed together daily, took frequent walks together into the country, and occasionally rested at a place, long known as "the heretics' hill."[2]

So striking a conversion gave fresh vigour to the evangelical movement. Hitherto Bilney and Latimer had been the most zealous champions of the two opposite causes; the one despised, the other honoured; the weak man had conquered the strong. This action of the Spirit of God was not thrown away upon Cambridge. Latimer's conversion, as of old the miracles of the apostles, struck men's minds; and was it not in truth a miracle? All the youth of the university ran to hear Bilney preach. He proclaimed "Jesus Christ as He who, having tasted death, has delivered His people from the penalty of sin." While the doctors of the schools (even the most pious of them) laid most stress upon *man's* part in the work of redemption, Bilney on the contrary emphasized the other term, namely, *God's* part. This doctrine of grace, said his adversaries, annuls the sacraments, and contradicts baptismal regeneration. The selfishness which forms the essence of fallen humanity rejected the evangelical doctrine, and felt that to accept it was to be lost. "Many listened with *the left ear*," to use an expression of Bilney's; "like Malchus, having their *right* ear cut off;" and they filled the university with their complaints.

But Bilney did not allow himself to be stopped. The idea of eternity had seized on his mind, and perhaps he still retained some feeble relics of the exaggerations of asceticism. He condemned every kind of recreation, even when innocent. Music in the churches seemed to him a mockery of God; and when Thurlby, who was afterwards a bishop, and who as a scholar lived at Cambridge in the room below his, used to begin playing on the recorder, Bilney would fall on his knees and pour out his soul in prayer: to him prayer was the sweetest melody. He prayed that the lively faith of the children of God might in

[1] A man of a very perfect life and angelic conversation. Becon's *Works* (Parker Society), p. 425.
[2] Foxe, *Acts* viii, p. 452.

all England be substituted for the vanity and pride of the priests. He believed—he prayed—he waited. His waiting was not to be in vain.

Latimer trod in his footsteps: the transformation of his soul was going on; and the more fanaticism he had shown for the sacerdotal system, which places salvation in the hands of the priest, the more zeal he now showed for the evangelical system, which places it in the hands of Christ. He saw that if the churches must needs have ministers, it is not because they require a human mediation, but from the necessity of a regular preaching of the Word and a steady direction of the flock; and accordingly he would have wished to call the servant of the Lord *minister* (ὑπηρέτης or διάκονος τοῦ λόγου), and not *priest* (ἱερεύς or *sacerdos*). In his view, it was not the imposition of hands by the bishop that gave grace, but grace which authorized the imposition of hands. He considered activity to be one of the essential features of the gospel ministry. "It is commonly seen," he said, "that fishers and hunters be very painful people both: they spare no labour to catch their game. . . . Therefore our Saviour chose fishers, because of these properties, that they should be painful and spare no labour: and then that they should be greedy to catch men, and to take them with the net of God's Word, to turn the people from wickedness to God. Ye see by daily experience what pain fishers and hunters take; how the fisher watcheth the day and night at his net, and is ever ready to take all such fishes that he can get, and that come in his way. So likewise the hunter runneth hither and thither after his game: leapeth over hedges, and creepeth through rough bushes; and all this labour he esteemeth for nothing because he is so desirous to obtain his prey and catch his venison. So all our prelates, bishops, and curates, parsons and vicars, should be as painful and greedy in casting their nets: that is to say, in preaching God's Word; in shewing unto the people the way to everlasting life; in exhorting them to leave their sins and wickedness . . . such a charge they have. But the most of them set aside this fishing; they put away this net; they take other business in hand; they will rather be surveyors or receivers, or clerks in the kitchen, than to cast out this net: they have the living of fishers, but they fish not, they are otherways occupied."[1]

[1] A sermon on Matt. iv. 18–20.

He regarded all confidence in human strength as a remnant of paganism. "Let us not do," he said, "as the haughty Ajax, who said to his father as he went to battle: Without the help of God I am able to fight, and I will get the victory with mine own strength."

The Reformation had gained in Latimer a very different man from Bilney. He had not so much discernment and prudence perhaps, but he had more energy and eloquence. What Tyndale was to be for England by his writings, Latimer was to be by his discourses. The tenderness of his conscience, the warmth of his zeal, and the vivacity of his understanding, were enlisted in the service of Jesus Christ; and, if at times he was carried too far by the liveliness of his wit, it only shows that the reformers were not *saints*, but sanctified men. "He was one of the first," says an historian, "who, in the days of King Henry VIII, set himself to preach the gospel in the truth and simplicity of it." He preached in Latin to the clergy, and in English to the people. He boldly placed the law with its curses before his hearers, and then conjured them to flee to the Saviour of the world. The same zeal which he had employed in saying mass, he now employed in preaching the true sacrifice of Christ. He said one day: "If one man had committed all the sins since Adam, you may be sure he should be punished with the same horror of death, in such a sort as all men in the world should have suffered. . . . Such was the pain Christ endured. . . . If our Saviour had committed all the sins of the world; all that I for my part have done, all that you for your part have done, and that any man else hath done; if He had done all this himself, His agony that He suffered should have been no greater nor grievouser than it was. . . . Believe in Jesus Christ, and you shall overcome death. . . . But, alas!" said he at another time, "the devil, by the help of that Italian bishop yonder, his chaplain, has laboured by all means that he might frustrate the death of Christ and the merits of his passion."

Thus began in British Christendom the preaching of the Cross. The Reformation was not the substitution of the catholicism of the first ages for the popery of the middle ages: it was a revival of the preaching of St Paul, and thus it was that on hearing Latimer everyone exclaimed with rapture: "Of a *Saul*, God has made him a very *Paul*."

P

To the inward power of faith, the Cambridge evangelists added the outward power of a godly life. Saul become Paul, the strong, the ardent Latimer, had need of action; and Biln y, the weak and humble Bilney, in delicate health, observing a severe diet, taking ordinarily but one meal a day, and never sleeping more than four hours, absorbed in prayer and in the study of the Word, displayed at that time all the energy of charity. These two friends devoted themselves not merely to the easy labours of Christian beneficence; but caring little for that formal Christianity so often met with among the comfortable classes, they explored the gloomy cells of the madhouse to bear the sweet and subtle voice of the gospel to the infuriate maniacs. They visited the miserable lazar-houses outside the city, in which poor lepers and other diseased persons were dwelling; they carefully tended them, wrapped them in clean sheets, and wooed them to be converted to Christ. The gates of the jail at Cambridge were opened to them, and they announced to the poor prisoners that word which gives liberty. Some were converted by it. One such is mentioned by Latimer in his Fifth Sermon preached long afterwards before King Edward VI: "This woman, when she came to prison, was all on her beads, and nothing else, a popish woman, and savoured not of Jesus Christ. In process (of time) she tasted that the Lord is gracious. She had such a savour, such a sweetness and feeling that she thought it long to the day of execution. She was with Christ already, as touching faith, longing to depart and to be with Him. The Word of God had so wrought in her."

Thus commenced the evangelical ministry of Hugh Latimer, afterwards Bishop of Worcester, one of the finest types of the Reformation in England! But he had many adversaries. In the front rank were the priests, who spared no endeavours to retain souls in bondage. "Beware," said Latimer to the new converts, "lest robbers overtake you, and plunge you into the pope's prison of purgatory." After these came the sons and favourites of the aristocracy, worldly and frivolous students, who felt little disposition to listen to the gospel. "By yeomen's sons the faith of Christ is and hath been chiefly maintained in the church,"[1] said Latimer. "Is this realm taught by rich men's

[1] Latimer's *Sermons*, p. 102.

sons? No, no; read the chronicles; ye shall find sometime noblemen's sons which have been unpreaching bishops and prelates, but ye shall find none of them learned men." He would have desired a mode of election which placed in the Christian pulpit, not the richest and most fashionable men, but the ablest and most pious. This important reform was reserved for other days. Lastly, the evangelists of Cambridge came into collision with the *brutality* of many, to use Latimer's own expression. "What need have we of universities and schools?" said the members of this class. The Holy Ghost "will give us always what to say."—"We must trust in the Holy Ghost," replied Latimer, "but not presume on the Holy Ghost. If you will not maintain schools and universities, you shall have a *brutality*. Preaching must not be allowed to decay: for surely, if preaching decay, ignorance and brutishness will enter again."[1] In this manner the Reformation restored to Cambridge gravity and knowledge, along with truth and charity.

Yet Bilney and Latimer often turned their eyes towards Oxford, and wondered how the light would be able to penetrate there. Wolsey provided for that. A Cambridge master of arts, John Clark, a conscientious man, of tender heart, great prudence, and unbounded devotion to his duty, had been enlightened by the Word of God. Wolsey, who since 1523 had been seeking everywhere for distinguished scholars to adorn his new college, invited Clark among the first. This doctor, desirous of bearing to Oxford the light which God had given Cambridge, immediately began to deliver a course of divinity lectures, to hold conferences, and to preach in his eloquent manner. He taught every day. Among the graduates and students who followed him was Anthony Dalaber, a young man of simple but profound feeling, who while listening to him had experienced in his heart the regenerating power of the gospel. Overflowing with the happiness which the knowledge of Jesus Christ imparted to him, he went to the Cardinal's college, knocked at Clark's door, and said: "Father, allow me never to quit you more!" The teacher, beholding the young disciple's enthusiasm, loved him, but thought it his duty to try him: "Anthony," said he, "you know not what you ask. My teaching is now pleasant to you, but the time will come when God will

[1] Ibid., p. 269.

lay the cross of persecution on you; you will be dragged before bishops; your name will be covered with shame in the world, and all who love you will be heart-broken on account of you. . . . Then, my friend, you will regret that you ever knew me."

Anthony believing himself rejected, and unable to bear the idea of returning to the barren instructions of the priests, fell on his knees, and weeping bitterly, exclaimed: "For the tender mercy of God, turn me not away." Touched by his sorrow, Clark folded him in his arms, kissed him, and with flowing tears exclaimed: "The Lord Almighty give thee what thou askest! . . . Take me for thy father, I take thee for my son in Christ." From that hour Anthony, all joy, was like Timothy at the feet of Paul. He united a quick understanding with tender affections. When any of the students had not attended Clark's conferences, the master commissioned his disciple to visit them weekly, to inquire into their doubts, and to impart to them his instructions. "This exercise did me much good," said Dalaber, "and I made great progress in the understanding of Scripture."

Thus the kingdom of God, which consists not in forms, but in the power of the Spirit, was set up in Cambridge and Oxford. The Lord Christ was building His church on Himself the Rock. His work was being set at nought of the foolish builders of the age, the worthlessness of whose hay, wood, and stubble was being daily revealed. The truth which is mighty, and must prevail over every lie, gigantic though that lie may be, was becoming the theme of attraction. The yeoman and the scholar were alike being drawn to the only true God and Jesus Christ whom He had sent. The centres of learning, the palaces of the bishops, the seats of the mighty, were being compelled to hear the trumpet blasts of the divine Word. It was as though the hosts of the Lord were marching around the all-but-impregnable walls of Antichrist's citadel, bearing in their van the ark of truth. Certainly the adversaries were many and strong, but the Lord mighty in battle was about to do, yea was already doing, great things. The Lord Omnipotent was with His Israel, and the shout of a King was among them. Clouds and darkness might be round about Him, but judgment and truth were the habitation of His throne. Evil had been arraigned and challenged in England as on the Continent of Europe. In the womb of the unknown morrow lay the church of the free.

CHAPTER NINE

Wolsey's Hopes and Fears

(1523–25)

ADRIAN VI died on the 14th September, 1523, before the end of the second year of his pontificate. Wolsey thought himself pope. At length he would no longer be the favourite only, but the arbiter of the kings of the earth; and his genius, for which England was too narrow, would have Europe and the world for its stage. Already revolving gigantic projects in his mind, the future pope dreamt of the destruction of heresy in the west, and in the east the cessation of the Greek schism, and new crusades to replant the cross on the walls of Constantinople. There is nothing that Wolsey would not have dared undertake when once seated on the throne of catholicism, and the pontificates of Gregory VII and Innocent III would have been eclipsed by that of the Ipswich butcher's son. The cardinal reminded Henry of his promise, and the very next day the king signed a letter addressed to the Emperor Charles V, the nephew of Catherine, Queen of England.

Believing himself sure of the Emperor, Wolsey turned all his exertions to the side of Rome. "The legate of England," said Henry's ambassadors to the cardinals, "is the very man for the present time. He is the only one thoroughly acquainted with the interests and wants of Christendom, and strong enough to provide for them. He is all kindness, and will share his dignities and wealth among all the prelates who support him."

But Julio de Medici, the titular Bishop of Worcester, himself aspired to the papacy and, as eighteen cardinals were devoted to him, the election could not take place without his support. "Rather than yield," said he in the conclave, "I would die in this prison." A month passed away, and nothing was done. New intrigues were then resorted to: there were cabals for Wolsey, cabals for Medici. The cardinals were besieged:

Into their midst, by many a secret path,
Creeps sly intrigue.

At length, on the 18th November 1523, the people collected under their windows, shouting: "No foreign pope." After forty-nine days of debating, Julio was elected and, according to his own expression, "bent his head beneath the yoke of apostolic servitude." He took the name of Clement VII.

Wolsey was exasperated. It was in vain that he presented himself before St Peter's chair at each vacancy: a more active or more fortunate rival always reached it before him. Master of England, and the most influential of European diplomatists, he saw men preferred to him who were his inferiors. This election was an event which favoured the Reformation in England. Wolsey as pope would, humanly speaking, have tightened the cords which already bound England so closely to Rome; but Wolsey, rejected, could hardly fail to throw himself into tortuous paths which would perhaps contribute to the emancipation of the Church. He became more crafty than ever; declared to Henry that the new election was quite in conformity with his wishes,[1] and hastened to congratulate the new pope. He wrote to Dr Pace at Rome: "This election, I assure you, is as much to the king's and my rejoicing, consolation, and gladness, as possibly may be devised or imagined. . . . Ye shall show unto his holiness what joy, comfort, and gladness it is both to the king's highness and me to perceive that once in our lives it hath pleased God of His great goodness to provide such a pastor unto His church, as his grace and I have long inwardly desired; who for his virtue, wisdom, and other high and notable qualities, we have always reputed the most able and worthy person to be called to that dignity." But the pope, divining his competitor's vexation, sent the king a golden rose, and a ring to Wolsey. "I am sorry," he said as he drew it from his finger, "that I cannot present it to his Eminence in person." Clement moreover conferred on him the quality of legate *for life*—an office which had hitherto been temporary only. Thus the popedom and England embraced each other, and nothing appeared more distant than that Christian revolution which was destined

[1] I take God to witness, I am more joyous thereof, than if it had fortuned upon my person. Wolsey to Henry VIII. Burnet, Records, p. cccxxviii. (Lond. 1841.)

very shortly to emancipate Britain from the tutelage of the Vatican.

Wolsey's disappointed ambition made him suspend the proceedings of the clergy at Cambridge. He had revenge in his heart, and cared not to persecute his fellow-countrymen merely to please his rival; and besides, like several popes, he had a certain fondness for learning. To send a few Lollards to prison was a matter of no difficulty; but learned doctors . . . this required a closer examination. Hence he gave Rome a sign of independence. And yet it was not specially against the pope that he began to entertain sinister designs: Clement had been more fortunate than himself; but that was no reason why he should be angry with him. . . . Charles V was the offender, and Wolsey swore a deadly hatred against him. Resolved to strike, he sought only the place where he could inflict the severest blow. To obtain his end, he resolved to dissemble his passion, and to distil drop by drop into Henry's mind that mortal hatred against Charles, which gave fresh energy to his activity.

Charles discovered the indignation that lay hid under Wolsey's apparent mildness and, wishing to retain Henry's alliance, made more pressing advances to the king. Having deprived the minister of a tiara, he resolved to offer the king a crown: this was, indeed, a noble compensation! "You are king of France," the Emperor said, "and I undertake to win your kingdom for you. Only send an ambassador to Italy to negotiate the matter." Wolsey, who could hardly contain his vexation, was forced to comply, in appearance at least, with the Emperor's views. The king, indeed, seemed to think of nothing but his arrival at St Germain's, and commissioned Pace to visit Italy for this important business. Wolsey hoped that he would be unable to execute his commission; it was impossible to cross the Alps, for the French troops blockaded every passage. But Pace, who was one of those adventurous characters whom nothing can stop, spurred on by the thought that the king himself had sent him, determined to cross the *Col di Tenda*. On the 27th July, 1524, he entered the mountains, traversed precipitous passes, sometimes climbing them on all-fours, and often falling during the descent. In some places he could ride on horseback; "but in the most part thereof I durst not either turn my horse traverse [he wrote to the king] for all the worldly riches, nor in manner look on my left hand, for the steep slope and deepness to the valley." After this passage, which lasted six days, Pace arrived in Italy worn out by fatigue. "If the king of England will enter France immediately by way of Normandy," said the constable of Bourbon to him, "I will give him leave to pluck out both my eyes if he is not master of Paris before All-Saints; and when Paris is taken, he will be master of the whole kingdom." But Wolsey, to whom these remarks were transmitted by the ambassador, slighted them, delayed furnishing the subsidies, and required certain conditions which were calculated to thwart the project. Pace, who was ardent and ever imprudent, but plain and straightforward, forgot himself, and in a moment of vexation wrote to Wolsey: "To speak frankly, if you do not attend to these things, I shall impute to your grace the loss of the crown of France." These words ruined Henry's envoy in the cardinal's mind. Was this man, who owed everything to him, trying to supplant him? . . . Pace in vain assured Wolsey that he should not take seriously what he had said, but the bolt had hit. Pace was associated with Charles in the cruel enmity of the minister, and he was one day to feel its terrible effects. It was not long before Wolsey was able to satisfy himself that the service Charles had desired to render the king of England was beyond the Emperor's strength.

No sooner at ease on one side, than Wolsey found himself attacked on another. This man, the most powerful among king's favourites, felt at this time the first breath of disfavour blow over him. On the pontifical throne, he would no doubt have attempted a reform after the manner of Sixtus V; and wishing to rehearse on a smaller stage, and regenerate after his own fashion the catholic church in England, he submitted the monasteries to a strict inquisition, patronized the instruction of youth, and was the first to set a great example, by suppressing certain religious houses whose revenues he applied to his college in Oxford.[1] Thomas Cromwell, his right-hand man, displayed much skill and industry in this business, and thus, under the orders of a cardinal of the Roman church, made his first campaign in a war of which he was in later days to hold the chief command. Wolsey and Cromwell, by their reforms, drew

[1] [Cardinal College: afterwards re-named Christ Church.]

down the hatred of certain monks, priests, and noblemen, always the very humble servants of the clerical party. The latter accused the cardinal of not having estimated the monasteries at their just value, and of having, in certain cases, encroached on the royal jurisdiction. Henry, whom the loss of the crown of France had put in a bad humour, resolved, for the first time, not to spare his minister: "There are loud murmurs throughout this kingdom," he said to him; "it is asserted that your new college at Oxford is only a convenient cloak to hide your malversations."—"God forbid," replied the cardinal, "that this virtuous foundation at Oxford, undertaken for the good of my poor soul, should be raised *ex rapinis!* (out of plunderings). But, above all, God forbid that I should ever encroach upon your royal authority." He then cunningly insinuated, that by his will he left all his property to the king. Henry was satisfied: he had a share in the business.

Events of very different importance drew the king's attention to another quarter. The two armies, of the Empire and of France, were met for battle before Pavia, in the Plain of Lombardy. Wolsey, who openly gave his right hand to Charles V, and secretly his left to Francis, repeated to his master: "If the Emperor gains the victory, are you not his ally? and if Francis, am I not in secret communication with him?" "Thus," added the cardinal, "whatever happens, your Highness will have great cause to give thanks to Almighty God."

On the 24th of February 1525, the battle of Pavia was fought. The army of Francis I was utterly routed. The king himself was taken prisoner to Madrid. "Of all things," he wrote to his mother, "nothing remains to me but honour and life." Charles V, who celebrated his twenty-fifth birthday on the day of the battle, was virtually Emperor of the West. England apart, he was supreme over all. Henry and Wolsey had in every sense been playing a double game. Professing friendship for Charles, and bound to support his cause by the Treaty of Windsor of August, 1522, they had at the same time been negotiating with Charles' enemy, Francis I of France. The agent employed in the negotiations was Giovanni Giovacchino di Passano, known to the English court as John Joachim, who passed for a merchant of Bologna and lived in concealment at Blackfriars. In fact, he was a Genoese attached to the household of Louise, mother of

the French king, and, after Pavia, regent of France until the
release of her son from custody at Madrid. De Praet, the Imperial
ambassador in London, had secret knowledge of Joachim's
presence in the city, and his master was not unaware that Henry
and Wolsey were not to be trusted. He was indeed much too
knowledgeable of the diplomatic situation to be deceived by
them. When, after Pavia, Wolsey urged upon him a joint
invasion of France, as a reward for which Henry was to become
its king, Charles bluntly refused to consider the proposal, and
for the rest of the year ignored English suggestions. Wisely so,
for meanwhile Wolsey re-opened negotiations with Louise,
accepted her secret present for himself of 100,000 crowns, and
concluded a treaty of peace between the two countries. In
March, 1526, Charles released his royal prisoner, after
obtaining his assent to onerous treaty terms, at the same time
requiring him to surrender to him his two sons as hostages for
his future good faith. To Louise Wolsey expressed the hope
that Francis would feel free to repudiate his solemn promises
at the first convenient opportunity. Feeling certain that Charles
had obstructed his accession to the popedom, Wolsey hoped to
prove to him by such actions that it was dangerous to thwart
the ambitions of a Cardinal and Chancellor.

While diplomatic moves of great intricacy and delicacy thus
occupied Wolsey's attention, he met with difficulties in home
affairs, particularly in matters of finance. Foreign policy, to be
effective, must be backed by adequate expenditure on armed
forces. In 1523 the Chancellor had himself visited the House of
Commons to demand four shillings in the pound of every
man's land and goods. The Commons administered to him a
humiliating rebuff, and voted a much smaller sum. In 1525,
he demanded no less than one-sixth of the movables and
incomes of the laity, and more still from the clergy. "You desire
to conquer France," said Wolsey; "you are right. Give me then
for that purpose the sixth part of your property; that is a trifle
to gratify so noble an inclination." England did not think so;
this illegal demand aroused universal complaint. "We are
English and not French, freemen and not slaves," was the
universal cry. Wolsey might tyrannize over the court, but not
lay hands on the property of the king's subjects.

The eastern counties rose in insurrection: four thousand

men were under arms in a moment; and Henry was guarded in his own palace by only a few servants. It was necessary to break down the bridges to stop the insurgents. The courtiers complained to the king; the king threw the blame on the cardinal; the cardinal laid it on the clergy, some of whom had encouraged him to impose this tax by quoting to him the example of Joseph demanding of the Egyptians the fifth part of their goods; and the clergy in their turn ascribed the insurrection to the gospellers, who (said they) were stirring up a peasant war in England, as they had done in Germany. Reformation produces revolution: this is the favourite text of the followers of the pope. Violent hands must be laid upon the heretics. *Non pluit Deus, duc ad christianos.*[1]

The charge of the priests was absurd; but the people are blind whenever the gospel is concerned, and occasionally the governors are blind also. Serious reasoning was not necessary to confute this invention. "Here, by the way, I will tell you a merry toy," said Latimer one day in the pulpit. "Master More was once sent in commission into Kent to help to try out, if it might be, what was the cause of Goodwin Sands and the shelf that stopped up Sandwich haven. He calleth the country afore him, such as were thought to be men of experience, and among others came in an old man with a white head, and one that was thought to be little less than a hundred years old. So Master More called the old aged man unto him, and said: Father, tell me if you can, what is the cause of this great arising of the sands and shelves hereabout, that stop up Sandwich haven? Forsooth, Sir, (quoth he) I am an old man, for I am well-nigh an hundred, and I think that Tenterden steeple is the cause of the Goodwin Sands. For I am an old man, Sir, and I may remember the building of Tenterden steeple, and before that steeple was in building, there was no manner of flats or sands." After relating this anecdote, Latimer slyly added: "Even so, to my purpose, is preaching of God's Word the cause of rebellion, as Tenterden steeple was the cause Sandwich haven is decayed."[2]

There was no persecution for the present, as there were

[1] "God sends no rain: lead us against the Christians." A cry ascribed by Augustine to the pagans of the first ages.
[2] Latimer's *Sermons*, p. 251.

other things to be done. Wolsey, still smarting at his failure to reach the pontifical throne, could only think of how he might repay Charles and obstruct his ambitions. But during this time Tyndale also was pursuing his aim; and the year 1525, memorable for the battle of Pavia, was destined to be no less so in the British Isles, for a still more important victory.

CHAPTER TEN

An Exile's Toil for a Nation's Life

(1524–26)

THE ship carrying Tyndale and his manuscripts cast anchor in the busy mercantile city of Hamburg, where the gospel had counted numerous friends. Encouraged by the presence of his brethren, the Oxford scholar had taken a quiet lodging in one of the narrow winding streets of that old city, and had immediately resumed his task. A secretary, whom he terms his "faithful companion," aided him in collating texts; but it was not long before this brother, whose name is unknown to us, thinking himself called to preach Christ in places where He had as yet never been proclaimed, left Tyndale. A former friar-observant of the Franciscan order at Greenwich, having abandoned the cloister, and being at this time without resources, offered his services to the translator. William Roye was one of those men (and they are always pretty numerous) whom impatience of the yoke alienates from Rome without their being attracted by the Spirit of God to Christ. Acute, insinuating, crafty, and yet of pleasing manners, he charmed all those who had mere casual relations with him. Tyndale banished to the distant shores of the Elbe, surrounded by strange customs, and hearing only a foreign tongue, often thought of England, and was impatient that his country should enjoy the result of his labours: he accepted Roye's aid. The Gospels of Matthew and Mark, translated at Hamburg, became, it would seem, the first fruits to England of his great task.

It is not possible from the evidence available to be completely certain about Tyndale's changes of residence during the period 1524–25. In all probability he and his assistant moved from Hamburg to Wittenberg in the late spring of 1524, and remained there until the spring of 1525. That Tyndale came into direct contact with Luther at Wittenberg is tolerably

certain.[1] Could he be in the reformer's own neighbourhood and
not desire to see him and speak with him? He did not need the
Saxon Valiant-for-the-Truth, either to teach him the Gospel
which he had already known at Oxford, or to instruct him in
the translation of the Scriptures. But did not all evangelical
foreigners flock to Luther's city? The strong personality of the
German reformer, his lectures, his table-talk, would doubtless
be potent sources of encouragement to the fugitive Englishman.
Above all he would be spurred on with his work of Bible
translation.

It may be the case that the two Gospels already translated
into English were printed at Wittenberg. Hamburg itself seems
to have had no resident printer at that time. During the period
1524–25 also, Tyndale must have worked with uncommon
energy at his translation of the remainder of the New Testament.
The work done, he probably moved with Roye to the Rhineland.

There were at Cologne some celebrated printers well known
in England, and among others, Peter Quentel and Arnold and
Francis Byrckmann. Francis Byrckmann had warehouses in
St Paul's churchyard in London—a circumstance that might
facilitate the introduction and sale of the Testament printed
on the banks of the Rhine. This providential circumstance
probably decided Tyndale in favour of Cologne, and thither he
repaired with Roye and his manuscripts. In the gloomy streets
of the city of Agrippina, he contemplated its innumerable
churches, and above all its ancient cathedral re-echoing to the
voices of its canons, and was oppressed with sorrow as he beheld
the priests and monks and mendicants and pilgrims who, from

[1] Not all historians believe that Tyndale and Luther met. We can
understand how Luther, at that time busily engaged in his dispute with
Carlstadt, does not mention Tyndale's visit in his letters. But, besides
Foxe, there are other contemporary authorities in favour of this fact.
Cochlæus, a German well informed on all the movements of the reformers,
and whom we shall presently see on Tyndale's traces, says of him and
Roye, that they had been to Wittenberg. And Sir Thomas More, having
said that Tyndale had gone to see Luther, Tyndale was content to reply:
"When Mr. More saith Tyndale was confederate with Luther, that is
not truth." *Answer to Sir Thos. More's Dialogue*, p. 147 (Parker Soc.). He
denied the *confederation*, but not the *visit*. If Tyndale had not *seen* Luther, he
would have been more explicit, and would probably have said that he
had never even met him. [J. F. Mozley in his *William Tyndale*, 1937, claims
that the university registers of Wittenberg for 1524 bear unmistakable proof
of our reformer's visit to that city, pp. 52–3.]

all parts of Europe, poured in to adore the pretended relics of the *three wise men* and of the *eleven thousand virgins*. And then Tyndale asked himself whether it was really in this superstitious city that the New Testament was to be printed in English. This was not all. The reform movement then at work in Germany had broken out at Cologne during the feast of Whitsuntide, and the archbishop had just forbidden all evangelical worship. Yet Tyndale persevered and, submitting to the most minute precautions so as not to compromise his work, he took an obscure lodging where he kept himself closely hidden.

Soon however, trusting in God, he called on the printer, presented his manuscripts to him, and ordered three thousand copies. The printing went on. The work was to appear as a quarto, with prologue and marginal notes and references. One sheet followed another. Gradually the gospel unfolded its mysteries in the English tongue, and Tyndale could not contain himself for very joy. He saw in his mind's eye the triumphs of the Scriptures over all the kingdom, and exclaimed with transport: "Whether the king wills it or not, erelong all the people of England, enlightened by the New Testament, will obey the gospel.

But on a sudden that sun whose earliest beams he had hailed with songs of joy was hidden by thick clouds. One day, just as the tenth sheet (making 80 quarto pages in all) had been thrown off, the printer hastened to Tyndale, and informed him that the senate of Cologne forbade him to continue the work. Everything was discovered then. No doubt Henry VIII, who had burnt Luther's books, wished to burn the New Testament also, to destroy Tyndale's manuscripts, and deliver him up to death. Who had betrayed him? He was lost in unavailing conjectures, and one thing only appeared certain: alas! his vessel, which was moving onwards in full sail, had struck upon a reef! The following is the explanation of this unexpected set-back.

One of the most violent enemies of the Reformation—we mean John Cochlæus—had arrived in Cologne. The wave of popular agitation which had stirred this city during the Whitsuntide holidays, had previously swept over Frankfort during the festival of Easter, and the Romish clergy had been threatened with violence. Cochlæus, the dean of Notre-Dame, taking advantage of a moment when the gates of the city were open, had escaped a few minutes before the burghers entered his house to arrest him. On arriving at Cologne, where he hoped to live unknown under the shadow of the powerful elector, he had gone to lodge with George Lauer, a canon in the church of the Apostles.

By a singular destiny the two most opposite men, Tyndale and Cochlæus, were in hiding in the same city; they could not long remain there without coming into collision.

On the right bank of the Rhine, and opposite Cologne, stood the monastery of Deutz, one of whose abbots, Rupert, who lived in the twelfth century, had said: "To be ignorant of Scripture is to be ignorant of Jesus Christ. This is *the scripture of nations!* This book of God, which is not pompous in words and poor in meaning like Plato, ought to be set before every people, and to proclaim aloud to the whole world the salvation of all." One day, when Cochlæus and his host were talking of Rupert, the canon informed the dean that the *heretic* Osiander of Nuremberg was in treaty with the abbot of Deutz about publishing the writings of this ancient doctor. Cochlæus guessed that Osiander was desirous of bringing forward the contemporary of Saint Bernard as a witness in defence of the Reformation. Hastening to the monastery he alarmed the abbot: "Intrust to me the manuscripts of your celebrated predecessor," he said; "I will undertake to print them and prove that he was one of us." The monks placed them in his hands, stipulating for an early publication, from which they expected no little renown. Cochlæus immediately went to Peter Quentel and Arnold Byrckmann to make the necessary arrangements. They were Tyndale's printers.

There Cochlæus made a more important discovery than that of Rupert's manuscripts. Byrckmann and Quentel having invited him one day to meet several of their colleagues at dinner, a printer, somewhat elevated by wine, declared in his cups, (to borrow the words of Cochlæus): "Whether the king and the cardinal of York wish it or not, all England will soon be Lutheran." Cochlæus listened and grew alarmed; he made inquiry; and was informed that *two Englishmen*, learned men and skilled in the languages, were concealed at Cologne. But all his efforts to discover more proved unavailing.

There was no more repose for the dean of Frankfort; his

imagination fermented, his mind became alarmed. "What," said he, "shall England, that faithful servant of the popedom, be perverted like Germany? Shall the English, the most religious people of Christendom, and whose king once ennobled himself by writing against Luther—shall they be invaded by heresy? . . . Shall the mighty cardinal-legate of York be compelled to flee from his palace, as I was from Frankfort?" Cochlæus continued his search; he paid frequent visits to the printers, spoke to them in a friendly tone, flattered them, invited them to visit him at the canon's; but as yet he dared not hazard the important question; it was sufficient for the moment to have won the good graces of the depositaries of the secret. He soon took a new step; he was careful not to question them before one another; but he procured a private interview with one of them, and supplied him plentifully with Rhenish wine—he himself is our informant. Artful questions embarrassed the unwary printer, and at last the secret was disclosed. "The New Testament," Cochlæus learnt, "is translated into English; three thousand copies are in the press; fourscore pages in quarto are ready; the expense is fully supplied by English merchants, who are secretly to convey the work when printed, and to disperse it widely through all England, before the king or the cardinal can discover or prohibit it. . . . Thus will Britain be converted to the opinions of Luther."

The surprise of Cochlæus equalled his alarm; he dissembled; he wished to learn, however, where the two Englishmen lay concealed; but all his exertions proved ineffectual, and he returned to his lodgings filled with emotion. The danger was very great. A stranger and an exile, what can he do to oppose this impious undertaking? Where shall he find a friend to England, prepared to show his zeal in warding off the threatened blow? . . . He was bewildered.

A flash of light suddenly dispelled the darkness. A person of some consequence at Cologne, Herman Rincke, a knight and an imperial councillor, had years before been sent on important business by the Emperor Maximilian to Henry VII, and from that time he had always shown a great attachment to England. Cochlæus determined to reveal the fatal secret to him; but, being still alarmed by the scenes at Frankfort, he was afraid to conspire openly against the Reformation. He had left an aged

Q

mother and a little niece at home, and was unwilling to do anything which might compromise them. He therefore crept stealthily towards Rincke's house (as he tells us himself), slipped in secretly, and unfolded the whole matter to him. Rincke could not believe that the New Testament in English was printing at Cologne; however, he sent a confidential person to make inquiries, who reported to him that Cochlæus's information was correct, and that he had found in the printing office a large supply of paper intended for the edition. The knight immediately proceeded to the senate, and spoke of Wolsey, of Henry VIII, and of the preservation of the Romish church in England; and that body which, under the influence of the archbishop, had long since forgotten the rights of liberty, forbade the printer to continue the work. Thus then there were to be no New Testaments for England! A practised hand had warded off the blow aimed at Roman-catholicism; Tyndale would perhaps be thrown into prison, and Cochlæus enjoy a complete triumph.

Tyndale was at first confounded. Were so many months of toil lost, then, for ever? His trial seemed beyond his strength. "They are ravening wolves," he exclaimed; "they preach to others, Steal not, and yet they have robbed the soul of man of the bread of life, and fed her with the shales [husks] and cods of the hope in their merits and confidence in their good works."[1] Yet Tyndale did not long remain cast down; for his faith was of that kind which removes mountains. Is it not the Word of God that is imperilled? Did God ever abandon those who trusted in Him? He must anticipate the senate of Cologne. Daring and prompt in all his movements, Tyndale bade Roye follow him, hastened to the printing office, collected the sheets, jumped into a boat, and rapidly ascended the river, carrying with him the hope of England.

When Cochlæus and Rincke, accompanied by the officers of the senate, reached the printing office, they were surprised beyond measure. The apostate had secured the abominable papers! ... Their enemy had escaped like a bird from the snare of the fowler. Where was he to be found now? He would no doubt go and place himself under the protection of some *Lutheran* prince, whither Cochlæus would take good care not to

[1] Tyndale, *Expositions*, p. 123 (Parker Society).

pursue him; but there was one resource left. These English books can do no harm in Germany; they must be prevented from reaching London. He wrote to Henry VIII, to Wolsey, and to the bishop of Rochester. "Two Englishmen," said he to the king, "like the two eunuchs who desired to lay hands on Ahasuerus, are plotting wickedly against the peace of your kingdom; but I, like the faithful Mordecai, will lay open their designs to you. They wish to send the New Testament in English to your people. Give orders at every seaport to prevent the introduction of this most baneful merchandise." Such was the name given by this zealous follower of the pope to the Word of God. An unexpected ally soon restored peace to the soul of Cochlæus. The celebrated Dr Eck, a champion of popery far more formidable than he was, had arrived at Cologne on his way to London, and he undertook to arouse the anger of the bishops and of the king. The eyes of the greatest opponents of the Reformation seemed now to be fixed on England. Eck, who boasted of having gained the most signal triumphs over Luther, would easily get the better of the humble tutor and his English New Testament.

Unhappily for Cochlæus, he does not appear to have received the material reward which he expected his startling news to have called forth. His "superlative merit" was recognized in words, but, as he himself lamented, "he was left like Mordecai at the gate without any substantial recompense for his disclosure of a plot as dangerous as that against the life of Ahasuerus."

His presence in Cologne thus disclosed, Tyndale had once more to resume his journeyings, and guarding his precious bales he ascended the rapid waters of the Rhine as quickly, and doubtless as secretly, as he could.

He passed the ancient cities and the smiling villages scattered along the banks amidst scenes of picturesque beauty. The mountains, glens, and rocks, the dark forests, the ruined fortresses, the gothic churches, the boats that passed and repassed each other, the birds of prey that soared over his head, as if they bore a mission from Cochlæus—nothing could turn his eyes from the treasure he was carrying with him. At last, after a voyage of five or six days, and probably in October, 1525, he reached Worms, where Luther, four years before, had

exclaimed: "Here I stand, I can do no other; so help me God!"
These words of the German reformer, so well known to Tyndale,
were the star that had guided him to Worms. He knew that
the gospel was preached in that ancient city. "The citizens are
subject to fits of Lutheranism," said Cochlæus. Tyndale arrived
there, not as Luther did, surrounded by an immense crowd, but
unknown, and imagining himself pursued by the myrmidons of
Charles and of Henry. As he landed from the boat he cast an
uneasy glance around him, and laid down his precious burden
on the bank of the river.

He had had time to reflect on the dangers which threatened
his work. As his enemies would have details of the edition, some
few sheets of it having fallen into their hands, he took steps to
mislead the inquisitors and began a new edition, striking out
the prologue and the notes, and substituting the more portable
octavo form for the original *quarto*. Peter Schæffer, the grandson
of Faust, one of the inventors of printing, lent his presses for
this important work. The two editions were quietly completed
about the end of the year 1525 or early in 1526.

Thus were the wicked deceived: they would have deprived
the English people of the oracles of God, and *two* editions were
now ready to enter England. "Give diligence," said Tyndale
to his fellow-countrymen, as he sent from Worms the Testament
he had just translated, "unto the words of eternal life, by the
which, if we repent and believe them, we are born anew,
created afresh, and enjoy the fruits of the blood of Christ."
About March, 1526, these books crossed the sea by way of
Antwerp or Rotterdam. Tyndale was happy; but he knew that
the unction of the Holy Ghost alone could enable the people of
England to understand these sacred pages; and accordingly he
followed them night and day with his prayers. "The scribes and
pharisees," said he, "had thrust up the sword of the Word of
God in a scabbard or sheath of glosses, and therein had knit it
fast, so that it could neither pierce nor cut. . . . Now, O God,
draw this sharp sword from the scabbard. Strike, wound, cut
asunder the soul and the flesh, so that man being divided in
two, and set at variance with himself, may be in peace with
Thee to all eternity!"

CHAPTER ELEVEN

The Awakening in Cambridge

(1524–25)

W HILE these works were accomplishing at Cologne and Worms, others were going on at Cambridge and Oxford. On the banks of the Rhine they were preparing the seed; in England they were drawing the furrows to receive it. The gospel produced a great agitation at Cambridge. Bilney, whom we may call the father of the English Reformation, since, being the first converted by the New Testament, he had brought to the knowledge of God the energetic Latimer, and so many other witnesses of the truth— Bilney did not at that time put himself forward, like many of those who had listened to him: his vocation was prayer. Timid before men, he was full of boldness before God, and day and night called upon Him for souls. But while he was kneeling in his chamber, others were at work in the world. Among these Stafford was particularly remarkable. "Paul is risen from the dead," said many as they heard him. And in fact Stafford explained with so much life the true meaning of the words of the apostle and of the four evangelists, that these holy men, whose faces had been so long hidden under the dense traditions of the schools, reappeared before the youth of the university such as the apostolic times had beheld them. But it was not only their *persons* (for that would have been a trifling matter), it was their *doctrine* which Stafford laid before his hearers. While the schoolmen of Cambridge were declaring to their pupils a reconciliation which was not yet worked out, and telling them that pardon must be purchased by the works prescribed by the church, Stafford taught that redemption was *accomplished*, that the satisfaction offered by Jesus Christ was *perfect*; and he added that, popery having revived the *kingdom of the law*, God, by the Reformation, was now reviving the *kingdom of grace*. The Cambridge students, charmed by their master's teaching, greeted him with applause, and, indulging a little too far in their enthusiasm, said to one another as they left the lecture-room: "Which is the most indebted to the other? Stafford to Paul, who left him the holy epistles; or Paul to Stafford, who has resuscitated that apostle and his holy doctrines, which the middle ages have obscured?"

Above Bilney and Stafford rose Latimer, who, by the power of the Holy Ghost, transfused into other hearts the learned lessons of his master.[1] Being informed of the work that Tyndale was preparing, he maintained from the Cambridge pulpits that the Bible ought to be read in the vulgar tongue.[2] "The author of Holy Scripture," said he, "is the Mighty One, the Ever-lasting. . . . *God Himself!* . . . and this Scripture partakes of the might and eternity of its author. There is neither king nor emperor that is not bound to obey it. Let us beware of those bypaths of human tradition, filled of stones, brambles, and uprooted trees. Let us follow the straight road of the Word. It does not concern us what the Fathers have done, but what they should have done."

A numerous congregation crowded to Latimer's preaching, and his hearers hung listening to his lips. One in particular attracted attention. He was a Norfolk youth, sixteen years of age, whose features were lighted up with understanding and piety. This poor scholar had received with eagerness the truth announced by the former crossbearer. He did not miss one of his sermons; with a sheet of paper on his knees, and a pencil in his hand, he took down part of the discourse, trusting the remainder to his memory.[3] This was Thomas Becon, afterwards chaplain to Thomas Cranmer, archbishop of Canterbury. "If I possess the knowledge of God," said he, "I owe it (under God) to Latimer."

Latimer had hearers of many sorts. By the side of those who gave way to their enthusiasm stood men "swelling, blown full, and puffed up like unto Æsop's frog, with envy and malice

[1] A private instructor to the rest of his brethren within the university by the space of three years. Foxe, *Acts*, vii, p. 438.

[2] He proved in his sermons that the Holy Scriptures ought to be read in the English tongue of all Christian people. Becon, vol. ii, p. 424 (Parker Society).

[3] A poor scholar of Cambridge . . . but a child of sixteen years. Becon's *Works*, ii, p. 424.

against him," said Becon; these were the partisans of traditional catholicism, whom curiosity had attracted, or whom their evangelical friends had dragged to the church. But as Latimer spoke a marvellous transformation was worked in them; by degrees their angry features relaxed, their fierce looks grew softer; and, if these friends of the priests were asked, after their return home, what they thought of the heretic preacher, they replied, in the exaggeration of their surprise and rapture: "*Nunquam sic locutus est homo, sicut hic homo!*" (John vii. 46.)

When he hastened from the pulpit, Latimer hastened to practise what he had taught. He visited the narrow chambers of the poor scholars, and the dark rooms of the working classes: "he watered with good deeds whatsoever he had before planted with godly words,"[1] said the student who collected his discourses. The disciples conversed together with joy and simplicity of heart; everywhere the breath of a new life was felt; as yet no external reforms had been effected, and yet the spiritual church of the gospel and of the Reformation was already there. And thus the recollection of these happy times was long commemorated in the adage:

> When Master Stafford read,
> And Master Latimer preached,
> Then was Cambridge blessed.[1]

The priests could not remain inactive: they heard speak of grace and liberty, and would have nothing to do with either. If *grace* is tolerated, will it not take from the hands of the clergy the manipulation of salvation, indulgences, penance, and all the rubrics of the canon law? If *liberty* is conceded, will not the hierarchy, with all its degrees, pomps, violence, and scaffolds, be shaken? Rome desires no other liberty than that of free-will, which, exalting the natural strength of fallen man, dries up as regards mankind the springs of divine life, withers Christianity, and changes that heavenly religion into a human moralism and legal observances.

The friends of popery, therefore, collected their forces to oppose the new religion. "Satan, who never sleeps," says the simple chronicler, "called up his familiar spirits, and sent them forth against the reformers." Meetings were held in the convents, but particularly in that belonging to the Greyfriars. They

---

[1] Becon's *Works*, ii, p. 425.

mustered all their forces. *An eye for an eye, and a tooth for a tooth*, said they. Latimer extols in his sermons the *blessings* of Scripture; we must deliver a sermon also to show its *dangers*. But where was the orator to be found who could cope with him? This was a very embarrassing question to the clerical party. Among the Dominicans there was a friar, adroit and skilful in little matters: it was the prior Bockenham. No one had shown more hatred against the evangelical Christians, and no one was in truth a greater stranger to the gospel. This was the man commissioned to set forth the dangers of the Word of God. He was by no means familiar with the New Testament; he opened it however, picked out a few passages here and there which seemed to favour his thesis; and then, arrayed in his costliest robes, with head erect and solemn step, already sure of victory, he went into the pulpit, combated the heretic, and with pompous voice stormed against the reading of the Bible; it was in his eyes the fountain of all heresies and misfortunes. "Scripture," he said, "is full of figurative language which the laity will be certain to misinterpret to their own ruin. If that heresy should prevail," he exclaimed, "there will be an end of everything useful among us. The ploughman, reading in the gospel that *no man having put his hand to the plough should look back*, would soon lay aside his labour. . . . The baker, reading that *a little leaven leaveneth the whole lump*, will in future make us nothing but very insipid bread; and the simple man finding himself commanded *to pluck out the right eye and cast it from thee*, England, after a few years, will be a frightful spectacle; it will be little better than a nation of blind and one-eyed men, sadly begging their bread from door to door."

This discourse moved that part of the audience for which it was intended. "The heretic is silenced," said the monks and clerks; but sensible people smiled, and Latimer was delighted that they had given him such an adversary. Being of a lively disposition and inclined to irony, he resolved to lash the platitudes of the pompous friar. There are some absurdities, he thought, which can only be refuted by showing how foolish they are. Does not even the grave Tertullian speak of things which are only to be laughed at, for fear of giving them importance by a serious refutation? "Next Sunday I will reply to him," said Latimer.

The church was crowded when Bockenham with the hood of St Francis on his shoulders and with a vain-glorious air, took his place solemnly in front of the preacher. Latimer began by recapitulating the least weak of his adversary's arguments; then taking them up one by one, he turned them over and over, and pointed out all their absurdity with so much wit, that the poor prior was buried in his own nonsense. Then turning towards the listening crowd, he exclaimed with warmth: "This is how your skilful guides abuse your understanding. They look upon you as children that must be for ever kept in leading-strings. Now, the hour of your majority has arrived; boldly examine the Scriptures, and you will easily discover the absurdity of the teaching of your doctors." And then desirous, as Solomon has it, of *answering a fool according to his folly*, he added: "As for the comparisons drawn from the *plough*, the *leaven*, and the *eye*, of which the reverend prior has made so singular a use, is it necessary to justify these passages of Scripture? Must I tell you what *plough*, what *leaven*, what *eye* is here meant? Is not our Lord's teaching distinguished by those expressions which, under a popular form, conceal a spiritual and profound meaning? Do not we know that in all languages and in all speeches, it is not on the *image* that we must fix our eyes, but on the *thing* which the image represents? . . . For instance," he continued, and as he said these words he cast a piercing glance on the prior, "if we see a fox painted preaching in a friar's hood, nobody imagines that a fox is meant, but that craft and hypocrisy are described, which are so often found disguised in that garb." At these words the prior, on whom the eyes of all the congregation were turned, rose and left the church hastily, and went off to hide his rage and confusion among his brethren. The monks and their creatures uttered loud cries against Latimer. It was unpardonable (they said) to have been thus wanting in respect to the cowl of St Francis. But his friends replied: "Do we not whip children? and he who treats Scripture worse than a child, does he not deserve to be well flogged?"

The Romish party did not consider themselves beaten. The heads of colleges and the priests held frequent conferences. The professors were desired to watch carefully over their pupils, and to lead them back to the teaching of the church by flattery and by threats. "We are putting our lance in rest," they told the students; "if you become evangelicals, your advancement is at an end." But these open-hearted generous youths loved rather to be poor with Christ, than rich with the priests. Stafford continued to teach, Latimer to preach, and Bilney to visit the poor: the doctrine of Christ ceased not to be spread abroad, and souls to be converted.

It was difficult, if not impossible, to silence a preacher so popular with the ordinary people as Latimer. A plan to do so had been in contemplation a considerable time before the encounter with Bockenham just recorded. The aid of the bishops was sought. Dr West, bishop of Ely, was ordinary of Cambridge; in response to an urgent request for his intervention, he ordered one of the doctors to inform him the next time Latimer was to preach; "but," added he, "do not say a word to any one. I wish to come without being expected."

One day as Latimer was preaching in Latin *ad clerum* (to the clergy), the bishop suddenly entered the university church, attended by a number of priests. Latimer stopped, waiting respectfully until West and his train had taken their places. "A new audience," he adroitly remarked, "and moreover, an audience of such rank, calls for a new theme. Leaving, therefore, the subject I had proposed, I will take up one that relates to the episcopal charge, and will preach on these words: *Christus existens Pontifex futurorum bonorum.*" (Hebrews ix. 11.) Then describing Jesus Christ, Latimer represented him as the "true and perfect pattern unto all other bishops." There was not a single virtue pointed out in the divine bishop that did not correspond with some defect in the Romish bishops. Latimer's caustic wit had a free course at their expense; but there was so much gravity in his sallies, and so lively a Christianity in his descriptions, that every one must have felt them to be the cries of a Christian conscience rather than the sarcasms of an ill-natured disposition. Never had bishop been taught by one of his priests like this man. "Alas!" said many, "our bishops are not of that breed: they are descended from Annas and Caiaphas." West was not more at his ease than Bockenham had been formerly. He stifled his anger, however; and after the sermon, said to Latimer with a gracious accent: "You have excellent talents, and if you would do one thing I should be ready to kiss your feet." . . . What humility in a bishop! . . . "Preach in this same church," continued West, "a sermon . . . against Martin Luther. That is the best way of checking heresy." Latimer understood the prelate's meaning, and replied calmly: "If Luther preaches the Word of God, I cannot oppose him. If he teaches the contrary, I am ready to attack him. But, my Lord, by command of my Cardinal of York, we are prohibited from reading Luther's works: therefore it were but a vain thing for me to attempt to refute them."—"Well, well, Master Latimer," exclaimed the bishop, "I perceive that you smell somewhat of the pan. . . . One day or another you will repent of this gear."

West having left Cambridge in great irritation against that rebellious clerk, hastened to convoke his chapter, and forbade Latimer to preach either in the university or in the diocese. "All that will live godly shall suffer persecution," Saint Paul had said; Latimer was now experiencing the truth of the saying. It was not enough that the name of heretic had been given him by the priests and their friends, and that the passers-by insulted him in the streets; . . . the work of God was violently checked. "Behold then," he exclaimed with a bitter sigh, "the use of the episcopal office . . . to hinder the preaching of Jesus Christ!" Some few years later he sketched, with his usual caustic irony, the portrait of a certain bishop, of whom Luther also used frequently to speak: "Do you know," said Latimer, "who is the most diligentest bishop and prelate in all England? . . . I see you listening and hearkening that I should name him. . . . I will tell you. . . . It is the devil. He is never out of his diocese; ye shall never find him out of the way; call for him when you will, he's ever at home. He is ever at his plough. Ye shall never find him idle, I warrant you. Where the devil is resident—there away with books and up with candles; away with Bibles and up with beads; away with the light of the gospel and up with the light of candles, yea at noondays; down with Christ's cross, up with purgatory pickpurse; away with clothing the naked, the poor, and impotent, up with decking of images and gay garnishing of stocks and stones; down with God's traditions and His most holy Word. . . . Oh! that our prelates would be as diligent to sow the corn of good doctrine as Satan is to sow cockle and darnel!" Truly may it be said, "There was never such a preacher in England as he is."

The reformer was not satisfied with merely speaking: he acted. "Neither the menacing words of his adversaries nor their cruel imprisonments," says one of his contemporaries, "could hinder him from proclaiming God's truth." Forbidden to preach in the churches, he went about from house to house. He longed for a pulpit however, and this he obtained. A haughty prelate had in vain interdicted his preaching; Jesus Christ, who is above all bishops, is able, when one door is shut, to open another. Instead of one great preacher there were soon two at Cambridge.

An Augustine monk named Robert Barnes, a native of the county of Norfolk, and a great scholar, had gone to Louvain to prosecute his studies. Here he received the degree of doctor of divinity and, having returned to Cambridge, was nominated prior of his monastery in 1523. It was his fortune to reconcile learning and the gospel in the university; but by leaning too much to learning he diminished the force of the Word of God. A great crowd collected every day in the Augustine lecture hall, to hear him discourse upon Terence and Plautus, and in particular upon Cicero. Many of those who were offended by the simple Christianity of Bilney and Latimer, were attracted by this reformer of another kind. Coleman, Coverdale, Field, Cambridge, Barley, and many other young men of the university, gathered round Barnes and proclaimed him "the restorer of letters."[1]

But the classics were only a preparatory teaching. The masterpieces of antiquity having aided Barnes to clear the soil, he opened before his class the epistles of St Paul. He did not understand their divine depth, like Stafford; he was not, like him, anointed with the Holy Ghost; he differed from him on several of the apostle's doctrines, on justification by faith, and on the new creature; but Barnes was an enlightened and liberal man, not without some degree of piety, and desirous, like Stafford, of substituting the teaching of Scripture for the barren disputations of the schools. But they soon came into collision, and Cambridge long remembered that celebrated discussion

---

[1] The great restorer of good learning. Strype, i, p. 568; Foxe, *Acts*, v, p. 415. [An excellent account of Barnes' teaching is in D. B. Knox, *The Doctrine of Faith* (James Clarke, 1961), pp. 63-69. This is the best modern treatment of the theology of the early English Reformers.]

in which Barnes and Stafford contended with so much renown, employing no other weapons than the Word of God, to the great astonishment of the blind doctors, and the great joy of the clear-sighted, says the chronicler.

Barnes was not as yet thoroughly enlightened, and the friends of the gospel were astonished that a man, a stranger to the truth, should deal such heavy blows against error. Bilney, whom we continually meet with when any secret work, a work of irresistible charity, is in hand—Bilney, who had converted Latimer, undertook to convert Barnes; and Stafford, Arthur, Thistel of Pembroke College, and Fooke of Benet's[1] earnestly prayed God to grant his assistance. The experiment was difficult: Barnes had reached that *juste milieu*, that "golden mean" of the humanists, that intoxication of learning and glory, which render conversion more difficult. Besides, could a man like Bilney really dare to instruct the restorer of antiquity? But the humble bachelor of arts, so simple in appearance, knew, like David of old, a secret power by which the Goliath of the university might be vanquished. He passed days and nights in prayer; and then urged Barnes openly to manifest his convictions without fearing the reproaches of the world. After many conversations and prayers, Barnes was converted to the gospel of Jesus Christ.[2] Still, the prior retained something undecided in his character, and only half relinquished that middle state with which he had begun. For instance, he appears to have always believed in the efficacy of sacerdotal consecration to transform the bread and wine into the body and blood of Christ. His eye was not single, and his mind was often agitated and driven to and fro by contrary thoughts: "Alas!" said this divided character one day, "I confess that my cogitations be innumerable."

Barnes, having come to a knowledge of the truth, immediately displayed a zeal that was somewhat imprudent. Men of the least decided character, and even those who are destined to make a signal fall, are often those who begin their course with the greatest ardour. Barnes seemed prepared at this time to withstand all England. Being now united to Latimer by a

---

[1] [St Benedict's, later re-named Corpus Christi.]

[2] Bilney converted Dr Barnes to the gospel of Jesus Christ. Foxe, *Acts*, iv, p. 620.

tender Christian affection, he was indignant that the powerful voice of his friend should be lost to the church. "The bishop has forbidden you to preach," he said to him, "but my monastery is not under episcopal jurisdiction. You can preach there." Latimer went into the pulpit at the Augustine's, and the church could not contain the crowd that flocked to it. At Cambridge, as at Wittenberg, the chapel of the Augustine monks was used for the first struggles of the gospel. It was here that Latimer delivered some of his best sermons.

A very different man from Latimer, and particularly from Barnes, was daily growing in influence among the English reformers: this was Fryth[1]. No one was more humble than he, and on that very account no one was stronger. He was less brilliant than Barnes, but more solid. He might have penetrated into the highest departments of science, but he was drawn away by the deep mysteries of God's Word; the call of conscience prevailed over that of the understanding. He did not devote the energy of his soul to difficult questions; he thirsted for God, for His truth, and for His love. Instead of propagating his particular opinions and forming divisions, he clung only to the faith which saves, and advanced the dominion of true unity. This is the mark of the great servants of God. Humble before the Lord, mild before men, and even in appearance somewhat timid, Fryth in the face of danger displayed an intrepid courage. "My learning is small," he said, "but the little I have I am determined to give to Jesus Christ for the building of His temple."

Latimer's sermons, Barnes' ardour, and Fryth's firmness, excited fresh zeal at Cambridge. They knew what was going on in Germany and Switzerland; shall the English, ever in front, now remain in the rear? Shall not Latimer, Bilney, Stafford, Barnes, and Fryth do what the servants of God are doing in other places?

A secret ferment announced an approaching crisis: every one expected some change for better or for worse. The evangelicals, confident in the truth, and thinking themselves sure of victory, resolved to fall upon the enemy simultaneously on several points. The Sunday before Christmas, in the year 1525, was chosen for this great attack. While Latimer should

[1] [For Fryth's teaching see Knox op. cit., pp. 43-51.]

address the crowds that continued to fill the Augustine chapel, and others were preaching in a variety of places, Barnes was to deliver a sermon in one of the churches in the town. But nothing compromises the gospel so much as a disposition turned towards outward things. God, who grants His blessing only to undivided hearts, permitted this general assault, of which Barnes was to be the hero, to be marked by a defeat. The prior, as he went into the pulpit, thought only of Wolsey. As the representative of the popedom in England, the cardinal was the great obstacle to the Reformation. Barnes preached from the epistle for the day: *Rejoice in the Lord alway.*[1] But instead of announcing Christ and the joy of the Christian, he imprudently declaimed against the luxury, pride, and diversions of the churchmen, and everybody understood that he aimed at the cardinal. He described those magnificent palaces, that brilliant suite, those scarlet robes, and pearls, and gold, and precious stones, and all the prelate's ostentation, so little in keeping (said he) with the stable of Bethlehem. Two fellows of King's College, Robert Ridley and Walter Preston, relations of Tunstall, bishop of London, who were intentionally among the congregation, noted down in their tablets the prior's imprudent expressions.

The sermon was scarcely over when the storm broke out. "These people are not satisfied with propagating monstrous heresies," exclaimed their enemies, "but they must find fault with the powers that be. To-day they attack the cardinal, to-morrow they will attack the king!" Ridley, Preston, and others, accused Barnes to the vice-chancellor. All Cambridge was in commotion. What! Barnes the Augustine prior, the restorer of letters, accused as a Wycliffite! . . . The gospel was threatened with a danger more formidable than a prison or a scaffold. The friends of the priests, knowing Barnes' weakness, and even his vanity, hoped to obtain of him a disavowal that would cover the evangelical party with shame. "What!" said these dangerous counsellors to him, "the noblest career was open to you, and would you close it? . . . Do, pray, explain away your sermon." They alarmed, they flattered him; and the poor prior was near yielding to their solicitations. "Next Sunday you will read this declaration," they said to him. Barnes

[1] Philippians iv. 4–7.

ran over the paper put into his hands, and saw no great harm in it. However he desired to show it to Bilney and Stafford. "Beware of such weakness," said these faithful men. Barnes then recalled his promise, and for a season the enemies of the gospel were silent.

Its friends worked with increased energy. The fall from which one of their companions had so narrowly escaped inspired them with fresh zeal. The more indecision and weakness Barnes had shown, the more did his brethren flee to God for courage and firmness. It was reported, moreover, that a powerful ally was coming across the sea, and that the Holy Scriptures, translated into the vulgar tongue, were at last to be given to the people. Whenever the Word was preached, there the congregation was largest. It was the seed-time of the church; all were busy in the fields to prepare the soil and trace the furrows. Seven colleges at least were in full ferment: Pembroke, St John's, Queens', King's, Caius, Benet's, and Peterhouse. The gospel was preached at the Augustine's, at Saint Mary's (the University church) and in other places, and when the bells rang to prayers, the streets were alive with students issuing from the colleges, and hastening to the sermon.

There was at Cambridge a house called the White Horse, so situated as to permit the most timid members of King's, Queens', and St John's Colleges, to enter at the rear without being perceived. In every age Nicodemus has had his followers. Here those persons used to assemble who desired to read the Bible and the works of the German reformers. The priests, looking upon Wittenberg as the focus of the Reformation, named this house Germany: the people will always have their bywords. At first the frequenters of the White Horse were called sophists; and now, whenever a group of "fellows" was seen walking in that direction, the cry was, "There are the Germans going to Germany."—"We are not Germans," was the reply, "neither are we Romans." The Greek New Testament had made them Christians. The gospel-meetings had never been more fervent. Some attended them to communicate the new life they possessed; others to receive what God had given to the more advanced brethren. The Holy Spirit united them all, and thus, by the fellowship of the saints, were real churches created. To these young Christians the Word of God was the source of so much light, that they imagined themselves transported to that heavenly city of which the Scriptures speak, *which had no need of the sun, for the glory of God did lighten it.* "So oft as I was in the company of these brethren," said a youthful student of St John's, "methought I was quietly placed in the new glorious Jerusalem."[1]

Similar things were taking place at Oxford. In 1524 and 1525, Wolsey had successively invited thither several Cambridge fellows, and although only seeking the most able, he found that he had taken some of the most pious. Besides John Clark, there were Richard Cox, John Fryer, Godfrey Harman, W. Betts, Henry Sumner, W. Baily, Michael Drumm, Th. Lawny, and, lastly, the excellent John Fryth. These Christians, associating with Clark, with his faithful Dalaber, and with other evangelicals of Oxford, held meetings, like their Cambridge brethren, at which God manifested His presence. The bishops made war upon the gospel; the king supported them with all his power; but the Word had gained the victory; there was no longer any doubt. The church was born again in England.

The great movement of the sixteenth century had begun more particularly among the younger doctors and students at Oxford and Cambridge. From them it was necessary that it should be extended to the people, and for that end the New Testament, hitherto read in Latin and in Greek, must be circulated in English. The voices of these youthful evangelists were heard, indeed, in London and in the provinces; but their exhortations would have been insufficient, if the mighty hand which directs all things had not made this Christian activity coincide with that holy work for which it had set Tyndale apart. While all was agitation in England, the waves of ocean were bearing from the continent to the banks of the Thames those Scriptures of God, which, three centuries later, multiplied by thousands and by millions, and translated into an ever-increasing number of tongues, were to be wafted from the same banks to the ends of the world. If in the fifteenth century, and even in the early years of the sixteenth, the English New Testament had been brought to London, it would only have fallen into the hands of a few Lollards. Now, in every place, in the parsonages, the universities, and the palaces, as well as in

[1] Becon, ii, p. 426 (Parker Society).

R

the cottages of the husbandmen and the shops of the tradesmen, there was an ardent desire to possess the Holy Scriptures.
The *fiat lux* was about to be uttered over the chaos of the
church, and light to be separated from darkness by the Word
of God.

BOOK THREE

The English New Testament **and the Court** *of Rome*

CHAPTER ONE

The Year of Grace

(1526)

THE Church and the State are essentially distinct. They both receive their task from God, but that task is different in each. The task of the church is to lead men to God; the task of the state is to secure the earthly development of a people in conformity with its peculiar character. There are certain bounds, traced by the particular spirit of each nation, within which the state should confine itself; while the church, whose limits are co-extensive with the human race, has a universal character, which raises it above all national differences. These two distinctive features should be maintained. A state which aims at universality loses itself; a church whose mind and aim are sectarian falls away. Nevertheless, the church and the state, the two poles of social life, while they are in many respects opposed to each other, are far from excluding each other absolutely. The church has need of that justice, order, and liberty, which the state is bound to maintain; but the state has especial need of the church. If Jesus can do without kings to establish His kingdom, kings cannot do without Jesus, if they would have their kingdoms prosper. Justice, which is the fundamental principle of the state, is continually fettered in its progress by the internal power of sin; and as force can do nothing against this power, the state requires the gospel in order to overcome it. That country will always be the most prosperous where the church is the most evangelical. These two communities having thus need one of the other, we must be prepared, whenever a great religious manifestation takes place in the world, to witness the appearance on the scene not only of the little ones, but of the great ones also, of the state. We must not then be surprised to meet with Henry VIII, but let us endeavour to appreciate accurately the part he played.

If the Reformation, particularly in England, happened

necessarily to be mixed up with the state, with the world even, it originated neither in the state nor in the world. There was much worldliness in the age of Henry VIII, passions, violence, festivities, a trial, a divorce; and some historians call that *the history of the Reformation in England*. We shall not pass by in silence these manifestations of the worldly life; opposed as they are to the Christian life, they are in history, and it is not our business to tear them out. But most assuredly they are not the Reformation. From a very different quarter proceeded the divine light which then rose upon the human race.

To say that Henry VIII was the reformer of his people is to betray ignorance of history. The kingly power in England by turns opposed and favoured the reform in the church; but it opposed before it favoured, and much more than it favoured. This great transformation was begun and extended by its own strength, by the Spirit from on high.

When the church has lost the life that is peculiar to it, it must again put itself in communication with its creative principle, that is, with the Word of God. Just as the buckets of a wheel employed in irrigating the meadows have no sooner discharged their reviving waters, than they dip again into the stream to be re-filled, so every generation, void of the Spirit of Christ, must return to the divine source for renewal. The primitive words which created the church have been preserved for us in the Gospels, the Acts, and the Epistles; and the humble reading of these divine writings will create in every age the communion of saints. God was the father of the Reformation, not Henry VIII. The visible world which then glittered with such brightness, those princes and sports, those noblemen, and trials and laws, far from effecting a reform, were calculated to stifle it. But the light and the warmth came from heaven, and the new creation was completed.

In the reign of Henry VIII a great number of citizens, priests, and noblemen possessed that degree of cultivation which favours the action of the holy books. It was sufficient for this divine seed to be scattered on the well-prepared soil for the work of germination to be accomplished.

A time not less important was also approaching—that in which the action of the popedom was to come to an end. The hour had not yet struck. God was first creating within by his

Word a spiritual church, before he broke without by his dispensations the bonds which had so long fastened England to the power of Rome. It was His good pleasure first to give truth and life, and then liberty. It has been said that if the pope had consented to a reform of abuses and doctrines, on condition of his keeping his position, the religious revolution would not have been satisfied at that price and that, after demanding *reform*, the next demand would have been for *liberty*. The only reproach that can be made to this assertion is that it is superabundantly true. Liberty was an integral part of the Reformation, and one of the changes imperatively required was to withdraw religious authority from the pope, and acknowledge it as belonging to the Word of God. In the sixteenth century there was a great outpouring of the Christian life in France, Italy, and Spain; it is attested by martyrs without number, and history shows that to transform these three great nations, all that the gospel wanted was liberty. "If we had set to work two months later," said a grand inquisitor of Spain who had dyed himself in the blood of the saints, "it would have been too late: Spain would have been lost to the Roman church." We may therefore believe that if Italy, France, and Spain had had some generous king to check the myrmidons of the pope, those three countries, carried along by the renovating power of the gospel, would have entered upon an era of liberty and faith.

The struggles of England with the popedom began shortly after the dissemination of the English New Testament by Tyndale. The epoch at which we are arrived accordingly brings in one view before our eyes both the Testament of Jesus Christ and the court of Rome. We can thus study the men— the reformers and the Romanists—and the works they produce, and arrive at a just valuation of the two great principles which dispute the possession of authority in the church.

It was probably in the early spring of 1526 that the English New Testaments were crossing the sea; pious Hanseatic merchants had taken charge of the books. Captivated by the Holy Scriptures they had taken them on board their ships, hidden them among their merchandise; and then made sail from Antwerp for London.

Thus those precious pages were approaching England, which

were to become its light and the source of its greatness. The
merchants, whose zeal unhappily cost them dear, were not
without alarm. Had not Cochlæus caused orders to be sent to
every port to prevent the entrance of the precious cargo they
were bringing to England? They arrived and cast anchor; they
lowered the boat to reach the shore; what were they likely to
meet there? Tunstall's agents, no doubt, and Wolsey's, and
Henry's, ready to take away their New Testaments! They
landed and soon again returned to the ship; boats passed to
and fro, and the vessel was unloaded. No enemy appeared;
and no one seemed to imagine that these ships contained so
great a treasure.

Just at the time this invaluable cargo was ascending the
river, an invisible hand had dispersed the preventive guard.
Tunstall, bishop of London, had been sent as ambassador to
Spain; Henry and Wolsey were occupied in political combinations with Scotland, France, and the Empire. God, if we may
so speak, had sent his angel to remove or otherwise occupy
the guards.

Seeing nothing that could stop them, the merchants, whose
establishment was at the Steelyard in Thames Street, hastened
to conceal their precious charge in their warehouses. But who
will receive them? Who will undertake to distribute these
Holy Scriptures in London, Oxford, Cambridge, and all
England? It is a little matter that they have crossed the sea.
The principal instrument God was about to use for their
dissemination was an humble servant of Christ.

In Honey Lane, a narrow thoroughfare adjoining Cheapside,
stood the old church of All Hallows, of which Dr Robert
Forman was rector. His curate was a plain man of lively
imagination, delicate conscience, and timid disposition, but
rendered bold by his faith, to which he was to become a martyr.
Thomas Garret, for that was his name, having believed in the
gospel, earnestly called his hearers to repentance; he urged
upon them that works, however good they might be in
appearance, were by no means capable of justifying the sinner,
and that faith alone could save him. He maintained that
every man had the right to preach the Word of God; and called
those bishops pharisees, who persecuted Christian men.
Garret's discourses, at once so quickening and so gentle,

attracted great crowds; and to many of his hearers, the street in which he preached was rightly named Honey Lane, for there they found the *honey out of the rock*.[1] But Garret was about to commit a fault still more heinous in the eyes of the priests than preaching faith. The Hanse merchants were seeking some sure place where they might store up the New Testaments and other books sent from Germany; the curate offered his house, stealthily transported the holy deposit thither, hid them in the most secret corners, and kept a faithful watch over this sacred library. He did not confine himself to this. Night and day he studied the holy books; he held gospel meetings, read the Word and explained its doctrines to the citizens of London. At last, not satisfied with being at once student, librarian, and preacher, he became a trader, and sold the New Testament to laymen, and even to priests and monks, so that the Holy Scriptures were dispersed over the whole realm.[2] Others, of whom we know nothing, must have given him their powerful, but secret, assistance.

And thus the Word of God, presented by Erasmus to the learned in 1516 was given to the people by Tyndale in 1526. In the parsonages and in the monastic cells, but particularly in shops and cottages, a crowd of persons were studying the New Testament. The clearness of the Holy Scriptures struck each reader. None of the systematic or aphoristic forms of the school were to be found there: it was the language of human life which they discovered in those divine writings: here a conversation, there a discourse; here a narrative, and there a comparison; here a command, and there an argument; here a parable, and there a prayer. It was not all doctrine or all history; but these two elements mingled together made an admirable whole. Above all, the life of our Saviour, so divine and so human, had an inexpressible charm which captivated the simple. One work of Jesus Christ explained another, and the great facts of the redemption, birth, death, and resurrection of the Son of God, and the sending of the Holy Ghost, followed and completed each other. The authority of Christ's teaching, so strongly contrasting with the doubts of the schools, increased

[1] Psalm xxxi. 16.
[2] Dispersing abroad of the said books within this realm. Foxe, *Acts*, v, p. 428. See also Strype, *Cranmer's Mem.*, p. 81.

the clearness of His discourses to His readers; for the more certain a truth is, the more distinctly it strikes the mind. Academical explanations were not necessary to those noblemen, farmers, and citizens. It is to me, for me, and of me that this book speaks, said each one. It is I whom all these promises and teachings concern. This *fall* and this *restoration* . . . they are mine. That old *death* and this new *life* . . . I have passed through them. That *flesh* and that *spirit* . . . I know them. This *law* and this *grace*, this *faith*, these *works*, this *slavery*, this *glory*, this *Christ* and this *Belial* . . . all are familiar to me. It is my own history that I find in this book. Thus by the aid of the Holy Ghost each one had in his own experience a key to the mysteries of the Bible. To understand certain authors and certain philosophers, the intellectual life of the reader must be in harmony with theirs; so must there be an intimate affinity with the holy books to penetrate their mysteries. "The man that has not the Spirit of God," said Martin Luther, "does not understand one jot or tittle of the Scripture." Now that this condition was fulfilled, the Spirit of God moved upon the face of the waters.

Such at that period were the hermeneutics of England. Tyndale had set the example himself by explaining many of the words which might stop the reader. "The *New Testament!*" we may suppose some farmer saying, as he took up the book; "what *Testament* is that?"—"Christ," replied Tyndale in his prologue, "commanded His disciples before His death to publish over all the world *His last will*, which is to give all his goods unto all that repent and believe. He bequeaths them His righteousness to blot out their sins—His salvation to overcome their condemnation; and this is why that document is called the *Testament* of Jesus Christ."

"The *law* and the *gospel*," says a citizen of London, in his shop; "what is that?"—"They are two *keys*," answered Tyndale. "The *law* is the key which shuts up all men under condemnation, and the *gospel* is the key which opens the door and lets them out. Or, if you like it, they are two salves. The law, sharp and biting, driveth out the disease and killeth it; while the gospel, soothing and soft, softens the wound and brings life." Every one understood and read, or rather devoured the inspired pages; and the hearts of the elect (to use Tyndale's words), warmed by the love of Jesus Christ, began to melt like wax.

This transformation was observed to take place even in the most catholic families. William Roper, More's son-in-law, having read the New Testament, received the truth. "I have no more need," said he, "of auricular confession, of vigils, or of the invocation of saints. The ears of God are always open to hear us. Faith alone is necessary to salvation. I believe . . . and I am saved. . . . Nothing can deprive me of God's favour."[1]

The amiable and zealous young man desired to do more. "Father," said he one day to Sir Thomas, "procure for me from the king, who is very fond of you, a licence to preach. God hath sent me to instruct the world." More was uneasy. Must this new doctrine, which he detested, spread even to his children? He exerted all his authority to destroy the work begun in Roper's heart. "What," said he with a smile, "is it not sufficient that we that are your friends should know that you are a fool, but you would proclaim your folly to the world? Hold your tongue: I will debate with you no longer." The young man's imagination had been struck, but his heart had not been changed. The discussions having ceased, the father's authority being restored, Roper became less fervent in his faith, and gradually he returned to popery, of which he was afterwards a zealous champion.

As for Thomas Garret, the humble curate of All Hallows having sold the New Testament to persons living in London and its neighbourhood, and to many pious men who would carry it to the farthest parts of England, he formed the resolution to introduce it into the University of Oxford, that citadel of traditional catholicism. It was there he had studied, and he felt towards that school the affection which a son bears to his mother: he set out with his books. Terror occasionally seized him, for he knew that the Word of God had many deadly enemies at Oxford; but his inexhaustible zeal overcame his timidity. In concert with Anthony Dalaber, he stealthily offered the mysterious book for sale; many students bought it, and Garret carefully entered their names in his account book. This was some time during 1526.

It was not only the New Testament and such doctrinal works as Luther's *Bondage of the Will* which Garret and others were quietly selling that men were starting to read. Another sort of

[1] More's Life, p. 134.

literature was also beginning to circulate and before long it added its testimony to the truth even within the walls of the Royal Palace. One morning when Edmund Moddis, one of Henry's valets-de-chambre, was in attendance on his master, the king, who was much attached to him, spoke to him of the new books come from beyond the sea. "If your Grace," said Moddis, "would promise to pardon me and certain individuals, I would present you a wonderful book which is dedicated to your Majesty."—"Who is the author?"—"A lawyer of Gray's Inn named Simon Fish, at present on the continent." "What is he doing there?"—"About three years ago, Mr Row, a fellow-student of Gray's Inn, composed for a private theatre a drama against my lord the cardinal." The king smiled; when his minister was attacked, his own yoke seemed lighter. "As no one was willing to represent the character employed to give the cardinal his lesson," continued the valet, "Master Fish boldly accepted it. The piece produced a great effect; and my lord, being informed of this impertinence, sent the police one night to arrest Fish. But he managed to escape, crossed the sea, joined one Tyndale, the author of some of the books so much talked of; and, carried away by his friend's example, he composed the book of which I was speaking to your Grace." —"What's the name of it?"—"*A Supplication for the Beggars.*"[1]— "Where did you see it?"—"At two of your tradespeople's, George Elyot and George Robinson; if your Grace desires it, they shall bring it you." The king appointed the day and the hour.

The book was written for the king, and everybody read it but the king himself. At the appointed day Moddis appeared with Elyot and Robinson, who were not entirely without fear, as they might be accused of proselytism even in the royal palace.

The king received them in his private apartments. "What do you want?" he said to them. "Sir," replied one of the merchants, "we are come about an extraordinary book that is addressed to you."—"Can one of you read it to me?"—"Yes, if it so please your Grace," replied Elyot. "You may repeat the contents from memory," rejoined the king . . . "but no, read it all; that will be better. I am ready." Elyot began,

[1] Published about 1529.

"A Supplication for the Beggars."

"To the king our sovereign lord—

"Most lamentably complaineth of their woeful misery, unto your Highness, your poor daily bedesmen,[1] the wretched hideous monsters, on whom scarcely, for horror, any eye dare look; the foul unhappy sort of lepers and other sore people, needy, impotent, blind, lame, and sick, that live only by alms; how that their number is daily sore increased, that all the alms of all the well-disposed people of this your realm are not half enough to sustain them, but that for very constraint they die for hunger.

"And this most pestilent mischief is come upon your said poor bedesmen, by the reason that there hath, in the time of your noble predecessors, craftily crept into this your realm, another sort, not of impotent, but of strong, puissant, and counterfeit, holy and idle beggars and vagabonds, who by all the craft and wiliness of Satan are now increased not only into a great number, but also into a kingdom."

Henry was very attentive: Elyot continued:

"These are not the shepherds, but the ravenous wolves going in shepherd's clothing, devouring the flock: bishops, abbots, priors, deacons, archdeacons, suffragans, priests, monks, canons, friars, pardoners, and summoners. . . . The goodliest lordships, manors, lands, and territories are theirs. Besides this, they have the tenth part of all the corn, meadow, pasture, grass, wood, colts, calves, lambs, pigs, geese, and chickens. Over and besides, the tenth part of every servant's wages, the tenth part of wool, milk, honey, wax, cheese, and butter. The poor wives must be accountable to them for every tenth egg, or else she getteth not her rights [*i.e.* absolution] at Easter. . . . Finally what get they in a year? Summa totalis: £430,333, 6s. 8d. sterling, whereof not four hundred years past they had not a penny. . . .

"What subjects shall be able to help their prince, that be after this fashion yearly polled? What good christian people can be able to succour us poor lepers, blind, sore, and lame, that be thus yearly oppressed? . . . The ancient Romans had never been able to have put all the whole world under their obeisance, if they had had at home such an idle sort of cormorants."

[1] A bedesman was a pensioner bound to pray for a benefactor.

No subject could have been found more likely to captivate the king's attention. "And what doth all this greedy sort of sturdy idle holy thieves with their yearly exactions that they take of the people? Truly nothing, but translate all rule, power, lordship, authority, obedience, and dignity from your Grace unto them. Nothing, but that all your subjects should fall into disobedience and rebellion. . . . Priests and doves make foul houses; and if you will ruin a state, set up in it the pope with his monks and clergy. . . . Send these sturdy loobies abroad in the world to take them wives of their own, instead of meddling with other men's wives, and to get their living with their labour in the sweat of their faces. . . . Then shall your commons increase in riches; then shall matrimony be much better kept; then shall not your sword, power, crown, dignity, and obedience of your people be translated from you."

When Elyot had finished reading, the king was silent, sunk in thought. The true cause of the ruin of the state had been laid before him; but Henry's mind was not ripe for these important truths. At last he said, with an uneasy manner: "If a man who desires to pull down an old wall, begins at the bottom, I fear the upper part may chance to fall on his head." Thus then, in the king's eyes, Fish by attacking the priests was disturbing the foundations of religion and society. It was imperative that the mischievous book should be withstood.

Of the Roman Church in England at this period, Sir Thomas More was the literary champion. Already famous as the author of *Utopia*, he now produced *The Supplications of the Souls in Purgatory*. "Suppress," said they, "the pious stipends paid to the monks, and then Luther's gospel will come in, Tyndale's testament will be read, heresy will be preached, fasts will be neglected, the saints will be blasphemed, God will be offended, virtue will be mocked at, vice will run riot, and England will be peopled with beggars and thieves." The Souls in Purgatory then call the author of the Beggars' Supplication "a goose, an ass, a mad dog." Thus did superstition degrade More's noble genius. Notwithstanding the abuse of the souls in purgatory, the New Testament was daily read more and more in England.

CHAPTER TWO

Oxford's Baptism of Suffering

(1526–28)

WE have already seen how Tyndale's New Testament had entered England by surprise early in 1526, and how in parsonages and monastic cells, shops and private houses, its startling message was entering the souls of men. Great were the fears of the bishops. They saw in the circulation of the "heretical" book the greatest threat to their power which had appeared in a thousand years. The gospellers who presumed to emancipate man from the priests, and put him in absolute dependence on God, were thereby undermining the very foundations of the papal system. What must be done?

Wolsey, as the greatest of the church dignitaries, hastened to assemble the bishops, and these, particularly Warham of Canterbury and Tunstall of London, gave immediate and diligent attention to the problem. With Wolsey they believed that the authority of the pope and of the clergy was a dogma to which all others were subordinate. They saw in the reform an uprising of the human mind, a desire in men to think for themselves, and to judge freely the doctrines and institutions which the nations had hitherto received humbly from the hands of the priests. The new teachers justified their attempt at enfranchisement by substituting a new authority for the old. It was the New Testament that compromised the absolute power of Rome. It must be seized and destroyed, said the bishops. London, Oxford and, above all, Cambridge, those three haunts of heresy, must be carefully searched. Definitive orders were issued in February 1528, and the work began immediately.

The first visit of the inquisitors was to Honey Lane, to the house of the curate of All Hallows. They did not find Garret; they sought after him at Monmouth's, and throughout the city, but he could not be met with. "He is gone to Oxford to sell his detestable wares," the inquisitors were informed, and they set off after him immediately, determined to burn the evangelist and his books; "so burning hot," says an historian, "was the charity of these holy fathers."

Early in February,[1] Garret was quietly selling his books at Oxford and carefully noting down his sales in his record, when two of his friends came to him exclaiming, "Fly! or else you will be taken before the cardinal, and thence . . . to the Tower." The poor curate was greatly agitated. "From whom did you learn that?"—"From Master Cole, the clerk of the assembly, who is deep in the cardinal's favour." Garret, who saw at once that the affair was serious, hastened to Anthony Dalaber, who held the stock of the Holy Scriptures at Oxford; others followed him; the news had spread rapidly, and those who had bought the book were seized with alarm, for they knew by the history of the Lollards what the Romish clergy could do. They took counsel together. The brethren, "for so did we not only call one another, but were in deed one to another," says Dalaber, decided that Garret should change his name; that Dalaber should give him a letter for his brother, the rector of Stalbridge, in Dorsetshire, who was in want of a curate; and that, once in this parish, he should seek the first opportunity of crossing the sea. The rector was in truth a "rank papist," says Dalaber, "afterwards the most mortal enemy that ever I had, for the gospel's sake;" but that did not alter their resolution. They knew of no other resource. Anthony wrote to him hurriedly; and Garret immediately left Oxford without being observed.

Having provided for Garret's safety, Dalaber next thought of his own. He carefully concealed in a secret recess of his chamber, at St Alban's Hall, Tyndale's Testament, and the works of Luther, Œcolampadius, and others, on the Word of God. Then, disgusted with the scholastic sophisms which he heard in that college, he took with him the New Testament and the Commentary on the Gospel of St Luke, by Lambert of Avignon, the second edition of which had just been published at Strasburg, and went to Gloucester College, where he

---

[1] [Foxe, *Acts*, v, p. 421, gives the date of these happenings as "1526, or thereabout." The true date, however, verifiable from sources not available to Foxe, is 1528. Additional documents relative to Garret are printed in Josiah Pratt's edition of the *Acts and Monuments*, Appendix to vol. V.]

intended to study the civil law, not caring to have anything more to do with the church.

During this time, poor Garret was making his way into Dorsetshire. His conscience could not bear the idea of being, although for a short time only, the curate of a bigoted priest—of concealing his faith, his desires, and even his name. He felt more wretched, although at liberty, than he could have been in Wolsey's prisons. It is better, he said within himself, to confess Christ before the judgment seat, than to seem to approve of the superstitious practices I detest. He went forward a little, then stopped—and then resumed his course. There was a fierce struggle between his fears and his conscience. At length, after a day and a half spent in doubt, his conscience prevailed; unable to endure any longer the anguish that he felt, he retraced his steps, returned to Oxford, which he entered on a Friday evening, and lay down calmly in his bed. It was barely past midnight when Wolsey's agents, who had received information of his return, arrived, and dragged him from his bed, and delivered him up to Dr Cottisford, the commissary of the university. The latter locked him up in one of his rooms, while London, warden of New College, and Higdon, dean of Frideswide, "two arch papists" (as the chronicler terms them) announced this important capture to the cardinal. They thought popery was saved, because a poor curate had been taken.

Dalaber, engaged in preparing his new room at Gloucester college, knew nothing of all this. On Saturday, at noon, having finished his arrangements, he double-locked his door, and began to read the Gospel according to St Luke. All of a sudden he hears a knock. Dalaber made no reply; it is no doubt the commissary's officers. A louder knock was given; but he still remained silent. Immediately after, there was a third knock, as if the door would be beaten in. "Perhaps somebody needs me," thought Dalaber. He laid his book aside, opened the door, and to his great surprise saw Garret, who, with alarm in every feature, exclaimed, "I am a lost man! They have caught me!" Dalaber, who thought his friend was with his brother at Stalbridge, could not conceal his astonishment, and at the same time he cast an uneasy glance on a stranger who accompanied Garret. He was one of the college servants who had led the fugitive curate to Dalaber's new room. As soon as

S

this man had gone away, Garret told Anthony everything:
"Observing that Dr Cottisford and his household had gone to
prayers, I put back the bolt of the lock with my finger . . . and
here I am."—"Alas! Master Garret," replied Dalaber, "the
imprudence you committed in speaking to me before that
young man has ruined us both!" At these words, Garret, whose
fear of the priests had returned, now that his conscience was
satisfied, exclaimed with a voice interrupted by sighs and tears:
"For mercy's sake, help me! Save me!" Without waiting for an
answer, he threw off his gown and hood, begged Anthony to
give him a sleeved coat and, thus disguised, he said: "I will
escape into Wales, and from there, if possible, to Germany."

Garret checked himself; there was something to be done
before he left. The two friends fell on their knees and prayed
together; they called upon God to lead His servant to a secure
retreat. That done, they embraced each other, their faces
bathed with tears, and unable to utter a word.

Silent on the threshold of his door, Dalaber followed both
with eyes and ears his friend's retreating footsteps. Having
heard him reach the bottom of the stairs, he returned to his
room, locked the door, took out his New Testament and, placing
it before him, read on his knees the tenth chapter of the Gospel
of St Matthew, breathing many a heavy sigh: . . . *Ye shall be
brought before governors and kings for my sake . . . but fear them not;
the very hairs of your head are all numbered.* This reading having
revived his courage, Anthony, still on his knees, prayed fervently
for the fugitive and for all his brethren: "O God, by Thy Holy
Spirit endue with heavenly strength this tender and new-born
little flock in Oxford. Christ's heavy cross is about to be laid
on the weak shoulders of Thy poor sheep. Grant that they may
bear it with godly patience and unflinching zeal!"

Rising from his knees, Dalaber put away his book, folded up
Garret's hood and gown, placed them among his own clothes,
locked his room door, and proceeded to the Cardinal's College,
(now Christ Church) to tell Clark and the other brethren what
had happened. They were in chapel: the evening service had
begun; the dean and canons, in full costume, were chanting in
the choir. Dalaber stopped at the door listening to the majestic
sounds of the organ at which Taverner presided, and to the
harmonious strains of the choristers. They were singing the

Magnificat: My soul doth magnify the Lord. . . . He hath holpen his servant Israel. It seemed to Dalaber that they were singing Garret's deliverance. But his voice could not join in their song of praise. "Alas!" he exclaimed, "all my singing and music is turned into sighing and musing."

As he listened, leaning against the entrance into the choir, Dr Cottisford, the university commissary, arrived with hasty step, "bare headed, and as pale as ashes." He passed Anthony without noticing him, and going straight to the dean appeared to announce some important and unpleasant news. "I know well the cause of his sorrow," thought Dalaber as he watched every gesture. The commissary had scarcely finished his report when the dean arose, and both left the choir with undisguised confusion. They had only reached the middle of the anti-chapel when Dr London came in, "puffing, blustering, and blowing, like a hungry and greedy lion seeking his prey." All three stopped, questioned one another, and deplored their misfortune. Their rapid and eager movements indicated the liveliest emotion; London above all could not restrain himself. He attacked the commissary, and blamed him for his negligence, so that at last Cottisford burst into tears. "Deeds, not tears," said the fanatical London; and forthwith they despatched officers and spies along every road.

Anthony having left the chapel hurried to Clark's to tell him of the escape of his friend. "We are walking in the midst of wolves and tigers," replied Clark; "prepare for persecution. *Prudentia serpentina et simplicitas columbina* (the wisdom of serpents and the harmlessness of doves) must be our motto. O God, give us the courage these evil times require." All in the little flock were delighted at Garret's deliverance. Sumner and Betts, who had come in, ran off to tell it to the other brethren in the college, and Dalaber hastened to Corpus Christi. All these pious young men felt themselves to be soldiers in the same army, travellers in the same company, brothers in the same family. Fraternal love nowhere shone so brightly in the days of the Reformation as among the Christians of Great Britain. This is a feature worthy of notice.

Fitzjames, Udal, and Diet were met together in the rooms of the last-named, at Corpus Christi college, when Dalaber arrived. They ate their frugal meal with downcast eyes and

broken voices, conversing of Oxford, of England, and of the
perils hanging over them. Then rising from table they fell on
their knees, called upon God for aid, and separated, Fitzjames
taking Dalaber with him to St Alban's Hall. They were afraid
that the servant of Gloucester College had betrayed him.

The disciples of the gospel at Oxford passed the night in
great anxiety. Garret's flight, the rage of the priests, the dangers
of the rising church, the roaring of a storm that filled the air
and re-echoed through the long cloisters—all filled them with
the liveliest apprehensions. The Lord's day came. Dalaber, who
was stirring at five in the morning, set out for his room in
Gloucester College. Finding the gates shut, he walked up and
down beneath the walls in the mud, for it had rained heavily.
As he paced to and fro along the solitary street in the obscure
dawn, a thousand thoughts alarmed his mind. It was known, he
said to himself, that he had assisted Garret's flight; he would be
arrested, and his friend's escape would be revenged on him. He
was weighed down by sorrow and alarm; he sighed heavily; he
imagined he saw Wolsey's commissioners demanding the names
of his accomplices, and pretending to draw up a proscription
list at his dictation; he recollected that on more than one
occasion cruel priests had extorted from the Lollards the names
of their brethren and, terrified at the possibility of such a
crime, he exclaimed; "O God, I swear to thee that I will
accuse no man. . . . I will tell nothing but what is perfectly
well known."

At last, after an hour of anguish, he was able to enter the
college. He hastened in, but when he tried to open his door, he
found that the lock had been tampered with. The door gave
way to a strong push, and what a sight met his eyes! his bedstead
overturned, the blankets scattered on the floor, his clothes all
confusion in his wardrobe, his study broken into and left open.
He doubted not that Garret's dress had betrayed him; and he
was gazing at this sad spectacle in alarm, when a monk who
occupied the adjoining rooms came and told him what had
taken place: "The commissary and two proctors, armed with
swords and bills, broke open your door in the middle of the
night. They pierced your bed-straw through and through to
make sure Garret was not hidden there; they carefully searched
every nook and corner, but were not able to discover any traces

of the fugitive." At these words Dalaber breathed again . . . but the monk had not ended. "I have orders," he added, "to send you to the prior." Anthony Dunstan, the prior, was a fanatical and avaricious monk; and the confusion into which this message threw Dalaber was so great, that he went just as he was, all bespattered with mud, to the rooms of his superior.

The prior, who was standing with his face towards the door, looked at Dalaber from head to foot as he came in. "Where did you pass the night?" he asked.—"At St Alban's Hall with Fitzjames." The prior with a gesture of incredulity continued: "Was not Master Garret with you yesterday?"—"Yes."— "Where is he now?"—"I do not know." During this examination, the prior had noticed a large double-gilt silver ring on Anthony's finger, with the initials A.D. "Show me that," said the prior. Dalaber gave him the ring and the prior, believing it to be of solid gold, put it on his own finger, adding with a cunning leer: "This ring is mine: it bears my name. A is for *Anthony*, and D for *Dunstan*."—"Would to God," thought Dalaber, "that I were as well delivered from his company, as I am sure of being delivered of my ring."

At this moment the chief beadle, with two or three of the commissary's men, entered and conducted Dalaber to the chapel of Lincoln College, where three ill-omened figures were standing beside the altar: they were Cottisford, London, and Higdon. "Where is Garret?" asked London; and pointing to his disordered dress, he continued: "Your shoes and garments covered with mud prove that you have been out all night with him. If you do not say where you have taken him, you will be sent to the Tower."—"Yes," added Higdon, "to *Little-ease* [one of the most horrible dungeons in the prison], and you will be put to the torture, do you hear?" Then the three doctors spent two hours attempting to shake the young man by flattering promises and frightful threats; but all was useless. The commissary then gave a sign, the officers stepped forward, and the judges ascended a narrow staircase leading to a large room situated above the commissary's chamber. Here Dalaber was deprived of his purse and girdle, and his legs were placed in the stocks, so that his feet were almost as high as his head. When that was done, the three doctors devoutly went to mass.

Left alone in this frightful position, Dalaber recollected the warning Clark had given him two years before. He groaned heavily and cried to God: "O Father! grant that my suffering may be for Thy glory, and for the consolation of my brethren! Happen what may, I will never accuse one of them." After this noble protest, Anthony felt an increase of peace in his heart; but a new sorrow was reserved for him.

Garret, who had directed his course south-westwards, was caught at Bedminster, near Bristol. He was brought back, and thrown into the dungeon in which Dalaber had been placed after the torture. Their gloomy presentiments were to be more than fulfilled.

In fact Wolsey was deeply irritated at seeing the college [Christ Church], which he had intended should be "the most glorious in the world," made the haunt of heresy, and the young men, whom he had so carefully chosen, become distributors of the New Testament. By favouring literature, he had had in view the triumph of the clergy, and literature had on the contrary served to the triumph of the gospel. He issued his orders without delay, and the university was filled with terror. John Clark, John Fryth, Henry Sumner, William Betts, Richard Taverner, Richard Cox, Michael Drumm, Godfrey Harman, Thomas Lawney, Radley, and others besides of Cardinal College; Udal, Diet, and others of Corpus Christi; Eden and several of his friends of Magdalene; Goodman, William Bayley, Robert Ferrar, John Salisbury of Gloucester, Barnard, and St Mary's Colleges; were seized and thrown into prison. Wolsey had promised them glory; he gave them a dungeon, hoping in this manner to save the power of the priests, and to repress that awakening of truth and liberty which was spreading from the continent to England.

Under Cardinal College there was a deep cellar sunk in the earth, in which the butler kept his salt fish. Into this hole these young men, the choice of England, were thrust. The dampness of this cave, the corrupted air they breathed, the horrible smell given out by the fish, seriously affected the prisoners, already weakened by study. Their hearts were bursting with groans, their faith was shaken, and the most mournful scenes followed one another in this foul dungeon. The wretched captives gazed on one another, wept, and prayed. This trial was destined to be a salutary one to them: "Alas!" said Fryth on a subsequent occasion, "I see that besides the Word of God, there is indeed a second purgatory . . . but it is not that invented by Rome; it is the cross of tribulation to which God has nailed us."

At last the prisoners were taken out one by one and brought before their judges; two only were released. The first was Betts, afterwards chaplain to Anne Boleyn: they had not been able to find any prohibited books in his room, and he pleaded his cause with great talent. The other was Taverner; he had hidden Clark's books under his school-room floor, where they had been discovered; but his love for the arts saved him: "Pshaw! he is only a musician," said the cardinal.

All the rest were condemned. A great fire was kindled at the top of Carfax, in the centre of Oxford, a long procession was marshalled, and these unfortunate men were led out, each bearing a faggot. When they came near the fire, they were compelled to throw into it the heretical books that had been found in their rooms, after which they were taken back to their noisome prison. There seemed to be a barbarous pleasure in treating these young and generous men so vilely. In other countries also, Rome was preparing to stifle in the flames the noblest geniuses of France, Spain, and Italy. Such was the reception letters and the gospel met with from popery in the sixteenth century. Every plant of God's must be beaten by the wind, even at the risk of its being uprooted; if it receives only the gentle rays of the sun, there is reason to fear that it will dry up and wither before it produces fruit. *Except a corn of wheat fall into the ground and die, it abideth alone.* There was to arise one day a true church in England; persecution was but the prelude to its appearing.

But we must now turn to give attention to the lot of confessors of the faith in another university city.

CHAPTER THREE

The Severities of Popery

(1526–28)

OXFORD and Cambridge, which alike shared the glories of the "new learning" in early Tudor days, and which were both deeply stirred by reformation teaching, were alike also in their experience of persecution. It was in 1526 that the party of reform in the city on the Cam received its baptism of suffering.

Early in February in that year, two of Wolsey's agents, Dr Capon, one of his chaplains, and Gibson, a sergeant-at-arms, notorious for his arrogance, left London for Cambridge. Submission, was the pass-word of popery. "Yes, submission," was responded from every part of Christendom by men of sincere piety and profound understanding; "submission to the legitimate authority against which Roman-catholicism has rebelled." According to their views the traditionalism and pelagianism of the Romish church had set up the supremacy of fallen reason in opposition to the divine supremacy of the Word and of grace. The external and apparent sacrifice of self which Roman-catholicism imposes—obedience to a confessor or to the pope, arbitrary penance, ascetic practices, and celibacy— only served to create, and so to strengthen and perpetuate, a delusion as to the egotistic preservation of a sinful personality. When the Reformation proclaimed liberty, so far as regarded ordinances of human invention, it was with the view of bringing man's heart and life into subjection to their real Sovereign. The reign of God was commencing; that of the priests must needs come to an end. No man can serve two masters. Such were the important truths which gradually dawned upon the world, and which Wolsey and countless others thought it necessary to extinguish without delay.

On the day after their arrival in Cambridge, Capon and Gibson went to the convocation house, where several of the doctors were talking together. Their appearance caused some anxiety among the spectators, who looked upon the strangers with distrust. On a sudden Gibson moved forward, put his hand on Barnes, and arrested him in the presence of his friends. The latter were frightened, and this was what the sergeant wanted. "What!" said they, "the prior of the Augustines, the restorer of letters in Cambridge, arrested by a sergeant!" This was not all. Wolsey's agents were to seize the books come from Germany, and their owners; Bilney, Latimer, Stafford, Arthur, and their friends, were all to be imprisoned, for they possessed the New Testament. Thirty members of the university were pointed out as suspected; and some miserable wretches, who had been bribed by the inquisitors, offered to show the place in every room where the prohibited books were hidden. But while the necessary preparations were making for this search, Bilney, Latimer, and their colleagues, being warned in time, got the books removed; they were taken away not only by the doors but by the windows, even by the roofs, and anxious inquiry was made for sure places in which they could be concealed.

This work was hardly ended, when the vice-chancellor of the university, the sergeant-at-arms, Wolsey's chaplain, the proctors, and the informers began their rounds. They opened the first room, entered, searched, and found nothing. They passed on to the second, there was nothing. The sergeant was astonished, and grew angry. On reaching the third room, he ran directly to the place that had been pointed out—still there was nothing. The same thing occurred everywhere; never was inquisitor more mortified. He dared not lay hands on the persons of the evangelical doctors; his orders read that he was to seize the books and *their owners*. But as no books were found, there could be no prisoners. However, there was one man (the prior of the Augustines) against whom there were particular charges. The sergeant promised to compensate himself at Barnes' expense for his useless labours.

The next day Gibson and Capon set out for London with Barnes. During this mournful journey the prior, in great agitation, at one time determined to brave all England, and at another trembled like a leaf. At last their journey was ended; the chaplain left his prisoner at Parnell's house, close by the stocks. Three students (Coverdale, Goodwin, and Field) had followed their master to cheer him with their tender affection.

On Thursday (8th February) the sergeant conducted Barnes to the cardinal's palace at Westminster; the wretched prior, whose enthusiasm had given way to dejection, waited all day before he could be admitted. What a day! Will no one come to his assistance? Doctor Gardiner, Wolsey's secretary, and Fox, his steward, both old friends of Barnes, passed through the gallery in the evening, and went up to the prisoner, who begged them to procure him an audience with the cardinal. These officers agreed to introduce the prior into the room where their master was sitting, and Barnes, as was customary, fell on his knees before him. "Is this the Doctor Barnes who is accused of heresy?" asked Wolsey, in a haughty tone, of Fox and Gardiner. They replied in the affirmative. The cardinal then turning to Barnes, who was still kneeling, said to him ironically, and not without reason: "What, master doctor, had you not sufficient scope in the Scriptures to teach the people; but my golden shoes, my poleaxes, my pillars, my golden cushions, my crosses, did so sore offend you, that you must make us a laughing-stock, *ridiculum caput*, amongst the people? We were jollily that day laughed to scorn. Verily it was a sermon more fit to be preached on a stage than in a pulpit; for at the last you said I wore a pair of *red* gloves. . . . Eh! what think you, master doctor?" Barnes, wishing to elude these embarrassing questions, answered vaguely: "I spoke nothing but the truth out of the Scriptures, according to my conscience and according to the old doctors." He then presented to the cardinal a statement of his teaching.

Wolsey received the papers with a smile: "Oh, ho!" said he, as he counted the six sheets, "I perceive you intend to stand to your articles and to show your learning."—"By the grace of God," said Barnes. Wolsey then began to read them, and stopped at the sixth article, which ran thus: "I will never believe that one man may, by the law of God, be bishop of two or three cities, yea, of a whole country, for it is contrary to St Paul, who saith: *I have left thee behind, to set in every city a bishop.*" Barnes did not quote correctly, for the apostle says: "*to ordain elders in every city.*"[1] Wolsey was displeased at this thesis: "Ah! this touches me," he said: "Do you think it wrong

[1] Titus i. 5.

(seeing the ordinance of the church) that one bishop should have so many cities underneath him?"—"I know of no ordinance of the church," Barnes replied, "as concerning this thing, but Paul's saying only."

Although this controversy interested the cardinal, the personal attack of which he had to complain touched him more keenly. "Good," said Wolsey; and then with a condescension hardly to be expected from so proud a man, he deigned almost to justify himself. "You charge me with displaying a royal pomp; but do you not understand that, being called to represent his Majesty, I must strive by these means to strike terror into the wicked?"—"It is not your pomp or your pole-axes," Barnes courageously answered, "that will save the king's person. . . . God will save him, who said: *Per me reges regnant.*" (By me kings reign.) Barnes, instead of profiting by the cardinal's kindness to present an humble justification, as Dean Colet had formerly done to Henry VIII, dared preach him a second sermon to his face. Wolsey felt the colour mount to his cheeks. "Well, gentlemen," said he, turning to Fox and Gardiner, "you hear him! Is this the wise and learned man of whom you spoke to me?"

At these words both steward and secretary fell on their knees, saying: "We desire your Grace to be good unto him, for he will be reformable."—"Do you not know," said Wolsey to Barnes, "that I am *Legatus de latere*, and that I am able to dispense in all matters concerning religion within this realm, as much as the pope may?" Barnes replied, "I know it to be so."—"Will you then be ruled by us, and we will do all things for your good, and for the good of the university." He answered: "I thank your grace for your goodwill; I will stick to the Holy Scripture, and to God's book, according to the simple talent that God hath lent me."—"Well," replied Wolsey, "thou shalt have thy learning tried to the utmost, and thou shalt have the law." Orders were then given that he should be taken to the Tower, but Gardiner and Fox offered to become his sureties, and Wolsey permitted him to pass the night at the house of a Master Parnell. He spent most of the night in writing, and did not sleep. The next day he was taken into the chapter house at Westminster and re-examined before Islip, abbot of Westminster, and sundry bishops. His judges laid before him a long statement, and said to him: "Promise to read this paper in public, without omitting or adding a single word." It was then read to him. "I would die first," was his reply. "Will you abjure or be burnt alive?" said his judges; "take your choice." The alternative was dreadful. A prey to the deepest agony, Barnes shrank at the thought of the stake; then, suddenly his courage revived, and he exclaimed: "I would rather be burnt than abjure." Gardiner and Fox did all they could to persuade him. "Listen to reason," said they craftily: "your articles are true; that is not the question. We want to know whether by your death you will let error triumph, or whether you would rather remain to defend the truth, when better days may come."

They entreated him; they put forward the most plausible motives; from time to time they uttered the terrible words, *burnt alive!* His blood froze in his veins; he knew not what he said or did . . . they placed a paper before him—they put a pen in his hand—his head was bewildered, he signed his name with a deep sigh. This unhappy man was destined at a later period to be a faithful martyr of Jesus Christ; but he had not yet learnt to "resist even unto blood." Barnes had fallen.

On the following Sunday morning a solemn spectacle was preparing at St Paul's. Before daybreak, all were astir in the prison of the unhappy prior; and at eight o'clock, the knight-marshal with his tipstaves, and the warden of the Fleet prison, with his billmen, conducted Barnes to St Paul's, along with four of the Hanse merchants who had first brought to London the New Testament of Jesus Christ in English. The fifth of these pious merchants held an immense taper, five pounds in weight, in his hands. A persevering search had discovered that it was these men to whom England was indebted for the so much dreaded book; their warehouses were surrounded and their persons arrested. On the top of St Paul's steps was a platform, and on the platform a throne, and on the throne the cardinal, dressed in purple. On his head glittered the mitre of which Barnes had spoken so ill; around him were thirty-six bishops, abbots, priors, and all his doctors, dressed in damask and satin; the cathedral held a vast congregation. The bishop of Rochester having gone into a pulpit placed at the top of the steps, Barnes and the merchants, each bearing a faggot, were compelled to kneel and listen to a sermon intended to cure these poor creatures of that taste for insurrection against popery which was beginning to spread in every quarter. The sermon ended, Dr Barnes was then required to declare that he was more charitably handled than he deserved, and to ask pardon for his heresies. All this done, the cardinal took his station under a magnificent canopy, moved with his escort of bishops to the cathedral gate, mounted his mule, and rode off. After this Barnes and his five companions walked three times round a fire, lighted before the cross at the north gate of the cathedral. The dejected prior, with downcast head, dragged himself along, rather than walked. After the third turn, the prisoners threw their faggots into the flames; some "heretical" books also were flung in; and the bishop of Rochester having given absolution to the six penitents, they were led back to prison to be kept there during the lord cardinal's pleasure. Barnes could not weep now; the thought of his relapse, and of the effects so guilty an example might produce, had deprived him of all moral energy. In the month of August, he was led out of prison and confined in the Augustine monastery.

Barnes was not the only man at Cambridge upon whom the blow had fallen. Since the year 1520, a monk named Richard Bayfield had been an inmate of the abbey of Bury St Edmunds. His affability delighted every traveller. One day, when engaged as chamberlain in receiving Barnes, who had come to visit Doctor Ruffam, his fellow-student at Louvain, two men entered the monastery. They were pious persons, and of great consideration in London, where they carried on the occupation of brick-making, and had risen to be wardens of their guild. Their names were Maxwell and Stacy, men "well grafted in the doctrine of Christ," says the historian, who had led many to the Saviour by their conversation and exemplary life. Being accustomed to travel once a year through the counties to visit their brethren, and extend a knowledge of the gospel, they used to lodge, according to the usages of the time, in the monasteries and abbeys. A conversation soon arose between Barnes, Stacy, and Maxwell, which struck the lay-brother. Barnes, who had observed his attention, gave him, as he was leaving the monastery, a New Testament in Latin, and the two brickmakers added a New Testament in English, with *The Wicked Mammon* and *The Obedience of a Christian Man*. The lay-brother ran and hid the books in his cell, and for two years read them constantly. At last he was discovered, and reprimanded; but he boldly confessed his faith. Upon this the monks threw him into prison, set him in the stocks, put a gag in his mouth, and cruelly whipped him, to prevent his speaking of grace. The unhappy Bayfield remained nine months in this condition.

When Barnes repeated his visit to Bury at a later period, he did not find the amiable chamberlain at the gates of the abbey. Upon inquiry he learnt his condition, and immediately took steps to procure his deliverance. Dr Ruffam came to his aid: "Give him to me," said Barnes, "I will take him to Cambridge." The prior of the Augustines was at that time held in high esteem; his request was granted, in the hope that he would lead back Bayfield to the doctrines of the church. But the very reverse took place: intercourse with the Cambridge brethren strengthened the young monk's faith. On a sudden his happiness vanished. Barnes, his friend and benefactor, was carried to London, and the monks of Bury St Edmunds, alarmed at the noise this affair created, summoned him to return to the abbey. But Bayfield, resolving to submit to their yoke no longer, went to London, and lay concealed with Maxwell and Stacy. One day, having left his hiding-place, he was crossing Lombard Street, when he met a priest named Pierson and two other members of his order, with whom he entered into a conversation which greatly scandalized them. "You must depart forthwith," said Maxwell and Stacy to him on his return. Bayfield received a small sum of money from them, went on board a ship and, as soon as he reached the continent, hastened to find Tyndale.

During this time scenes of a very different nature from those which had taken place at Cambridge, but not less heart-rending, were passing at Oxford. The storm of persecution was raging there with more violence than at Cambridge. Clark and the other confessors of the name of Christ were still confined in their underground prison. The air they breathed, the food they took (and they were given nothing but salt fish), the burning thirst this created, the thoughts by which they were agitated, all together combined to crush these noble-hearted men. Their bodies wasted day by day; they wandered like spectres up and down their gloomy cellar. Those animated discussions in which the deep questions then convulsing

Christendom were so eloquently debated were at an end; they were like shadow meeting shadow. Their hollow eyes cast a vague and haggard glance on one another and, after gazing for a moment, they passed on without speaking. Clark, Sumner, Bayley, and Goodman, consumed by fever, feebly crawled along, leaning against their dungeon walls. The first, who was also the eldest, could not walk without the support of one of his fellow-prisoners. Soon he was quite unable to move, and lay stretched upon the damp floor. The brethren gathered round him, sought to discover in his features whether death was not about to cut short the days of him who had brought many of them to the knowledge of Christ. They repeated to him slowly the words of Scripture, and then knelt down by his side and uttered a fervent prayer.

Clark, feeling his end draw near, asked for the communion.

The jailers conveyed his request to their master; the noise of the bolts was soon heard, and a turnkey, stepping into the midst of the disconsolate band, pronounced a cruel *no!* On hearing this, Clark looked towards heaven, and exclaimed with a father of the church: *Crede et manducasti* (Believe and thou hast eaten). He was lost in thought: he contemplated the crucified Son of God; by faith he ate and drank the flesh and blood of Christ, and experienced in his inner life the strengthening action of the Redeemer. Men might refuse him the host, but Jesus had given him His body; and from that hour he felt strengthened by a living union with the King of heaven.

Not alone did Clark descend into the shadowy valley: Sumner, Bayley, and Goodman were sinking rapidly. Death, the gloomy inhabitant of this foul prison, had taken possession of these four friends. Their brethren addressed fresh solicitations to the cardinal, at that time closely occupied in negotiations with France, Rome, and Venice. He found means, however, to give a moment to the Oxford martyrs; and just as these Christians were praying over their four dying companions, the commissioner came and informed them, that "his lordship, of his great goodness, permitted the sick persons to be removed to their own chambers." Litters were brought, on which the dying men were placed and carried to their rooms; the doors were closed again upon those whose lives this frightful dungeon had not yet attacked.

It was the middle of August, 1528. The wretched men who had passed six months in the cellar were transported in vain to their chambers and their beds; several members of the university ineffectually tried by their cares and their tender charity to recall them to life. It was too late. The severities of popery had killed these noble witnesses. The approach of death soon betrayed itself; their blood grew cold, their limbs stiff, and their bedimmed eyes sought only Jesus Christ, their everlasting hope. Clark, Sumner, and Bayley died in the same week. Goodman followed close upon them.

This unexpected catastrophe softened Wolsey. He was cruel only as far as his interest and the safety of the church required. He feared that the death of so many young men would raise public opinion against him, or that these catastrophes would damage his college; perhaps even some sentiment of humanity may have touched his heart. "Set the rest at liberty," he wrote to his agents, "but upon condition that they do not go above ten miles from Oxford." The university beheld these young men issue from their living tomb pale, wasted, weak, and with faltering steps. At that time they were not men of mark; it was their youth that touched the spectators' hearts; but in after-years they all occupied an important place in the church. They were Cox, who became Bishop of Ely, and tutor to Edward the Prince Royal; Drumm, who under Cranmer became one of the six preachers at Canterbury; Udal, afterwards master of Westminster and Eton schools; Salisbury, dean of Norwich, and then bishop of Sodor and Man, who in all his wealth and greatness often recalled his frightful prison at Oxford as a title to glory; Ferrar, afterwards Cranmer's chaplain, bishop of St David's, and a martyr even unto death, after an interval of thirty years; Fryth, Tyndale's friend, to whom this deliverance proved only a delay; and several others. When they came forth from their terrible dungeon, their friends ran up to them, supported their faltering steps, and embraced them amidst floods of tears. Fryth quitted the university not long after and went to Flanders. Thus was the tempest stayed which had so fearfully ravaged Oxford. But the calm was of no long duration; an unexpected circumstance became perilous to the cause of the Reformation.

CHAPTER FOUR

The Tempest against the Truth

(1526)

IN 1526 the peace of mind of Henry, king of England, was disturbed, not only by the circulation of unauthorized New Testaments from the continent, but by the reception of a communication from Martin Luther. The letter which, at the advice of Christian II, king of Denmark, this reformer had written to him in September 1525, had miscarried. The Wittenberg doctor hearing nothing of it, had boldly printed it, and sent a copy to the king. "I am informed," said Luther, "that your Majesty is beginning to favour the gospel, and to be disgusted with the perverse race that fights against it in your noble kingdom. . . . It is true that, according to Scripture, *the kings of the earth take counsel together against the Lord,* and we cannot, consequently, expect to see them favourable to the truth. How fervently do I wish that this miracle may be accomplished in the person of your Majesty."

We may imagine Henry's wrath as he read this letter. "What!" said he, "does this apostate monk dare print a letter addressed to us, without having even sent it, or at the least without knowing if we have ever received it? . . . And as if that were not enough, he insinuates that we are among his partisans. . . . He wins over also one or two wretches, born in our kingdom, and engages them to translate the New Testament into English, adding thereto certain prefaces and poisonous glosses." Thus spoke Henry. The idea that his name should be associated with that of the Wittenberg monk called all the blood into his face. He will reply right royally to such unblushing impudence. He summoned Wolsey forthwith. "Here!" said he, pointing to a passage concerning the prelate, "here! read what is said of you!" And then he read aloud: "*Illud monstrum et publicum odium Dei et hominum, cardinalis Eboracensis, pestis illa regni tui.* You see, my lord, you are a *monster,* an object of *hatred*

271

T

both to God and man, the *plague* of my kingdom!" The king
had hitherto allowed the bishops to do as they pleased, and
observed a sort of neutrality. He now determined to lay it
aside and begin a crusade against the gospel of Jesus Christ,
but he must first answer this impertinent letter. He consulted
Sir Thomas More, shut himself in his chamber, and dictated
to his secretary a reply to the reformer: "You are ashamed of
the book you have written against me," he said, "I would
counsel you to be ashamed of all that you have written. They
are full of disgusting errors and frantic heresies; and are
supported by the most audacious obstinacy. Your venomous
pen mocks the church, insults the fathers, abuses the saints,
despises the apostles, dishonours the holy virgin, and blas-
phemes God, by making him the author of evil. . . . And after
all that, you claim to be an author whose like does not exist
in the world!"

"You offer to publish a book in my praise. . . . I thank you!
. . . You will praise me most by abusing me; you will dishonour
me beyond measure if you praise me. I say with Seneca: "Let
it be as disgraceful to you to be praised by the vile, as if you
were praised for vile deeds.""

This letter, written by the *king of the English to the king of the
heretics*, was immediately circulated throughout England bound
up with Luther's epistle.[1] Henry, by publishing it, put his
subjects on their guard against the *unfaithful* translations of the
New Testament, which were besides about to be burnt everywhere. "The grapes seem beautiful," he said, "but beware
how you wet your lips with the wine made from them, for the
adversary hath mingled poison with it."

Luther, agitated by this rude lesson, tried to excuse himself.
"I said to myself, *There are twelve hours in the day*. Who knows?
perhaps I may find one favourable hour to gain the King of
England. I therefore laid my humble epistle at his feet; but
alas! the swine have torn it. I am willing to be silent . . . but as
regards my doctrine, I cannot impose silence on it. It must cry
aloud, it must bite. If any king imagines he can make me
retract my faith, he is a dreamer. So long as one drop of blood
remains in my body, I shall say NO. Emperors, kings, the devil,
and even the whole universe, cannot frighten me when faith

[1] [The date of publication appears to have been February 1527.]

is concerned. I claim to be proud, very proud, exceedingly proud. If my doctrine had no other enemies than the king of England, Duke George, the pope and their allies, all these soap-bubbles . . . one little prayer would long ago have worsted them all. Where are Pilate, Herod, and Caiaphas now? Where are Nero, Domitian, and Maximilian? Where are Arius, Pelagius, and Manes?—Where are they? . . . Where all our scribes and all our tyrants will soon be.—But Christ? Christ is the same always.

"For a thousand years the Holy Scriptures have not shone in the world with so much brightness as now. I wait in peace for my last hour; I have done what I could. O princes, my hands are clean from your blood; it will fall on your own heads."

Bowing before the supreme royalty of Jesus Christ, Luther spoke thus boldly to King Henry, who contested the rights of the Word of God.

A letter written against the reformer was not enough for the bishops. Profiting by the wound Luther had inflicted on Henry's self-esteem, they urged him to put down this revolt of the human understanding, which threatened (as they averred) both the popedom and the monarchy. They commenced the persecution. Latimer was summoned before Wolsey, but his learning and presence of mind procured his dismissal. Bilney also, who had been ordered to London, received an injunction not to preach *Luther's doctrines*. "I will not preach Luther's doctrines, if there are any peculiar to him," he said; "but I can and I must preach the doctrine of Jesus Christ, although Luther should preach it too." And finally Garret, led into the presence of his judges, was seized with terror, and fell before the cruel threats of the bishop. When restored to liberty, he fled from place to place, endeavouring to hide his sorrow, and to escape from the despotism of the priests, awaiting the moment when he should give his life for Jesus Christ.

The adversaries of the Reformation were not yet satisfied. The New Testament continued to circulate, and depots were formed in several monasteries. Barnes, a prisoner in the Augustine monastery in London, had regained his courage, and loved his Bible more and more. One day about the end of September, as three or four friends were reading in his chamber, two simple peasants, John Tyball and Thomas Hilles, natives of

Bumpstead in Essex, came in. "How did you come to a knowledge of the truth?" asked Barnes. They drew from their pockets some old volumes containing the Gospels, and a few of the Epistles in English. Barnes returned them with a smile. "They are nothing," he told them, "in comparison with the new edition of the New Testament," a copy of which the two peasants bought for three shillings and twopence. "Hide it carefully," said Barnes. When this came to the ears of the clergy, Barnes was removed to Northampton to be burnt at the stake; but he managed to escape; his friends reported that he was drowned; and while strict search was making for him during a whole week along the sea-coast, he secretly went on board a ship, and was carried to Germany. "The cardinal will catch him even now," said the bishop of London, "whatever amount of money it may cost him." When Barnes was told of this, he remarked: "I am a poor simple wretch, not worth the tenth penny they will give for me. Besides, if they burn me, what will they gain by it? . . . The sun and the moon, fire and water, the stars and the elements—yea, and also stones shall defend this cause against them, *rather than the truth should perish.*" Faith had returned to Barnes' feeble heart.

His escape added fuel to the wrath of the clergy. They proclaimed, throughout the length and breadth of England, that the English translations of the Holy Scriptures contained an *infectious poison*, and ordered a general search after the Word of God. On the 24th of October, 1526, the bishop of London enjoined on his archdeacons to seize all translations of the New Testament in English with or without glosses; and, a few days later, the archbishop of Canterbury issued a mandate against all the books which should contain "any particle of the New Testament." The primate remembered that a spark was sufficient to kindle a large fire.

On hearing of this order, William Roye, a sarcastic writer, published a violent satire, in which figured *Judas* (Standish), *Pliate* (Wolsey), and *Caiaphas* (Tunstall). The author exclaimed with energy:

> God, of his goodness, grudged not to die,
>   Man to deliver from deadly damnation;
> Whose will is, that we should know perfectly
>   What he here hath done for our salvation.

O cruel Caiaphas! full of crafty conspiration,
How durst thou give them false judgment
To burn God's word—the Holy Testament.

The efforts of Caiaphas and his colleagues were indeed
useless: the priests were undertaking a work beyond their
strength. If by some terrible revolution all social forms should
be destroyed in the world, the living church of the elect, a
divine institution in the midst of human institutions, would
still exist by the power of God, like a rock in the midst of the
tempest, and would transmit to future generations the seeds of
Christian life and civilization. It is the same with the Word, the
creative principle of the church. It cannot perish here below.
The priests of England had something to learn on this matter.

While the agents of the clergy were carrying out the
archiepiscopal mandate, and a merciless search was made
everywhere for the New Testaments from Worms, a new edition
was discovered, fresh from the press, of a smaller and more
portable, and consequently more dangerous size. It was printed
by Christopher Eyndhoven of Antwerp, who had consigned it
to his correspondents in London. The annoyance of the priests
was extreme, and Hackett, the agent of Henry VIII in the
Low Countries, immediately received orders to get this man
punished. "We cannot deliver judgment without inquiry into
the matter," said the lords of Antwerp; "we will therefore have
the book translated into Flemish."—"God forbid," said Hackett
in alarm, "What! would you also on your side of the ocean
translate this book into the language of the people?"—"Well
then," said one of the judges, less conscientious than his
colleagues, "let the king of England send us a copy of each of
the books he has burnt, and we will burn them likewise."
Hackett wrote to Wolsey for them, and as soon as they arrived
the court met again. Eyndhoven's counsel called upon the
prosecutor to point out the *heresies* contained in the volume.
The margrave (an officer of the imperial government) shrank
from the task, and said to Hackett, "I give up the business!"
The charge against Eyndhoven was dismissed.

Thus did the Reformation awaken in Europe the slumbering
spirit of law and liberty. By enfranchising thought from the
yoke of popery, it prepared the way for other enfranchisements;
and by restoring the authority of the Word of God, it brought

back the reign of the law among nations long the prey of
turbulent passions and arbitrary power. Then, as at all times,
religious society forestalled civil society, and gave it those two
great principles of order and liberty, which popery compromises
or annuls. It was not in vain that the magistrates of a Flemish
city, enlightened by the first dawn of the Reformation, set so
noble an example; the English, who were very numerous in
the Hanse Towns, thus recovered that civil and religious liberty
which is the time-honoured right of England, and of which
they were in after-years to give other nations the so much
needed lessons.

"Well then," said Hackett, who was annoyed at their setting
the law above his master's will, "I will go and buy all these
books, and send them to the cardinal, that he may burn them."
With these words he left the court. But his anger evaporating,
he set off for Malines to complain to the regent and her council
of the Antwerp decision. "What!" said he, "you punish those
who circulate false money, and you will not punish still more
severely the man who coins it?—in this case, he is the printer."
—"But that is just the point in dispute," they replied; "we are
not sure the money is *false*."—"How can it be otherwise,"
answered Henry's agent, "since the bishops of England have
declared it so?" The imperial government, which was not very
favourably disposed towards England, ratified Eyndhoven's
acquittal, but permitted Hackett to burn all the copies of the
New Testament he could seize. He hastened to profit by this
concession, and began hunting after the Holy Scriptures, while
the priests eagerly came to his assistance. In their view, as well
as in that of their English colleagues, the supreme decision in
matters of faith rested not with the Word of God but with the
pope; and the best means of securing this privilege to the
pontiff was to reduce the Bible to ashes.

Notwithstanding these trials, the year 1526 was a memorable
one for England. The English New Testament had been
circulated from the shores of the Channel to the borders of
Scotland, and the Reformation had begun in that island by
the Word of God. The revival of the sixteenth century was in
no country less than in England the outcome of a royal mandate.
But God, who had disseminated the Scriptures over Britain, in
defiance of the rulers of the nation, was about to make use of

their passions to remove the difficulties which opposed the final triumph of His plans. We here enter upon a new phase in the history of the Reformation; and, having studied the work of God in the faith of the little ones, we proceed to contemplate the work of man in the intrigues of the great ones of the earth.

CHAPTER FIVE

The Divorce Question Opens

(1526–27)

WOLSEY, mortified at not being able to obtain the pontifical throne, to which he had so ardently aspired, and being especially irritated by the ill-will of Charles V, meditated a plan which, entirely unsuspected by him, was to lead to the enfranchisement of England from the papal yoke. "They laugh at me, and thrust me into the second rank," he had exclaimed. "So be it! I will create such a confusion in the world as has not been seen for ages. . . . I will do it, even should England be swallowed up in the tempest!" Desirous of exciting imperishable hatred between Henry VIII and Charles V, he had undertaken to break the marriage which Henry VII and Ferdinand the Catholic had planned to unite for ever their families and their crowns. His hatred of Charles was not his only motive. Catherine had reproached him for his dissolute life, and he had sworn to be revenged. There can be no doubt about Wolsey's share in the matter.[1] "The *first terms* of the divorce were put forward by me," he told the French ambassador. "I did it," he added, "to cause a lasting separation between the houses of England and Burgundy." The best informed writers of the sixteenth century, men of the most opposite parties, Pole, Polydore Virgil, Tyndale, Meteren, Pallavicini, Sanders, and Roper, More's son-in-law, all agree in pointing to Wolsey as the instigator of that divorce, which has become so famous. He desired to go still farther and, after inducing the king to put away his queen, he hoped to prevail

---

[1] [Merle d'Aubigné presents a reasoned case for regarding Wolsey as the originator of the divorce proposal, but some modern historians do not agree with his views and conclusions. One of them fitly says that almost the only statement about the question which one can make without fear of contradiction from some quarter is that Henry VIII, shortly after his accession, married Catherine of Aragon, his brother's widow. Readers who wish to explore the matter further will have no difficulty in finding histories, ancient and modern, which present widely-contrasted views.]

on the pope to depose the Emperor. It was not the king's passion for Anne Boleyn, as so many of the Romish fabulists have repeated; but the passion of a cardinal for the triple crown which gave the signal of England's emancipation. Offended pride is one of the most active principles of human nature.

Wolsey's design was a strange one, and difficult of execution, but not impossible. Henry was living apparently on the best terms with Catherine; on more than one occasion Erasmus had spoken of the royal family of England as the pattern of the domestic virtues. But the most ardent of Henry's desires was not satisfied; he had no son; those whom the queen had borne him had died in their infancy, and Mary alone survived. The deaths of these little children, at all times so heart-rending, were particularly so in the palace of Greenwich. It appeared to Catherine that the shade of the last Plantagenet, immolated on her marriage altar, came forth to seize one after another the heirs she gave to the throne of England, and to carry them away to his tomb.[1] The queen shed tears almost unceasingly, and implored the divine mercy, while the king cursed his unhappy fate. The people seemed to share in the royal sorrow; and men of learning and piety (Longland was among their number) declared against the validity of the marriage. They said that "the papal dispensations had no force when in opposition to the law of God." Yet hitherto Henry had rejected every idea of a divorce.

The times had changed since 1509. The king appears genuinely to have loved Catherine: her reserve, mildness, and dignity, had charmed him. Greedy of pleasure and applause, he was delighted to see his wife content to be the quiet witness of his joys and of his triumphs. But gradually the queen had grown older, her Spanish gravity had increased, her devout practices were multiplied, and her infirmities, become more frequent, had left the king no hope of having a son to succeed him on the throne. From that hour, even while continuing to praise her virtues, Henry grew cold towards her person, and his love by degrees changed into repugnance. And then he thought that the death of his children might be a sign of God's anger. This idea had taken hold of him, and induced him to occupy apartments separate from the queen's.

[1] [The reference is to the death of Warwick, cf. pp. 111-112.]

Wolsey judged the moment favourable for beginning the attack. It was in the latter months of 1526, when calling Longland, Bishop of Lincoln and the king's confessor, to him, and concealing his principal motive, he said: "You know his majesty's anguish. The stability of his crown and his everlasting salvation seem to be compromised alike. To whom can I unbosom myself, if not to you, who must know the inmost secrets of his soul?" The two bishops resolved to awaken Henry to the perils incurred by his union with Catherine; but Longland insisted that Wolsey should take the first steps.

The cardinal waited upon the king, and reminded him of his scruples before the betrothal; he exaggerated those entertained by the nation and, speaking with unusual warmth, he entreated the king to remain no longer in such danger: "The holiness of your life and the legitimacy of your succession are at stake."—"My good father," said Henry, "you would do well to consider the weight of the stone that you have undertaken to move. The queen is a woman of such exemplary life that I have no motive for separating from her."

The cardinal did not consider himself beaten; three days later he appeared before the king accompanied by the bishop of Lincoln. "Most mighty prince," said the confessor, who felt bold enough to speak after the cardinal, "you cannot, like Herod, have your brother's wife. I exhort and conjure you, as having the care of your soul, to submit the matter to competent judges." Henry consented, and perhaps not unwillingly.

It was not enough for Wolsey to separate Henry from the Emperor; he must, for greater security, unite him to Francis I. The King of England shall repudiate the aunt of Charles V, and then marry the sister of the French king. Proud of the success he had obtained in the first part of his plan, Wolsey entered upon the second. "There is a princess," he told the king, "whose birth, graces, and talents charm all Europe. Margaret of Valois, sister of King Francis, is superior to all of her sex, and no one is worthier of your alliance." Henry made answer that it was a serious matter, requiring deliberate examination. Wolsey, however, placed in the king's hands a portrait of Margaret, and it has been imagined that he even privily caused her sentiments to be sounded. Be that as it may, the sister of Francis I having learnt that she was pointed at as the future queen of England, rebelled at the idea of taking from an innocent woman a crown she had worn so nobly. "The French king's sister knows too much of Christ to consent unto such wickedness," said Tyndale. Margaret of Valois replied: "Let me hear no more of a marriage that can be effected only at the expense of Catherine of Aragon's happiness and life." Shortly after this, on the 24th of January 1527, the sister of Francis I married Henry d'Albret, king of Navarre.

Henry VIII, desirous of information with regard to his favourite's suggestion, commissioned Fox, his almoner, Pace, dean of St Paul's, and Wakefield, professor of Hebrew at Oxford, to study the passages of Leviticus and Deuteronomy which related to marriage with a brother's wife. Wakefield, who had no wish to commit himself, asked whether Henry was *for* or *against* the divorce. Pace replied to this servile hebraist that the king wanted nothing but the truth.

But who would take the first public step in an undertaking so hazardous? Every one shrank back; the terrible Emperor alarmed them all. It was a French bishop that hazarded the step; bishops meet us at every turn in this affair of the divorce, with which bishops have so violently reproached the Reformation. Henry, desirous of excusing Wolsey, pretended afterwards that the objections of the French prelate had preceded those of Longland and the cardinal. In February 1527, Francis I had sent an embassy to London, at the head of which was Gabriel de Grammont, bishop of Tarbes, with the intention to procure the hand of Mary of England. Henry's ministers having inquired whether the engagement of Francis with the queen dowager of Portugal did not oppose the commission with which the French bishop was charged, the latter answered: "I will ask you in turn what has been done to remove the impediments which opposed the marriage of which the Princess Mary is issue." They laid before the ambassador the dispensation of Julius II, which he returned, saying, that the bull was not *sufficient*, seeing that such a marriage was forbidden *jure divino*; and he added: "Have you English a different gospel from ours?"

The king, when he heard these words (as he informs us himself) was filled with fear and horror. Three of the most respected bishops of Christendom united to accuse him of incest! He began to speak of it to certain individuals: "The scruples of my conscience have been terribly increased (he said) since the bishop spoke of this matter before my council in exceedingly plain words." There is no reason to believe that these *terrible* troubles of which the king speaks were a mere invention on his part. A disputed succession might again plunge England into civil war. Even if no pretenders should spring up, might they not see a rival house, a French prince for instance, wedded to Henry's daughter, reigning over England? The king, in his anxiety, had recourse to his favourite author, Thomas Aquinas, and this *angel of the schools* declared his marriage unlawful. Henry next opened the Bible, and found this threat against the man who took his brother's wife: "He shall be *childless*!" The denunciation increased his trouble, for he had no heir. In the midst of this darkness a new perspective opened before him. His conscience might be unbound; his desire to have a younger wife might be gratified; he might have a son! . . . The king resolved to lay the matter before a commission of lawyers, and this commission soon wrote volumes.

During all this time Catherine, suspecting no evil, was occupied in her devotions. Her heart, bruised by the death of her children and by the king's coldness, sought consolation in prayer both privately and in the royal chapel. She would rise at midnight and kneel down upon the cold stones, and never missed any of the canonical services. But one day (probably in May or June 1527) some officious person informed her of the rumours circulating in the city and at court. Bursting with anger and alarm, and all in tears, she hastened to the king, and addressed him with the bitterest complaints. Henry was content to calm her by vague assurances; but the unfeeling Wolsey, troubling himself still less than his master about Catherine's emotion, called it, with a smile, "a short tragedy."

The offended wife lost no time: it was necessary that the Emperor should be informed promptly, surely, and accurately of this unprecedented insult. A letter would be insufficient, even were it not intercepted. Catherine therefore determined to send her servant Francis Philip, a Spaniard, to her nephew; and to conceal the object of his journey, they proceeded, after the *tragedy*, to play a *comedy* in the Spanish style. "My mother is sick and desires to see me," said Philip. Catherine begged the king to refuse her servant's prayer; and Henry, divining the stratagem, resolved to employ trick against trick. "Philip's request is very proper," he made answer; and Catherine, *from regard to her husband*, consented to his departure. Henry meantime had given orders that, "notwithstanding any safe conduct, the said Philip should be arrested and detained at Calais, in such a manner, however, that no one should know whence the stoppage proceeded."

It was to no purpose that the queen indulged in a culpable dissimulation; a poisoned arrow had pierced her heart, and her words, her manners, her complaints, her tears, the numerous messages she sent, now to one and now to another, betrayed the secret which the king wished still to conceal. Her friends blamed her for this publicity; men wondered what Charles would say when he heard of his aunt's distress; they feared that peace would be broken; but Catherine, whose heart was "rent in twain," was not to be moved by diplomatic considerations. Her sorrow did not check Henry; with the two motives which made him eager for a divorce—the scruples of his conscience and the desire of an heir—was now combined a third still more forcible. A woman was about to play an important part in the destinies of England.

CHAPTER SIX

Anne Boleyn

(1522–27)

ABOUT the year 1522, or possibly a little earlier, Anne Boleyn had returned from the court of France. It is probable that she was little more than fifteen years of age.[1] Historians hold widely differing views about her charms, but when she appeared in the English court an unfriendly contemporary was compelled to own that she eclipsed her companions "by her excellent gesture and behaviour." Her chief attractiveness appears to have been in her eyes, which are described as "black and beautiful and of great effect." Cranmer, some ten years later, found her appearance very impressive as she "sat in her hair" (it seems that on great occasions she appeared with her hair falling over her shoulders) upon a horse litter, richly apparelled at her coronation.

Anne Boleyn brought to the English court the polished manners and deportment of the court of France. But more important, as later events were to show, she also brought home something of the influence which reached her through Margaret of Angoulême, the sister of the French king. This gracious woman became renowned for the support and protection she afforded to advocates and preachers of reformation doctrine and practice. It is probable that, before Anne left France, she had begun to read, without thoroughly understanding it, the holy book in which Margaret found consolation and repose,

[1] [The date of Anne Boleyn's birth is uncertain. 1501 and 1507 have both been claimed. The place of her birth was probably Blickling Hall, Norfolk. At a later date she lived at Hever Castle, Kent. Her father permitted her to accompany Mary Tudor, Henry VIII's sister, to France, on the marriage of that princess to Louis XII in 1514. Remaining at the French court after the death of Louis in 1515, she served Queen Claude, the wife of Francis I, for several years, and thus came into contact with Margaret of Valois, better known as Margaret of Angoulême, or Margaret of Navarre.]

and to direct a few light and passing thoughts to that "mild Emmanuel" to whom the latter addressed such beautiful verses.

Among the young noblemen in the cardinal's household was Lord Percy, eldest son of the Earl of Northumberland. While Wolsey was in conference with the king, Percy was accustomed to resort to the queen's apartments, where he passed the time among her ladies. He soon felt a sincere passion for Anne, and the young maid of honour, who had been cold to the addresses of the gentlemen at the court of Francis, replied to the affections of the heir of Northumberland. The two young people already indulged in day-dreams of a quiet, elegant, and happy life in their noble castles of the north; but such dreams were fated to be of short duration.

Wolsey hated the Norfolks, and consequently the Boleyns. It was to counterbalance their influence that he had been first introduced at court. He became angry, therefore, when he saw one of his household suing for the hand of the daughter and niece of his enemies. Besides, certain partisans of the clergy accused Anne of being friendly to the Reformation. One day, therefore, when Percy was in attendance upon the cardinal, the latter rudely addressed him: "I marvel at your folly, that you should attempt to contract yourself with that girl without your father's or the king's consent. I command you to break with her." Percy burst into tears, and besought the cardinal to plead his cause. "I charge you to resort no more into her company," was Wolsey's cold reply, after which he rose up and left the room.[1] Anne received an order at the same time to leave the court. Proud and bold, and ascribing her misfortune to Wolsey's hatred, she exclaimed as she quitted the palace,

[1] [On the evidence of Cavendish's *Life of Wolsey* (written between 1554 and 1557) it was long believed that as early as 1523 Wolsey had discovered Henry's eyes turned complacently on the young maid of honour, and that this induced him to thwart Percy's love, but it has now been conclusively shown that Henry had quite different motives. Thomas Boleyn, father to Anne, had a claim to certain Irish estates through his mother, but was strongly opposed in this matter by a member of the Butler family living in Ireland. It suited Henry's schemes to seek for a reconciliation between the rival families, and this, he thought, could best be effected by a marriage between Anne and Sir James Butler. She would in time become Lady Ormonde and live in Kilkenny Castle. But the marriage never came about; perhaps Anne herself refused to be drawn into it.]

"I will be revenged for this insult." But she had scarcely taken up her abode in the gothic halls of Hever Castle, when news still more distressing overwhelmed her. Percy was married to Lady Mary Talbot. She wept long and bitterly, and vowed against the young nobleman who had deserted her a contempt equal to her hatred of the cardinal. Anne was reserved for a more illustrious, but more unhappy fate.

While life at the court of Henry VIII was thus perturbed by these seemingly small and comparatively unimportant affairs, a strange report filled all England with surprise. It was reported that the imperialist soldiers of Charles V had taken Rome by assault, and that the pope was a prisoner in his own city.

Shortly, the captive pope and cardinals wrote letters "filled with tears and groans." Full of zeal for the papacy, Wolsey ordered a public fast. "The Emperor will never release the pope, unless he be compelled," he told the king. "Sir, God has made you *defender of the faith*; save the church and its head!"— "My lord," answered the king with a smile, "I assure you that this war between the Emperor and the pope is not for the faith, but for temporal possessions and dominions."

But Wolsey would not be discouraged; and, on the 3rd of July, he passed through the streets of London, riding a richly caparisoned mule, and resting his feet on gilt stirrups, while nine hundred gentlemen accompanied him on horseback. He was going to entreat Francis to aid his master in saving Clement VII. He had found no difficulty in prevailing upon Henry; Charles talked of carrying the pope to Spain, and of permanently establishing the apostolic see in that country.[1] Now, how could they obtain the divorce from a *Spanish* pope? During the procession, Wolsey seemed oppressed with grief, and even shed tears; but he soon raised his head and exclaimed: "My heart is inflamed, and I wish it may be said of the pope *per secula sempiterna*,

"Rediit Henrici octavi virtute serena."

Desirous of forming a close union between France and England for the accomplishment of his designs, he had cast

---

[1] The see apostolic should perpetually remain in Spain. State Papers, i, p. 227.

his eyes on the princess Renée, daughter of Louis XII, and sister-in-law to Francis I, as a possible future wife of Henry VIII. A treaty of alliance between the two crowns was signed at Amiens on the 18th of August (1527), after which Francis, with his mother and the cardinal, proceeded to Compiègne, and there Wolsey, styling Charles the most obstinate defender of Lutheranism, promising "perpetual *conjunction* on the one hand [between France and England], and perpetual *disjunction* on the other" [between England and Germany], sought to discover whether the French saw advantages in a marriage between Renée and King Henry. Staffileo, dean of Rota, affirmed that the pope had been able to permit the marriage between Henry and Catherine only by an error of the keys of St Peter. This avowal, so remarkable on the part of the dean of one of the first jurisdictions of Rome, induced Francis' mother to listen favourably to the cardinal's demand. But whether this proposal was displeasing to Renée, who was destined on a future day to profess the pure faith of the Gospel with greater earnestness than Margaret of Valois, or whether Francis was not over-anxious for a union that would have given Henry rights over the duchy of Brittany, she was promised to the son of the Duke of Ferrara. It was a check to the cardinal; but it was his ill fortune to receive one still more severe on his return to England.

The daughter of Sir Thomas Boleyn (who had been created Viscount Rochford in 1525) was constantly at court, "where she flourished in great estimation and favour," says Cavendish, "having always a private indignation against the cardinal for breaking off the pre-contract made between Lord Percy and her." Her beauty, her graceful carriage, her black hair, oval face, and bright eyes, her sweet voice in singing, her skill and dignity in the dance, her desire to please which was not entirely devoid of coquetry, her sprightliness, the readiness of her repartees, and above all the amiability of her character, won every heart. Every day (it was reported) she invented a new style of dress, and set the fashion in England. But to all these qualities, she added modesty, and even imposed it on others by her example. The ladies of the court, who had hitherto adopted a different fashion (says her greatest enemy), covered the neck and bosom as she did; and the malicious, unable to

U

appreciate Anne's motives, ascribed this modesty on the young lady's part to a desire to hide a secret deformity. Numerous admirers once more crowded round Anne Boleyn, and among others, one of the most illustrious noblemen and poets of England, Sir Thomas Wyatt, a follower of Wycliffe. He, however, was not the man destined to replace the son of the Percies.

Henry, absorbed in anxiety about his divorce from Catherine, had become low-spirited and melancholy. The laughter, songs, repartees, and beauty of Anne Boleyn struck and captivated him, and his eyes were soon fixed complacently on the young maid of honour. Catherine was more than forty years old, and it was hardly to be expected that so susceptible a man as Henry would have made, as Job says, *a covenant with his eyes not to think upon a maid*. Desirous of showing his admiration, he presented Anne, according to usage, with a costly jewel; she accepted and wore it, and continued to dance, laugh, and chatter as before, without attaching particular importance to the royal present. Henry's attentions became more continuous; and he took advantage of a moment when he found Anne alone to declare his sentiments. With mingled emotion and alarm, the young lady fell trembling at the king's feet, and exclaimed, bursting into tears: "I think, most noble and worthy king, your majesty speaks these words in mirth to prove me. . . . I will rather lose my life than my virtue." Henry gracefully replied that he should at least continue to hope. But Anne, rising up, proudly made answer: "I understand not, most mighty king, how you should retain any such hope; your wife I cannot be, both in respect of mine own unworthiness, and also because you have a queen already. Your mistress I will not be." Anne kept her word. She continued to show the king, even after this interview, all the respect that was due to him; but on several occasions she proudly, violently even, repelled his advances. In this age of gallantry, we find her resisting for nearly six years all the seductions Henry scattered round her. Such an example is not often met with in the history of courts. The books she had read in Margaret's palace gave her a secret strength. All looked upon her with respect; and even the queen treated her with politeness. Catherine showed, however, that she had remarked the king's preference. One day, as she was playing at cards with her maid of honour, while Henry was in the room, Anne frequently holding the *king*, she said: "My Lady Anne, you have good hap to stop ever at a *king*; but you are not like others, you will have all or none." Anne blushed: from that moment Henry's attentions acquired more importance; she resolved to withdraw from them, and quitted the court with Lady Rochford.

The king, who was not accustomed to resistance, was extremely grieved; and having learnt that Anne would not return to the court either with or without her mother, sent a courier to Hever with a message and a letter for her. If we recollect the manners of the age of Henry VIII, and how far the men, in their relations with the gentler sex, were strangers to that reserve which society now imposes upon them, we cannot but be struck by the king's respectful tone: He writes thus in French:

"As the time seems to me very long since I heard from you or concerning your health, the great love I have for you has constrained me to send this bearer to be better informed both of your health and pleasure; particularly, because since my last parting with you, I have been told that you have entirely changed the mind in which I left you, and that you neither mean to come to court with your mother nor any other way; which report, if true, I cannot enough marvel at, being persuaded in my own mind that I have never committed any offence against you; and it seems hard, in return for the great love I bear you, to be kept at a distance from the person and presence of the woman in the world that I value the most. And if you love me with as much affection as I hope you do, I am sure the distance of our two persons would be equally irksome to you, though this does not belong so much to the mistress as to the servant.

"Consider well, my mistress, how greatly your absence afflicts me. I hope it is not your will that it should be so; but if I heard for certain that you yourself desired it, I could but mourn my ill-fortune, and strive by degrees to abate of my great folly.

'And so for lack of time I make an end of this rude letter, beseeching you to give the bearer credence in all he will tell you from me. Written by the hand of your entire servant,

"H. R."[1]

The word *servant* (serviteur) employed in this letter explains the sense in which Henry used the word *mistress*. In the language of chivalry, the latter term expressed a person to whom the lover had surrendered his heart.

It would seem that Anne's reply to this letter was the same she had made to the king from the very first; and Cardinal Pole mentions more than once her obstinate refusal of an adulterous love. At last Henry understood Anne's virtue; but he was far from *abating of his great folly*, as he had promised. That tyrannical selfishness, which the prince often displayed in his life, was shown particularly in his amours. Seeing that he could not attain his end by illegitimate means, he determined to break, as quickly as possible, the bonds which united him to the queen. Anne's virtue was the third cause of Henry's divorce.

His resolution being once taken, it must needs be carried out. Henry having succeeded in bringing Anne back to court, procured a private interview with her, offered her his crown, and, seizing her hand, took off one of her rings. But Anne, who would not be the king's mistress, refused also to be his wife. The glory of a crown could not dazzle her, said Wyatt, and two motives in particular counterbalanced all the prospects of greatness which were set before her eyes. The first was her respect for the queen: "How could I injure a princess of such great virtue?" she exclaimed. The second was the fear that a union with "one that was her lord and her king," would not give her that freedom of heart and that liberty which she would enjoy by marrying a man of the same rank with herself.

Yet the noblemen and ladies of Henry's court whispered to one another that Anne would certainly become queen of England. Some were tormented by jealousy; others, her friends, were delighted at the prospect of a rapid advancement. Wolsey's

[1] It is difficult to fix the order and chronology of Henry's letters to Anne Boleyn. This is the second in the Vatican Collection, but it appears to us to be of older date. It is considered as written in May 1528; we are inclined to place it in the autumn of 1527. The originals of these letters, chiefly in old French, are still preserved in the Vatican, having been stolen from Anne's cabinet and conveyed thither.

enemies in particular were charmed at the thought of ruining the favourite. It was at the very moment when all these emotions were so variously agitating the court that the cardinal, returning from his embassy to Francis, re-appeared in London, where an unexpected blow struck him.

Wolsey was expressing his grief to Henry at having failed in obtaining either Margaret or Renée for him, when the king interrupted him: "Console yourself, I shall marry Anne Boleyn." The cardinal remained speechless for a moment. What would become of him, if the king placed the crown of England on the head of the daughter and niece of his greatest enemies? What would become of the church, if a second Anne of Bohemia should ascend the throne? Wolsey threw himself at the feet of his master, and entreated him to renounce so fatal a project. It was then no doubt that he remained (as he afterwards said) *an hour or two* on his knees before the king in his privy chamber, but without prevailing on Henry to give up his design. Wolsey, persuaded that if he continued openly to oppose Henry's will, he would for ever lose his confidence, dissembled his vexation, waiting an opportunity to get rid of this unfortunate rival by some intrigue. He began by writing to the pope, informing him that a young lady, brought up by the queen of Navarre, and consequently tainted by the Lutheran heresy, had captivated the king's heart; and from that hour Anne Boleyn became the object of the hatred and calumnies of Rome. But at the same time, to conceal his intentions, Wolsey received Henry at a series of splendid entertainments, at which Anne outshone all the ladies of the court.

CHAPTER SEVEN

Bilney in Strength and Weakness
(1527)

WHILE these passions were agitating Henry's palace, the most moving scenes, produced by Christian faith, were stirring the nation. Bilney, animated by that courage which God sometimes gives to the weakest men, seemed to have lost his natural timidity, and preached for a time with an energy quite apostolic. He taught that all men should first acknowledge their sins and condemn them, and then hunger and thirst after that righteousness which Jesus Christ gives. To this testimony borne to the truth, he added his testimony against error. "These five hundred years," he added, "there hath been no good pope ... for they have neither preached nor lived well, nor conformably to their dignity; wherefore, unto this day, they have borne the keys of simony."

As soon as he descended from the pulpit, this pious scholar, with his friend, Thomas Arthur, visited the neighbouring towns and villages. "The Jews and Saracens would long ago have become believers," he once said at Wilsdon, "had it not been for the idolatry of Christian men in offering candles, wax, and money to stocks and stones." One day when he visited Ipswich, where there was a Franciscan monastery, he exclaimed: "The cowl of St Francis wrapped round a dead body hath no power to take away sins. . . . *Ecce agnus Dei qui tollit peccata mundi.*" (John i. 29.) The monks, who were little versed in Scripture, had recourse to the *Almanac* to convict the *Bible* of error. "St Paul did rightly affirm," said Friar John Brusierd, "that there is but one mediator of God and man, because as yet there was no *saint* canonized or put into the calendar."—"Let us ask of the Father in the name of the Son," rejoined Bilney, "and he will give unto us. He says not, whatsoever ye shall ask of the Father in the name of St Peter, St Paul, or other saints, but in My name."—"You are always speaking of the Father and never of the *saints*," replied the friar; "you are like a man who has been looking so long upon the sun, that he can see nothing else." As he uttered these words the monk seemed bursting with anger. "If I did not believe and know that God and all His saints would take everlasting vengeance upon you, I would surely with these nails of mine be your death." Twice in fact did two monks pull him out of his pulpit. He was arrested and taken to London.

Arthur, instead of fleeing, began to visit the flocks which his friend had converted. "Good people," said he, "if I should suffer persecution for the preaching of the gospel, there are seven thousand more that would preach it as I do now. Therefore, good people! good people!" (and he repeated these words several times in a sorrowful voice) "think not that if these tyrants and persecutors put a man to death, the preaching of the gospel therefore is to be forsaken. Every Christian man, yea every layman, is a priest. Let our adversaries preach by the authority of the cardinal; others by the authority of the university; others by the pope's; we will preach by the authority of God. It is not the man who brings the Word that saves the soul, but the Word which the man brings. Neither bishops nor popes have the right to forbid any man to preach the gospel; and if they kill him he is not a heretic but a martyr." The priests were horrified at such doctrines. In their opinion, there was no God out of their church, no salvation out of their sacrifices. Arthur was thrown into the same prison as Bilney.

On the 27th of November 1527 the cardinal and the archbishop of Canterbury, with a great number of bishops, divines, and lawyers, met in the chapter-house of Westminster, when Bilney and Arthur were brought before them. But the king's prime minister thought it beneath his dignity to occupy his time with miserable heretics. Wolsey had hardly commenced the examination, when he rose, saying: "The affairs of the realm call me away; all such as are found guilty, you will compel them to abjure, and those who rebel you will deliver over to the secular power." After a few questions proposed by the bishop of London, the two accused men were led back to prison.

Abjuration or death—that was Wolsey's order. But the conduct of the trial was confided to Tunstall; Bilney conceived some hope. "Is it possible," he said to himself, "that the bishop of London, the friend of Erasmus, will gratify the monks? . . . I must tell him that it was the Greek Testament of his learned master that led me to the faith." Upon which the humble evangelist, having obtained paper and ink, set about writing to the bishop from his gloomy prison those admirable letters which have been transmitted to posterity. Tunstall, who was not a cruel man, was deeply moved, and then a strange struggle took place: a judge wishing to save the prisoner, the prisoner desiring to give up his life. Tunstall, by acquitting Bilney, had no desire to compromise himself. "Submit to the church," said the bishop, "for God speaks only through it." But Bilney, who knew that God speaks in the Scriptures, remained inflexible. "Very well, then," said Tunstall, taking up the prisoner's eloquent letters, "in discharge of my conscience I shall lay these letters before the court." He hoped, perhaps, that they would touch his colleagues, but he was deceived. He determined, therefore, to make a fresh attempt. On the 4th of December, Bilney was brought again before the court. "Abjure your errors," said Tunstall. Bilney refusing by a shake of the head, the bishop continued: "Retire into the next room and consider." Bilney withdrew, and returning shortly after with joy beaming in his eyes, Tunstall thought he had gained the victory. "You will return to the church, then?" said he. . . . Bilney answered calmly:" Let judgment be done in the Name of the Lord."— "Be quick," continued the bishop, "this is the last moment, and you will be condemned."—"This is the day which the Lord hath made," answered Bilney, "we will rejoice and be glad in it." Upon this Tunstall took off his cap, and said: "In the Name of the Father and of the Son and of the Holy Ghost . . . let God arise and let His enemies be scattered." Then making the sign of the cross on his forehead and on his breast, he gave judgment: "Thomas Bilney, I pronounce thee convicted of heresy." He was about to name the penalty . . . a last hope restrained him; he stopped: "For the rest of the sentence we take deliberation until to-morrow." Thus was the struggle prolonged between two men, one of whom desired to walk to the stake, the other to bar the way as it were with his own body.

"Will you return to the unity of the church?" asked Tunstall the next day. "I hope I was never separated from the church," answered Bilney. "Go and consult with some of your friends," said the bishop, who was resolved to save his life; "I will give you till one o'clock in the afternoon." In the afternoon Bilney made the same answer. "I will give you two nights' respite to deliberate," said the bishop; "on Saturday at nine o'clock in the forenoon, the court will expect a plain definitive answer." Tunstall reckoned on the night with its dreams, its anguish, and its terrors, to bring about Bilney's recantation.

This extraordinary struggle occupied many minds both in court and city. Anne Boleyn and Henry VIII watched with interest the various phases of this tragic history. What will happen? was the general question. Will he give way? Shall we see him live or die? One day and two nights still remained; everything was tried to shake the Cambridge doctor. His friends crowded to his prison; he was overwhelmed with arguments and examples; but an inward struggle, far more terrible than those without, agitated the pious Bilney. "Whoever will save his soul shall lose it," Christ had said. That selfish love of his soul, which is found even in the advanced Christian—that self, which, after his conversion had been not absorbed, but overruled by the Spirit of God, gradually recovered strength in his heart, in the presence of disgrace and death. His friends who wished to save him, not understanding that the fallen Bilney would be Bilney no longer, conjured him with tears to have pity on himself; and by these means his firmness was overcome. The bishop pressed him, and Bilney asked himself: "Can a young soldier like me know the rules of war better than an old soldier like Tunstall? Or can a poor silly sheep know his way to the fold better than the chief pastor of London?" His friends quitted him neither night nor day and, entangled by their fatal affection, he believed at last that he had found a compromise which would set his conscience at rest. "I will preserve my life," he said, "to dedicate it to the Lord." This delusion had scarcely laid hold of his mind before his views were confused, his faith was veiled, the Holy Ghost departed from him, God gave him over to his carnal thoughts and, under the pretext of being useful to Jesus Christ for many years, Bilney disobeyed Him at the present moment. Being led before the bishops on the morning of Saturday the 7th of December, at nine o'clock, he fell . . . (Arthur had fallen before him), and whilst the false friends who had misled him hardly dared raise their eyes, the living church of Christ in England uttered a cry of anguish. "If ever you come in danger, in durance, in prison," said Latimer, "for God's quarrel, I would advise you, above all things, to abjure all your friends, all your friendships; leave not one unabjured. It is they that shall undo you, and not your enemies. It was his very friends that brought Bilney to it."[1]

On the following day (Sunday, 8th December) Bilney was placed at the head of a procession, and the fallen disciple, bareheaded, with a faggot on his shoulders, stood in front of St Paul's cross, while a priest from the pulpit exhorted him to repentance; after which he was led back to prison.

What a solitude for the wretched man! At one time the cold darkness of his cell appeared to him as a burning fire; at another he fancied he heard accusing voices crying to him in the silence of the night. Death, the very enemy he had wished to avoid, fixed his icy glance upon him and filled him with fear. He strove to escape from the horrible spectre, but in vain. Then the friends who had dragged him into this abyss, crowded round and endeavoured to console him; but if they gave utterance to any of Christ's gentle promises, Bilney started back with affright and shrank to the farthest part of the dungeon, with a cry "as though a man had run him through the heart with a sword."[2] Having denied the Word of God, he could no longer endure to hear it. The curse of the Apocalypse: *Ye mountains, hide me from the wrath of the Lamb!* was the only passage of Scripture in harmony with his soul. His mind wandered, the blood froze in his veins, he sank under his terrors; he lost all sense, and almost his life, and lay motionless in the arms of his astonished friends. "God," exclaimed those unhappy individuals who had caused his fall, "God, by a just judgment, delivers up to the tempests of their conscience all who deny his truth."

This was not the only sorrow of the church. As soon as Richard Bayfield, the late chamberlain of St Edmunds' Bury, had joined Tyndale and Fryth, he said to them: "I am at your disposal; you shall be my head and I will be your hand; I will sell your books and those of the German reformers in the Low Countries, France, and England." It was not long indeed before he returned to London. But Pierson, the priest whom he

[1] Latimer's *Sermons* (Parker Society), p. 222.   [2] Ibid.

had formerly met in Lombard Street, found him again, and accused him to the bishop. The unhappy man was brought before Tunstall. "You are charged," said the prelate, "with having asserted that praise is due to God alone, and not to saints or creatures." Bayfield acknowledged the charge to be true. "You are accused of maintaining that every priest may preach the Word of God by the authority of the gospel without the licence of the pope or cardinals." This also Bayfield acknowledged. A penance was imposed on him; and then he was sent back to his monastery with orders to show himself there on the 25th of April. But he crossed the sea once more, and hastened to join Tyndale.

The New Testaments, however, sold by him and others remained in England. At that time the bishops subscribed to suppress the Scriptures, as so many persons have since done to circulate them; and, accordingly, a great number of the copies brought over by Bayfield and his friends were bought up. A scarcity of food was erelong added to the scarcity of the Word of God; for as the cardinal was endeavouring to foment a war between Henry and the Emperor, the Flemish ships ceased to enter the English ports. It was in consequence of this that the lord mayor and aldermen of London hastened to express their apprehensions to Wolsey almost before he had recovered from the fatigues of his return from France. "Fear nothing," he told them; "the king of France assured me, that if he had three bushels of wheat, England should have two of them." But none arrived, and the people were on the point of breaking out into violence, when a fleet of ships suddenly appeared off the mouth of the Thames. They were German and Flemish vessels laden with corn, in which the worthy people of the Low Countries had also concealed the New Testament. An Antwerp bookseller, named John Raimond or Ruremond, from his birthplace, had printed a fourth edition more beautiful than the previous ones. It was enriched with references and engravings on wood, and each page bordered with red lines. Raimond himself had embarked on board one of the ships with five hundred copies of his New Testament. About Christmas 1527, the book of God was circulated in England along with the bread that nourishes the body. But certain priests and monks, having discovered the Scriptures among the sacks of corn, carried several copies to the bishop of London, who threw Raimond into prison. The greater part, however, of the new edition escaped him. The New Testament was read everywhere, and even the court did not escape the contagion. Anne Boleyn, notwithstanding her smiling face, often withdrew to her rooms at Greenwich or at Hampton Court, to study the gospel. Frank, courageous, and proud, she did not conceal the pleasure she found in such reading; her boldness astonished the courtiers, and exasperated the clergy. In the city things went still further: the New Testament was explained in frequent conventicles, particularly in the house of one Russell, and great was the joy among the faithful. "It is sufficient only to enter London," said the priests, "to become a heretic!" The Reformation was taking root among the people before it arrived at the upper classes.

CHAPTER EIGHT

The Campaign for Henry's Divorce
(1527)

THE sun of the Word of God, which daily grew brighter in the sky of the sixteenth century, was sufficient to scatter all the darkness in England; but popery, like an immense wall, intercepted its rays. Britain had hardly received the Scriptures in Greek and Latin, and then in English, before the priests began to make war upon them with indefatigable zeal. It was necessary that the wall should be thrown down in order that the sun might penetrate freely among the Anglo-Saxon people. And now events were ripening in England, destined to make a great breach in popery. The negotiations of Henry VIII with Clement VII play an important part in the Reformation. By showing up the Court of Rome, they destroyed the respect which the people felt for it; they took away that *power and strength*, as Scripture says, which the monarchy had given it; and the throne of the pope once fallen in England, Jesus Christ uplifted and strengthened His own.

Henry, ardently desiring an heir, and thinking that he had found the woman that would ensure his own and England's happiness, conceived the design of severing the ties that united him to the queen, and with this view he consulted his most favourite councillors about the divorce. There was one in particular whose approval he coveted: this was Sir Thomas More. One day as Erasmus' friend was walking with his master in the beautiful gallery at Hampton Court, giving him an account of a mission he had just executed on the continent, the king suddenly interrupted him: "My marriage with the queen," he said, "is contrary to the laws of God, of the church, and of nature." He then took up the Bible, and pointed out the passages in his favour. "I am not a theologian," said More, somewhat embarrassed; "your majesty should consult a council of doctors."

Accordingly, by Henry's order, Warham assembled the most learned canonists at Hampton Court; but weeks passed away before they could agree. Most of them quoted in the king's favour those passages in Leviticus (xviii. 16; xx. 21,) which forbid a man to take *his brother's wife*. But Fisher, bishop of Rochester, and the other opponents of the divorce, replied that, according to Deuteronomy (xxv. 5,) when a woman is left a widow without children, her brother-in-law ought to take her to wife, to perpetuate his brother's name in Israel. "This law concerned the Jews only," replied the partisans of the divorce; they added that its object was "to maintain the inheritances distinct, and the genealogies intact, until the coming of Christ. The Judaical dispensation has passed away; but the law of Leviticus, which is a moral law, is binding upon all men in all ages."

To free themselves from their embarrassment, the bishops demanded that the most eminent universities should be consulted; and commissioners were forthwith despatched to Oxford, Cambridge, Paris, Orleans, Toulouse, Louvain, Padua, and Bologna, furnished with money to reward the foreign doctors for the time and trouble this question would cost them. This caused some little delay, and every means was now to be tried to divert the king from his purpose.

Wolsey, who was the first to suggest the idea of a divorce, was now thoroughly alarmed. It appeared to him that a nod from the daughter of the Boleyns would hurl him from the post he had so laboriously won, and this made him vent his ill-humour on all about him, at one time threatening Warham, and at another persecuting Pace. But fearing to oppose Henry openly, he summoned from Paris, Clarke, bishop of Bath and Wells, at that time ambassador to the French court. The latter entered into his views, and after cautiously preparing the way, he ventured to say to the king: "The progress of the inquiry will be so slow, your majesty, that it will take more than seven years to bring it to an end!"—"Since my patience has already held out for *eighteen* years," the king replied coldly, "I am willing to wait *four* or *five* more."

As the political party had failed, the clerical party set in motion a scheme of another kind. A young woman, Elizabeth Barton, known as *the holy maid of Kent*, had been subject from childhood to epileptic fits. The priest of her parish, named Masters, had persuaded her that she was inspired of God and, confederating with one Bocking, a monk of Canterbury, he turned the weakness of the prophetess to account. Elizabeth wandered over the country, passing from house to house, and from convent to convent; on a sudden her limbs would become rigid, her features distorted; violent convulsions shook her body, and strange unintelligible sounds fell from her lips, which the amazed bystanders received as revelations from the Virgin and the saints. Fisher, bishop of Rochester, Abel, the queen's ecclesiastical agent, and even Sir Thomas More, were among the number of Elizabeth's partisans. Rumours of the divorce having reached the maid's ears, an angel commanded her to appear before the cardinal. As soon as she stood in his presence, the colour fled from her cheeks, her limbs trembled and, falling into an ecstasy, she exclaimed: "Cardinal of York, God has placed three swords in your hand: the spiritual sword, to range the church under the authority of the pope; the civil sword, to govern the realm; and the sword of justice, to prevent the divorce of the king. . . . If you do not wield these three swords faithfully, God will lay it sore to your charge." After these words the prophetess withdrew.

But other influences were then dividing Wolsey's breast: hatred, which induced him to oppose the divorce; and ambition, which foreboded his ruin in this opposition. At last ambition prevailed, and he resolved to make his objections forgotten by the energy of his zeal.

Henry hastened to profit by this change. "Declare the divorce yourself," said he to Wolsey, "has not the pope named you his vicar-general?" The cardinal was not anxious to raise himself so high. "If I were to decide the affair," said he, "the queen would appeal to the pope; we must therefore either apply to the holy father for special powers, or persuade the queen to retire to a nunnery. And if we fail in either of these expedients, we will obey the voice of conscience, even in despite of the pope." It was arranged to begin with the more regular attempt, and Gregory Da Casale, secretary Knight, and the prothonotary Gambara, were appointed to an extraordinary mission at the pontifical court. Casale was Wolsey's man, and Knight was Henry's. Wolsey told the envoys: "You will demand of the pope. 1*stly*, a *commission* authorizing me to inquire into this matter; 2*ndly*, his promise to pronounce the nullity of Catherine's marriage with Henry, if we should find that her marriage with Arthur was consummated; and 3*rdly*, a *dispensation* permitting the king to marry again." In this manner Wolsey hoped to make sure of the divorce without damaging the papal authority. It was insinuated that false representations, with regard to the consummation of the first marriage, had been sent from England to Julius II, which had induced the pontiff to permit the second. The pope being deceived as to the *fact*, his infallibility was untouched. Wolsey desired something more; knowing that no confidence could be put in the good faith of the pontiff, he demanded a fourth instrument by which the pope should bind himself *never to recall the other three;* he only forgot to take precautions in case Clement should withdraw *the fourth.* "With these four snares, skilfully combined," said the cardinal, "I shall catch the hare; if he escapes from one, he will fall into the other." The courtiers anticipated a speedy termination of the affair. Was not the Emperor the declared enemy of the pontiff? Had not Henry, on the contrary, made himself *protector of the Clementine league?* Could Clement hesitate, when called upon, to choose between his jailer and his benefactor?

Indeed, Charles V, at this moment, was in a very embarrassing position. It is true, his guards were posted at the gates of the castle of St Angelo, where Clement was a prisoner, and people in Rome said to one another with a smile: "Now indeed it is true, *Papa non potest errare.*"[1] But it was not possible to keep the pope a prisoner in Rome; and then what was to be done with him? The viceroy of Naples proposed to Alercon, the governor of St Angelo, to remove Clement to Gaeta; but the affrighted colonel exclaimed: "Heaven forbid that I should drag after me the very body of God!" Charles thought at one time of transporting the pontiff to Spain; but might not an enemy's fleet carry him off the road? The pope in prison was far more embarrassing to Charles than the pope at liberty.

It was at this critical time that Francis Philip, Queen Catherine's servant, having escaped the snares laid by Henry

---

[1] The pope cannot err—a play upon the double meaning of the word *errare.*

The banks of the Thames where Tyndale's New Testament was first landed in 1526, and hidden in the cellars of men like Thomas Garret, in defiance of the Bishop of London's ban. From the painting *Old London Bridge* by Claude de Jongh. See page 246.

[*To face p.* 320

Cardinal Wolsey at the Trial of Catherine of Aragon and Henry VIII at Blackfriars 1529.
The painting by F. O. Salisbury in the House of Lords.

VIII and Wolsey, arrived at Madrid, where he passed a whole day in conference with Charles V. This prince was at first astonished, shocked even, by the designs of the king of England. The curse of God seemed to hang over his house. Charles' mother was a lunatic; his sister of Denmark expelled from her dominions; his sister of Hungary made a widow by the battle of Mohacz; the Turks were encroaching upon his territories; Lautrec was victorious in Italy, and the catholics, irritated by the pope's captivity, detested his ambition. This was not enough. Henry VIII was striving to divorce his aunt, and the pope would naturally give his aid to this criminal design. Charles must choose between the pontiff and the king. The friendship of the king of England might aid him in breaking the league formed to expel him from Italy, and by sacrificing Catherine he would be sure to obtain his support; but placed between reasons of state and his aunt's honour, the Emperor did not hesitate; he even renounced certain projects of reform that he had at heart. He suddenly decided for the pope, and from that very hour followed a new course.

Charles, who possessed great discernment, had understood his age; he had seen that concessions were called for by the movement of the human mind, and would have desired to carry out the change from the middle ages to modern times by a carefully-managed transition. He had consequently demanded a council to reform the church and weaken the Romish dominion in Europe. But very different was the result. If Charles turned away from Henry, he was obliged to turn towards Clement; and after having compelled the head of the church to enter a prison, it was necessary to place him once more upon the throne. Charles V sacrificed the interests of Christian society to the interests of his own family. This divorce, which in England has been looked upon as the ruin of the popedom, was what saved it in continental Europe.

But how could the Emperor win the heart of the pontiff, filled as it was with bitterness and anger? He selected for this difficult mission a friar of great ability, De Angelis, general of the Spanish Observance, and ordered him to proceed to the castle of St Angelo under the pretext of negotiating the liberation of the holy father. The cordelier was conducted to the strongest part of the fortress, called the Rock, where Clement

x

was lodged; and the two priests brought all their craft to bear on each other. The monk, assisted by the artful Moncade, adroitly mingled together the pope's deliverance and Catherine's marriage. He affirmed that the Emperor wished to open the gates of the pontiff's prison, and had already given the order; and then he added immediately: "The Emperor is determined to maintain the rights of his aunt, and will never consent to the divorce."—"If you are a *good shepherd* to me," wrote Charles to the pope with his own hand on the 22nd of November, 1527, "I will be a *good sheep* to you." Clement smiled as he read these words; he understood his position; the Emperor had need of the priest, Charles was at his captive's feet; Clement was saved! The divorce was a rope fallen from the skies which could not fail to drag him out of the pit; he had only to cling to it quietly to reascend his throne. Accordingly from that hour Clement appeared less eager to quit the castle than Charles to liberate him. "So long as the divorce is in suspense," thought the crafty De Medici, "I have two great friends; but as soon as I declare for one, I shall have a mortal enemy in the other." He promised the monk to come to no decision in the matter without informing the Emperor.

Meantime Knight, the envoy of the impatient monarch, having heard, as he crossed the Alps, that the pope was at liberty, hastened on to Parma, where he met Gambara: "He is not free yet," replied the prothonotary; "but the general of the Franciscans hopes to terminate his captivity in a few days. Continue your journey," he added. Knight could not do so without great danger. He was told at Foligno, sixty miles from the metropolis, that if he had not a safe-conduct he could not reach Rome without exposing his life; Knight halted. Just then a messenger from Henry brought him despatches more pressing than ever; Knight started again with one servant and a guide. At Monte Rotondo he was nearly murdered by the inhabitants; but on the next day (25th November), protected by a violent storm of wind and rain, Henry's envoy entered Rome at ten o'clock without being observed, and kept himself concealed.

It was impossible to speak with Clement, for the Emperor's orders were positive. Knight, therefore, began to *practise* upon the cardinals; he gained over the Cardinal of Pisa, by whose means his despatches were laid before the pontiff. Clement after reading them laid them down with a smile of satisfaction. "Good!" said he, "here is *the other* coming to me now!" But night had hardly closed in before the Cardinal of Pisa's secretary hastened to Knight and told him: "Don Alercon is informed of your arrival; and the pope entreats you to depart immediately." This officer had scarcely left him, when the prothonotary Gambara arrived in great agitation: "His holiness presses you to leave; as soon as he is at liberty, he will attend to your master's request." Two hours after this, two hundred Spanish soldiers arrived, surrounded the house in which Knight had concealed himself, and searched it from top to bottom, but to no purpose; the English agent had escaped.

Knight's safety was not the true motive which induced Clement to urge his departure. The very day on which the pope received the message from the king of England, he signed a treaty with Charles V, restoring him, under certain conditions, to both his powers. At the same time the pontiff, for greater security, pressed the French general Lautrec to hasten his march to Rome in order to save him from the hands of the Emperor. Clement, a disciple of Machiavelli, thus gave the right hand to Charles and the left to Francis; and as he had not another for Henry, he made him the most positive promises. Each of the three princes could reckon on the pope's friendship, and on the same grounds.

The 10th of December (1527) was the day on which Clement's imprisonment would terminate; but he preferred to owe his freedom to intrigue rather than to the Emperor's generosity. He therefore procured the dress of a tradesman, and, on the evening before the day fixed for his deliverance, his ward being already much relaxed, he escaped from the castle, and, accompanied only by Louis of Gonzago in his flight, he made his way to Orvieto.[1]

[1] [The vacillations of Pope Clement VII (1523–34) are noteworthy. He was distressed by the long rivalry between the Houses of Hapsburg (Spain and the Empire) and Valois (France). At length he decided to side with Francis I of France, but that king's crushing defeat at Pavia (1525) caused him to come to terms with Charles, only to depart from him again by joining a League of Freedom which aimed at asserting the independence of Italy from foreign powers. On the failure of this movement, Clement again submitted to Charles the Emperor, but a year later he absolved Francis from his oath to submit to Charles (entered into at Madrid after a long captivity), and helped to form the Holy League of Cognac, by which

While Clement was experiencing all the joy of a man just escaped from prison, Henry was a prey to the most violent agitation. Having ceased to love Catherine, he persuaded himself that he was the victim of his father's ambition, a martyr to duty, and the champion of conjugal sanctity. His very gait betrayed his vexation and, even among the gay conversation of the court, deep sighs would escape from his bosom. He had frequent interviews with Wolsey. "I regard the safety of my soul above all things," he said; "but I am concerned also for the peace of my kingdom. For a long while an unceasing remorse has been gnawing at my conscience, and my thoughts dwell upon my marriage with unutterable sorrow. God, in His wrath, has taken away my sons, and if I persevere in this unlawful union, He will visit me with still more terrible chastisements. My only hope is in the holy father." Wolsey replied with a low bow: "Please your majesty, I am occupied with this business, as if it were my only means of winning heaven."

And indeed he redoubled his exertions. He wrote to Sir Gregory Da Casale on the 5th of December (1527): "You will procure an audience of the pope at any price. Disguise yourself, appear before him as the servant of some nobleman, or as a messenger from the duke of Ferrara. Scatter money plentifully; sacrifice everything, provided you procure a secret interview with his holiness; ten thousand ducats are at your disposal. You will explain to Clement the king's scruples, and the necessity of providing for the continuance of his house and the peace of his kingdom. You will tell him that in order to restore him to liberty, the king is ready to declare war against the Emperor, and thus show himself to all the world to be a true son of the church."

Wolsey saw clearly that it was essential to represent the

he, France, and the leading Italian states, bound themselves to resist the ambitions of Charles. Then followed the Imperial invasion of Italy to break the League, and the sack of Rome (May 1527) which horrified the West. Clement remained Charles' prisoner from June to December 1527. In 1528 Francis once more made war in Italy, but eventually Charles again proved victorious, and for several years Clement VII became dependent upon him. This dependence had important bearings on the English divorce question, for Clement would not nullify the marriage between Henry and Catherine while he was in the power of Charles, the nephew of Catherine. Hence Wolsey could make no real progress in his suit.]

divorce to Clement VII as a means likely to secure the safety of the popedom. The cardinal, therefore, wrote again to Da Casale on the 6th of December: "Night and day, I revolve in my mind the actual condition of the church, and seek the means best calculated to extricate the pope from the gulf into which he has fallen. While I was turning these thoughts over in my mind during a sleepless night . . . one way suddenly occurred to me. I said to myself, the king must be prevailed upon to undertake the defence of the holy father. This was no easy matter, for his majesty is strongly attached to the Emperor; however, I set about my task. I told the king that his holiness was ready to satisfy him; I staked my honour; I succeeded. . . . To save the pope, my master will sacrifice his treasures, subjects, kingdom, and even his life. . . . I therefore conjure his holiness to entertain our just demand."

Never before had such pressing entreaties been made to a pope by the government of England.

The Dilemma and Duplicity of Clement VII

(1527–28)

THE envoys of the king of England appeared in the character of the saviours of Rome. This was doubtless no stratagem; and Wolsey probably regarded that thought as coming from heaven, which had visited him during the weary sleepless night. The zeal of his agents increased. The pope was hardly set at liberty, before Knight and Da Casale appeared at the foot of the precipitous rock on which Orvieto is built, and demanded to be introduced to Clement VII. Nothing could be more compromising to the pontiff than such a visit. How could he appear on good terms with England, when Rome and all his states were still in the hands of Catherine's nephew? The pope's mind was utterly bewildered by the demand of the two envoys. He recovered however; to reject the powerful hand extended to him by England, was not without its danger; and as he knew well how to bring a difficult negotiation to a successful conclusion, Clement regained confidence in his skill, and gave orders to introduce Henry's ambassadors.

Their discourse was not without eloquence. "Never was the church in a more critical position," said they. "The unmeasured ambition of the kings who claim to dispose of spiritual affairs at their own pleasure (this was aimed at Charles V) holds the apostolical bark suspended over an abyss. The only port open to it in the tempest is the favour of the august prince whom we represent, and who has always been the shield of the faith. But, alas! this monarch, the impregnable bulwark of your holiness, is himself the prey of tribulations almost equal to your own. His conscience torn by remorse, his crown without an heir, his kingdom without security, his people exposed once more to perpetual disorders. . . . Nay, the whole Christian world given up to the most cruel discord. . . . Such are the consequences of a fatal union which God has marked with his displeasure. . . . There are also," they added in a lower tone, "certain things of which his majesty cannot speak in his letter . . . certain incurable disorders under which the queen suffers, which will never permit the king to look upon her again as his wife. If your holiness puts an end to such wretchedness by annulling his unlawful marriage, you will attach his majesty by an indissoluble bond. Assistance, riches, armies, crown, and even life—the king our master is ready to employ all in the service of Rome. He stretches out his hand to you, most holy father . . . stretch out yours to him; by your union the church will be saved, and Europe will be saved with it."

Clement was cruelly embarrassed. His policy consisted in holding the balance between the two princes, and he was now called upon to decide in favour of one of them. He began to regret that he had ever received Henry's ambassadors. "Consider my position," he said to them, "and entreat the king to wait until more favourable events leave me at liberty to act."— "What!" replied Knight proudly, "has not your holiness promised to consider his majesty's prayer? If you fail in your promise now, how can I persuade the king that you will keep it some future day?" Da Casale thought the time had come to strike a decisive blow. "What evils," he exclaimed, "what inevitable misfortunes your refusal will create! . . . The Emperor thinks only of depriving the church of its power, and the king of England alone has sworn to maintain it." Then speaking lower, more slowly, and dwelling upon every word, he continued: "We fear that his majesty, reduced to such extremities . . . of the two evils will choose the *least*, and supported by the purity of his intentions, will do *of his own authority* . . . what he now so respectfully demands. . . . What should we see then? . . . I shudder at the thought. . . . Let not your holiness indulge in a false security which will inevitably drag you into the abyss. . . . Read all . . . remark all . . . divine all . . . take note of all. . . . Most holy father, this is a question of life and death." And Da Casale's tone said more than his words.

Clement understood that a positive refusal would expose him to lose England. Placed between Henry and Charles, as between the hammer and the anvil, he resolved to gain time. "Well then," he said to Knight and Da Casale, "I will do what you ask; but I am not familiar with the *forms* these dispensations require. . . . I will consult the Cardinal *Sanctorum Quatuor* on the subject . . . and then will inform you."

Knight and Da Casale, wishing to anticipate Clement VII, hastened to Lorenzo Pucci, cardinal Ṣanctorum Quatuor, and intimated to him that their master would know how to be grateful. The cardinal assured the deputies of his affection for Henry VIII, and they, in the fulness of their gratitude, laid before him the four documents which they were anxious to get executed. But the cardinal had hardly looked at the first—the proposal that Wolsey should decide the matter of the divorce in England—when he exclaimed: "Impossible! . . . a bull in such terms would cover with eternal disgrace not only his holiness and the king, but even the cardinal of York himself." The deputies were confounded, for Wolsey had ordered them to ask the pope for nothing but his signature. Recovering themselves, they rejoined: "All that we require is a *competent* commission." On his part, the pope wrote Henry a letter, in which he managed to say nothing.

Of the four required documents there were two on whose immediate despatch Knight and Da Casale insisted: these were the *commission* to pronounce the divorce, and the *dispensation* to contract a second marriage. The *dispensation* without the *commission* was of no value; this the pope knew well; accordingly he resolved to give the *dispensation* only. It was as if Charles had granted Clement when in prison permission to visit his cardinals, but denied him liberty to leave the castle of St Angelo. It is in such a manner as this that a religious system transformed into a political system has recourse, when it is without power, to stratagem. "The *commission*," said the artful Medici to Knight, "must be corrected according to the style of our court; but here is the *dispensation*." Knight took the document; it was addressed to Henry VIII and ran thus: "We accord to you, in case your marriage with Catherine shall be declared null, free liberty to take another wife, provided she have not been the wife of your brother. . . ." The Englishman was duped by the Italian. "In my poor judgment," he said, "this document will be of use to us." After this Clement appeared to concern himself solely about Knight's health, and suddenly manifested the greatest interest for him. "It is proper that you should hasten your departure," said he, "for it is necessary that you should travel *at your ease*. Gambara will follow you post, and bring the commission." Knight thus mystified, took leave of the pope, who got rid of Da Casale and Gambara in a similar manner. He then began to breathe once more. There was no diplomacy in Europe which Rome, even in its greatest weakness, could not easily dupe.

It had now become necessary to elude the commission. While the king's envoys were departing in good spirits, reckoning on the document that was to follow them, the general of the Spanish Observance reiterated to the pontiff in every tone: "Be careful to give no document authorizing the divorce and, above all, do not permit this affair to be judged in Henry's realm." The cardinals drew up the document under the influence of De Angelis, and made it a masterpiece of insignificance. If good theology ennobles the heart, bad theology, so fertile in subtleties, imparts to the mind a skill by no means common; and hence the most celebrated diplomatists have often been churchmen. The act being thus drawn up, the pope despatched three copies, to Knight, to Da Casale, and to Gambara. Knight was near Bologna when the courier overtook him. He was stupified, and taking post-horses returned with all haste to Orvieto. Gambara proceeded through France to England with the useless *dispensation* which the pope had granted.

Knight had thought to meet with more good faith at the court of the pope than with kings, and he had been outwitted. What would Wolsey and Henry say of his folly? His wounded self-esteem began to make him believe all that Tyndale and Luther said of the popedom. The former had just published the *Obedience of a Christian Man*, and the *Parable of the Wicked Mammon*, in which he represented Rome as one of the transformations of Antichrist. "Antichrist," said he in the latter treatise, "is not a man that should suddenly appear with wonders; he is a spiritual thing, who was in the Old Testament and also in the time of Christ and the apostles, and is now and shall (I doubt not) endure till the world's end. His nature is (when he is overcome with the Word of God) to go out of the play for a season, and to disguise himself, and then to come in again with a new name and new raiment. The Scribes and

Pharisees in the gospel were very Antichrists; popes, cardinals, and bishops have gotten their new names, but the thing is all one. Even so now, when we have uttered [vanquished] him, *he will change himself once more*, and turn himself into an angel of light. Already *the beast*, seeing himself now to be sought for, roareth and seeketh new holes to hide himself in, and changeth himself into a thousand fashions with all manner of wiliness, falsehood, subtlety, and craft."[1] This idea, paradoxical at first, gradually made its way into men's minds. The Romans, by their practices, familiarized the English to the somewhat coarse descriptions of the reformers. England was to have many such lessons, and thus by degrees learn to set Rome aside for the sake of her own glory and prosperity.

Knight and Da Casale reached Orvieto about the same time. Clement replied with sighs: "Alas! I am the Emperor's prisoner. The imperialists are every day pillaging towns and castles in our neighbourhood. . . . Wretch that I am! I have not a friend except the king your master, and he is far away. . . ". If I should do anything now to displease Charles, I am a lost man. . . . To sign the commission would be to sign an eternal rupture with him." But Knight and Da Casale pleaded so effectually with Cardinal Sanctorum Quatuor, and so pressed Clement, that the pontiff, without the knowledge of the Spaniard De Angelis, gave them a more satisfactory document, but not such as Wolsey required. "In giving you this commission," said the pope, "I am giving away my liberty, and perhaps my life. I listen not to the voice of prudence, but to that of affection only. I confide in the generosity of the king of England, he is the master of my destiny." He then began to weep, and seemed ready to faint. Knight, forgetting his vexation, promised Clement that the king would do everything to save him.— "Ah!" said the pope, "there is one effectual means."—"What is that?" inquired Henry's agents.—"M. Lautrec, who says daily that he will come, but never does," replied Clement, "has only to bring the French army promptly before the gates of Orvieto; then I could excuse myself by saying that he constrained me to sign the commission."—"Nothing is easier," replied the envoys, "we will go and hasten his arrival."

Clement was not even now at ease. The safety of the Roman

[1] Tyndale, *Doctrinal Treatises*, p. 42, 43.

church troubled him not less than his own. . . . Charles might discover the trick and make the popedom suffer for it. There was danger on all sides. If the English spoke of *independence*, did not the Emperor threaten a *reform*? . . . The catholic princes, said the papal councillors, are capable, without perhaps a single exception, of supporting the cause of Luther to gratify a criminal ambition. The pope reflected and, withdrawing his word, promised to give the commission when Lautrec was under the walls of Orvieto; but the English agents insisted on having it immediately. To conciliate all, it was agreed that the pope should give the required document at once, but as soon as the French army arrived, he should send another copy bearing the date of the day on which he saw Lautrec. "Beseech the king to keep secret the commission I give you," said Clement VII to Knight; "if he begins the process immediately he receives it, I am undone for ever." The pope thus gave permission to act, on condition of not acting at all. Knight took leave on the 1st of January 1528; he promised all the pontiff desired, and then, as if fearing some fresh difficulty, he departed the same day. Da Casale, on his side, after having offered the Cardinal Sanctorum Quatuor a gift of 4000 crowns, which he refused, repaired to Lautrec, to beg him to *constrain* the pope to sign a document which was already on its way to England.

But while the business seemed to be clearing at Rome, it was becoming more complicated in London. The king's project got wind, and Catherine gave way to the liveliest sorrow. "I shall protest," said she, "against the commission given to the cardinal of York. Is he not the king's subject, the vile flatterer of his pleasures?" Catherine did not resist alone; the people, who hated the cardinal, could not with pleasure see him invested with such authority. To obviate this inconvenience, Henry resolved to ask the pope for another cardinal, who should be empowered to terminate the affair in London with or without Wolsey.

The latter agreed to the measure: it is even possible that he was the first to suggest it, for he feared to bear alone the responsibility of so hateful an inquiry. Accordingly, on the 27th of December, he wrote to the king's agents at Rome: "Procure the envoy of a legate, and particularly of an able, easy, *manageable* legate . . . desirous of meriting the king's favour, Campeggio for instance. You will earnestly request the cardinal who may be selected, to travel with all diligence, and you will assure him that the king will behave liberally towards him."

Knight reached Asti in Savoy on the 10th of January, where he found letters with fresh orders. This was another check: at one time it is the pope who compels him to retrace his steps, at another it is the king. Henry's unlucky valetudinarian secretary, a man very susceptible to fatigue, and already wearied and exhausted by ten painful journeys, was in a very bad humour. He determined to permit Gambara to carry the two documents to England; to commission Da Casale, who had not left the pope's neighbourhood, to solicit the despatch of the legate; and as regarded himself, to go and wait for further orders at Turin:—"If it be thought good unto the king's highness that I do return unto Orvieto, I shall do as much as *my poor carcass* may endure."

When Da Casale reached Bologna, he pressed Lautrec to go and constrain the pontiff to sign the act which Gambara was already bearing to England. On receiving the new despatches he returned in all haste to Orvieto, and the pope was very much alarmed when he heard of his arrival. He had feared to grant a simple paper, destined to remain *secret;* and now he is required to send a prince of the church! Will Henry never be satisfied? "The mission you desire would be full of dangers," he replied; "but we have discovered another means, alone calculated to finish this business. Mind you do not say that I pointed it out to you," added the pope in a mysterious tone; "but that it was suggested by Cardinal Sanctorum Quatuor and Simonetta." Da Casale was all attention. "There is not a doctor in the world who can better decide on this matter, and on its most private circumstances, than the king himself. If therefore he sincerely believes that Catherine had really become his brother's wife, let him empower the cardinal of York to pronounce the divorce, and let him take another wife without any further ceremony; he can then afterwards demand the confirmation of the consistory. The affair being concluded in this way, I will take the rest upon myself."—"But," said Da Casale, somewhat dissatisfied with this new intrigue, "I must fulfil my mission, and the king demands a legate."—

"And whom shall I send," asked Clement. "Da Monte? he cannot move. De Cæsis? he is at Naples. Ara Cœli? he has the gout. Piccolomini? he is of the imperial party . . . Campeggio would be the best, but he is at Rome, where he supplies my place, and cannot leave without peril to the church." . . . And then with some emotion he added, "I throw myself into his majesty's arms. The Emperor will never forgive what I am doing. If he hears of it he will summon me before *his council;* I shall have no rest until he has deprived me of my throne and my life."

Da Casale hastened to forward to London the result of the conference. Clement being unable to untie the knot, requested Henry to cut it. Will this prince hesitate to employ so easy a means, the pope (Clement declared it himself) being willing to ratify everything?

Here closes Henry's first campaign in the territories of the popedom. We shall now see the results of so many efforts.

CHAPTER TEN

Royal Threats Counter Papal Cunning

(January to March, 1528)

NEVER was disappointment more complete than that felt by Henry and Wolsey after the arrival of Gambara with the commission; the king was angry, the cardinal vexed. What Clement called the *sacrifice of his life* was in reality but a sheet of paper fit only to be thrown into the fire. "This commission is of no value," said Wolsey.—"And even to put it into execution," added Henry, "we must wait until the imperialists have quitted Italy! The pope is putting us off to the Greek calends."—"His holiness," observed the cardinal, "does not bind himself to pronounce the divorce; the queen will therefore appeal from our judgment."—"And even if the pope had bound himself," added the king, "it would be sufficient for the Emperor to smile upon him, to make him retract what he had promised."—"It is all a cheat and a mockery," concluded both king and minister.

What was to be done next? The only way to make Clement ours, thought Wolsey, is to get rid of Charles; it is time his pride was brought down. Accordingly, on the 22nd of January 1528, Clarencieux,[1] being sent to France with instructions which had not been revealed to Henry VIII or to his Council, made a formal proclamation of hostilities against Charles. The king of France acted likewise. When Charles heard of this proceeding he exclaimed: "I know the hand that has flung the torch of war into the midst of Europe. My crime is not having placed the cardinal of York on St Peter's throne."

A mere declaration of hostilities was not enough for Wolsey; the bishop of Bayonne, ambassador from France, seeing him one day somewhat excited, whispered in his ear: "In former

---

[1] [Clarencieux is the second King-of-Arms in England. He is so named after the Duke of Clarence, son of Edward III.]

times popes have deposed emperors for smaller offences." The deposition of Charles would have delivered the king of France from a troublesome rival; but Du Bellay, fearing to take the initiative in so bold an enterprise, suggested the idea to the cardinal. Wolsey reflected: such a thought had never before occurred to him. Taking the ambassador aside to a window, he there swore *stoutly*, said Du Bellay, that he should be delighted to use all his influence to get Charles deposed by the pope. "No one is more likely than yourself," replied the bishop, "to induce Clement to do it."—"I will use all my credit," rejoined Wolsey, and the two priests separated. This bright idea the cardinal never forgot. Charles had robbed him of the tiara; he would retaliate by depriving Charles of his crown. *An eye for an eye, and a tooth for a tooth.* Staffileo, dean of the Rota, was then in London, and still burning with resentment against the author of the Sack of Rome, he favourably received the suggestions Wolsey made to him; and, finally, the envoy from John Zapolyai, king-elect of Hungary, supported the project. But the kings of France and England were not so easily induced to put the thrones of kings at the disposal of the priests. It appears, however, that the pope was sounded on the subject; and if the Emperor had been beaten in Italy, it is probable that the bull would have been fulminated against him. His sword preserved his crown, and the plot of the two bishops failed.

The king's councillors began to seek for less heroic means. "We must prosecute the affair at *Rome*," said some.—"No," said others, "in *England*. The pope is too much afraid of the Emperor to pronounce the divorce in person."—"If the pope fears the Emperor more than the king of England," exclaimed the proud Tudor, "we shall find some other way to set him at ease." Thus, at the first contradiction, Henry placed his hand on his sword, and threatened to sever the ties which bound his kingdom to the throne of the Italian pontiff.

"I have hit it!" said Wolsey at length; "we must combine the two plans—judge the affair in London, and at the same time bind the pontiff at Rome." And then the able cardinal proposed the draft of a bull, by which the pope, delegating his authority to two legates, should declare that the acts of that delegation should have a perpetual effect, notwithstanding any contrary decrees that might subsequently emanate from his infallible authority. A new mission was decided upon for the accomplishment of this bold design.

Wolsey, annoyed by the weakness of Knight and his colleagues, desired men of another stamp. He therefore cast his eyes on his own secretary, Stephen Gardiner, an active man, intelligent, supple, and crafty, a learned canonist, desirous of the king's favour, and, above all, a good Romanist, which at Rome was not without its advantage. Gardiner was in miniature the living image of his master; and hence the cardinal sometimes styled him *the half of himself.* Edward Fox, the chief almoner, was joined with him—a moderate, influential man, a particular friend of Henry's, and a zealous advocate of the divorce. Fox was named first in the commission; but it was agreed that Gardiner should be the real head of the embassy. "Repeat without ceasing," Wolsey told them, "that his majesty cannot do otherwise than separate from the queen. Attack each one on his weak side. Declare to the pope that the king promises to defend him against the Emperor; and to the cardinals that their services will be nobly rewarded. If that does not suffice, let the energy of your words be such as to excite a wholesome fear in the pontiff."

Fox and Gardiner, after a gracious reception at Paris (23rd February) by Francis I, arrived at Orvieto on the 21st of March, after many perils, and with their dress in such disorder on account of foul weather, that no one could have taken them for the ambassadors of Henry VIII. "What a city!" they exclaimed, as they passed through its streets; "what ruins, what misery! It is indeed truly called Orvieto (the aged city)!" The state of the town gave them no very grand idea of the state of the popedom, and they imagined that with a pontiff so poorly lodged, their negotiation could not be otherwise than easy. "I give you my house," said Da Casale, to whom they went, "my room and my own bed;" and as they made some objections, he added: "It is not possible to lodge you elsewhere; I have even been forced to borrow what was necessary to receive you." Da Casale pressing them to change their clothes, which were still dripping (they had just crossed a river on their mules) they replied that being obliged to travel post, they had not been able to bring a change of raiment. "Alas!" said Casale, "what is to be done? There are few persons in Orvieto

Gloucester College (now Worcester College) Oxford, into which Anthony Dalaber brought Tyndale's New Testament in 1526. The progress of the truth in the Universities was an important feature of the English Reformation. See page 254.

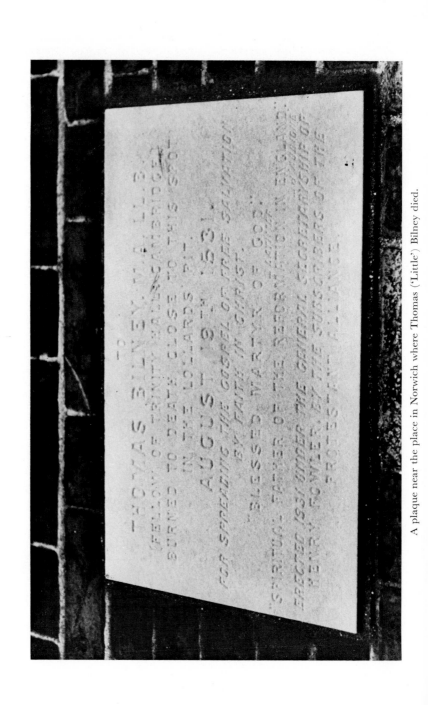

A plaque near the place in Norwich where Thomas ('Little') Bilney died.

who have more garments than one; even the shopkeepers have no cloth for sale; this town is quite a prison. People say the pope is at liberty here. A pretty liberty indeed! Want, impure air, wretched lodging, and a thousand other inconveniences keep the holy father closer than when he was in the Castle of St Angelo. Accordingly, he told me the other day, it was better to be in captivity at Rome than at liberty here."[1]

Shortly, however, they managed to procure some new clothing; and being now in a condition to show themselves, Henry's agents were admitted to an after-dinner audience on Monday the 25th of March (1528).

Da Casale conducted them to an old building in ruins. "This is where his holiness lives," he said. They looked at one another with astonishment and, crossing the rubbish lying about, passed through three chambers whose ceilings had fallen in, whose windows were curtainless, and in which thirty persons "*riff-raff* were standing against the bare walls for a garnishment." This was the pope's court.

At length the ambassadors reached the pontiff's room, and placed Henry's letters in his hands. "Your holiness," said Gardiner, "when sending the king a dispensation, was pleased to add, that if this document were not sufficient, you would willingly give a better. It is that favour the king now desires." The pope with embarrassment strove to soften his refusal. "I am informed," he said, "that the king is led on in this affair by a secret inclination, and that the lady he loves is far from being worthy of him." Gardiner replied with firmness: "The king truly desires to marry again after the divorce, that he may have an heir to the crown; but the woman he proposes to take is animated by the noblest sentiments; the cardinal of York and all England do homage to her virtues." The pope appeared convinced. "Besides," continued Gardiner, "the king has written a book on the motives of his divorce."—"Good! come and read it to me to-morrow," rejoined Clement.

The next day the English envoys had hardly appeared, before Clement took Henry's book, ran over it as he walked up and down the room, and then seating himself on a long bench covered with an old carpet, "not worth twenty pence," says an annalist, he read the book aloud. He counted the number of

[1] State Papers, vii, p. 63.

arguments, made objections as if Henry were present, and piled them one upon another without waiting for an answer. "The marriages forbidden in Leviticus," said he, in a short and quick tone of voice, "are permitted in Deuteronomy; now Deuteronomy coming after Leviticus, we are bound by the latter. The honour of Catherine and the Emperor is at stake, and the divorce would give rise to a terrible war." The pope continued speaking, and whenever the Englishmen attempted to reply, he bade them be silent, and kept on reading. "It is an excellent book," said he, however, in a courteous tone, when he had ended; "I shall keep it to read over again at my leisure." Gardiner then presenting a draft of the commission which Henry required, Clement made answer: "It is too late to look at it now; leave it with me."—"But we are in haste," added Gardiner.—"Yes, yes, I know it," said the pope. All his efforts tended to protract the business.

On the 28th of March, the ambassadors were conducted to the room in which the pope slept; the cardinals Sanctorum Quatuor and De Monte, as well as the councillor of the Rota, Simonetta, were then with him. Chairs were arranged in a semicircle. "Be seated," said Clement, who stood in the middle. "Master Gardiner, now tell me what you want."—"There is no question between us but one of *time*," said Gardiner. "You promised to ratify the divorce, as soon as it was pronounced; and we require you to do *before* what you engage to do *after*. What is right on one day, must be right on another." Then, raising his voice, the Englishman added: "If his majesty perceives that no more respect is paid to him than to a common man, he will have recourse to a *remedy* which I will not name, but which will not fail in its effect."

The pope and his councillors looked at one another in silence; they had understood him. The imperious Gardiner, remarking the effect which he had produced, then added in an absolute tone: "We have our instructions, and are determined to keep to them."—"I am ready to do everything compatible with my honour," exclaimed Clement, in alarm.— "What your honour would not permit you to grant," said the proud ambassador, "the honour of the king, my master, would not permit him to ask." Gardiner's language became more imperative every minute. "Well, then," said Clement, driven to extremity, "I will do what the king demands, and if the Emperor is angry, I cannot help it." The interview, which had commenced with a storm, finished with a gleam of sunshine.

That bright gleam soon disappeared: Clement, who imagined he saw in Henry a Hannibal at war with Rome, wished to play the temporizer, the *Fabius Cunctator* (Fabius the Delayer.) "He gives twice who gives quickly," said Gardiner sharply, who observed this manœuvre.—"It is a question of law," replied the pope, "and as I am very ignorant in these matters, I must give the doctors of the canon law the necessary time to make it all clear."—"By his delays Fabius Maximus saved Rome," rejoined Gardiner; "you will destroy it by yours."—"Alas!" exclaimed the pope, "if I say the king is right, I shall have to go back to prison."—"When truth is concerned," said the ambassador, "of what consequence are the opinions of men?" Gardiner was speaking at his ease, but Clement found that the castle of St Angelo was not without weight in the balance. "You may be sure that I shall do everything for the best," replied the modern Fabius. With these words the conference terminated.

Such were the struggles of England with the popedom— struggles which were to end in a definitive rupture. Gardiner knew that he had a skilful adversary to deal with; too cunning to allow himself to be irritated, he coolly resolved to frighten the pontiff: that was in his instructions. On the Friday before Palm Sunday, he was ushered into the pope's private room; there he found Clement attended by De Monte, Sanctorum Quatuor, Simonetta, Staffileo, Paul, auditor of the Rota, and Gambara. "It is impossible," said the cardinals, "to grant a decretal commission in which the pope pronounces *de jure* in favour of the divorce, with a promise of confirmation *de facto*." Gardiner insisted; but no persuasion, "neither dulce nor poynante," could move the pontiff. The envoy judged the moment had come to discharge his strongest battery. "O perverse race," said he to the pontiff's ministers, "instead of being harmless as doves, you are as full of dissimulation and malice as serpents; promising everything but performing nothing. England will be driven to believe that God has taken from you the key of knowledge, and that the laws of the popes, ambiguous to the popes themselves, are only fit to be cast into

the fire. The king has hitherto restrained his people, impatient
of the Romish yoke; but he will now give them the rein." A long
and gloomy silence followed. Then the Englishman, suddenly
changing his tone, softly approached Clement, who had left
his seat, and conjured him in a low voice to consider carefully
what justice required of him. "Alas!" replied Clement, "I tell
you again, I am ignorant in these matters. According to the
maxims of the canon law *the pope carries all laws in the tablets of
his heart*, but unfortunately God has never given me the *key*
that opens them." As he could not escape by silence, Clement
retreated under cover of a jest, and heedlessly pronounced the
condemnation of the popedom. If he had never received the
famous *key*, there was no reason why other pontiffs should have
possessed it. The next day he found another loophole; for when
the ambassadors told him that the king would carry on the
matter without him, he sighed, drew out his handkerchief and
said, as he wiped his eyes: "Would to God that I were dead!"
Clement employed tears as a political engine.

"We shall not get the *decretal* commission," (that which
pronounced the divorce) said Fox and Gardiner after this, "and
it is not really necessary. Let us demand the *general* commission
(authorizing the legates to pronounce it) and exact a promise
that shall supply the place of the act which is denied us."
Clement, who was ready to make all the promises in the world,
agreed to ratify the sentence of the legates without delay. Fox
and Gardiner then presented to Simonetta a draft of the act
required. The dean, after reading it, returned it to the envoys,
saying, "It is very well, I think, except *the end;* show it Sanctorum Quatuor." The next morning they carried the draft to
that cardinal: "How long has it been the rule for the patient
to write the prescription? I always thought it was the physician's
business."—"No one knows the disease so well as the patient,"
replied Gardiner; "and this disease may be of such a nature
that the doctor cannot prescribe the remedy without taking
the patient's advice." Sanctorum Quatuor read the prescription, and then returned it, saying: "It is not bad, with the
exception of *the beginning.* Take the draft to De Monte and the
other councillors." The latter liked neither beginning, middle,
nor end. "We will send for you this evening," said De Monte.

Three or four days having elapsed, Henry's envoys again

waited on the pope, who showed them the draft prepared by his councillors. Gardiner remarking in it additions, retrenchments, and corrections, threw it disdainfully from him, and said coldly: "Your holiness is deceiving us; you have selected these men to be the instruments of your duplicity." Clement, in alarm, sent for Simonetta; and after a warm discussion, the envoys, more discontented than ever, quitted the pope at one in the morning.

The night brings wisdom. "I only desire two little words more in the commission," said Gardiner next day to Clement and Simonetta. The pope requested Simonetta to wait upon the cardinals immediately; the latter sent word that they were at dinner, and adjourned the business until the morrow.

When Gardiner heard of this epicurean message, he thought the time had come for striking a decisive blow. A new tragedy began. "We are deceived," exclaimed he, "you are laughing at us. This is not the way to gain the favour of princes. Water mixed with wine spoils it; your corrections nullify our document. These ignorant and suspicious priests have spelled over our draft as if a scorpion was hidden under every word.—You made us come to Italy," said he to Staffileo and Gambara, "like hawks which the fowler lures by holding out to them a piece of meat; and now that we are here, the bait has disappeared, and, instead of giving us what we sought, you pretend to lull us to sleep by the sweet voice of the sirens." Then, turning to Clement, the English envoy added, "Your holiness will have to answer for this." The pope sighed and wiped away his tears. "It was God's pleasure," continued Gardiner, whose tone became more threatening every minute, "that we should see with our own eyes the disposition of the people here. It is time to have done. Henry is not an ordinary prince—bear in mind that you are insulting *the defender of the faith*. . . . You are going to lose the favour of the only monarch who protects you, and the apostolical chair, already tottering, will fall into dust, and disappear entirely amidst the applause of all Christendom."

Gardiner paused. The pope was moved. The state of Italy seemed to confirm but too strongly the sinister predictions of the envoy of Henry VIII. The imperial troops, terrified and pursued by Lautrec, had abandoned Rome and retired on

Naples. The French general was following up this wretched army of Charles V, decimated by pestilence and debauchery; Andrea Doria, at the head of his galleys, had destroyed the Spanish fleet; Gaeta and Naples only were left to the imperialists; and Lautrec, who was besieging the latter place, wrote to Henry on the 26th of August that all would soon be over. The timid Clement VII had attentively watched all these catastrophes. Accordingly, Gardiner had hardly spoken of the danger which threatened the popedom, before he turned pale with affright, rose from his seat, stretched out his arms in terror, as if he had desired to repel some monster ready to devour him, and exclaimed, "Write, write! Insert whatever words you please." As he said this, he paced up and down the room, raising his hands to heaven and sighing deeply, while Fox and Gardiner, standing motionless, looked on in silence. A tempestuous wind seemed to be stirring the depths of the abyss; the ambassadors waited until the storm was abated. At last Clement recovered himself, made a few trivial excuses, and dismissed Henry's ministers. It was an hour past midnight.

It was neither morality, nor religion, nor even the laws of the church which led Clement to refuse the divorce; ambition and fear were his only motives. He would have desired that Henry should first constrain the Emperor to restore him his territories. But the king of England, who felt himself unable to protect the pope against Charles, required, however, this unhappy pontiff to provoke the Emperor's anger. Clement reaped the fruits of that fatal system which had transformed the church of Jesus Christ into a pitiful combination of policy and cunning.

On the next day, the tempest having thoroughly abated, Sanctorum Quatuor corrected the commission. It was signed, completed by a leaden seal attached to a piece of string, and then handed to Gardiner, who read it. The bull was addressed to Wolsey, and "authorized him, in case he should acknowledge the nullity of Henry's marriage, to pronounce judicially the sentence of divorce, but without noise or display of judgment; for that purpose he might take any English bishop for his colleague."—"All that we can do, you can do," said the pope. "We are very doubtful," said the importunate Gardiner after reading the bull, "whether this commission, without the clauses of *confirmation* and *revocation*, will satisfy his majesty; but we will do all in our power to get him to accept it."—"Above all, do not speak of our altercations," said the pope. Gardiner, like a discreet diplomatist, did not scruple to note down every particular in cipher in the letters whence these details are procured. "Tell the king," continued the pontiff, "that this commission is on my part a declaration of war against the Emperor, and that I now place myself under his majesty's protection." The chief-almoner of England departed for London with the precious document.

But one storm followed close upon another. Fox had not long quitted Orvieto when new letters arrived from Wolsey, demanding the fourth of the acts previously requested, namely, the *engagement* to ratify at Rome whatever the commissioners might decide in England. Gardiner was to set about it *in season and out of season;* the verbal promise of the pope counted for nothing; this document must be had, whether the pope was ill, dying, or dead. "*Ego et Rex meus,* his majesty and I command you;" said Wolsey; "this divorce is of more consequence to us than twenty popedoms." The English envoy renewed his demand. "Since you refuse the decretal," he said, "there is the greater reason why you should not refuse *the engagement.*" This application led to fresh discussion and fresh tears. Clement gave way once more; but the Italians, more crafty than Gardiner, reserved a loophole in the document through which the pontiff might escape. The messenger Thaddeus carried it to London; and Gardiner left Orvieto for Rome to confer with Campeggio.

Clement was a man of penetrating mind and, although he knew as well as any how to deliver a clever speech, he was irresolute and timid; and accordingly the commission had not long been despatched before he repented. Full of distress, he paced the ruined chambers of his old palace, and imagined he saw hanging over his head that terrible sword of Charles the Fifth, whose edge he had already felt. "Wretch that I am," said he; "cruel wolves surround me; they open their jaws to swallow me up. . . . I see none but enemies around me. At their head is the Emperor. . . . What will he do? Alas! I have yielded that fatal commission which the general of the Spanish Observance had enjoined me to refuse. Behind Charles come the Venetians, the Florentines, the duke of Ferrara. . . . They have cast lots upon my vesture. . . . Next comes the king of France, who promises nothing, but looks on with folded arms; or rather, what perfidy! calls upon me at this critical moment to deprive Charles V of his crown. . . . And last, but not least, Henry VIII, *the defender of the faith,* indulges in frightful menaces against me. . . . The Emperor desires to maintain the queen on the throne of England; the latter, to put her away. . . . Would to God that Catherine were in her grave! But, alas! she lives . . . to be the apple of discord dividing the two greatest monarchies, and the inevitable cause of the ruin of the popedom. . . . Wretched man that I am! how cruel is my perplexity, and around me I can see nothing but horrible confusion."

CHAPTER ELEVEN

Wolsey's Desperate Demands

(April to July, 1528)

DURING this time Fox was making his way to England. On the 27th of April (1528) he reached Paris; on the 2nd of May he landed at Sandwich, and hastened to Greenwich, where he arrived the next day at five in the evening, just as Wolsey had left for London. Fox's arrival was an event of great importance. "Let him go to Lady Anne's apartments," said the king, "and wait for me there." Fox told Anne Boleyn of his and Gardiner's exertions, and the success of their mission, at which she expressed her very great satisfaction. It is clear that she no longer resisted Henry's project for divorce. "Mistress Anne always called me Master Stephen," wrote Fox to Gardiner, "her thoughts were so full of you." The king appeared and Anne withdrew.

"Tell me as briefly as possible what you have done," said Henry. Fox placed in the king's hands the pope's insignificant letter, which he bade his almoner read; then that from Staffileo, which was put on one side; and lastly Gardiner's letter, which Henry took hastily and read himself. "The pope has promised us," said Fox, as he terminated his report, "to confirm the sentence of the divorce, as soon as it has been pronounced by the commissioners."—"Excellent!" exclaimed Henry; and then he ordered Anne to be called in. "Repeat before this lady," he said to Fox, "what you have just told me." The almoner did so. "The pope is convinced of the justice of your cause," he said in conclusion, "and the cardinal's letter has convinced him that my lady is worthy of the throne of England."— "Make your report to Wolsey this very night," said the king.

It was ten o'clock when the chief almoner reached the cardinal's palace; he had gone to bed, but immediate orders were given that Fox should be conducted to his room. Being a churchman, Wolsey could understand the pope's artifices better than Henry; accordingly, as soon as he learnt that Fox had brought the commission only, he became alarmed at the task imposed upon him. "What a misfortune!" he exclaimed; "your commission is no better than Gambara's. . . . However, go and rest yourself; I will examine these papers to-morrow." Fox withdrew in confusion. "It is not bad," said Wolsey the next day, "but the whole business still falls on me alone!—Never mind, I must wear a contented look, or else. . . ." In the afternoon he summoned into his chamber Fox, Dr Bell, and Viscount Rochford: "Master Gardiner has surpassed himself," said the crafty supple cardinal; "What a man! what an inestimable treasure! what a jewel in our kingdom!"

He did not mean a word he was saying. Wolsey was dissatisfied with everything—with the refusal of the *decretal*, and with the drawing up of the *commission*, as well as of the *engagement* (which arrived soon after in good condition, so far as the outside was concerned). But the king's ill humour would infallibly recoil on Wolsey; so putting a good face on a bad matter, he ruminated in secret on the means of obtaining what had been refused him. "Write to Gardiner," said he to Fox, "that everything makes me desire the pope's *decretal*—the need of unburdening my conscience, of being able to reply to the calumniators who will attack my judgment, and the thought of the accidents to which the life of man is exposed. Let his holiness, then, pronounce the divorce himself; we engage on our part to keep his resolution secret. But order Master Stephen to employ every kind of persuasion that his *rhetoric* can imagine." In case the pope should positively refuse the decretal, Wolsey required that at least Campeggio should share the responsibility of the divorce with him.

This was not all: while reading the engagement, Wolsey discovered the loophole which had escaped Gardiner, and this is what he contrived: "The *engagement* which the pope has sent us," he wrote to Gardiner, "is drawn up in such terms that he can retract it at pleasure; we must therefore find some *good way* to obtain another. You may do it under this pretence. You will appear before his holiness with a dejected air, and tell him that the courier, to whom the conveyance of the said engagement was intrusted, fell into the water with his despatches, so that the rescripts were totally defaced and illegible; that I have not dared deliver it into the king's hands, and unless his holiness will grant you a duplicate, some notable blame will be imputed unto you for not taking better care in its transmission. And further, you will continue: I remember the expressions of the former document, and to save your holiness trouble, I will dictate them to your secretary. Then," added Wolsey, "while the secretary is writing, you will find means to introduce, without its being perceived, as many *fat, pregnant*, and available words as possible, to bind the pope and enlarge my powers, the politic handling of which the king's highness and I commit unto your good discretion."

Such was the expedient invented by Wolsey. The papal secretary, imagining he was making a fresh copy of the original document (which was, by the way, in perfect condition) was at the dictation of the ambassador to draw up another of a different tenor. The "politic handling" of the cardinal-legate, which was not very unlike forgery, throws a disgraceful light on the policy of the sixteenth century.

Wolsey read this letter to the chief-almoner; and then, to set his conscience at rest, he added piously: "In an affair of such high importance, on which depends the glory or the ruin of the realm—my honour or my disgrace—the condemnation of my soul or my everlasting merit—I will listen solely to the voice of my conscience, and I shall act in such a manner as to be able to render an account to God without fear."

Wolsey did more; it seems that the boldness of his declarations reassured him with regard to the baseness of his works. Being at Greenwich on the following Sunday, he said to the king in the presence of Fox, Bell, Wolman, and Tuke: "I am bound to your royal person more than any subject was ever bound to his prince. I am ready to sacrifice my goods, my blood, my life for you. . . . But my obligations towards God are greater still. For that cause, rather than act against His will, I would endure the extremest evils. I would suffer your royal indignation, and, if necessary, deliver my body to the executioners that they might cut it in pieces." What could be the spirit then impelling Wolsey? Was it blindness or impudence? He may have been sincere in the words he addressed to Henry; at the bottom of his heart he may have desired to set the pope above the king, and the church of Rome above the kingdom of England; and this desire may have appeared to him a sublime virtue, such as would hide a multitude of sins. What the public conscience would have called treason was heroism to the Romish priest. This zeal for the papacy is sometimes met with in conjunction with the most flagrant immorality. If Wolsey deceived the pope, it was to save popery in the realm of England. Fox, Bell, Wolman, and Tuke listened to him with astonishment. Henry, who thought he knew his man, received these holy declarations without alarm, and the cardinal having thus eased his conscience, proceeded boldly in his iniquities. It seems, however, that the inward reproaches which he silenced in public, had their revenge in secret. One of his officers, entering his private room shortly afterwards, presented a letter addressed to Campeggio for his signature. It ended thus: "I hope all things shall be done according to the will of God, the desire of the king, the quiet of the kingdom, and to our honour *with a good conscience.*" The cardinal having read the letter, dashed out the last four words. Conscience has a sting from which none can escape, not even a Wolsey.

However, Gardiner lost no time in Italy. When he met Campeggio (to whom Henry VIII had given a palace at Rome, and a bishopric in England) he entreated him to go to London and pronounce the divorce. This prelate, who was to be empowered in 1530 with authority to crush Protestantism in Germany, seemed bound to undertake a mission that would save Romanism in Britain. But proud of his position at Rome, where he acted as the pope's representative, he cared not for a charge that would undoubtedly draw upon him either Henry's hatred or the Emperor's anger. He begged to be excused. The pope spoke in a similar tone. When he was informed of this, the terrible Tudor, beginning to believe that Clement desired to entangle him, as the hunter entangles the lion in his toils, gave vent to his anger on Tuke, Fox, and Gardiner, but particularly on Wolsey. Nor were reasons wanting for this explosion. The cardinal, perceiving that his hatred against Charles had carried him too far, pretended that it was without his orders that Clarencieux, bribed by France, had combined with the French ambassador to declare war against the Emperor; and added that he would have the English king-at-arms put to death as he passed through Calais. This was an infallible means of preventing disagreeable revelations. But the herald, who had been forewarned, crossed by way of Boulogne, and, without the cardinal's knowledge, obtained an interview with Henry, before whom he placed the *orders* he had received from Wolsey in *three* consecutive letters. The king was astonished at his minister's impudence. With an oath he exclaimed: "The man in whom I had most confidence told me quite the contrary." He then summoned Wolsey before him, and reproached him severely for his falsehoods. The wretched man shook like a leaf. Henry appeared to pardon him, but the season of his favour had passed away. Henceforward he kept the cardinal as one of those instruments we make use of for a time, and then throw away when we have no further need of them.

The king's anger against the pope far exceeded that against Wolsey; he trembled from head to foot, rose from his seat, then sat down again, and vented his wrath in the most violent language: "What!" he exclaimed, "I shall exhaust my political combinations, empty my treasury, make war upon my friends, consume my forces . . . and for whom? . . . for a heartless priest who, considering neither the exigencies of my honour, nor the peace of my conscience, nor the prosperity of my kingdom, nor the numerous benefits which I have lavished on him, refuses me a favour, which he ought, as the common father of the faithful, to grant even to an enemy. . . . Hypocrite! . . . You cover yourself with the cloak of friendship, you flatter us by crafty practices, but you give us only a bastard document, and you say like Pilate: It matters little to me if this king perishes, and all his kingdom with him; take him and judge him according to your law! . . . I understand you . . . you wish to entangle us in the briers, to catch us in a trap, to lure us into a pitfall. . . . But we have discovered the snare; we shall escape from your ambuscade, and brave your power."

Such was the language then heard at the court of England, says John Strype, the historian. The monks and priests began to grow alarmed, while the more enlightened minds already saw in the distance the first gleams of religious liberty. One day, at a time when Henry was proving himself a zealous follower of the Romish doctrines, Sir Thomas More was sitting in the midst of his family, when his son-in-law, William Roper, now become a warm papist, exclaimed: "Happy kingdom of England, where no heretic dares show his face!"—"That is

true, son Roper," said More; "we seem to sit now upon the
mountains, treading the heretics under our feet like ants; but
I pray God that some of us do not live to see the day when we
gladly would wish to be at league with them, to suffer them to
have their churches quietly to themselves, so that they would
be content to let us have ours peaceably to ourselves." Roper
angrily replied: "By my word, sir, that is very desperately
spoken!" More, however, was in the right; genius is sometimes
a great diviner. The Reformation was on the point of inaugur-
ating religious liberty, and by that means placing civil liberty
on an immovable foundation.

Henry himself grew wiser by degrees. He began to have
doubts about the Roman hierarchy, and to ask himself
whether a priest-king, embarrassed in all the political com-
plications of Europe, could be the head of the church of Jesus
Christ. Pious individuals in his kingdom recognized in Scripture
and in conscience a law superior to the law of Rome, and
refused to sacrifice at the command of the church their moral
convictions, sanctioned by the revelation of God. The hierarchical system, which claims to absorb man in the papacy,
had oppressed the consciences of Christians for centuries. When
the Romish Church had required from such as Berengarius,
John Huss, Savonarola, John Wesel, and Martin Luther the
denial of their consciences enlightened by the Word, that is to
say, by the voice of God, it had shown most clearly how great
is the iniquity of its claim to substitute papal domination for
the sovereignty of Almighty God. "If the Christian consents to
this enormous demand of the hierarchy," said the most
enlightened men; "if he renounces his own notions of good
and evil in favour of the clergy; if he reserves not his right to
obey God, who speaks to him in the Bible, rather than men,
even if their agreement is universal; if Henry VIII, for instance,
should silence his conscience, which condemns his union with
his brother's widow, to obey the clerical voice which approves
of it; by that very act he renounces truth, duty, and even God
Himself." But we must add, that if the rights of conscience were
beginning to be understood in England, it was not about
such holy matters as these that the pope and Henry were
contending. They were both intriguers—both dissatisfied, the
one desirous of love, the other of power.

Be that as it may, a feeling of disgust for Rome then took root in the king's heart, and nothing could afterwards eradicate it. He immediately made every exertion to attract Erasmus to London. Indeed, if Henry separated from the pope, his old friends, the humanists, must be his auxiliaries, and not the heretical doctors. But Erasmus, in a letter dated 1st June, alleged the weak state of his health, the robbers who infested the roads, the wars and rumours of wars then afloat. "Our destiny leads us," he said; "let us yield to it." It is a fortunate thing for England that Erasmus was not its reformer.

Wolsey noted this movement of his master's, and resolved to make a strenuous effort to reconcile Clement and Henry; his own safety was at stake. He wrote to the pope, to Campeggio, to Da Casale, to all Italy. He declared that if he was ruined, the popedom would be ruined too, so far at least as England was concerned: "I would obtain the *decretal* bull with my own blood, if possible," he added. "Assure the holy father on my life that no mortal eye shall see it." Finally, he ordered the chief-almoner to write to Gardiner: "If Campeggio does not come, *you shall never return* to England;" an infallible means of stimulating the secretary's zeal.

This was the last effort of Henry VIII. The duke of Bourbon and the Prince of Orange had not employed more zeal a year before in scaling the walls of Rome. Wolsey's fire had inflamed his agents; they argued, entreated, stormed, and threatened. The alarmed cardinals and theologians, assembling at the pope's call, discussed the matter, mixing political interests with the affairs of the church. At last they understood what Wolsey now communicated to them. "Henry is the most energetic defender of the faith," they said. "It is only by acceding to his demand that we can preserve the kingdom of England to the popedom. The army of Charles is in full flight, and that of Francis triumphs." The last of these arguments decided the question; the pope suddenly felt a great sympathy for Wolsey and for the English Church; the Emperor was beaten; therefore he was wrong. Clement granted everything.

First, Campeggio was desired to go to London. The pontiff knew that he might reckon on his intelligence and inflexible adhesion to the interests of the hierarchy; even the cardinal's gout was of use, for it might help to innumerable delays. Next,

on the 8th of June, the pope, then at Viterbo, gave a new
commission, by which he conferred on Wolsey and Campeggio
the power to declare null and void the marriage between
Henry and Catherine, with liberty for the king and queen to
form new matrimonial ties. A few days later he signed the
famous *decretal* by which he himself annulled the marriage
between Henry and Catherine; but instead of intrusting it to
Gardiner, he gave it to Campeggio, with orders not to let it
go out of his hands. Clement was not sure of the course of
events: if Charles should decidedly lose his power, the bull
would be published in the face of Christendom; if he should
recover it, the bull would be burnt. In fact the flames did
actually consume some time afterwards this decree which
Clement had wetted with his tears as he put his name to it.
Finally, on the 23rd of July, the pope signed a valid *engagement*,
by which he declared beforehand that all retraction of these
acts should be *null and void*. Campeggio and Gardiner departed.
Charles' defeat was as complete at Rome as at Naples; the
justice of his cause had vanished with his army.

Nothing, therefore, was wanting to Henry's desires. He had
Campeggio, the commission, the decretal bull of divorce signed
by the pope, and the engagement giving an irrevocable value
to all these acts. Wolsey was conqueror—the conqueror of
Clement! . . . He had often wished to mount the restive courser
of the popedom and to guide it at his will, but each time the
unruly steed had thrown him from the saddle. Now he was
firm in his seat, and held the horse in hand. Thanks to Charles'
reverses, he was master at Rome. The popedom, whether it was
pleased or not, must take the road he had chosen, and before
which it had so long recoiled. The king's joy was unbounded,
and equalled only by Wolsey's. The cardinal, in the fulness of
his heart, wishing to show his gratitude to the officers of the
Roman court, made them presents of carpets, horses, and
vessels of gold. All near Henry felt the effects of his good
humour. Anne smiled; the court indulged in amusements; the
great affair was about to be accomplished. The union between
England and the popedom appeared confirmed for ever, and
the victory which Rome seemed about to gain in the British
Isles might secure her triumph in the west. Vain omens! Far
different were the events in the womb of the future.

BOOK FOUR

The Two Divorces

CHAPTER ONE

"A Thousand Wolseys for One Anne Boleyn"

(1528)

WHILE England seemed binding herself to the court of Rome, the general course of the church and of the world gave stronger presage every day of the approaching emancipation of Christendom. The respect which for so many centuries had hedged in the Roman pontiff was everywhere shaken; the Reform, already firmly established in several states of Germany and Switzerland, was extending in France, the Low Countries, and Hungary, and beginning in Sweden, Denmark, and Scotland. The South of Europe appeared indeed submissive to the Romish church; but Spain, at heart, cared little for the pontifical infallibility; and even Italy began to inquire whether the papal dominion was not an obstacle to her prosperity. England, notwithstanding appearances, was also going to throw off the yoke of the bishops of the Tiber, and many faithful voices might already be heard demanding that the Word of God should be acknowledged the supreme authority in the church.

The conquest of Christian Britain by the papacy occupied all the seventh century, as we have seen. The sixteenth was the counterpart of the seventh. The struggle which England then had to sustain, in order to free herself from the power that had enslaved her during nine hundred years, was full of sudden changes; like those of the times of Augustine and Oswiu. This struggle indeed took place in each of the countries where the church was reformed; but nowhere can it be traced in all its diverse phases so distinctly as in Great Britain. The positive work of the Reformation—that which consisted in recovering the truth and life so long lost—was nearly the same everywhere; but as regards the negative work—the struggle with the popedom—we might almost say that other nations committed to England the task by which they were all to profit. An

unenlightened piety may perhaps look upon the relations of the
court of London with the court of Rome, at the period of the
Reformation, as void of interest to the faith; but history will
not think the same. It has been too often forgotten that the
main point in this contest was not the divorce (which was only
the occasion) but the contest itself and its important consequences. The divorce of Henry Tudor and Catherine of
Aragon is a secondary event; but the divorce of England and
the popedom is a primary event, one of the great watersheds
of history, a creative act (so to speak) which still exercises a
profound influence over the destinies of mankind. And
accordingly everything connected with it is full of instruction
for us. Already a great number of pious men had attached
themselves to the authority of God; but the king and that part
of the nation who were strangers to the evangelical faith, clung
to Rome, which Henry had so valiantly defended. The Word
of God had spiritually separated England from the papacy; the
"great matter" separated it materially. There is a close relation-
ship between these two divorces, which gives extreme importance
to the process between Henry and Catherine. When a great
revolution is to be effected in the bosom of a people (we have
the Reformation particularly in view), God instructs the
minority by the Holy Scriptures, and the majority by the
dispensations of the divine government. Facts undertake to
push forward those whom the more spiritual voice of the Word
leaves behind. England, profiting by this great teaching of
facts, has thought it her duty ever since[1] to avoid all contact
with a power that had deceived her; she has thought that
popery could not have the dominion over a people without
infringing on its vitality, and that it was only by emancipating
themselves from this priestly dictatorship that modern nations
could advance safely in the paths of liberty, order, and greatness.

For more than a year, as Henry's complaints testify, Anne
hesitated to give Henry encouragement in his love-suit. She
seems to have halted between two opinions. The despairing
king saw that he must set other springs to work and, taking
Lord Rochford aside, he unfolded his plans to him. The
ambitious father promised to do all in his power to influence

---

[1] [Readers will remember that these words were written in the middle
of the nineteenth century.]

his daughter. "The divorce is a settled thing," he said to her; "you have no control over it. The only question is, whether it shall be you or another who shall give an heir to the crown. Bear in mind that terrible revolutions threaten England, if the king has no son." Thus did everything combine to weaken Anne's resolution. The voice of her father, the interests of her country, the king's love, and doubtless some secret ambition, influenced her to grasp the proffered sceptre. These thoughts haunted her in society, in solitude, and even in her dreams. At one time she imagined herself on the throne, distributing to the people her charities and the Word of God; at another, in some obscure exile, leading a useless life, in tears and ignominy. When, in the sports of her imagination, the crown of England appeared all glittering before her, she at first rejected it; but afterwards that regal ornament seemed so beautiful, and the power it conferred so enviable, that she repelled it less energetically. Anne still refused, however, to give the so ardently solicited assent.

Henry, troubled by her hesitation, wrote to her frequently, and usually in French. As the court of Rome makes use of these letters, which are kept in the Vatican, to abuse the Reformation, we think it our duty to quote them.[1] The theft committed by a cardinal has preserved them for us; and we shall see that, far from supporting the calumnies that have been spread abroad, they tend, on the contrary, to refute them. We are far from approving their contents as a whole; but we cannot deny to the young lady, to whom they are addressed, the possession of noble and generous sentiments.

Henry, unable to support the anguish caused by Anne's refusal, wrote to her, as it is generally supposed, in May 1528:

> "By revolving in my mind the contents of your last letters, I have put myself into great agony, not knowing how to interpret them, whether to my disadvantage, as I understand some passages, or not, as I conclude from others. I beseech you earnestly to let me know your real mind as to the love between us two. It is needful for me to obtain this

[1] [The *Love-letters of Henry VIII*, reprinted from the Harleian Miscellany, with an introduction by Ladbroke Black, were reprinted by the Blandford Press in 1933.]

answer of you, having been for a whole year wounded with
the dart of love, and not yet assured whether I shall succeed
in finding a place in your heart and affection. This uncertainty
has hindered me of late from declaring you my mistress, lest
it should prove that you only entertain for me an ordinary
affection. But if you please to do the duty of a true and loyal
mistress, and to give up yourself, body and heart to me, . . .
I promise you that not only the name shall be given to you,
but also that I will take you for my mistress, casting off all
others that are in competition with you, out of my thoughts,
and affection, and serving you only. I beg you to give an
entire answer to this my rude letter, that I may know on
what and how far I may depend. But if it does not please
you to answer me in writing, let me know some place where
I may have it by word of mouth, and I will go thither with
all my heart. No more for fear of tiring you. Written by the
hand of him who would willingly remain yours,

"H. REX."

Such were the affectionate, and we may add (if we think of
the time and the man) the respectful terms employed by Henry
in writing to Anne Boleyn. The latter, without making any
promises, betrayed some little affection for the king, and added
to her reply an emblematical jewel, representing "a solitary
damsel in a boat tossed by the tempest," wishing thus to make
the prince understand the dangers to which his love exposed
her. Henry was ravished and immediately replied:

"For a present so valuable, that nothing could be more
(considering the whole of it), I return you my most hearty
thanks, not only on account of the costly diamond, and the
ship in which the solitary damsel is tossed about, but chiefly
for the fine interpretation, and the too humble submission
which your goodness hath made to me. Your favour I will
always seek to preserve, and this is my firm intention and
hope, according to the matter, *aut illic aut nullibi* (either here
or nowhere).

"The demonstrations of your affections are such, the fine
thoughts of your letter so cordially expressed, that they
oblige me for ever to honour, love, and serve you sincerely.

I beseech you to continue in the same firm and constant purpose, and assuring you that, on my part, I will not only make you a suitable return, but outdo you, so great is the loyalty of the heart that desires to please you. I desire, also, that if, at any time before this, I have in any way offended you, that you would give me the same absolution that you ask, assuring you, that hereafter my heart shall be dedicated to you alone. . . . God can do it, if he pleases, *to whom I pray once a day* for that end, hoping that at length *my prayers will be heard*. I wish the time may be short, but I shall think it long till we see one another. Written by the hand of that secretary, who in heart, body, and will, is

"Your loyal and most faithful Servant,
"H. T. Rex." [1]

Henry was a passionate lover, and history is not called upon to vindicate that cruel prince; but in the preceding letter we cannot discover the language of a seducer. It is impossible to imagine the king praying to God *once a day* for anything but a lawful union. These daily prayers seem to present the matter in a different light from that which Romanist writers have imagined.

Henry thought himself more advanced than he really was. Anne then shrank back; embarrassed by the position she held at court, she begged for one less elevated. The king submitted, although very vexed at first:

"Nevertheless that it belongeth not to a gentleman," he wrote to her, "to put his *mistress* in the situation of a *servant*, yet, by following your wishes, I would willingly concede it, if by that means you are less uncomfortable in the place you shall choose than in that where you have been placed by me.

[1] After the signature comes the following device:

Nulle autre que   A B   *ne cherche H.T.*

(Henry seeks Anne Boleyn, no other)

I thank you most cordially that you are pleased still to bear me in your remembrance.

"H. T."

Anne, having retired in May to Hever Castle, her father's residence, the king wrote to her as follows:

"My Mistress and my Friend,

"My heart and I surrender ourselves into your hands, and we supplicate to be commended to your good graces, and that by absence your affections may not be diminished to us. For that would be to augment our pain, which would be a great pity, which absence alone does sufficiently, and more than I could ever have thought. This brings to my mind a fact in astronomy, which is, that the farther off is the sun, yet the more scorching is his heat. Thus is it with our love; absence has placed distance between us, nevertheless fervour increases, at least on my part. I hope the same from you, assuring you that in my case the anguish of absence is so great that it would be intolerable were it not for the firm hope I have of your indissoluble affection towards me. In order to remind you of it, and because I cannot in person be in your presence, I send you the thing which comes nearest that is possible, that is to say, my picture, . . . set in bracelets; wishing myself in their place when it pleases you. This is from the hand of

"Your Servant and Friend,
"H. T. Rex."

Pressed by her father, her uncles, and by Henry, Anne's firmness was shaken. That crown, rejected by Renée and by Margaret, dazzled the young Englishwoman; every day she found some new charm in it; and gradually familiarizing herself with her new future, she said at last: "If the king becomes free, I shall be willing to marry him." This was a great fault; but Henry was at the height of joy.

The courtiers watched with observant eyes these developments of the king's affection, and were already preparing the homage which they proposed to lay at Anne Boleyn's feet. But there was one man at court whom Henry's resolution filled with sorrow; this was Wolsey. He had been the first to suggest to the king the idea of separating from Catherine; but if Anne is to succeed her, there must be no divorce. He had first alienated Catherine's party; he was now going to irritate that of the Boleyns; accordingly he began to fear that whatever might be the issue of this affair, it would cause his ruin. He took frequent walks in his park at Hampton Court, accompanied by the French ambassador, John du Bellay, the confidant of his sorrows: "I would willingly lose one of my fingers," he said, "if I could only have two hours' conversation with the king of France." At another time, fancying all England was pursuing him, he said with alarm, "The king my master and all his subjects will cry murder against me; they will fall upon me more fiercely than on a Turk, and all Christendom will rise against me!" The next day Wolsey, to gain the French ambassador, gave him a long history of what he had done for France *against the wishes of all England:* "I need much dexterity in my affairs," he added, "and must use a terrible *alchemy.*" But alchemy could not save him. Rarely has so much anguish been veiled beneath such grandeur. Du Bellay was moved with pity at the sight of the unhappy man's sufferings. "When he gives way," he wrote to Montmorency, "it lasts a day together—he is continually sighing.—You have never seen a man in such anguish of mind."

In truth Wolsey's reason was tottering. That fatal idea of the divorce was the cause of all his woes, and to be able to recall it, he would have given, not a *finger* only, but an arm, and perhaps more. It was too late; Henry had started his car down the steep, and whoever attempted to stop it must needs be crushed beneath its wheels. However, the cardinal tried to obtain something. Francis I had intercepted a letter from Charles V in which the Emperor spoke of the divorce as likely to raise the English nation in revolt. Wolsey caused this letter to be read to the king, in the hope that it would excite his serious apprehensions; but Henry only *frowned,* and Du Bellay, to whom the monarch ascribed the report on these troubles foreboded by Charles, received a "gentle lash." This was the sole result of the manœuvre.

Wolsey now resolved to broach this important subject in a straightforward manner. The step might prove his ruin; but if he succeeded he was saved and the popedom with him. Accordingly one day (shortly before the sweating sickness broke out, says Du Bellay, probably in June 1528) Wolsey openly prayed the king to renounce his design; his own reputation, he told him, the prosperity of England, the peace of Europe, the safety of the church—all required it; besides the pope would never grant the divorce. While the cardinal was speaking, Henry's face grew black; and before he had concluded the king's anger broke out. "The king used terrible words," said Du Bellay. He would have given a thousand Wolseys for one Anne Boleyn. "No other than God shall take her from me," was his most decided resolution.

Wolsey, now no longer doubting of his disgrace, began to take his measures accordingly. He commenced building in several places, in order to win the affections of the common people; he took great care of his bishoprics, in order that they might ensure him an easy retreat; he was affable to the courtiers; and thus covered the earth with flowers to deaden his fall. Then he would sigh as if he were disgusted with honours, and would celebrate the charms of solitude. He did more than this. Seeing plainly that the best way of recovering the king's favour would be to conciliate Anne Boleyn, he made her the most handsome presents, and assured her that all his efforts would now be directed to raise her to the throne of England. Anne believing these declarations, replied that she would help him in her turn, "as long as any breath was in her body." Even Henry had no doubt that the cardinal had profited by his lesson.

Thus were all parties restless and uneasy—Henry desiring to marry Lady Anne, the courtiers to get rid of Wolsey, and the latter to remain in power—when a serious event appeared to put everyone in harmony with his neighbour. About the middle of June, the terrible sweating sickness (*sudor anglicus*) broke out in England. The citizens of London, "thick as flies," said Du Bellay, suddenly feeling pains in the head and heart, rushed from the streets or shops to their chambers, began to sweat, and took to their beds. The disease made frightful and rapid progress, a burning heat preyed on their limbs; if they chanced to uncover themselves, the perspiration ceased, delirium came on, and in four hours the victim was dead and "stiff as a wall," says the French ambassador. Every family was in mourning. Sir Thomas More, kneeling by his daughter's bedside, burst into tears, and called upon God to save his beloved Margaret. Wolsey, who was at Hampton Court, suspecting nothing amiss, arrived in London as usual to preside in the Court of Chancery; but he ordered his horses to be saddled again immediately and rode back. In four days, 2000 persons died in London.

The court was at first safe from the contagion; but on the fourth day one of Anne Boleyn's ladies was attacked; it was as if a thunderbolt had fallen on the palace. The king removed with all haste, and stayed at a place twelve miles off, for he was not prepared to die. He ordered Anne to return to her father, invited the queen to join him, and took up his residence at Waltham. His real conscience awoke only in the presence of death. Four of his attendants and a friar, Anne's confessor, as it would appear, falling ill, the king departed for Hunsdon. He had been there two days only when Powis, Carew, Carton, and others of his court, were carried off in two or three hours. Henry had met an enemy whom he could not vanquish. He quitted the place attacked by the disease; he removed to another quarter; and when the sickness laid hold of any of his attendants in his new retreat, he again left that for a new asylum. Terror froze his blood; he wandered about pursued by that terrible scythe whose sweep might perhaps reach him; he cut off all communication, even with his servants; shut himself up in a room at the top of an isolated tower; ate all alone, and would see no one but his physician; he prayed, fasted, confessed, became reconciled with the queen; took the sacrament every Sunday and feast day; received *his Maker*, to use the words of a gentleman of his chamber; and the queen and Wolsey did the same. Nor was that all: his councillor, Sir Brian Tuke, was sick in Essex; but that mattered not; the king ordered him to come to him, even in his litter; and on the 20th of June, Henry after hearing three masses (he had never done so much before in one day) said to Tuke: "I want you to write *my will*." He was not the only one who took that precaution. "There were *a hundred thousand* made," says Du Bellay.

During this time, Anne in her retirement at Hever was calm and collected; she prayed much, particularly for the king and for Wolsey. But Henry, far less submissive, was very anxious. "The uneasiness my doubts about your health gave me," he wrote to her, "disturbed and frightened me exceedingly; but now, since you have as yet felt nothing, I hope it is with you as it is with us. . . . I beg you, my entirely beloved, not to frighten yourself, or be too uneasy at our absence, for wherever I am, I am yours. And yet we must sometimes submit to our misfortunes, for whoever will struggle against fate, is generally but so much the farther from gaining his end. Wherefore, comfort yourself and take courage, and make this misfortune as easy to you as you can."

As he received no news, Henry's uneasiness increased; he sent to Anne a messenger and a letter: "To acquit myself of the duty of a true servant, I send you this letter, beseeching you to apprise me of your welfare, which I pray may continue as long as I desire mine own."

Henry's fears were well founded; the malady became more severe; in four hours eighteen persons died at the archbishop of Canterbury's; Anne Boleyn herself and her brother also caught the infection. The king was exceedingly agitated; Anne alone appeared calm; the strength of her character raised her above exaggerated fears; but her enemies ascribed her calmness to other motives. "Her ambition is stronger than death," they said. "The king, queen, and cardinal tremble for their lives, but she . . . she would die content if she died a queen." Henry once more changed his residence. All the gentlemen of his privy-chamber were attacked with one exception; "he remained alone, keeping himself apart," says Du Bellay, and confessed every day. He wrote again to Anne, sending her his physician, Dr Butts: "The most displeasing news that could occur came to me suddenly at night. On three accounts I must lament it. One, to hear of the illness of my mistress, whom I esteem more than all the world, and whose health I desire as I do my own. I would willingly bear half of what you suffer to cure you. The second, from the fear that I shall have to endure my wearisome absence much longer, which has hitherto given me all the vexation that was possible; and when gloomy thoughts fill my mind, then I pray God to remove far from me such troublesome and rebellious ideas. The third, because my physician, in whom I have most confidence, is absent. Yet, from the want of him, I send you my second, and hope that he will soon make you well. I shall then love him more than ever. I beseech you to be guided by his advice in your illness. By your doing this, I hope soon to see you again, which will be to me a greater comfort than all the precious jewels in the world."

The pestilence soon broke out with more violence around Henry; he fled in alarm to Hatfield, taking with him only the gentlemen of his chamber; he next quitted this place for Tittenhanger, a house belonging to Wolsey, whence he commanded "general processions" throughout the kingdom in order to avert this scourge of God. At the same time he wrote to Wolsey: "As soon as any one falls ill in the place where you are, fly to another; and go thus from place to place." The poor cardinal was still more alarmed than Henry. As soon as he felt the slightest perspiration, he fancied himself a dead man. "I entreat your highness," he wrote trembling to the king on the 5th of July, "to show yourself full of pity for my soul; these are perhaps the last words I shall address to you . . . the whole world will see by my last testament that you have not bestowed your favour upon an ungrateful man." The king, perceiving that Wolsey's mind was affected, bade him "put apart fear and fantasies," and wear a cheerful humour in the midst of death.

At last the sickness began to diminish, and immediately the desire to see Anne revived in Henry's bosom. On the 18th of August she reappeared at court, and all the king's thoughts were now bent on the divorce.

But this business seemed to proceed in inverse ratio to his desires. There was no news of Campeggio; was he lost in the Alps or at sea? Did his gout detain him in some village, or was the announcement of his departure only a feint? Anne Boleyn herself was uneasy, for she attached great importance to Campeggio's coming. If the church annulled the king's marriage, Anne seeing the principal obstacle removed, thought she might accept Henry's hand. She therefore wrote to Wolsey: "I long to hear from you news of the legate, for I do hope (an' they come from you) they shall be very good." The king added in a postscript: "The not hearing of the legate's arrival in France causeth us somewhat to muse. Notwithstanding we trust by your diligence and vigilancy (with the assistance of Almighty God) shortly to be eased out of that trouble."

But still there was no news. While waiting for the long-desired ambassador, every one at the English court played his part as well as he could. Anne, whether from conscience, prudence, or modesty, refused the honours which the king would have showered upon her, and never approached Catherine but with marks of profound respect. Wolsey appeared to desire the divorce, while in reality he dreaded it, as fated to cause his ruin and that of the popedom. Henry strove to conceal the motives which impelled him to separate from the queen; to the bishops, he spoke of his *conscience*, to the nobility *of an heir*, and to all of the sad obligation which compelled him to put away so justly beloved a princess. In the meanwhile, he seemed to live on the best terms with her, from what Du Bellay says. But Catherine was the one who best dissembled her sentiments; she lived with the king as during their happiest days, treated Anne with every kindness, adopted an elegant costume, encouraged music and dancing in her apartments, often appeared in public, and seemed desirous of captivating by her gracious smiles the goodwill of England. This was a mournful comedy, destined to end in tragedy full of tears and agony.

CHAPTER TWO

Scripture and the Spreading Revival
(1527–29)

WHILE these scenes were acting in the royal palaces, far different discussions were going on among the people. After having dwelt for some time on the agitations of the court, we gladly return to the lowly disciples of the divine Word. The Reformation in England (and this is its characteristic) brings before us by turns the king upon his throne, and the laborious artisan in his humble cottage; and between these two extremes we meet with the doctor in his college, and the priest in his pulpit.

Among the young men trained at Cambridge under Barnes' instruction, and who had aided him at the time of his trial, was Miles Coverdale, afterwards bishop of Exeter, a man distinguished by his zeal for the gospel of Jesus Christ. Some time after the prior's fall, on Easter Eve, 1527, Coverdale and Cromwell met at the house of Sir Thomas More, when Cromwell exhorted the Cambridge student to apply himself to the study of sacred learning.[1] The lapse of his unhappy master had alarmed Coverdale, and he felt the necessity of withdrawing from that outward activity which had proved so fatal to Barnes. He therefore turned to the Scriptures, read them again and again, and perceived, like Tyndale, that the reformation of the church must be effected by the Word of God. The inspiration of that Word, the only foundation of its sovereign authority, had struck Coverdale. "Wherever the Scripture is known it reformeth all things, and setteth everything in order. And why? Because it is given *by the inspiration of God*."[2] This fundamental principle of the Reformation in England must, in every age, be that of the church.

Coverdale found happiness in his studies: "Now," he said,

---

[1] *Coverdale's Remains* (Parker Society), p. 490. The editor of the "*Remains*" dates this letter to Cromwell, 1st May, 1527. Others assign it to a later period. [2] *Ibid.*, p. 10.

"I begin to taste of Holy Scriptures! Now, honour be to God! I am set to the most sweet smell of holy letters."[1] He did not stop there, but thought it his duty to attempt in England the work which Tyndale was prosecuting in Germany. The Bible was so important in the eyes of these Christians, that two translations were undertaken simultaneously. "Why should other nations," said Coverdale, "be more plenteously provided for with the Scriptures in their mother-tongue than we?"[2]— "Beware of translating the Bible!" exclaimed the partisans of the schoolmen; "your labour will only make divisions in the faith and in the people of God."[3]—"God has now given His church," replied Coverdale, "the gifts of translating and of printing; we must improve them." And if any friends spoke of Tyndale's translation, he answered: "Do not you know that when many are shooting together, every one doth his best to be nighest the mark?"[4]—"But Scripture ought to exist in Latin only," objected the priests.—"No," replied Coverdale again, "the Holy Ghost is as much the author of it in the Hebrew, Greek, French, Dutch, and English, as in Latin. . . . The Word of God is of like worthiness and authority, in what language soever the Holy Ghost speaketh it."[5] This does not mean that translations of Holy Scripture are inspired, but that the Word of God, faithfully translated, always possesses a divine authority.

Coverdale determined therefore to translate the Bible, and, to procure the necessary books, he wrote to Cromwell, who, during his travels, had made a collection of these precious writings. "Nothing in the world I desire but books, as concerning my learning," he wrote; "like Jacob, you have drunk of the dew of heaven. . . . I ask to drink of your waters."[6] Cromwell did not refuse Coverdale his treasures. "Since the Holy Ghost has moved other men to bear the cost of this work," exclaimed the latter, "God gives me boldness to labour in the same."[7] He commenced without delay, saying: "Whosoever believeth not the Scripture, believeth not Christ; and whoso refuseth it, refuseth God also."[8] Such were the foundations of the reformed church in England.

---

[1] *Coverdale's Remains*, p. 490.   [2] Ibid., p. 12.   [3] Ibid.
[4] Ibid., p. 14.   [5] Ibid., p. 26.   [6] Ibid., p. 491.
[7] Ibid., p. 10.   [8] Ibid., p. 19.

Coverdale did not undertake to translate the Scriptures as a mere literary task: the Spirit which had moved him spoke to his heart; and tasting their life-giving promises, he expressed his happiness in pious songs:

> Be glad now, all ye christen men,
>   And let us rejoyce unfaynedly.
> The kyndnesse cannot be written with penne,
>   That we have receaved of God's mercy;
> Whose love towarde us hath never ende:
> He hath done for us as a frende;
>   Now let us thanke him hartely.
>
> These lovynge wordes he spake to me:
>   I wyll delyver thy soule from payne;
> I am desposed to do for thee,
>   And to myne owne selfe thee to retayne.
> Thou shalt be with me, for thou art myne;
> And I with thee, for I am thyne;
>   Soch is my love, I can not layne.
>
> They wyll shed out my precyous bloude,
>   And take away my lyfe also;
> Which I wyll suffre all for thy good:
>   Beleve this sure, where ever thou go.
> For I wyll yet ryse up agayne;
> Thy synnes I beare, though it be payne,
>   To make thee safe and free from wo.

Coverdale did not remain long in the solitude he desired. The study of the Bible, which had attracted him to it, soon drew him out of it. A revival was going on in Essex; John Tyball, an inhabitant of Bumpstead, having learnt to find in Jesus Christ the *true bread from heaven*, did not stop there. One day as he was reading the first epistle to the Corinthians, these words: "eat of this *bread*," and "drink of this *cup*," repeated four times within a few verses, convinced him that there was no transubstantiation. "A priest has no power to create the body of the Lord," said he ; "Christ truly is present in the Eucharist, but He is there only *for him that believeth*, and by a spiritual presence and action only." Tyball, disgusted with the Romish clergy and worship, and convinced that Christians are called to a universal priesthood, soon thought that men could do

AA

without a special ministry and, without denying the offices
mentioned in Scripture, as some Christians have done since,
he attached no importance to them. "Priesthood is not
necessary," he said: "every layman may administer the
sacraments as well as a priest." The minister of Bumpstead,
one Richard Foxe, and next a greyfriar of Colchester named
Meadow, were successively converted by Tyball's energetic
preaching.

Coverdale, who was living not far from these parts, having
heard speak of this religious revival, came to Bumpstead, and
went into the pulpit on the 29th of March 1528, to proclaim
the treasures contained in Scripture. Among his hearers was
an Augustine monk, named Topley, who was supplying Foxe's
place during his absence. This monk, while staying at the
parsonage, had found a copy of Wycliffe's *Wicket*, which he
read eagerly. His conscience was wounded by it, and all
seemed to totter about him. He had gone to church full of
doubt, and after divine service he waited upon the preacher,
exclaiming: "O my sins, my sins!"—"Confess yourself to
God," said Coverdale, "and not to a priest. God accepteth
the confession which cometh from the heart, and blotteth out
all your sins."[1] The monk believed in the forgiveness of God,
and became a zealous evangelist for the surrounding country.

The divine Word had hardly lighted one torch, before that
kindled another. At Colchester, in the same county, a worthy
man named Pykas, had received a copy of the Epistles of
Saint Paul from his mother, with this advice: "My son, live
according to these writings, and not according to the teaching
of the clergy." Some time after, Pykas having bought a New
Testament, and "read it thoroughly many times," a total
change took place in him. "We must be baptized by the Holy
Ghost," he said, and these words passed like a breath of life
over his simple-minded hearers. One day, Pykas having learnt
that Bilney, the first of the Cambridge doctors who had known
the power of God's Word, was preaching at Ipswich, he
proceeded thither, for he never refused to listen to a priest,
when that priest proclaimed the truth. "O, what a sermon!
how full of the Holy Ghost!" exclaimed Pykas.

From that period meetings of the brothers in Christ (for thus

[1] *Coverdale's Remains*, p. 481.

they were called) increased in number. They read the New
Testament, and each imparted to the others what he had
received for the instruction of all. One day when the twenty-
fourth chapter of Matthew had been read, Pykas, who was
sometimes wrong in the spiritual interpretation of Scripture,
remarked: "When the Lord declares that *not one stone of the
temple shall be left upon another*, he speaks of those haughty priests
who persecute those whom they call heretics, and who pretend
to be the temple of God. God will destroy them all." After
protesting against the priest, he protested against the host:
"The real body of Jesus Christ is in the Word," he said; "God
is in the Word, the Word is in God. God and the Word cannot
be separated. Christ is the living Word that nourishes the soul."
These humble preachers increased. Even women knew the
Epistles and Gospels by heart; Marion Matthew, Dorothy
Long, Catherine Swain, Alice Gardiner, and, above all,
Gyrling's wife, who had been in service with a priest lately
burnt for heresy, took part in these gospel meetings. And it
was not in cottages only that the glad tidings were then
proclaimed; Bower Hall, the residence of the squires of Bumpstead, was open to Foxe, Topley, and Tyball, who often read
the Holy Scriptures in the great hall of the mansion, in the
presence of the master and all their household: a humble
Reformation more real than that effected by Henry VIII.

There was, however, some diversity of opinion among these
brethren. "All who have begun to believe," said Tyball,
Pykas, and others, "ought to meet together to hear the Word
and increase in faith. We pray in common . . . and that
constitutes a church." Coverdale, Bilney, and Latimer willingly
recognized these incomplete societies, in which the members
met simply as *disciples;* they believed them necessary at a period
when the church was forming. These societies (in the reformers'
views) proved that organization has not the priority in the
Christian church, as Rome maintains, and that this priority
belongs to the faith and the life. But this imperfect form they
also regarded as provisional. To prevent numerous dangers, it
was necessary that this society should be succeeded by another,
the church of the New Testament, with its elders or bishops,
and deacons. The Word, they thought, rendered a ministry of
the Word necessary; and for its proper exercise not only piety

was required, but a knowledge of the sacred languages, the gift of eloquence, its exercise and perfection. However, there was no division among these Christians upon primary matters.

For some time the bishop of London watched this movement with uneasiness. He caused Hacker to be arrested, who, for six years past, had gone from house to house reading the Bible in London and Essex; examined and threatened him, inquired carefully after the names of those who had shown him hospitality; and the poor man in alarm had given up about forty of his brethren. Sebastian Harris, priest of Kensington, Forman, rector of All Hallows, John and William Pykas, and many others, were summoned before the bishop. They were taken to prison; they were led before the judges; they were put in the stocks; they were tormented in a thousand ways. Their minds became confused; their thoughts wandered; and many made the confessions required by their persecutors.

The adversaries of the gospel, proud of this success, now desired a more glorious victory. If they could not reach Tyndale, had they not in London the patron of his work, Monmouth, the most influential of the merchants, and a follower of the true faith? The clergy had made religion their business, and the Reformation was restoring it to the people. Nothing offended the priests so much, as that laymen should claim the right to believe without their intervention, and even to propagate the faith. Sir Thomas More, one of the most amiable men of the sixteenth century, participated in their hatred. He wrote to Cochlæus: "Germany now daily bringeth forth monsters more deadly than what Africa was wont to do;"[1] "But, alas! she is not alone. Numbers of Englishmen, who would not a few years ago even hear Luther's name mentioned, are now publishing his praises! England is now like the sea, which swells and heaves before a great storm, without any wind stirring it."[2] More felt particularly irritated, because the boldness of the gospellers had succeeded to the timidity of the Lollards. "The heretics," he said, "have put off hypocrisy, and put on impudence." He therefore resolved to set his hand to the work.

On the 14th of May 1529, Monmouth was in his shop, when an usher came and summoned him to appear before Sir John

[1] *More's Life*, p. 82.   [2] Ibid., p. 117.

Dauncies, one of the privy council. The pious merchant obeyed, striving to persuade himself that he was wanted on some matter of business; but in this he was deceived, as he soon found out. On arrival he was interrogated by Sir Thomas More, who, with Sir William Kingston, was Sir John's colleague. "What letters and books have you lately received from abroad?" asked Sir Thomas More, with some severity.—"None," replied Monmouth.—"What aid have you given to any persons living on the continent?"—"None, for these last three years. William Tyndale abode with me six months," he continued, "and his life was what a good priest's ought to be. I gave him ten pounds at the period of his departure, but nothing since. Besides, he is not the only one I have helped; the bishop of London's chaplain, for instance, has received of me more than £50."—"What books have you in your possession?" The merchant named the New Testament and some other works. "All these books have lain more than two years on my table, and I never heard that either priests, friars, or laymen learnt any great errors from them." More tossed his head. "It is a hard matter," he used to say, "to put a dry stick in the fire without its burning, or to nourish a snake in our bosom and not be stung by it.[1]—That is enough," he continued, "we shall go and search your house." Not a paper escaped their curiosity; but they found nothing to compromise Monmouth; he was however sent to the Tower.

After some interval the merchant was again brought before his judges. "You are accused," said More, "of having bought Martin Luther's tracts; of maintaining those who are translating the Scriptures into English; of subscribing to get the New Testament printed in English, with or without glosses; of having imported it into the kingdom; and, lastly, of having said that faith alone is sufficient to save a man."

Here was matter enough to burn several men. Monmouth, feeling convinced that Wolsey alone had power to deliver him, resolved to apply to him. "What will become of my poor workmen in London and in the country during my imprisonment?" he wrote to the cardinal. "They must have their money every week; who will give it them? . . . Besides, I make considerable sales in foreign countries, which bring large

[1] *More's Life*, p. 116.

returns to his majesty's customs. If I remain in prison, this commerce is stopped, and of course all the proceeds for the exchequer." Wolsey, who was as much a statesman as a churchman, began to melt; on the eve of a struggle with the pope and the Emperor, he feared, besides, to make the people discontented. Monmouth was released from prison. As alderman, and then as sheriff of London, he was faithful until death, and ordered in his last will that thirty sermons should be preached by the most evangelical ministers in England, "to make known the holy word of Jesus Christ."—"That is better," he thought, "than founding masses." The Reformation showed, in the sixteenth century, that great activity in commerce might be allied to great piety.

CHAPTER THREE

Campeggio Arrives in England

(July to November, 1528)

WHILE these persecutions were agitating the fields and the capital of England, all had changed in the ecclesiastical world, because all had changed in the political. The pope, pressed by Henry VIII and intimidated by the armies of Francis I, had granted the decretal and despatched Campeggio. But, on a sudden, there was a new development; a change of events brought a change of counsels. Doria had gone over to the Emperor; his fleet had restored abundance to Naples; the army of Francis I, ravaged by famine and pestilence, had capitulated, and Charles V, triumphant in Italy, had said proudly to the pope: "We are determined to defend the queen of England against King Henry's injustice."

Charles having recovered his superiority, the affrighted pope opened his eyes to the justice of Catherine's cause. "Send four messengers after Campeggio," said he to his officers; "and let each take a different road; bid them travel with all speed and deliver our despatches to him." They overtook the legate, who opened the pope's letters. "In the first place," said Clement VII to him, "protract your journey. In the second place, when you reach England, use every endeavour to reconcile the king and queen. In the third place, if you do not succeed, persuade the queen to take the veil. And in the last place, if she refuses, do not pronounce any sentence favourable to the divorce without a new and express order from me. This is the essential: *Summum et maximum mandatum.*[1]" The ambassador of the sovereign pontiff had a mission to do nothing. This instruction is sometimes as effective as any.

Campeggio, the youngest of the cardinals, was the most intelligent and the slowest; and this slowness caused his selection by the pope. He understood his master. If Wolsey was Henry's

[1] The chief and greatest commandment.

spur to urge on Campeggio, the latter was Clement's bridle to check Wolsey.[1] One of the judges of the divorce was about to pull forwards, the other backwards; thus the business stood a chance of not advancing at all, which was just what the pope required.

The legate, very eager to relax his speed, spent three months on his journey from Italy to England. He should have embarked for France on the 23rd of July; but the end of August was approaching, and no one knew in that country what had become of him.[2] At length they learnt that he had reached Lyons on the 22nd of August. The English ambassador in France sent his horses, carriages, plate, and money, in order to hasten his progress; the legate complained of the *gout*, and Gardiner found the greatest difficulty in getting him to move. Henry wrote every day to Anne Boleyn, complaining of the slow progress of the nuncio. "He arrived in Paris last Sunday or Monday," he says at the beginning of September; "Monday next we shall hear of his arrival in Calais, and then I shall obtain what I have so longed for, to God's pleasure and both our comforts."

At the same time this impatient prince sent message after message to accelerate the legate's rate of travelling.

Anne began to desire a future which surpassed all that her youthful imagination had conceived, and her agitated heart expanded to the breath of hope. She wrote to Wolsey:

"This shall be to give unto your Grace, as I am most bound, my humble thanks for the great pain and travail that your Grace doth take in studying, by your wisdom and great diligence, how to bring to pass honourably the greatest wealth [well-being] that is possible to come to any creature living; and in especial remembering how wretched and unworthy I am in comparison to his Highness. . . . Now, good my lord, your discretion may consider as yet how little it is in my power to recompense you but alonely [only] with my good will; the which I assure you, look what thing in this world I can imagine to do you pleasure in, you shall find me the gladdest woman in the world to do it."

[1] Fuller, *Church History of Britain* (1655) Book v, p. 172.
[2] State Papers, vii, p. 91, 92.

But the impatience of the king of England and of Anne seemed as if it would never be satisfied. Campeggio, on his way through Paris, told Francis I that the divorce would never take place, and that he should soon go to *Spain* to see Charles V. . . . This was significative. "The king of England ought to know," said the indignant Francis to the duke of Suffolk, "that Campeggio is *imperialist* at heart, and that his mission in England will be a mere mockery."[1]

In truth, the Spanish and Roman factions tried every manœuvre to prevent a union they detested. Anne Boleyn, queen of England, signified not only Catherine humbled, but Charles offended; the clerical party weakened, perhaps destroyed, and the evangelical party probably strengthened. The Romish faction found accomplices even in Anne's own family. Her brother George's wife, a proud and passionate woman, and a rigid Roman catholic, had sworn an implacable hatred against her young sister. By this means wounds might be inflicted, even in the domestic sanctuary, which would not be the less deep because they were the work of her own kindred. One day we are told that Anne found in her chamber a book of pretended prophecies, in which was a picture representing a king, a queen shedding tears, and at their feet a young lady headless. Anne turned away her eyes with disgust. She desired, however, to know what this emblem signified, and officious friends brought to her one of those pretended wise men, so numerous at all times, who abuse the credulity of the ignorant by professing to interpret such mysteries. "This prophetic picture," he said, "represents the history of the king and his wife." Anne was not credulous, but she understood what her enemies meant to insinuate, and dismissed the mock interpreter without betraying any signs of fear; then turning to her favourite attendant, Anne Saville, "Come hither, Nan," said she, "look at this book of prophecies; this is the king, this is the queen wringing her hands and mourning, and this (putting her finger on the bleeding body) is *myself*, with my head cut off."—The young lady answered with a shudder: "If I thought it were true, I would not myself have him were he an emperor."

---

[1] "The cardinal intended not that your Grace's matter should take effect, but only to use dissimulation with your Grace, for he is entirely imperial." Suffolk to Henry, State Papers, vii, p. 183.

—"Tut, Nan," replied Anne Boleyn with a smile, "I think the book a bauble, and am resolved to have him, that my issue may be royal, whatever may become of me." This story is based on good authority, and there were so many predictions of this kind afloat that it was very possible one of them might come true; people afterwards recollected only the prophecies confirmed by the events. But, be that as it may, this young lady, so severely chastised in afterdays, found in her God an abundant consolation.

At length Campeggio embarked at Calais on the 29th of September, and unfortunately for him he had an excellent passage across the channel. A storm to drive him back to the French coast would have suited him admirably. But on the 1st of October he was at Canterbury, whence he announced his arrival to the king. At this news, Henry forgot all the delays which had so irritated him. "His majesty can never be sufficiently grateful to your holiness for so great a favour," wrote Wolsey to the pope; "but he will employ his riches, his kingdom, his life even, and deserve the name of *Restorer of the Church* as justly as he has gained that of *Defender of the Faith*." This zeal alarmed Campeggio, for the pope wrote to him that any proceeding which might irritate Charles would inevitably cause the ruin of the church. The nuncio became more dilatory than ever, and although he reached Canterbury on the 1st of October, he did not arrive at Dartford until the 5th, thus taking four days for a journey of about thirty miles.

Meanwhile preparations were making to receive him in London. Wolsey, feeling contempt for the poverty of the Roman cardinals, and very uneasy about the equipage with which his colleague was likely to make his entrance into the capital, sent a number of showy chests, rich carpets, litters hung with drapery, and harnessed mules. On the other hand Campeggio, whose secret mission was to keep in the background, and above all to do nothing, feared these banners, and trappings, and all the parade of a triumphal entry. Alleging therefore an attack of gout in order to escape from the pomps his colleague had prepared for him, he quietly took a boat, and thus reached the palace of the bishop of Bath, where he was to lodge.

While the nuncio was thus proceeding unnoticed up the

Thames, the equipages sent by Wolsey entered London through the midst of a gaping crowd, who looked on them with curiosity as if they had come from the banks of the Tiber. Some of the mules however took fright and ran away, the coffers fell off and burst open, when there was a general rush to see their contents; but to the surprise of all they were empty. This was an excellent jest for the citizens of London. "Fine outside, empty inside; a just emblem of the popedom, its embassy, and foolish pomps," they said; "a sham legate, a procession of masks, and the whole a farce!"

Campeggio was come at last, and now what he dreaded most was an audience. "I cannot move," he said, "or endure the motion of a litter." Never had an attack of gout been more seasonable. Wolsey, who paid him frequent visits, soon found him to be his equal in cunning. To no purpose did he treat him with every mark of respect, shaking his hand and making much of him; it was labour lost, the Roman nuncio would say nothing, and Wolsey began to despair. The king, on the contrary, was full of hope, and fancied he already had the act of divorce in his portfolio, because he had the nuncio in his kingdom.

The greatest effect of the nuncio's arrival was the putting an end to Anne Boleyn's indecision. She had several relapses: the trials which she foresaw, and the grief Catherine must necessarily feel, had agitated her imagination and disturbed her mind. But when she saw the church and her own enemies prepared to pronounce the king's divorce, her doubts were removed, and she regarded as legitimate the position that was offered her. The king, who suffered from her scruples, was delighted at this change. "I desire to inform you," he wrote to her in English, "what joy it is to me to understand of your conformableness with reason, and of the suppressing of your inutile and vain thoughts and fantasies with the bridle of reason. I assure you all the greatness of this world could not counterpoise for my satisfaction the knowledge and certainty thereof. . . . The unfeigned sickness of this well-willing legate doth somewhat retard his access to your person." It was therefore the determination of the pope that made Anne Boleyn resolve to accept Henry's hand; this is an important lesson for which we are indebted to the *Vatican letters*. We should be grateful to the papacy for having so carefully preserved them.

But the more Henry rejoiced, the more Wolsey despaired; he would have desired to penetrate into pope Clement's thoughts, but could not succeed. Imagining that De Angelis, the general of the Spanish Observance, knew all the secrets of the pope and of the Emperor, he conceived the plan of kidnapping him. "If he goes to Spain by sea," said he to Du Bellay, "a good brigantine or two would do the business; and if by land, it will be easier still." Du Bellay failed not (as he informs us himself) "to tell him plainly that by such proceedings he would entirely forfeit the pope's good will."—"What matter?" replied Wolsey, "I have nothing to lose." As he said this, tears started to his eyes. At last he made up his mind to remain ignorant of the pontiff's designs, and wiped his eyes, awaiting, not without fear, the interview between Henry and Campeggio.

On the 22nd of October, a month after his arrival, the nuncio, borne in a sedan chair of red velvet, was carried to court. He was placed on the right of the throne, and his secretary in his name delivered a high-sounding speech, saluting Henry with the name of Saviour of Rome, *Liberator urbis.* "His majesty," replied Fox in the king's name, "has only performed the duties incumbent on a Christian prince, and he hopes that the holy see will bear them in mind."—"Well attacked, well defended," said Du Bellay. For the moment, a few Latin declamations got the papal nuncio out of his difficulties.

Campeggio did not deceive himself: if the divorce were refused, he foresaw the reformation of England. Yet he hoped still, for he was assured that Catherine would submit to the judgment of the church; and being fully persuaded that the queen would refuse the holy father nothing, the nuncio began "his approaches," as Du Bellay calls them. On the 22nd of October, and again on the 27th, the two cardinals waited on Catherine, and in flattering terms insinuated that she might prevent the blow which threatened her by voluntary retirement into a convent. And, then, to end all indecision in the queen's mind, Campeggio put on a severe look and exclaimed: "How is it, madam, explain the mystery to us? From the moment the holy father appointed us to examine the question of your divorce, you have been seen not only at court, but in public, wearing the most magnificent ornaments, participating with an appearance of gaiety and satisfaction at amusements and festivities which you had never tolerated before. . . . The church is in the most cruel embarrassment with regard to you; the king, your husband, is in the greatest perplexity; the princess, your daughter, is taken from you . . . and instead of shedding tears, you give yourself up to vanity. Renounce the world, madam; enter a nunnery. Our holy father himself requires this of you."

The agitated queen was almost fainting; stifling her emotion, however, she said mildly but firmly: "Alas! my lords, is it now a question whether I am the king's lawful wife or not, when I have been married to him almost twenty years and no objection raised before? . . . Divers prelates and lords are yet alive who then adjudged our marriage good and lawful—and now to say it is detestable! this is a great marvel to me, especially when I consider what a wise prince the king's father was, and also the natural love and affection my father, King Ferdinand, bare unto me. I think that neither of these illustrious princes would have made me contract an illicit union." At these words, Catherine's emotion compelled her to stop—"If I weep, my lords," she continued almost immediately, "it is not for myself, it is for a person dearer to me than my life. What! I should consent to an act which deprives my daughter of a crown? No, I will not sacrifice my child. I know what dangers threaten me. I am only a weak woman, a stranger, without learning, advisers or friends . . . and my enemies are skilful, learned in the laws, and desirous to merit their master's favour . . . and more than that, even my judges are my enemies. Can I receive as such," she said as she looked at Campeggio, "a man extorted from the pope by manifest lying? . . . And as for you," added she, turning haughtily to Wolsey, "having failed in attaining the tiara, you have sworn to revenge yourself on my nephew the Emperor . . . and you have kept him true promise; for of all his wars and vexations, he may only thank you. One victim was not enough for you. Forging abominable suppositions, you desire to plunge his aunt into a frightful abyss. . . . But my cause is just, and I trust it in the Lord's hand." After this bold language, the unhappy Catherine withdrew to her apartments. The imminence of the danger effected a salutary revolution in her; she laid aside her brilliant ornaments, assumed the sober garments in which she is usually represented, and passed days and nights in mourning and in tears.

Thus Campeggio saw his hopes deceived; he had thought to find a nun, and had met a queen and a mother. . . . He now proceeded to set every imaginable spring at work; as Catherine would not renounce Henry, he must try and prevail upon Henry to renounce his idea of separating from the queen. The Roman legate therefore changed his batteries, and turned them against the king.

Henry, always impatient, went one day unannounced to Campeggio's lodging, accompanied by Wolsey only: "As we are without witnesses," he said, taking his seat familiarly between the two cardinals, "let us speak freely of our affairs.— How shall you proceed?" But to his great astonishment and grief, the nuncio prayed him, with all imaginable delicacy, to renounce the divorce. At these words the fiery Tudor burst out: "Is this how the pope keeps his word? He sends me an ambassador to annul my marriage, but in reality to confirm it." He made a pause. Campeggio knew not what to say. Henry and Catherine being equally persuaded of the justice of their cause, the nuncio was in a dilemma. Wolsey himself suffered a martyrdom. The king's anger grew fiercer; he had thought the legate would hasten to withdraw an imprudent expression, but Campeggio was dumb. "I see that you have chosen your part," said Henry to the nuncio; "mine, you may be sure, will soon be taken also. Let the pope only persevere in this way of acting, and the apostolical see, covered with perpetual infamy, will be visited with a frightful destruction." The lion had thrown off the lamb's skin which he had momentarily assumed. Campeggio felt that he must appease the monarch. "Craft and delay" were his orders from Rome; and with that view the pope had provided him with the necessary arms. He hastened to produce the famous *decretal* which pronounced the divorce. "The holy father," he told the king, "ardently desires that this matter should be terminated by a happy reconciliation between you and the queen; but if that is impossible, you shall judge yourself whether or not his holiness can keep his promises." He then read the bull, and even showed it to Henry, without permitting it, however, to leave his hands. This exhibition produced the desired effect: Henry grew calm. "Now I am at ease again," he said; "this miraculous talisman revives all my courage. This decretal is the efficacious remedy that will restore peace to my oppressed conscience, and joy to my bruised heart. Write to his holiness, that this immense benefit binds me to him so closely, that he may expect from me more than his imagination can conceive."

And yet a few clouds gathered shortly after in the king's mind.

Campeggio having shown the bull had hastened to lock it up again. Would he presume to keep it in his own hands? Henry and Wolsey will leave no means untried to get possession of it; that point gained, and victory is theirs.

Wolsey having returned to the nuncio, he asked him for the decretal with an air of candour as if it was the most natural thing in the world. He desired, he said, to show it to the king's privy-councillors. "The pope," replied Campeggio, "has granted this bull, not to be used, but to be kept secret; he simply desired to show the king the good feeling by which he was animated." Wolsey having failed, Henry tried his skill. "Have the goodness to hand me the bull which you showed me," said he. The nuncio respectfully refused. "For a single moment," he said. Campeggio still refused. The haughty Tudor retired, stifling his anger. Then Wolsey made another attempt, and founded his demand on justice. "Like you, I am delegated by his holiness to decide this affair," he said, "and I wish to study the important document which is to regulate our proceedings." —This was met by a new refusal. "What!" exclaimed the minister of Henry VIII, "am I not, like you, a cardinal? . . . like you, a judge? your colleague?" It mattered not, the nuncio would not, by any means, let the decretal go. Clement was not deceived in the choice he had made of Campeggio; the ambassador was worthy of his master.

It was evident that the pope in granting the bull had been acting a part: this trick revolted the king. It was no longer anger that he felt, but disgust. Wolsey knew that Henry's contempt was more to be feared than his wrath. He grew alarmed, and paid the nuncio another visit. "The *general* commission," he said, "is insufficient, the *decretal* commission alone can be of service, and you do not permit us to read a word of it. . . . The king and I place the greatest confidence in the good intentions of his holiness, and yet we find our expectations frustrated. Where is that paternal affection with which we had flattered ourselves? What prince has ever been trifled with as the king of England is now? If this is the way in which the *Defender of the Faith* is rewarded, Christendom will know what those who serve Rome will have to expect from her, and every power will withdraw its support. Do not deceive yourselves: the foundation on which the holy see is placed is so very insecure that the least movement will suffice to precipitate it into everlasting ruin. What a sad futurity! . . . what inexpressible torture! . . . whether I wake or sleep, gloomy thoughts continually pursue me like a frightful nightmare." This time Wolsey spoke the truth.

But all his eloquence was useless; Campeggio refused to give up the so much desired bull. When sending him, Rome had told him: "Above all, do not succeed!" This means having failed, there remained for Wolsey one other way of effecting the divorce. "Well then," he said to Campeggio, "let us pronounce it ourselves."—"Far be it from us," replied the nuncio; "the anger of the Emperor will be so great, that the peace of Europe will be broken for ever."—"I know how to arrange all that," replied the English cardinal, "in political matters you may trust to me." The nuncio then took another tone and, proudly wrapping himself up in his morality, he said: "I shall follow the voice of my conscience; if I see that the divorce is possible, I shall leap the ditch; if otherwise, I shall not."—"Your conscience! that may be easily satisfied," rejoined Wolsey. "Holy Scripture forbids a man to marry his brother's widow; now no pope can grant what is forbidden by the law of God."— "The Lord preserve us from such a principle," exclaimed the Roman prelate; "the power of the pope is unlimited."—The nuncio had hardly put his conscience forward, before it stumbled; it bound him to Rome and not to heaven. But for that matter, neither public opinion nor Campeggio's own friends had any great idea of his morality; they thought that to make him *leap the ditch*, it was only requisite to know the price at which he might be bought. The bishop of Bayonne wrote to Montmorency: "Put at the close of a letter which I can show Campeggio something *promissory*, that he shall have *benefices*. . . . That will cost you nothing, and may serve in this matter of the marriage; for I know that he is longing for something of the sort."—"What is to be done then," said Wolsey at last, astonished at meeting with a resistance to which he was unaccustomed. "I shall inform the pope of what I have seen and heard," replied Campeggio, "and I shall wait for his instructions." Henry was forced to consent to this new course, for the nuncio hinted that if it were opposed he would go in person to Rome to ask the pontiff's orders, and he never would have returned. By this means several months were gained.

During this time men's minds were troubled. The prospect of a divorce between the king and queen had stirred the nation; and the majority, particularly among the women, declared against the king. "Whatever may be done," the people said boldly, "whoever marries the Princess Mary will be king of England." Wolsey's spies informed him that Catherine and Charles V had many devoted partisans even at the court. He wished to make sure of this. "It is pretended," he said one day in an indifferent tone, "that the Emperor has boasted that he will get the king driven from his realm, and that by his majesty's own subjects. . . . What do you think of it, my lords?" —"Tough against the spur," says Du Bellay, the lords remained silent. At length, however, one of them more imprudent than the rest, exclaimed: "Such a boast will make the Emperor lose more than a hundred thousand Englishmen." This was enough for Wolsey. To *lose* them, he thought, Charles must *have* them. If Catherine thought of levying war against her husband, following the example of former queens of England, she would have, then, a party ready to support her; this became dangerous.

The king and the cardinal immediately took their measures. More than 15,000 of Charles' subjects were ordered to leave London; the arms of the citizens were seized, "in order that they might have no worse weapon than the tongue;" the Flemish councillors accorded to Catherine were dismissed, after they had been heard by the king and Campeggio, "for they had no commission to speak to *the other* [Wolsey]"—and finally, they kept "a great and constant watch" upon the country. Men feared an invasion of England, and Henry was not of a humour to subject his kingdom to the pope.

This was not enough; the alarmed king thought it his duty

BB

to come to an explanation with his people; and having summoned the lords spiritual and temporal, the judges, the members of the privy-council, the mayor and aldermen of the city, and many of the gentry, to meet him at his palace of Bridewell on the 13th of November, he said to them with a very condescending air: "You know, my lords and gentlemen, that for these twenty years past divine Providence has granted our country such prosperity as it has never known before. But in the midst of all the glory that surrounds me, the thought of my last hour often occurs to me, and I fear that if I should die without an heir, my death would cause more damage to my people than my life has done them good. God forbid that for want of a legitimate king England should be again plunged into the horrors of civil war!" Then calling to mind the illegalities invalidating his marriage with Catherine, the king continued: "These thoughts have filled my mind with anxiety, and are continually pricking my conscience. This is the only motive, and God is my witness, which has made me lay this matter before the pontiff. As touching the queen, she is a woman incomparable in gentleness, humility and buxomness, as I these twenty years have had experiment of; so that if I were to marry again, if the marriage might be good, I would surely choose her above all other women. But if it be determined by judgment that our marriage was against God's law, and surely void, then I shall not only sorrow in departing from so good a lady and loving companion, but much more lament and bewail my unfortunate chance, that I have so long lived in adultery, to God's great displeasure, and have no true heir of my body to inherit this realm. . . . Therefore I require of you all to pray with us that the very truth may be known, for the discharging of our conscience and the saving of our soul." These words, though wanting in sincerity, were well calculated to soothe men's minds. Unfortunately, it appears that after this *speech from the crown*, the official copy of which has been preserved, Henry added a few words of his own. "If however," he said, according to Du Bellay, casting a threatening glance around him, "there should be any man whatsoever who speaks of his prince in other than becoming terms, I will show him that I am the master, and there is no head so high that I will not roll it from his shoulders." This was a speech in Henry's style;

but we cannot give unlimited credit to Du Bellay's assertions, this diplomatist being very fond, like others of his class, of "seasoning" his despatches. But whatever may be the fact as regards the postscript, the speech on the divorce produced an effect. From that time there were no more jests, not even on the part of the Boleyns' enemies. Some supported the king, others were content to pity the queen in secret; the majority prepared to take advantage of a court-revolution which every one foresaw. "The king *so plainly* gave them to understand his pleasure," says the French ambassador, "that they speak more soberly than they have done hitherto."

Henry wishing to silence the clamours of the people, and to allay the fears felt by the higher classes, gave several magnificent entertainments, at one time in London, at another at Greenwich, now at Hampton Court, and then at Richmond. The queen accompanied him, but Anne generally remained "in a very handsome lodging which Henry had furnished for her," says Du Bellay. The cardinal, following his master's example, gave representations of French plays with great magnificence. All his hope was in France. "I desire nothing in England, neither in word nor in deed, which is not French," he said to the bishop of Bayonne. At length Anne Boleyn had accepted the brilliant position she had at first refused, and every day her stately mansion (Suffolk House) was filled with a numerous court—"more than ever had crowded to the queen."—"Yes, yes," said Du Bellay, as he saw the crowd turning towards the *rising sun*, "they wish by these *little* things to accustom the people to endure her, that when *great* ones are attempted, they may not be found so strange."

In the midst of these festivities the grand business did not slumber. When the French ambassador solicited the subsidy intended for the ransom of the sons of Francis I, the cardinal required of him in exchange a paper proving that the marriage had never been valid. Du Bellay excused himself on the ground of his age and want of learning; but being given to understand that he could not have the subsidy without it, he wrote the memoir in a single day. The enraptured cardinal and king entreated him to speak with Campeggio. The ambassador consented, and succeeded beyond all expectation. The nuncio, fully aware that a bow too much bent will break, made Henry by turns become the sport of hope and fear. "Take care how you assert that the pope had not the right to grant a dispensation to the king," said he to the French bishop, "this would be denying *his power, which is infinite.* But," added he in a mysterious tone, "I will point out a road that will infallibly lead you to the mark. Show that the holy father has been deceived by false information. *Push me hard on that,*" he continued, "so as to force me to declare that the dispensation was granted on erroneous grounds." Thus did the legate himself reveal the breach by which the fortress might be surprised. "Victory!" exclaimed Henry, as he entered Anne's apartments all beaming with joy.

But this confidence on the part of Campeggio was only a new trick. "There is a great rumour at court," wrote Du Bellay soon after, "that the Emperor and the king of France are coming together, and leaving Henry alone, so that all will fall on his shoulders." Wolsey, finding that the intrigues of diplomacy had failed, thought it his duty to put fresh springs in motion, "and by all good and honest means to gain the pope's favour." He saw, besides, to his great sorrow, the new catholicity then forming in the world, and uniting, by the closest bonds, the Christians of England to those of the continent. To strike down one of the leaders of this evangelical movement might incline the court of Rome in Henry's favour. The cardinal undertook, therefore, to persecute Tyndale; and this resolution will now transport us to Germany.

CHAPTER FOUR

The Search for William Tyndale

(1528–30)

THE residence of Tyndale and his friends in foreign countries, and the connections there formed with pious Christians, testify to the fraternal spirit which the Reformation then restored to the church. It is in protestantism that true catholicity is to be found. The Romish church is not a catholic church. Separated from the churches of the east, which are the oldest in Christendom, and from the reformed churches, which are the purest, it is nothing but a sect, and that a degenerate one. A church which should profess to believe in an episcopal unity, but which kept itself separate from the episcopacy of Rome and of the East, and from the evangelical churches, would be no longer a catholic church; it would be a sect more sectarian still than that of the Vatican, a fragment of a fragment. The church of the Saviour requires a truer, a diviner unity than that of priests, who condemn one another. It was the reformers, and particularly Tyndale, who proclaimed throughout Christendom the existence of a *body of Christ*, of which all the children of God are members. The disciples of the Reformation are the true catholics.

It was a catholicity of another sort that Wolsey desired to uphold. He did not reject certain reforms in the church, particularly such as brought him any profit; but, before all, he wished to preserve for the hierarchy their privileges and uniformity. The Romish Church in England was then personified in him, and if he fell, its ruin would be near. His political talents and multiplied relations with the continent, caused him to discern more clearly than others the dangers which threatened the popedom. The publication of the Scriptures of God in English appeared to some a cloud without importance, which would soon disappear from the horizon; but to the foreseeing glance of Wolsey, it betokened a mighty tempest. Besides, he

371

loved not the fraternal relations then forming between the evangelical Christians of Great Britain and of other nations. Annoyed by this spiritual catholicity, he resolved to procure the arrest of Tyndale, who was its principal organ.[1]

Already had Hackett, Henry's envoy to the Low Countries, caused the imprisonment of Harman, an Antwerp merchant, one of the principal supporters of the English reformer. But Hackett had in vain asked Wolsey for such documents as would convict him of *treason* (for the crime of loving the Bible was not sufficient to procure Harman's condemnation in Brabant); the envoy had remained without letters from England, and the last term fixed by the law having expired, Harman and his wife were liberated after seven months' imprisonment.

And yet Wolsey had not been inactive. The cardinal hoped to find elsewhere the co-operation which Margaret of Austria refused. It was Tyndale that he wanted, and everything seemed to indicate that he was then hidden at Cologne or in its neighbourhood. Wolsey, recollecting senator Rincke and the services he had already performed, determined to send to him one John West, a friar of the Franciscan house at Greenwich. West, a somewhat narrow-minded but energetic man, was very desirous of distinguishing himself, and he had already gained some notoriety in England among the adversaries of the Reformation. Flattered by his mission, this vain monk immediately set off for Antwerp, accompanied by another friar, in order to seize Tyndale, and even Roye, once his colleague at Greenwich, and against whom he had there ineffectually contended in argument.

While these men were conspiring his ruin, Tyndale composed several works, got them printed, and sent to England, and prayed God night and day to enlighten his fellow-countrymen. "Why do you give yourself so much trouble?" said some of his friends. "They will burn your books as they have burnt the Gospel." "They will only do what I expect," replied he, "if they burn me also." Already he beheld his own burning pile in the distance; but it was a sight which only served to increase his zeal. Hidden, like Luther at the Wartburg, not however in

[1] [In this work Wolsey did not himself take the initiative. Rather was his name and authority used by other leaders of the Church in England who pressed on with the persecutions.]

a castle, but in a humble lodging, Tyndale, like the Saxon reformer, spent his days and nights translating the Bible. But not having an elector of Saxony to protect him, he was forced to change his residence from time to time.

Before the close of 1528, Fryth, who had escaped from the prisons of Oxford, rejoined Tyndale, and the sweets of friendship softened the bitterness of their exile. Tyndale having finished the New Testament, and begun the translation of the Old, the learned Fryth was of great use to him. The more they studied the Word of God, the more they admired it. During 1529 they were busily occupied in seeing through the press the translation of the five Books of Moses on which Tyndale had been engaged since the completion of his work on the New Testament. Early in 1530 this first instalment of the Old Testament was in circulation. Addressing his fellow-countrymen in his Prologue to the Book of Genesis, Tyndale said: "As thou readest, think that every syllable pertaineth to thine own self, and suck out the pith of the Scripture."[1] Then denying that visible signs naturally impart grace, as the schoolmen had pretended, Tyndale maintained that the sacraments are effectual only when the Holy Ghost sheds his influence upon them. "The ceremonies of the law," he wrote in his Prologue to Leviticus, "stood the Israelites in the same stead as the sacraments do us. We are saved not by the power of the sacrifice or the deed itself, but by virtue of *faith in the promise*, whereof the sacrifice or ceremony was a token or sign. The Holy Ghost is no dumb God, no God that goeth a mumming. Wherever the Word is proclaimed, this inward witness worketh. If baptism preach me the washing in Christ's blood, so doth the Holy Ghost accompany it; and that deed of preaching through faith doth put away my sins. The ark of Noah saved them in the water through faith."[2]

The man who dared address England in language so contrary to the teaching of the middle ages must be imprisoned. John West, who had been sent with this object, arrived at Antwerp; Hackett procured for him as interpreter a friar of English descent, made him assume a secular dress, and gave him "three pounds" on the cardinal's account; the less attention the

---

[1] Prologue to the Book of Genesis (*Doctrinal Treatises*), pp. 398–403.
[2] Prologue to the Book of Leviticus (*Doctrinal Treatises*), pp. 421-8.

embassy attracted, the more likely it would be to succeed. But great was West's vexation, on reaching Cologne, to learn that Rincke was at Frankfort. But that mattered not; the Greenwich monk could search for Tyndale at Cologne, and desire Rincke to do the same at Frankfort; thus there would be two searches instead of one. West procured a "swift" messenger (he too was a monk) and gave him the letter Wolsey had addressed to Rincke.

It was fair-time at Frankfort, and the city was filled with merchants and their wares. As soon as Rincke had finished reading Wolsey's letter, he hastened to the burgomasters, and required them to confiscate the English translations of the Scriptures, and, above all, to seize "the heretic who was troubling England as Luther troubled Germany."—"Tyndale and his friends have not appeared in our fairs since the month of March 1528," replied the magistrates, "and we know not whether they are dead or alive."

Rincke was not discouraged. John Schott of Strasburg, who was said to have printed Tyndale's books, and who cared less about the works he published than the money he drew from them, happened to be at Frankfort. "Where is Tyndale?" Rincke asked him. "I do not know," replied the printer; but he confessed that he had printed a thousand volumes at the request of Tyndale and Roye. "Bring them to me," continued the senator of Cologne—"If a fair price is paid me, I will give them up to you." Rincke paid all that was demanded.

Wolsey would now be gratified, for the New Testament annoyed him almost as much as the divorce; this book, so dangerous in his eyes, seemed on the point of raising a conflagration which would infallibly consume the edifice of Roman traditionalism. Rincke, who participated in his patron's fear, impatiently opened the volumes made over to him; but there was a sad mistake, they were not the New Testament, not even a work of Tyndale's, but one written by William Roye, a changeable and violent man, whom the reformer had employed for some time at Hamburg, and who had followed him to Cologne, but with whom he had soon become disgusted. "I bade him farewell for our two lives," said Tyndale, "and a day longer." Roye, on quitting the reformer, had gone to Strasburg, where he boasted of his relations with him, and had got a

satire in that city printed against Wolsey and the monastic
orders, entitled *The Burial of the Mass:* this was the book
delivered to Rincke. The monk's sarcastic spirit had exceeded
the legitimate bounds of controversy, and the senator accordingly dared not send the volumes to England. He did not
however discontinue his inquiries, but searched every place
where he thought he could discover the New Testament and,
having seized all the suspected volumes, set off for Cologne.

Yet he was not satisfied. He wanted Tyndale, and went
about asking everyone if they knew where to find him. But the
reformer, whom he was seeking in so many places, and especially
at Frankfort and Cologne, chanced to be residing at about
equal distances from these two towns, so that Rincke, while
travelling from one to the other, might have met him face to
face, as Ahab's messenger met Elijah. Tyndale was at Marburg,
whither he had been drawn by several motives. Prince Philip
the Magnanimous, of Hesse-Cassel, was the great protector of
the evangelical doctrines. The university had attracted attention in the Reform by the paradoxes of Lambert of Avignon.
Here a young Scotsman named Hamilton, afterwards illustrious
as a martyr, had studied shortly before, and here too the
celebrated printer, John Luft, had his presses. In this city
Tyndale and Fryth had taken up their abode, in September
1528, and, hidden on the quiet banks of the Lahn, were
translating the Old Testament. If Rincke had searched this
place he could not have failed to discover them. But either he
thought not of it, or was afraid of the terrible landgrave. The
direct road by the Rhine was that which he followed, and
Tyndale escaped.

When he arrived at Cologne, Rincke had an immediate
interview with West. Their investigations having failed, they
must have recourse to more vigorous measures. The senator,
therefore, sent the monk back to England, accompanied by his
son Hermann, charging them to tell Wolsey: "To seize Tyndale
we require fuller powers, ratified by the Emperor. The traitors
who conspire against the life of the king of England are not
tolerated in the Empire, much less Tyndale and all those who
conspire against Christendom. He must be put to death;
nothing but some striking example can check the Lutheran
heresy.—And as to ourselves," they were told to add, "by the

favour of God there may possibly be an opportunity for his royal highness and your grace to recompense us." Rincke had not forgotten the subsidy of ten thousand pounds which he had received from Henry VII for the Turkish war, when he had gone to London as Maximilian's envoy.

West returned to England sorely vexed that he had failed in his mission. What would they say at court and in his monastery? A fresh humiliation was in reserve for him. Roye, whom West had gone to look for on the banks of the Rhine, had paid a visit to his mother on the banks of the Thames; and to crown all, the new doctrines had penetrated into his own house. The warden, Father Robinson, had embraced them, and night and day the Greenwich monks read that New Testament which West had gone to Cologne to burn. The Antwerp friar, who had accompanied him on his journey, was the only person to whom he could confide his sorrows; but the Franciscans sent him back again to the continent, and then amused themselves at poor West's expense. If he desired to tell of his adventures on the banks of the Rhine, he was laughed at; if he boasted of the names of Wolsey and Henry VIII, they jeered at him still more. He desired to speak to Roye's mother, hoping to gain some useful information from her; this the monks prevented. "It is in my commission," he said. They ridiculed him more and more. Robinson, perceiving that the commission made West assume unbecoming airs of independence, requested Wolsey to withdraw it; and West, fancying he was about to be thrown into prison, exclaimed in alarm: "I am weary of my life!" and conjured a friend whom he had at court to procure him before Christmas an *obedience* under his lordship's hand and seal, enabling him to leave the monastery; "What you pay him for it," he added, "I shall see you be reimbursed." Thus did West expiate the fanatical zeal which had urged him to pursue the translator of the oracles of God. What became of him, we know not: he is never heard of more.

At that time Wolsey had other matters to engage him than this "obedience." While West's complaints were going to London, those of the king were travelling to Rome. The great business in the cardinal's eyes was to maintain harmony between Henry and the church. There was no more thought about investigations in Germany, and for a time Tyndale was saved.

CHAPTER FIVE

The Pope Burns his Bull

(November, 1528)

THE king and a part of his people still adhered to the popedom, and so long as these bonds were not broken the Word of God could not have free course. But to induce England to renounce Rome, there must indeed be powerful motives: and these were not wanting.

Wolsey had never given such pressing orders to any of Henry's ambassadors: "The king," he wrote to Da Casale on the 1st of November 1528, "commits this business to your prudence, dexterity, and fidelity; and I conjure you to employ all the powers of your genius, and even to surpass them. Be very sure that you have done nothing and can do nothing that will be more agreeable to the king, more desirable by me, and more useful and glorious for you and your family."

Da Casale possessed a tenacity which justified the cardinal's confidence, and an active excitable mind: trembling at the thought of seeing Rome lose England, he immediately requested an audience of Clement VII. "What!" said he to the pope, "just as it was proposed to go on with the divorce, your nuncio endeavours to dissuade the king! . . . There is no hope that Catherine of Aragon will ever give an heir to the crown. Holy father, there must be an end of this. Order Campeggio to place the *decretal* in his majesty's hands."—"What say you?" exclaimed the pope. "I would gladly lose one of my fingers to recover it again, and you ask me to make it public . . . it would be my ruin." Da Casale insisted: "We have a duty to perform," he said; "we remind you at this last hour of the perils threatening the relations which unite Rome and England. The crisis is at hand. We knock at your door, we cry, we urge, we entreat, we lay before you the present and future dangers which threaten the papacy. . . . The world shall know that the king at least has fulfilled the duty of a devoted son of the church. If your holiness

377

desires to keep England in St Peter's fold, I repeat . . . now is the time . . . now is the time." At these words, Da Casale, unable to restrain his emotion, fell down at the pope's feet, and begged him to save the church in Great Britain. The pope was moved. "Rise," said he, with marks of unwonted grief, "I grant you all that is in my power; I am willing to confirm the judgment which the legates may think it their duty to pass; but I acquit myself of all responsibility as to the untold evils which this matter may bring with it. . . . If the king, after having defended the faith and the church, desires to ruin both, on him alone will rest the responsibility of so great a disaster." Clement granted nothing. Da Casale withdrew disheartened, and feeling convinced that the pontiff was about to treat with Charles V.

Wolsey desired to save the popedom; but the popedom resisted. Clement VII was about to lose that island which Gregory the Great had won with such difficulty. The pope was in the most cruel position. The English envoy had hardly left the palace before the Emperor's ambassador entered breathing threats. The unhappy pontiff escaped the assaults of Henry only to be exposed to those of Charles; he was thrown backwards and forwards like a ball. "I shall assemble a general council," said the Emperor through his ambassador, "and if you are found to have infringed the canons of the church in any point, you shall be proceeded against with every rigour. Do not forget," added his agent in a low tone, "that your birth is *illegitimate*, and consequently excludes you from the pontificate." The timid Clement, imagining that he saw the tiara falling from his head, swore to refuse Henry everything. "Alas!" he said to one of his dearest confidants, "I repent in dust and ashes that I ever granted this decretal bull. If the king of England so earnestly desires it to be given him, certainly it cannot be merely to know its contents. He is but too familiar with them. It is only to tie my hands in this matter of the divorce; I would rather die a thousand deaths." Clement, to calm his agitation, sent one of his ablest gentlemen of the bed-chamber, Francis Campana, apparently to feed the king with fresh promises, but in reality to cut the only thread on which Henry's hopes still hung. "We embrace your majesty," wrote the pope in the letter given to Campana, "with the paternal love your numerous merits deserve." Now Campana was sent to England to burn clandestinely the famous decretal; Clement concealed his blows by an embrace. Rome had granted many divorces not so well founded as that of Henry VIII; but a very different matter from a divorce was in question here; the pope, desirous of upraising in Italy his shattered power, was about to sacrifice the Tudor, and to prepare the triumph of the Reformation. Rome was separating herself from England.

All Clement's fear was that Campana would arrive too late to burn the bull; he was soon reassured; a dead calm prevented the *great matter* from advancing. Campeggio, who took care to be in no hurry about his mission, gave himself up, like a skilful diplomatist, to his worldly tastes; and when he could not, due respect being had to the state of his legs, indulge in the chase, of which he was very fond, he passed his time in gambling, to which he was much addicted. Respectable historians assert that he indulged in still more illicit pleasures. But this could not last for ever, and the nuncio sought some new means of delay, which offered itself in the most unexpected manner. One day an officer of the queen presented to the Roman legate a *brief* of Julius II, bearing the same date as the *bull* of dispensation, signed too, like that, by the secretary Sigismond, and in which the pope expressed himself in such a manner, that Henry's objections fell of themselves. "The Emperor," said Catherine's messenger, "has discovered this brief among the papers of Puebla, the Spanish ambassador in England, at the time of the marriage."—"It is impossible to go on," said Campeggio to Wolsey; "all your reasoning is now cut from under you. *We must wait for fresh instructions.*" This was the cardinal's conclusion at every new incident, and the journey from London to the Vatican being very long (without reckoning the Roman dilatoriness) the expedient was infallible.

Thus there existed two acts of the same pope, signed on the same day—the one secret, the other public, in contradiction to each other. Henry determined to send a new mission to Rome. Anne proposed for this embassy one of the most accomplished gentlemen of the court, her cousin, Sir Francis Bryan. With him was joined an Italian, Peter Vannes, Henry's Latin secretary. "You will search all the registers of the time of Julius II," said Wolsey to them; "you will study the handwriting of secretary Sigismond, and you will attentively

examine the ring of the fisherman used by that pontiff.—
Moreover you will inform the pope that it is proposed to set a
certain greyfriar, named De Angelis, in his place, to whom
Charles would give the *spiritual* authority, reserving the
temporal for himself. You will manage so that Clement takes
alarm at the project, and you will then offer him a presidy
(guard) of 2000 men to protect him. You will ask whether, in
case the queen should desire to embrace a religious life, on
condition of the king's doing the same, and Henry should yield
to this wish, he could have the assurance that the pope would
afterwards release him from his vows. And, finally, you will
inquire whether, in case the queen should refuse to enter a
convent, the pope would permit the king to have *two wives*, as
we see in the Old Testament." This idea, which brought so
much reproach on the landgrave of Hesse, was not a new one;
the honour of it belongs to a cardinal and legate of Rome,
whatever Bossuet may say. "Lastly," continued Wolsey, "as
the pope is of a timid disposition, you will not fail to season
your remonstrances with threats. You, Peter, will take him
aside and tell him that, as an Italian, having more at heart
than any one the glory of the holy see, it is your duty to warn
him that, if he persists, the king, his realm, and many other
princes, will for ever separate from the papacy."

It was not on the mind of the pope alone that it was necessary
to act; the rumour that the Emperor and the king of France
were treating together disturbed Henry. Wolsey had vainly
tried to sound Du Bellay; these two priests tried craft against
craft. Besides, the Frenchman was not always seasonably
informed by his court, letters taking *ten days* to come from Paris
to London. Henry resolved to have a conference with the
ambassador. He began by speaking to him of *his matter*, says
Du Bellay, "and I promise you," he added, "that he needs no
advocate, he understands the whole business so well." Henry
next touched upon the *wrongs* of Francis I, "recalling so many
things that the envoy knew not what to say."—"I pray you,
Master Ambassador," said Henry in conclusion, "to beg the
king, my brother, to give up a little of his amusements during
a year only for the prompt despatch of his affairs. Warn those
whom it concerns." Having given this spur to the king of
France, Henry turned his thoughts towards Rome.

In truth, the fatal brief from Spain tormented him day and night, and the cardinal tortured his mind to find proofs of its non-authenticity; if he could do so, he would acquit the papacy of the charge of duplicity, and accuse the Emperor of forgery. At last he thought he had succeeded. "In the first place," he said to the king, "the brief has the same date as the bull. Now, if the errors in the latter had been found out on the day it was drawn up, it would have been more natural to make another than to append a brief pointing out the errors. What! the same pope, the same day, at the petition of the same persons, give out two rescripts for one effect,[1] one of which contradicts the other! Either the bull was good, and then, why the brief? Or the bull was bad, and then, why deceive princes by a worthless bull? Certain names are found in the brief incorrectly spelt, and these are faults which the pontifical secretary, whose accuracy is so well known, could not have committed.[2] Lastly, no one in England ever heard mention of this brief; and yet it is here that it ought to be found." Henry charged Knight, his principal secretary, to join the other envoys with all speed, in order to prove to the pope the supposititious character of the document.

This important paper revived the irritation felt in England against Charles V, and it was resolved to come to extremities. Every one discontented with Austria took refuge in London, particularly the Hungarians. The ambassador from Hungary proposed to Wolsey to adjudge the imperial crown of Germany to the elector of Saxony or the landgrave of Hesse, the two chiefs of Protestantism. Wolsey exclaimed in alarm: "It will be an inconvenience to Christendom, *they are so Lutheran.*" But the Hungarian ambassador so satisfied him that in the end he did not find the matter quite so inconvenient. These schemes were prospering in London, when suddenly a new metamorphosis took place under the eyes of Du Bellay. The king, the cardinal, and the ministers appeared in strange consternation. Vincent da Casale had just arrived from Rome with a letter from his cousin the prothonotary, informing Henry

[1] State Papers, vol. vii, p. 130.
[2] Queen *Isabella* was called *Elizabeth* in the brief; but I have seen a document from the court of Madrid in which Queen Elizabeth of England was called Isabella; it is not therefore an error without a parallel.

that the pope, seeing the triumph of Charles V, the indecision of Francis I, the isolation of the king of England, and the distress of his cardinal, had flung himself into the arms of the Emperor. At Rome they went so far as to jest about Wolsey, and to say that since he could not be St Peter they would make him St Paul.

While they were ridiculing Wolsey at Rome, at St Germain's they were joking about Henry. "I will make him get rid of the notions he has in his head," said Francis; and the Flemings, who were again sent out of the country, said as they left London, "that this year they would carry on the war so vigorously, that it would be really a sight worth seeing."

Besides these public griefs, Wolsey had his private ones. Anne Boleyn, who had already begun to use her influence on behalf of the despotic cardinal's victims, gave herself no rest until Cheyney, a courtier disgraced by Wolsey, had been restored to the king's favour. Anne even gave utterance to several biting sarcasms against the cardinal, and the duke of Norfolk and his party began "to speak big," says Du Bellay. At the moment when the pope, scared by Charles V, was separating from England, Wolsey himself was tottering. Who shall uphold the papacy? . . . After Wolsey, nobody! Rome was on the point of losing the power which for nine centuries she had exercised in the bosom of this illustrious nation. The cardinal's anguish cannot be described; unceasingly pursued by gloomy images, he saw Anne on the throne causing the triumph of the Reformation: this nightmare was stifling him. "His grace, the legate, is in great trouble," wrote the bishop of Bayonne. "However . . . he is more cunning than they are."

To still the tempest Wolsey had only one resource left: this was to render Clement favourable to his master's designs. The crafty Campana, who had burnt the decretal, conjured him not to believe all the reports transmitted to him concerning Rome. "To satisfy the king," said he to the cardinal, "the holy father will, if necessary, descend from the pontifical throne." Wolsey therefore resolved to send to Rome a more energetic agent than Vannes, Bryan, or Knight, and cast his eyes on Gardiner. His courage began to revive, when an unexpected event fanned once more his loftiest hopes.

CHAPTER SIX

Wolsey between Scylla and Charybdis
(1529)

Oᴺ the 11th of January 1529, just as the pope was performing mass, he was attacked by a sudden illness; he was taken to his room, apparently in a dying state. When this news reached London, the cardinal resolved to hasten to abandon England, where the soil trembled under his feet, and to climb boldly to the throne of the pontiffs. Bryan and Vannes, then at Florence, hurried on to Rome through roads infested with robbers. At Orvieto they were informed the pope was better; at Viterbo, no one knew whether he was alive or dead; at Ronciglione, they were assured that he had expired; and, finally, when they reached the metropolis of the popedom, they learnt that Clement could not survive, and that the imperialists, supported by the Colonnas, were striving to have a pope devoted to Charles V.

But great as might be the agitation at Rome, it was greater still at Whitehall. If God caused Clement to descend from the pontifical throne, it could only be, thought Wolsey, to make him mount it. "It is expedient to have such a pope as may save the realm," said he to Gardiner. "And although it cannot but be incommodious to me in this mine old age to be the common father, yet, when all things be well pondered, the qualities of all the cardinals well considered, I am the only one, without boasting, that can and will remedy the king's secret matter. And were it not for the re-integration of the state of the church, and especially to relieve the king and his realm from their calamities, all the riches and honour of the world should not cause me to accept the said dignity.[1] Nevertheless I conform myself to the necessities of the times, and am content to apply all my wit and study, and to set forth all means and ways for the attaining of the said dignity. . . . Wherefore, Master Stephen, that this matter may succeed, I

[1] [Foxe caustically comments: "You may long say so, before we will believe you."]

pray you to apply all your ingenuity, spare neither money nor labour. I give you the amplest powers, without restriction or limitation."[1] Gardiner departed to win for his master the coveted tiara.

Henry VIII and Wolsey, who could hardly restrain their impatience, soon heard of the pontiff's death from different quarters. "The Emperor has taken away Clement's life," said Wolsey, blinded by hatred. "Charles," rejoined the king, "will endeavour to obtain by force or fraud a pope according to his desires."—"Yes, to make him his chaplain," replied Wolsey, "and to put an end by degrees both to pope and popedom."— "We must fly to the defence of the church," resumed Henry, "and with that view, my lord, make up your mind to be pope."—"That alone," answered the cardinal, "can bring your majesty's weighty matter to a happy termination, and by saving you, save the church . . . and myself also," he thought in his heart.—"Let us see, let us count the voters."

Henry and his minister then wrote down on a strip of parchment the names of all the cardinals, marking with the letter *A* those who were on the side of the kings of England and France, and with the letter *B* all who favoured the Emperor. "There was no *C*," says a chronicler sarcastically, "to signify any on *Christ's* side." The letter *N* designated the neutrals. "The cardinals present," said Wolsey, "will not exceed thirty-nine, and we must have two-thirds, that is, twenty-six. Now, there are twenty upon whom we can reckon; we must therefore, at any price, gain six of the neutrals."

Wolsey, deeply sensible of the importance of an election that would decide whether England was to be reformed or not, carefully drew up the instructions, which Henry signed, and which history must register. "We desire and ordain," the ambassadors were informed in them, "that you secure the election of the cardinal of York; not forgetting that next to the salvation of his own soul, there is nothing the king desires more earnestly.

"To gain over the neutral cardinals you will employ two methods in particular. The first is, the cardinals being present, and having God and the Holy Ghost before them, you shall remind them that the cardinal of York alone can save Christendom.

[1] Foxe, *Acts*, iv, pp. 600-1.

"The second is, because human fragility suffereth not all things to be pondered and weighed in a just balance, it appertaineth in matter of so high importance, to the comfort and relief of all Christendom, to succour the infirmity that may chance . . . not for corruption, you will understand . . . but rather to help the lacks and defaults of human nature. And, therefore, it shall be expedient that you promise spiritual offices, dignities, rewards of money, or other things which shall seem meet to the purpose.

"Then shall you, with good dexterity, combine and knit those favourable to us in a perfect fastness and indissoluble knot. And that they may be the better animated to finish the election to the king's desire, you shall offer them a guard of 2000 or 3000 men from the kings of England and France, from the viscount of Turin, and the republic of Venice.

"If, notwithstanding all your exertions, the election should fail, then the cardinals of the king shall repair to some sure place, and there proceed to such an election as may be to God's pleasure.

"And to win more friends for the king, you shall promise, on the one hand, to the Cardinal de Medici and his party our special favour; and the Florentines, on the other hand, you shall put in comfort of the exclusion of the said family De Medici.

"Likewise you shall put the cardinals in perfect hope of recovering the patrimony of the church; and you shall contain the Venetians in good trust of a reasonable way to be taken for Cervia and Ravenna [which formed part of the patrimony] to their contentment."

Such were the means by which the cardinal hoped to win the papal throne. To the right he said *yes*, to the left he said *no*. What would it matter that these perfidies were one day discovered, provided it were after the election. Christendom might be very certain that the choice of the future pontiff would be the work of the Holy Ghost. Alexander VI had been a poisoner; Julius II had given way to ambition, anger, and vice; the liberal Leo X had passed his life in worldly pursuits; the unhappy Clement VII had lived on stratagems and lies; Wolsey would be their worthy successor:

"All the seven deadly sins have worn the triple crown."

Wolsey found his excuse in the thought that if he succeeded, the divorce was secured, and England enslaved for ever to the court of Rome.

Success at first appeared probable. Many cardinals spoke openly in favour of the English prelate; one of them asked for a detailed account of his life, in order to present it as a model to the church; another worshipped him (so he said) as a divinity. . . . Among the gods and popes adored at Rome there were some no better than he. But ere long alarming news reached England. What grief! the pope was getting better. "Conceal your instructions," wrote the cardinal.

Wolsey not having obtained the tiara, it was necessary at least to gain the divorce. "God declares," said the English ambassadors to the pope, *"except the Lord build the house, they labour in vain that build it.*[1] Therefore, the king, taking God alone for his guide, requests of you, in the first place, an engagement to pronounce the divorce in the space of three months, and in the second the avocation to Rome."—"The promise first, and only after that the avocation," Wolsey had said; "for I fear that if the pope begins with the avocation, he will never pronounce the divorce."—"Besides," added the envoys, "the king's second marriage admits of no refusal, whatever bulls or briefs there may be. The only issue of this matter is the divorce; the divorce in one way or another must be procured."

Wolsey had instructed his envoys to pronounce these words with a certain air of familiarity, and at the same time with a gravity calculated to produce an effect. His expectations were deceived: Clement was colder than ever. He had determined to abandon England in order that he might secure the States of the Church, of which Charles was then master, thus sacrificing the spiritual to the temporal. "The pope will not do the least thing for your majesty," wrote Bryan to the king; "your matter may well be in his *Pater noster*, but it certainly is not in his *Credo*."—"Increase in importunity," answered the king; "the cardinal of Verona should remain about the pope's person and counterbalance the influence of De Angelis and the archbishop of Capua. I would rather lose my two crowns than be beaten by these two friars."

[1] Where Christ is not the foundation, surely no building can be of good work. State Papers, vii, p. 122.

Thus was the struggle about to become keener than ever, when Clement's relapse once more threw doubt on everything. He was always between life and death; and this perpetual alternation agitated the king and the impatient cardinal in every way. The latter considered that the pope had need of *merits* to enter the kingdom of heaven. "Procure an interview with the pope," he wrote to the envoys, "even though he be in the very agony of death;[1] and represent to him that nothing will be more likely *to save his soul* than the bill of divorce." Henry's commissioners were not admitted; but towards the end of March, the deputies appearing in a body, the pope promised to examine the letter from Spain. Vannes began to fear this document; he represented that those who had fabricated it would have been able to give it an appearance of authenticity. "Rather declare immediately that this brief is not a brief," said he to the pope. "The king of England, who is your holiness's son, is not so like the rest of the world. We cannot put the same shoe on every foot." This rather vulgar argument did not touch Clement. "If to content your master in this business," said he, "I cannot employ my head, at least I will my finger."—"Be pleased to explain yourself," replied Vannes, who found the *finger* a very little matter.—"I mean," resumed the pontiff, "that I shall employ every means, provided they are *honourable*." Vannes withdrew disheartened.

He immediately conferred with his colleagues, and all together, alarmed at the idea of Henry's anger, returned to the pontiff; they thrust aside the lackeys, who endeavoured to stop them, and made their way into his bed-chamber. Clement opposed them with that resistance of inertia by which the popedom has gained its greatest victories: *siluit*, he remained silent. Of what consequence to the pontiff were Tudor, his island, and his church, when Charles of Austria was threatening him with his armies? Clement, less proud than Hildebrand, submitted willingly to the Emperor's power, provided the Emperor would protect him. "I had rather," he said, "be Cæsar's servant, not only in a temple, but in a stable if necessary, than be exposed to the insults of rebels and vagabonds." At the same time he wrote to Campeggio: "Do not irritate the king, but spin out this matter as much as possible; the Spanish brief gives us the means."

[1] Burnet's *Reformation*, i, p. 49.

In fact, Charles V had twice shown Lee, Henry's ambassador, the original document, and Wolsey, after this report, began to believe that it was not Charles who had forged the brief, but that Pope Julius II had really given two contradictory documents on the same day. Accordingly the cardinal now feared to see this letter in the pontiff's hands. "Do all you can to dissuade the pope from seeking the original in Spain," wrote he to one of his ambassadors; "it may exasperate the Emperor." We know how cautious the cardinal was towards Charles. Intrigue attained its highest point at this epoch, and Englishmen and Romans encountered craft with craft. "In such ticklish negotiations," says Burnet (who had had some little experience in diplomacy), "ministers must say and unsay as they are instructed, which goes of course as a part of their business." Henry's envoys to the pope intercepted the letters sent from Rome, and had Campeggio's seized. On his part the pope indulged in flattering smiles and perfidious equivocations. Bryan wrote to Henry VIII: "Always your grace hath done for him in deeds, and he hath recompensed you with fair *words* and fair *writings*, of which both I think your grace shall lack none; but as for the *deeds*, I never believe to see them, and especially at this time." Bryan had comprehended the court of Rome better perhaps than many politicians. Finally, Clement himself, wishing to prepare the king for the blow he was about to inflict, wrote to him: "We have been able to find nothing that would satisfy your ambassadors."

Henry thought he knew what this message meant: that he had found nothing, and would find nothing; and accordingly this prince, who, if we may believe Wolsey, had hitherto shown incredible patience and gentleness, gave way to all his violence. "Very well then," said he; "my lords and I well know how to withdraw ourselves from the authority of the Roman see." Wolsey turned pale, and conjured his master not to rush into that fearful abyss; Campeggio, too, endeavoured to revive the king's hopes. But it was all of no use. Henry recalled his ambassadors.

Henry, it is true, had not yet reached the age when violent characters become inflexible from the habit they have encouraged of yielding to their passions. But the cardinal, who knew his master, knew also that his inflexibility did not depend upon the number of his years; he thought Rome's power in England was lost, and placed between Henry and Clement, he exclaimed: "How shall I avoid Scylla, and not fall into Charybdis?" He begged the king to make one last effort by sending Dr Bennet to the pope with orders to support the avocation to Rome, and he gave him a letter in which he displayed all the resources of his eloquence. "How can it be imagined," he wrote, "that the persuasions of sense urge the king to break a union in which the ardent years of his youth were passed with such purity? . . . The matter is very different. I am on the spot, I know the state of men's minds. . . . Pray, believe me. . . . The divorce is the secondary question; the primary one is *the fidelity of this realm* to the papal see. The nobility, gentry, and citizens all exclaim with indignation: Must our fortunes, and even our lives, depend upon the nod of a foreigner? We must abolish, or at the very least diminish, the authority of the Roman pontiff. . . . Most holy father, we cannot mention such things without a shudder." . . . This new attempt was also unavailing. The pope demanded of Henry how he could doubt his good will, seeing that the king of England had done so much for the apostolic see. This appeared a cruel irony to Tudor; the king requested a favour of the pope, and the pope replied by calling to mind those which the papacy had received from his hands. "Is this the way," men asked in England, "in which Rome pays her debts?"

Wolsey had not reached the end of his misfortunes. Gardiner and Bryan had just returned to London: they declared that to demand an avocation to Rome was to lose their cause. Accordingly Wolsey, who turned to every wind, ordered Da Casale, in case Clement should pronounce the avocation, to appeal from the pope, the false head of the church, *to the true vicar of Jesus Christ*.[1] This was almost in Luther's style. Who was this true vicar? Probably a pope nominated by the influence of England.

But this proceeding did not assure the cardinal: he was losing his judgment. A short time before this, Du Bellay, who had just returned from Paris, whither he had gone to retain France on the side of England, had been invited to Richmond by Wolsey. As the two prelates were walking in the park, on

[1] State Papers, vii, p. 191.

that hill whence the eye ranges over the fertile and undulating
fields through which the winding Thames pours its tranquil
waters, the unhappy cardinal observed to the bishop: "My
trouble is the greatest that ever was! . . . I have excited and
carried on this matter of the divorce, to dissolve the union
between the two houses of Spain and England, by sowing
misunderstanding between them, as if I had no part in it.
You know it was in the interest of France; I therefore entreat
the king your master and her majesty to do everything that
may forward the divorce. I shall esteem such a favour more than
if they made me pope; but if they refuse me, my ruin is inevitable." And then giving way to despair, he exclaimed: "Alas!
would that I were going to be buried to-morrow!"

The wretched man was drinking the bitter cup his perfidies
had prepared for him. All seemed to conspire against Henry,
and Bennet was recalled shortly after. It was said at court and
in the city: "Since the pope sacrifices us to the Emperor, let
us sacrifice the pope." Clement VII, intimidated by the threats
of Charles V, and tottering upon his throne, madly repelled
with his foot the bark of England. Europe was all attention,
and began to think that the proud vessel of Albion, cutting the
cable that bound her to the pontiffs, would boldly spread her
canvas to the winds, and ever after sail the sea alone, wafted
onwards by the breeze that comes from heaven.

The influence of Rome over Europe is in great measure
political. It loses a kingdom by a royal quarrel, and might in
this same way lose ten.

CHAPTER SEVEN

More and Tyndale: A Theological Duel

(1528–29)

OTHER circumstances from day to day rendered the emancipation of the church more necessary. If behind these political debates there had not been found a Christian people, resolved never to temporize with error, it is probable that England, after a few years of independence, would have fallen back into the bosom of Rome. The affair of the divorce was not the only one agitating men's minds; the religious controversies, which for some years filled the continent, were always more animated at Oxford and Cambridge. The *Evangelicals* and the *Catholics* (not very catholic indeed) warmly discussed the great questions which the progress of events brought before the world. The former maintained that the primitive church of the apostles and the actual church of the papacy were not identical; the latter affirmed, on the contrary, the identity of popery and apostolic Christianity. Other Romish doctors in later times, finding this position somewhat embarrassing, have asserted that Catholicism existed only *in the germ* in the apostolic church, and had subsequently developed itself. But a thousand abuses, a thousand errors may creep into a church under cover of this theory. A plant springs from the seed and grows up in accordance with immutable laws; whilst a doctrine cannot be transformed in the mind of man without falling under the influence of sin. It is true that the disciples of popery have supposed a constant action of the Divine Spirit in the Catholic church, which excludes every influence of error. To stamp on the development of the church the character of truth, they have stamped on the church itself the character of infallibility; *quod erat demonstrandum*. Their reasoning is a mere begging of the question. To know whether the Romish development is identical with the gospel, we must examine it by Scripture.

It was not university men alone who occupied themselves with Christian truth. The separation which has been remarked in other times between the opinions of the people and of the learned, did not now exist. What the doctors taught, the citizens practised; Oxford and London embraced each other. The theologians knew that learning has need of life, and the citizens believed that life has need of that learning which derives the doctrine from the wells of the Scriptures of God. It was the harmony between these two elements, the one theological, the other practical, which constituted the strength of the English reformation.

The evangelical life in the capital alarmed the clergy more than the evangelical doctrine in the colleges. Since Monmouth had escaped, they must strike another. Among the London merchants was John Tewkesbury, one of the oldest friends of the Scriptures in England. As early as 1512 he had become possessor of a manuscript copy of the Bible, and had attentively studied it; when Tyndale's New Testament appeared, he read it with avidity; and, finally, *The Wicked Mammon* had completed the work of his conversion. Being a man of heart and understanding, clever in all he undertook, a ready and fluent speaker, and liking to get to the bottom of everything, Tewkesbury, like Monmouth, became very influential in the city, and one of the most learned in Scripture of any of the evangelicals. These generous Christians, being determined to consecrate to God the good things they had received from him, were the first among that long series of laymen who were destined to be more useful to the truth than many ministers and bishops. They found time to interest themselves about the most trifling details of the kingdom of God; and in the history of the Reformation in Britain their names should be inscribed beside those of Latimer and Tyndale.

The activity of these laymen could not escape the cardinal's notice. Clement VII was abandoning England: it was necessary for the English bishops, by crushing the heretics, to show that they would not abandon the popedom. We can understand the zeal of these prelates and, without excusing their persecutions, we are disposed to extenuate their crime. The bishops determined to ruin Tewkesbury. One day in April 1529, as he was busy among his peltries, the officers entered his warehouse, arrested him and led him away to the bishop of London's chapel, where, besides the ordinary (Tunstall) the bishops of Ely, St Asaph, Bath, and Lincoln, with the abbot of Westminster, were on the bench. The composition of this tribunal indicated the importance of his case. The emancipation of the laity, thought these judges, is perhaps a more dangerous heresy than justification by faith.

"John Tewkesbury," said the bishop of London, "I exhort you to trust less to your own wit and learning, and more unto the doctrine of the holy mother the church." Tewkesbury made answer that in his judgment he held no other doctrine than that of the church of Christ. Tunstall then broached the principal charge, that of having read the *Wicked Mammon*, and after quoting several passages, he exclaimed: "Renounce these errors."—"I find no fault in the book," replied Tewkesbury. "It has enlightened my conscience and consoled my heart. But it is not my gospel. I have studied the Holy Scriptures these seventeen years and, as a man sees the spots of his face in a glass, so by reading them I have learnt the faults of my soul. If there is a disagreement between you and the New Testament, put yourselves in harmony with it, rather than desire to put that in accord with you." The bishops were surprised that a leather-seller should speak so well, and quote Scripture so happily that they were unable to resist him. Annoyed at being catechized by a layman, the bishops of Bath, St Asaph, and Lincoln thought they could conquer him more easily by the rack than by their arguments. He was taken to the Tower, where they ordered him to be put to the torture. His limbs were crushed, which was contrary to the laws of England, and the violence of the rack tore from him a cry of agony to which the priests replied by a shout of exultation. The inflexible merchant had promised at last to renounce Tyndale's *Wicked Mammon*. Tewkesbury left the Tower "almost a cripple," and returned to his house to lament the fatal word which the question had extorted from him, and to prepare in the silence of faith to confess in the burning pile the precious name of Christ Jesus.

We must, however, acknowledge that the "question" was not Rome's only argument. The gospel had two classes of opponents in the sixteenth century, as in the first ages of the church. Some attacked it with the torture, others with their writings. Sir Thomas More, a few years later, was to have recourse to the first of these arguments; but for the moment he took up his pen. He had first studied the writings of the Fathers of the church and of the Reformers, but rather as an advocate than as a theologian; and then, armed at all points, he rushed into the arena of polemics, and in his attacks dealt those "technical convictions and that malevolent subtlety," says one of his greatest admirers, "from which the honestest men of his profession are not free." Jests and sarcasms had fallen from his pen in his discussion with Tyndale, as in his controversy with Luther. In 1528 there appeared *A Dialogue of Sir Thomas More, Knt., touching the pestilent Sect of Luther and Tyndale, by the one begun in Saxony, and by the other laboured to be brought into England.*[1]

Tyndale soon became informed of More's publication, and a remarkable combat ensued between these two representatives of the two doctrines that were destined to divide Christendom— Tyndale the champion of Scripture,[2] and More the champion of the church. More having called his book a *dialogue*, Tyndale adopted this form in his reply, and the two combatants valiantly crossed their swords, though wide seas lay between them.

This theological duel is not without importance in the history of the Reformation. The struggles of diplomacy, of sacerdotalism, and of royalty were not enough; there must be struggles of doctrine. Rome had set the hierarchy above the faith; the Reformation was to restore faith to its place above the hierarchy.

MORE. Christ said not, the Holy Ghost shall *write*, but shall

[1] [Sir Thomas More, regarded by his church as the greatest English scholar of his time, was invited by Tunstall to read the works of the reformers in order that he might use his pen to refute them. The *Dialogue* was the outcome. It was intended to be a popular work, intermingling "merry tales" with somewhat shallow theological disquisitions. C. S. Lewis, in his *English Literature in the sixteenth century*, speaks of it as a weak defence of Romanism but as "great Platonic dialogue, perhaps the best specimen of that form ever produced in English" (p. 172).]

[2] The *Dialogue* consisted of 250 pages, and was printed by Rastell, More's brother-in-law. Tyndale's answer did not appear until later; we have thought it best to introduce it here.

[Tyndale's *Answer to Sir Thomas More's Dialogue* roots the Christian faith firmly in Scripture, and is to be found in the Parker Society Publications.]

teach. Whatsoever the church says, it is the word of God, though it be not in Scripture.

TYNDALE. It is not the custom of Scripture to say the Holy Ghost writeth but inspireth the writer . . . and it is manifest that . . . love compelled the apostles to leave nothing unwritten that should be necessarily required, and that, if it were left out, should hurt the soul. . . . *These are written,* says St John, *that ye may believe and through belief have life.* (1 John ii. 1; Rom. xv. 4; Matthew xxii. 29.)

MORE. The apostles have taught by *mouth* many things they did not *write,* because they should not come into the hands of the heathen for mocking.

TYNDALE. I pray you what thing more to be mocked by the heathen could they teach than the resurrection; and that Christ was God and man, and died between two thieves? And yet all these things the apostles *wrote.* And again, purgatory, penance, and satisfaction for sin, and praying to saints, are marvellous agreeable unto the superstition of the heathen people, so that they needed not to abstain from writing of them for fear lest the heathen should have mocked them.

MORE. We must not examine the teaching of the church by Scripture, but understand Scripture by means of what the church says.

TYNDALE. What! Does the air give light to the sun, or the sun to the air? Is the church before the gospel, or the gospel before the church? Is not the father older than the son? *God begat us with his own will, with the word of truth,* says St James (i. 18.) If he who begetteth is before him who is begotten, the *word* is before the *church,* or, to speak more correctly, before the *congregation.*

MORE. Why do you say *congregation* and not *church?*

TYNDALE. Because by that word *church,* you understand nothing but a multitude of shaven, shorn and oiled, which we now call the spiritualty or clergy; while the word of right is common unto all the congregation of them that believe in Christ.

MORE. The church is the pope and his sect or followers.

TYNDALE. The pope teacheth us to trust in holy works for salvation, as penance, saints' merits, and friars' coats. Now, he that hath no faith to be saved through Christ, is not of Christ's church.

MORE. The Romish church from which the Lutherans came out, was before them, and therefore is the right one.

TYNDALE. In like manner you may say, the church of the Pharisees, whence Christ and His apostles came out, was before them, and was therefore the right church, and consequently Christ and his disciples are heretics.

MORE. No: the apostles came out from the church of the Pharisees because they found not Christ there; but your priests in Germany and elsewhere, have come out of our church, because they wanted wives.

TYNDALE. Wrong . . . these priests were at first attached to what you call *heresies*, and then they took wives; but yours were first attached to the *holy* doctrine of the pope, and then they took harlots.

MORE. Luther's books be open, if ye will not believe us.

TYNDALE. Nay, ye have shut them up, and have even burnt them. . . .

MORE. I marvel that you deny *purgatory*, Sir William, except it be a plain point with you to go straight to hell.

TYNDALE. I know no other purging but faith in the cross of Christ; while you, for a groat or a sixpence, buy some secret pills [indulgences] which you take to purge yourselves of your sins.

MORE. Faith, then, is your purgatory, you say; there is no need, therefore, of works—a most immoral doctrine!

TYNDALE. It is faith *alone* that saves us, but not a *bare faith*. When a horse beareth a saddle and a man thereon, we may well say that the horse only and alone beareth the saddle, but we do not mean the saddle empty, and no man thereon.

In this manner did the catholic and the evangelical carry on the discussion. According to Tyndale, what constitutes the true church is the work of the Holy Ghost within; according to More, the constitution of the papacy without. The spiritual character of the gospel is thus put in opposition to the formalist character of the Roman church. The Reformation restored to our belief the solid foundation of the Word of God; for the sand it substituted the rock.[1] In the discussion to which we have

---

[1] [The latest Roman Catholic historian of the Reformation in England (*The Reformation in England*, Vol. I. '*The King's Proceedings*' by Philip Hughes, 1950) necessarily devotes considerable attention to Tyndale's attack on the Roman church. While he classes Tyndale as "the greatest English light in

just been listening, the advantage remained not with the catholic. Erasmus, a friend of More, embarrassed by the course the latter was taking, wrote to Tunstall: "I cannot heartily congratulate More."

Henry interrupted the celebrated knight in these contests to send him to Cambray, where a peace was negotiating between France and the Empire. Wolsey would have been pleased to go himself; but his enemies suggested to the king, "that it was only that he might not expedite the matter of the divorce." Henry, therefore, despatched More, Knight, and Tunstall; but Wolsey had created so many delays that they did not arrive until after the conclusion of the *Ladies' Peace* (August, 1529). The king's vexation was extreme. Du Bellay had in vain helped him to

---

the heretical firmament in these first years, and the most powerful solvent in English Catholicism since Wycliffe (p. 133, 4th ed.), he strangely states that "Tyndale can hardly be reckoned a religious thinker of any real importance. The ideas he puts forth are none of them his own." In this respect, says Hughes, all other English reformers of the period are like Tyndale: "all are derivative." The verdict is not justified. It is easy to claim originality for a pioneer and to deny it to those who follow. The fact is that, although Tyndale was thoroughly well acquainted with Luther's writings—their influence certainly appears in his treatises—his doctrine came, not from Luther, but from his own independent study of the Scriptures. Hughes rightly links Tyndale's recalling of his countrymen to the Word with the following: "The whole Catholic conception of sacraments, of the sacramental sacrifice and the sacramentally qualified and endowed priesthood that offered it, was violently rejected. The Mass was idolatry, an abomination. And all the elaborately wrought system of the mediaeval and patristic theologians was swept aside also." (p. 135). Exactly so! That Luther and Tyndale put forth the same teachings is proof, not that the one was the mere copyist of the other, but that both alike, illumined by the same Holy Spirit, had drunk deeply of the enlightening Word.

The best that Hughes can say of Tyndale reads as follows: "But Tyndale's passion and his skill in languages is another matter: and of his own language he showed himself a master indeed. His fiery zeal, and burning hate; the vicious bite of his attack; the unfailing, simple, clear style; the real eloquence when indignation drives him, or the thought of all that the "gospel" will one day accomplish, or the thought of God's saving love; it is the rhetorician who is powerful, who will convert men and hold them to his school" (p. 138.)

That Tyndale often used words of "bitterest hatred" in denouncing a delusive Romanism is undeniable. Romanism was, in his eyes, the "abomination that made the land desolate of truth." But equally strong terms were used of Tyndale by his adversaries. And if an apostle was moved by the Spirit of God to anathematize teachers in Galatia who, though nominally Christian, desired to add man's works and ceremonies to faith as the instrument of justification before God, it is not surprising that Tyndale and his fellow-reformers used the strongest expressions to denounce a system which departed so grievously from the plain "truth as it is in Jesus."]

spend a *good preparatory July* to make him *swallow the dose*. Henry
was angry with Wolsey, Wolsey threw the blame on the
ambassador, and the ambassador defended himself, he tells us,
"with tooth and nail."

By way of compensation, the English envoys concluded with
the Emperor a treaty prohibiting on both sides the printing
and sale of "any Lutheran books." Some of them could have
wished for a good persecution, for a few burning piles, it may be.
A singular opportunity occurred. In the spring of 1529,
Tyndale and Fryth had left Marburg for Antwerp, and were
thus in the vicinity of the English envoys. What West had been
unable to effect, it was thought the two most intelligent men in
Britain could not fail to accomplish. "Tyndale must be captured," said More and Tunstall.—"You do not know what sort
of a country you are in," replied Hackett. "Will you believe
that on the 7th of April, Harman arrested me at Antwerp for
damages caused by his imprisonment? If you can lay anything
to my charge as a private individual, I said to the officer, I am
ready to answer for myself; but if you arrest me as ambassador,
I know no judge but the Emperor. Upon which the procurator
had the audacity to reply, that I was arrested *as ambassador;*
and the lords of Antwerp only set me at liberty on condition
that I should appear again at the first summons. These merchants
are so proud of their franchises, that they would resist even
Charles himself." This anecdote was not at all calculated to
encourage More; and not caring about a pursuit, which
promised to be of little use, he returned to England. But the
bishop of London, who was left behind, persisted in the project,
and repaired to Antwerp to put it in execution.

Tyndale was at that time greatly embarrassed; considerable
debts, incurred with his printers, compelled him to suspend
his labours. Nor was this all: the prelate who had spurned him
so harshly in London, had just arrived in the very city where
he lay concealed. . . . What would become of him? . . . A
merchant, named Augustin Packington, a clever man, but
somewhat inclined to dissimulation, happening to be at
Antwerp on business, hastened to pay his respects to the bishop.
The latter observed, in the course of conversation: "I should
like to get hold of the books with which England is poisoned."
—"I can perhaps serve you in that matter," replied the

merchant. "I know the Flemings, who have bought Tyndale's books; so that if your lordship will be pleased to pay for them, I will make sure of them all."—"Oh, oh!" thought the bishop, "Now, as the proverb says, I shall have God by the toe. Gentle Master Packington," he added in a flattering tone, "I will pay for them whatsoever they cost you. I intend to burn them at St Paul's cross." The bishop, having his hand already on Tyndale's Testaments, fancied himself on the point of seizing Tyndale himself.

Packington, being one of those men who love to conciliate all parties, ran off to Tyndale, with whom he was intimate, and said: "William, I know you are a poor man, and have a heap of New Testaments and books by you, for which you have beggared yourself; and I have now found a merchant who will buy them all, and with ready money too."—"Who is the merchant?" said Tyndale.—"The bishop of London."— "Tunstall? . . . If he buys my books, it can only be to burn them."—"No doubt," answered Packington; "but what will he gain by it? The whole world will cry out against the priest who burns God's Word, and the eyes of many will be opened. Come, make up your mind, William; the bishop shall have the books, you the money, and I the thanks." . . . Tyndale resisted the proposal; Packington became more pressing. "The question comes to this," he said; "shall the bishop pay for the books or shall he not? for, make up your mind . . . he will have them."— "I consent," said the Reformer at last; "I shall pay my debts, and bring out a new and more correct edition of the Testament." The bargain was made.

Ere long the danger thickened around Tyndale. Placards, posted at Antwerp and throughout the province, announced that the Emperor, in conformity with the treaty of Cambray, was about to proceed against the reformers and their writings. Not an officer of justice appeared in the street but Tyndale's friends trembled for his liberty. Under such circumstances, how could he print his translations? It appears probable that he made up his mind about the end of August to go to Hamburg, and took his passage in a vessel loading for that port. Embarking with his books, his manuscripts, and the rest of his money, he glided down the Scheldt, and soon found himself afloat on the German ocean.

DD

But one danger followed close upon another. He had scarcely passed the mouth of the Meuse when a tempest burst upon him, and his ship, like that of old which bore St Paul, was almost swallowed up by the waves.—"Satan, envying the happy course and success of the gospel," says a chronicler, "set to his might how to hinder the blessed labours of this man." The seamen toiled, Tyndale prayed, all hope was lost. The reformer alone was full of courage, not doubting that God would preserve him for the accomplishment of his work. All the exertions of the crew proved useless; the vessel was dashed on the coast, and the passengers escaped with their lives. Tyndale gazed with sorrow upon that ocean which had swallowed up his beloved books and precious manuscripts, and deprived him of his resources. What labours, what perils! banishment, poverty, thirst, insults, watchings, persecution, imprisonment, the stake! ... Like Paul, he was in perils by his own countrymen, in perils among strange people, in perils in the city, in perils in the sea. Recovering his spirits, however, he went on board another ship, entered the Elbe, and at last reached Hamburg.[1]

Great joy was in store for him in that city. Coverdale, Foxe informs us, was waiting there to confer with him, and to help him in his labours. It has been supposed that Coverdale went to Hamburg to invite Tyndale, in Cromwell's name, to return to England; but it is merely a conjecture, lacking confirmation. As early as 1527, Coverdale had made known to Cromwell his desire to translate the Scriptures.[2] It was natural that, meeting with difficulties in this undertaking, he should desire to converse with Tyndale. The two friends lodged with a pious woman named Margaret van Emmersen, and spent some time together in the autumn of 1529, undisturbed by the sweating sickness which was making such cruel havoc all around them. Coverdale returned to England shortly after; the two reformers had, no doubt, discovered that it was better for each of them to translate the Scriptures separately.

Before Coverdale's return, Tunstall had gone back to London, exulting at carrying with him the books he had bought

---

[1] [A number of historians have seen fit to cast doubt on this part of Tyndale's history, which is narrated by Foxe alone. J. F. Mozley however, in his *William Tyndale*, 1937, gives substantial reasons for accepting it.]

[2] This is the date assigned in *Coverdale's Remains* (Parker Society), p. 490.

so dearly. But when he reached the capital, he thought he had better defer the meditated *auto da fé* until some striking event should give it increased importance. And besides, just at that moment, very different matters were engaging public attention on the banks of the Thames, and the liveliest emotions agitated every mind.

CHAPTER EIGHT

A Queen's Pleadings Convict a Court

(1529)

AFFAIRS had changed in England during the absence of Tunstall and More; and even before their departure, events of a certain importance had occurred. Henry, finding there was nothing more to hope from Rome, had turned to Wolsey and Campeggio. The Roman nuncio had succeeded in deceiving the king. "Campeggio is very different from what he is reported," said Henry to his friends; "he is not for the Emperor, as I was told; I have said somewhat to him which has changed his mind." No doubt he had made some brilliant promise.

Henry therefore, imagining himself sure of his two legates, desired them to proceed with the matter of the divorce without delay. There was no time to lose, for the king was informed that the pope was on the point of recalling the commission given to the two cardinals; and as early as the 19th of March, Salviati, the pope's uncle and secretary of state, wrote to Campeggio about it. Henry's process, once in the court of the pontifical chancery, it would have been long before it got out again. Accordingly, on the 31st of May, the king, by a warrant under the great seal, gave the legates *leave* to execute their commission, "without any regard to his own person, and having the fear of God only before their eyes." The legates themselves had suggested this formula to the king.

On the same day the commission was opened; but to begin the process was not to end it. Every letter which the nuncio received forbade him to do so in the most positive manner. "Advance slowly and never finish," were Clement's instructions. The trial was to be a farce, played by a pope and two cardinals.

The ecclesiastical court met in the Great Hall of the Blackfriars, commonly called the "parliament chamber." The two legates having successively taken the commission in their hands, devoutly declared that they were resolved to execute it (they should have said, to elude it) made the required oaths, and ordered a peremptory citation of the king and queen to appear on the 18th of June at nine in the morning. Campeggio was eager to proceed *slowly;* the session was adjourned for three weeks. The citation caused a great stir among the people. "What!" said they, "a king and a queen constrained to appear, in their own realm, before their own subjects." The papacy set an example which was to be strictly followed in after-years both in England and in France.

On the 18th of June, Catherine appeared before the commission in the parliament chamber and, stepping forward with dignity, said with a firm voice: "I protest against the legates as incompetent judges, and appeal to the pope." This proceeding of the queen, her pride and firmness, troubled her enemies, and in their vexation they grew exasperated against her. "Instead of praying God to bring this matter to a good conclusion," they said, "she endeavours to turn away the people's affections from the king. Instead of showing Henry the love of a youthful wife, she keeps away from him night and day. There is even cause to fear," they added, "that she is in concert with certain individuals who have formed the horrible design of killing the king and the cardinal." But persons of generous heart, seeing only a queen, a wife, and a mother, attacked in her dearest affections, showed themselves full of sympathy for her.

On the 21st of June, the day to which the court adjourned, the two legates entered the parliament chamber with all the pomp belonging to their station, and took their seats on a raised platform. Near them sat the bishops of Bath and Lincoln, the abbot of Westminster, and Doctor Taylor, master of the Rolls, whom they had added to their commission. Below them were the secretaries, among whom the skilful Stephen Gardiner held the chief rank. On the right beneath a canopy of cloth of gold sat the king surrounded by his officers; and on the left, a little lower, and under a similar canopy, was the queen, attended by her ladies. The archbishop of Canterbury and the bishops were seated between the legates and Henry VIII, and on both sides of the throne were stationed the counsellors of the king and queen—Fisher, bishop of Rochester, Standish of St

Asaph, West of Ely and Doctor Ridley. The people, when they saw this procession pass before them, were far from being dazzled by the pomp. "Less show and more virtue," they said, "would better become such judges."

The pontifical commission having been read, the legates declared that they would judge without fear or favour, and would admit of neither recusation nor appeal. Then the usher cried: "Henry, king of England, come into court." The king, cited in his own capital to accept as judges two priests, his subjects, repressed the throbbing of his proud heart, and replied, in the hope that this strange trial would have a favourable issue, "Here I am." The usher continued: "Catherine, queen of England, come into court." The queen handed the cardinals a paper in which she protested against the legality of the court, as the judges were the subjects of her opponent, and appealed to Rome. The cardinals declared they could not admit this paper, and consequently Catherine was again called into court. After the king and Wolsey had in turn briefly spoken, the queen devoutly crossed herself, made the circuit of the court to where the king sat, bending with dignity as she passed in front of the legates, and fell on her knees before her husband. Every eye was turned upon her. Then speaking in English, but with a Spanish accent, which by recalling the distance she was from her native home, pleaded eloquently for her, Catherine said with tears in her eyes, and in a tone at once dignified and impassioned:

"SIR—I beseech you, for all the love that hath been between us, and for the love of God, let me have justice and right; take some pity on me, for I am a poor woman and a stranger, born out of your dominions. I have here no assured friend, much less impartial counsel, and I flee to you as to the head of justice within this realm. Alas! Sir, wherein have I offended you, or what occasion given you of displeasure, that you should wish to put me from you? I take God and all the world to witness, that I have been to you a true, humble, and obedient wife, ever conformable to your will and pleasure. Never have I said or done aught contrary thereto, being always well pleased and content with all things wherein you had delight; neither did I ever grudge in word or countenance, or show a visage or spark of discontent. I loved all those whom you loved, only for your sake. This twenty years I have been your true wife, and by me ye have had divers children, although it hath pleased God to call them out of this world, which yet hath been no default in me."

The judges, and even the most servile of the courtiers, were touched when they heard these simple and eloquent words, and the queen's sorrow moved them almost to tears. Catherine continued:

"Sir—When ye married me at the first, I take God to be my judge I was a true maid; and whether it be true or not, I put it to your conscience. . . . If there be any just cause that ye can allege against me, I am contented to depart from your kingdom, albeit to my great shame and dishonour; and if there be none, then let me remain in my former estate until death. Who united us? The king, your father, who was called the second Solomon; and my father, Ferdinand, who was esteemed one of the wisest princes that, for many years before, had reigned in Spain. It is not, therefore, to be doubted that the marriage between you and me is good and lawful. Who are my judges? Is not one the man that has put sorrow between you and me? . . . a judge whom I refuse and abhor!—Who are the counsellors assigned me? Are they not officers of the crown, who have made oath to you in your own council? . . . Sir, I conjure you not to call me before a court so formed. Yet, if you refuse me this favour . . . your will be done . . . I shall be silent, I shall repress the emotions of my soul and remit my just cause to the hands of God."

Thus spoke Catherine through her tears; humbly bending, she seemed to embrace Henry's knees. She rose and made a low obeisance to the king. It was expected that she would return to her seat; but leaning on the arm of Master Griffiths, her receiver-general, she moved towards the door. The king, observing this, ordered her to be recalled; and the usher following her, thrice cried aloud: "Catherine, queen of England, come into court."—"Madam," said Griffiths, "you are called back."—"I hear it well enough," replied the queen, "but go you on, for this is no court wherein I can have justice: let us proceed." Catherine returned to the palace, and never again appeared before the court either by proxy or in person.

She had gained her cause in the minds of many. The dignity

of her person, the quaint simplicity of her speech, the propriety with which, relying upon her innocence, she had spoken of the most delicate subjects, and the tears which betrayed her emotion, had created a deep impression. But "the sting in her speech," as an historian says, was her appeal to the king's conscience, and to the judgment of Almighty God, on the capital point in the cause. "How could a person so modest, so sober in her language," said many, "dare utter such a falsehood? Besides, the king did not contradict her."

Henry was greatly embarrassed: Catherine's words had moved him. Catherine's defence, one of the most touching in history, had gained over the accuser himself. He therefore felt constrained to render this testimony to the accused: "Since the queen has withdrawn, I will, in her absence, declare to you all present, that she has been to me as true and obedient a wife as I could desire. She has all the virtues and good qualities that belong to a woman. She is as noble in character as in birth."

But Wolsey was the most embarrassed of all. When the queen had said, without naming him, that one of her judges was the cause of all her misfortunes, looks of indignation were turned upon him. He was unwilling to remain under the weight of this accusation. As soon as the king had finished speaking, he said: "Sir, I humbly beg your majesty to declare before this audience, whether I was the first or chief mover in this business, for I am greatly suspected of all men herein." Wolsey had formerly boasted to Du Bellay, "that the first project of the divorce was set on foot by himself, to create a perpetual separation between the houses of England and Spain;" but now it suited him to affirm the contrary. The king, who needed his services, took care not to contradict him. "My lord cardinal," he said, "I can well excuse you herein. Marry, so far from being a mover, ye have been rather against me in attempting thereof. It was the bishop of Tarbes, the French ambassador, who begot the first scruples in my conscience by his doubts on the legitimacy of the princess Mary." This was not correct. The bishop of Tarbes was not in England before the year 1527, and we have proof that the king was meditating a divorce in 1526.[1]

---

[1] See Pace's letter to Henry in 1526. Pace there shows that it is incorrect to say: *Deuteronomium abrogare Leviticum* (Deuteronomy abrogates Leviticus), so far as concerns the prohibition to take the wife of a deceased brother.

"From that hour," he continued. "I was much troubled, and thought myself in danger of God's heavy displeasure, who, wishing to punish my incestuous marriage, had taken away all the sons my wife had borne me. I laid my grief before you, my lord of Lincoln, then being my ghostly father; and by your advice I asked counsel of the rest of the bishops, and you all informed me under your seals, that you shared in my scruples."—"That is the truth," said the archbishop of Canterbury.—"No, Sir, not so, under correction," quoth the bishop of Rochester, "you have not my hand and seal."—"No?" exclaimed the king, showing him a paper which he held in his hand; "is not this your hand and seal?"—"No, forsooth," he answered. Henry's surprise increased, and turning with a frown to the archbishop of Canterbury, he asked him: "What say you to that?"—"Sir, it is his hand and seal," replied Warham.—"It is not," rejoined Rochester; "I told you I would never consent to any such act."—"You say the truth," responded the archbishop, "but you were fully resolved at the last, that I should subscribe your name and put your seal."—"All which is untrue," added Rochester, in a passion. The bishop was not very respectful to his primate. "Well, well," said the king, wishing to end the dispute, "we will not stand in argument with you; for you are but one man." The court adjourned. The day had been better for Catherine than for the prelates.

In proportion as the first sitting had been pathetic, so the discussions in the second between the lawyers and bishops were calculated to revolt a delicate mind. The advocates of the two parties vigorously debated *pro* and *con* respecting the consummation of Arthur's marriage with Catherine. "It is a very difficult question," said one of the counsel; "none can know the truth."—"But I know it," replied the bishop of Rochester.—"What do you mean?" asked Wolsey.—"My lord," he answered, "he was the very Truth who said: *What God hath joined together, let not man put asunder:* that is enough for me."—"So everybody thinks," rejoined Wolsey; "but whether it was God who united Henry of England and Catherine of Aragon, *hoc restat probandum* (that remains to be proved). The king's council decides that the marriage is unlawful, and consequently it was not *God who joined them together.*" The two bishops then exchanged a few words less edifying than those of the preceding day. Several of the hearers expressed a sentiment of disgust. "It is a disgrace to the court," said Doctor Ridley with no little indignation, "that you dare discuss questions which fill every right-minded man with horror." This sharp reprimand put an end to the debate.

The agitations of the court spread to the religious houses; priests, monks, and nuns were everywhere in commotion. It was not long before astonishing revelations began to circulate through the cloisters. There was no talk then of an old portrait of the Virgin that winked its eyes; but other miracles were invented. "An angel," it was rumoured, "has appeared to Elizabeth Barton, the maid of Kent, as he did formerly to Adam, to the patriarchs, and to Jesus Christ." At the epochs of the creation and of the redemption, and in the times which lead from one to the other, miracles are natural; God then appeared, and His coming without any signs of power would be as surprising as the rising of the sun unattended by its rays of light. But the Romish Church does not stop there; it claims in every age, for its saints, the privilege of miraculous powers, and the miracles are multiplied in proportion to the ignorance of the people. And accordingly the angel said to the epileptic maid of Kent: "Go to the unfaithful king of England, and tell him there are three things he desires, which I forbid now and for ever. The first is the power of the pope; the second the new doctrine; the third Anne Boleyn. If he takes her for his wife, God will visit him." The vision-seeing maid delivered the message to the king, whom nothing could now stop.

On the contrary, he began to find out that Wolsey proceeded too slowly, and the idea sometimes crossed his mind that he was betrayed by this minister. One fine summer's morning, Henry, as soon as he rose, summoned the cardinal to him at Bridewell. Wolsey hastened thither, and remained closeted with the king from eleven till twelve. The latter gave way to all the fury of his passion and the violence of his despotism. "We must finish this matter promptly," he said, "we must positively." Wolsey retired very uneasy, and returned by the Thames to Westminster. The sun darted his bright rays on the water. The bishop of Carlisle, who sat by the cardinal's side, as he wiped his forehead: "A very warm day, my lord."—"Yes," replied the unhappy Wolsey, "if you had been *chafed* for an hour as I have been, you would say it was a *hot* day." When he reached his palace, the cardinal lay down on his bed to seek repose; he was not quiet long.

Catherine had grown in Henry's eyes, as well as in those of the nation. The king shrank from a judgment; he even began to doubt of his success. He wished that the queen would consent to a separation. This idea occurred to his mind after Wolsey's departure, and the cardinal had hardly closed his eyes before the Earl of Wiltshire (Anne Boleyn's father) was announced to him with a message from the king. "It is his majesty's pleasure," said Wiltshire, "that you represent to the queen the shame that will accrue to her from a judicial condemnation, and persuade her to confide in his wisdom." Wolsey, commissioned to execute a task he knew to be impossible, exclaimed: "Why do you put such fancies in the king's head?" and then he spoke so reproachfully that Wiltshire, with tears in his eyes, fell on his knees beside the cardinal's bed. Boleyn, desirous of seeing his daughter queen of England, feared perhaps that he had taken a wrong course. "It is well," said the cardinal, recollecting that the message came from Henry VIII, "I am ready to do everything to please his majesty." He rose, went to Bath-Place to fetch Campeggio, and together they waited on the queen.

The two legates found Catherine quietly at work with her maids of honour. Wolsey addressed the queen in Latin: "Nay, my lord," she said, "speak to me in English; I wish all the world could hear you."—"We desire, madam, to communicate to *you alone* our counsel and opinion."—"My lord," said the queen, "you are come to speak of things beyond my capacity;" and then, with noble simplicity, showing a skein of white thread hanging about her neck, she continued: "These are my occupations and all that I am capable of. I am a poor woman, without friends in this foreign country and lacking wit to answer persons of wisdom as ye be; and yet, my lords, to please you, let us go to my withdrawing room."

At these words the queen rose, and Wolsey gave her his hand. Catherine earnestly maintained her rights as a woman and a queen. "We who were in the outer chamber," says Cavendish, "from time to time could hear the queen speaking very loud, but could not understand what she said." Catherine, instead of justifying herself, boldly accused her judge. "I know,

Sir Cardinal," she said with noble candour, "I know who has given the king the advice he is following: it is you. I have not ministered to your pride—I have blamed your conduct—I have complained of your tyranny, and my nephew the Emperor has not made you pope. . . . Hence all my misfortunes. To revenge yourself you have kindled a war in Europe and have stirred up against me this most wicked matter. God will be my judge . . . and yours!" Wolsey would have replied, but Catherine haughtily refused to hear him and, while treating Campeggio with great civility, declared that she would not acknowledge either of them as her judge. The cardinals withdrew, Wolsey full of vexation and Campeggio beaming with joy, for the business was getting more complicated. Every hope of accommodation was lost: nothing remained now but to proceed judicially.

CHAPTER NINE

The Trial Ends in Farce

(July, 1529)

THE trial was resumed. The bishop of Bath and Wells waited upon the queen at Greenwich and peremptorily summoned her to appear in the parliament-chamber. On the day appointed Catherine limited herself to sending an appeal to the pope. She was declared contumacious, and the legates proceeded with the cause.

Twelve articles were prepared, which were to serve for the examination of the witnesses and the summary of which was that the marriage of Henry with Catherine, being forbidden both by the law of God and of the church, was null and void.

The hearing of the witnesses began, and Dr Taylor, arch-deacon of Buckingham, conducted the examination.[1] The duke of Norfolk, high-treasurer of England, the duke of Suffolk, Maurice St John, gentleman-carver to Prince Arthur, the viscount Fitzwalter and Anthony Willoughby, his cup-bearers, testified to their being present on the morrow of the wedding at the breakfast of the prince, then in sound health, and reported the conversation that took place. The old duchess of Norfolk, the earl of Shrewsbury and the marquis of Dorset, confirmed these declarations, which proved that Arthur and Catherine were really married. It was also called to mind that, at the time of Arthur's death, Henry was not permitted to take the title of Prince of Wales, because Catherine hoped to give an heir to the crown of England.

"If Arthur and Catherine were really married," said the king's counsellors after these extraordinary depositions, "the marriage of this princess with Henry, Arthur's brother, was forbidden by the divine law, by an express command of God contained in Leviticus, and no dispensation could permit what

[1] The evidence is to be found recorded in Lord Herbert of Cherbury's *History of Henry VIII* (first published in 1649).

God had forbidden." Campeggio would never concede this argument, which limited the right of the popes; it was necessary therefore to abandon the *divine right* (which was in reality to lose the cause) and to seek in the bull of Julius II and in his famous brief for flaws that would invalidate them both; and this the king's counsel did, although they did not conceal the weakness of their position. "The motive alleged in the dispensation," they said, "is the necessity of preserving a cordial relation between Spain and England; now, there was nothing that threatened their harmony. Moreover, it is said in this document that the pope grants it at the prayer of Henry, Prince of Wales. Now as this prince was only thirteen years old, he was not of age to make such a request. As for the brief, it is found neither in England nor in Rome; we cannot therefore admit its authenticity." It was not difficult for Catherine's friends to invalidate these objections. "Besides," they added, "a union that has lasted twenty years sufficiently establishes its own lawfulness. And will you declare the Princess Mary illegitimate, to the great injury of this realm?"

The king's advocates then changed their course. Was not the Roman legate provided with a decretal pronouncing the divorce, in case it should be proved that Arthur's marriage had been really consummated? Now, this fact had been proved by the depositions. "This is the moment for delivering judgment," said Henry and his counsellors to Campeggio. "Publish the pope's decretal." But the pope feared the sword of Charles V, then hanging over his head; and accordingly, whenever the king advanced one step, the Romish prelate took several in an opposite direction. "I will deliver judgment in *five* days," said he; and when the five days were expired, he bound himself to deliver it in six. "Restore peace to my troubled conscience," exclaimed Henry. The legate replied in courtly phrase; he had gained a few days' delay, and that was all he desired.

Such conduct on the part of the Roman legate produced an unfavourable effect in England, and a change took place in the public mind. The first movement had been for Catherine; the second was for Henry. Clement's endless delays and Campeggio's stratagems exasperated the nation. The king's argument was simple and popular: "The pope cannot dispense with the laws of God;" while the queen, by appealing to the authority of the

Roman pontiff, displeased both high and low. "No precedent," said the lawyers, "can justify the king's marriage with his brother's widow."

There were, however, some evangelical Christians who thought Henry was "troubled" more by his passions than by his conscience; and they asked how it happened that a prince, who represented himself to be so disturbed by the possible transgression of a law of doubtful interpretation, could desire, after twenty years, to violate the indisputable law which forbade the divorce? . . . On the 21st of July, the day fixed *ad concludendum*, the cause was adjourned until the Friday following, and no one doubted that the matter would then be terminated.

All prepared for this important day. The king ordered the dukes of Norfolk and Suffolk to be present at the sitting of the court; and, being himself impatient to hear the so much coveted judgment, he stole into a gallery of the parliament-chamber facing the judges.

The legates of the holy see having taken their seats, the attorney-general signified to them, "that everything necessary for the information of their conscience having been judicially laid before them, that day had been fixed for the conclusion of the trial." There was a pause; every one feeling the importance of this judgment, waited for it with impatience. "Either the papacy pronounces my divorce from Catherine," the king had said, "or I shall divorce myself from the papacy." That was the way Henry put the question. All eyes, and particularly the king's, were turned on the judges; Campeggio could not retreat; he must now say *yes* or *no*. For some time he was silent. He knew for certain that the queen's appeal had been admitted by Clement VII, and that the latter had concluded an alliance with the Emperor. It was no longer in his power to grant the king's request. Clearly foreseeing that a *no* would perhaps forfeit the power of Rome in England, while a *yes* might put an end to the plans of religious emancipation which alarmed him so much, he could not make up his mind to say either *yes* or *no*.

At last the nuncio rose slowly from his chair, and all the assembly listened with emotion to the oracular decision which for so many years the powerful king of England had sought from the Roman pontiff. "The general vacation of the harvest and vintage," he said, "being observed every year by the court of Rome, dating from to-morrow the 24th of July, the beginning of the dog-days, we adjourn, to some future period, the conclusion of these pleadings."

The auditors were thunderstruck. "What! because the *malaria* renders the air of Rome dangerous at the end of July, and compels the Romans to close their courts, must a trial be broken off on the banks of the Thames, when its conclusion is looked for so impatiently?" The people hoped for a judicial sentence, and they were answered with a jest; it was thus Rome made sport of Christendom. Campeggio, to disarm Henry's wrath, gave utterance to some noble sentiments; but his whole line of conduct raises legitimate doubts as to his sincerity. "The queen," he said, "denies the competency of the court; I must therefore make my report to the pope, who is the source of life and honour, and wait his sovereign orders. I have not come so far to please any man, be he king or subject. I am an old man, feeble and sickly, and fear none but the Supreme Judge, before whom I must soon appear. I therefore adjourn this court until the 1st of October." It was evident that this adjournment was only a formality intended to signify the definitive rejection of Henry's demand.

The king, who from his place of concealment had heard Campeggio's speech, could scarcely control his indignation. He wanted a regular judgment; he clung to forms; he desired that his cause should pass successfully through all the windings of ecclesiastical procedure, and yet here it is wrecked upon the vacations of the Romish court. Henry was silent, however, either from prudence, or because surprise deprived him of the power of speech, and he hastily left the gallery.

Norfolk, Suffolk, and the other courtiers, did not follow him. The king and his ministers, the peers and the people, and even the clergy, were almost unanimous, and yet the pope pronounced his *veto*. He humbled the Defender of the Faith to flatter the author of the sack of Rome. This was too much. The impetuous Suffolk started from his seat, struck his hand violently on the table in front of him, cast a threatening look upon the judges and exclaimed: "By the mass, the old saying is confirmed to-day, that no cardinal has ever brought good to England."—"Sir, of all men in this realm," replied Wolsey, "you have the least cause to disparage cardinals, for if I, poor cardinal, had not been, you would not have a head on your shoulders." It would seem that Wolsey pacified Henry at the time of the duke's marriage with the Princess Mary. "I cannot pronounce sentence," continued Wolsey, "without knowing the good pleasure of his holiness." The two dukes and the other noblemen left the hall in anger, and hastened to the palace. The legates, remaining with the officers, looked at each other for a few moments. At last Campeggio, who alone had remained calm during this scene of violence, arose, and the audience dispersed.

Henry did not allow himself to be crushed by this blow. Rome, by her strange proceedings, aroused in him that suspicious and despotic spirit, of which he gave such tragic proofs in after-years. The papacy was making sport of him. Clement and Wolsey tossed his divorce from one to the other like a ball which, now at Rome and now at London, seemed fated to remain perpetually in the air. The king thought he had been long enough the plaything of his holiness and of the crafty cardinal; his patience was exhausted, and he resolved to show his adversaries that Henry VIII was more than a match for these bishops. We shall find him seizing this favourable opportunity, and giving an unexpected solution to the matter.

Wolsey sorrowfully hung his head; by taking part with the nuncio and the pope, he had signed the warrant of his own destruction. So long as Henry had a single ray of hope, he thought proper still to dissemble with Clement VII; but he might vent all his anger on Wolsey. From the period of the *Roman Vacations* the cardinal was ruined in his master's mind. Wolsey's enemies, seeing his favour decline, hastened to attack him. Suffolk and Norfolk in particular, impatient to get rid of an insolent priest who had so long chafed their pride, told Henry that Wolsey had been continually playing false; they went over all his negotiations month by month and day by day, and drew the most overwhelming conclusions from them. Sir William Kingston and Lord Manners laid before the king one of the cardinal's letter which Sir Francis Bryan had obtained from the papal archives. In it the cardinal desired Clement to spin out the divorce question, and finally to oppose it, seeing (he added) that if Henry was separated from Catherine, a friend

EE

to the reformers would become queen of England. This letter clearly expressed Wolsey's inmost thoughts: Rome at any price ... and perish England and Henry rather than the popedom! We can imagine the king's anger.

Anne Boleyn's friends were not working alone. There was not a person at court whom Wolsey's haughtiness and tyranny had not offended; no one in the king's council in whom his continual intrigues had not raised serious suspicions. He had, they said, betrayed in France the cause of England; kept up in time of peace and war secret intelligence with Madam, mother of Francis I; received great presents from her; oppressed the nation, and trodden under foot the laws of the kingdom. The people called him *Frenchman* and *traitor*, and all England seemed to vie in throwing burning brands at the superb edifice which the pride of this prelate had so laboriously erected.

Wolsey was too clearsighted not to discern the signs of his approaching fall. "Both the rising and the setting sun (for thus an historian calls Anne Boleyn and Catherine of Aragon) frowned upon him,"[1] and the sky, growing darker around him, gave token of the storm that was to overwhelm him. If the *cause* failed, Wolsey incurred the vengeance of the king; if it succeeded, he would be delivered up to the vengeance of the Boleyns, without speaking of Catherine's, the Emperor's, and the pope's. Happy Campeggio! thought the cardinal, he has nothing to fear. If Henry's favour is withdrawn from him, Charles and Clement will make him compensation. But Wolsey lost everything when he lost the king's good graces. Detested by his fellow-citizens, despised and hated by all Europe, he saw to whatever side he turned nothing but the just reward of his avarice and falseness. He strove in vain, as on other occasions, to lean on the ambassador of France; Du Bellay was solicited on the other side. "I am exposed here to such a heavy and continual fire that I am half dead," exlaimed the French Ambassador; and the cardinal met with an unusual reserve in his former confidant.

Yet the crisis approached. Like a skilful but affrighted pilot, Wolsey cast his eyes around him to discover a port in which he could take refuge. He could find none but his see of York. He therefore began once more to complain of the fatigues of

[1] Thomas Fuller's *Church History of Britain* (1655), Bk. V, p. 176.

power, of the weariness of the diplomatic career, and to extol the sweetness of an episcopal life. On a sudden he felt a great interest about the flock of whom he had never thought before. Those around him shook their heads, well knowing that such a retreat would be to Wolsey the bitterest of disgraces. One single idea supported him; if he fell, it would be because he had clung more to the pope than to the king: he would be the martyr of his faith.—What a faith! what a martyr!

CHAPTER TEN

'Tyndale' Received in a King's Palace

(1529)

WHILE these things were taking place Anne was living at Hever Castle in retirement and sadness. Scruples from time to time still alarmed her conscience. It is true, the king represented to her unceasingly that his salvation and the safety of his people demanded the dissolution of a union condemned by the divine law, and that what he solicited several popes had granted. Had not Alexander VI annulled, after ten years, the marriage of Ladislaus and Beatrice of Naples? Had not Louis XII, the father of his people, been divorced from Joan of France? Nothing was more common, he said, than to see the divorce of a prince authorized by a pope; the security of the state must be provided for before everything else. Carried away by these arguments and dazzled by the splendour of a throne, Anne Boleyn consented to usurp at Henry's side the rank belonging to another. Yet, if she was imprudent and ambitious, she was feeling and generous, and the misfortunes of a queen whom she respected soon made her reject with terror the idea of taking her place. The fertile pastures of Kent and the gothic halls of Hever Castle were by turns the witnesses of the mental conflicts this young lady experienced. The fear she entertained of seeing the queen again, and the idea that the two cardinals, her enemies, were plotting her ruin, made her adopt the resolution of not returning to court, and she shut herself up in her solitary chamber.

Anne had neither the deep piety of a Bilney, nor the somewhat vague and mystic spirituality observable in Margaret of Valois; it was not feeling which prevailed in her religion, it was knowledge, and a horror of superstition and pharisaism. Her mind required light and activity, and at that time she sought in reading the consolations so necessary to her position.

One day she opened one of the books prohibited in England, which a friend of the Reformation had given her: *The Obedience of a Christian Man*. Its author was William Tyndale, that invisible man whom Wolsey's agents were hunting for in Brabant and Germany, and this was a recommendation to Anne. "If thou believe the promises," she read, "then God's truth justifieth thee; that is, forgiveth thy sins and sealeth thee with His Holy Spirit. If thou have true faith, so seest thou the exceeding and infinite love and mercy which God hath shown thee freely in Christ: then must thou needs love again: and love cannot but compel thee to work. If when tyrants oppose thee thou hast power to confess, then art thou sure that thou art safe. If thou be fallen from the way of truth, come thereto again and thou art safe. Yea, Christ shall save thee, and the angels of heaven shall rejoice at thy coming." These words did not change Anne's heart, but she marked with her nail, as was her custom, other passages which struck her more, and which she desired to point out to the king if, as she hoped, she was ever to meet him again. She believed that the truth was there, and took a lively interest in those whom Wolsey, Henry, and the pope were at that time persecuting.

Anne was soon dragged from these pious lessons, and launched into the midst of a world full of dangers. Henry, convinced that he had nothing to expect henceforward from Campeggio, neglected those proprieties which he had hitherto observed, and immediately after the adjournment required Anne Boleyn to return to court; he restored her to the place she had formerly occupied, and even surrounded her with increased splendour. Everyone saw that Anne, in the king's mind, was queen of England; and a powerful party was formed around her, which proposed to accomplish the definitive ruin of the cardinal.

After her return to court, Anne read much less frequently *The Obedience of a Christian Man* and the *Testament of Jesus Christ*. Henry's homage, her friends' intrigues, and the whirl of festivities, bade fair to stifle the thoughts which solitude had aroused in her heart. One day having left Tyndale's book in a window, Miss Gainsford, a fair young gentlewoman attached to her person, took it up and read it. A gentleman of handsome mien, cheerful temper, and extreme mildness, named George Zouch, also belonging to Anne's household, and betrothed to

Miss Gainsford, profiting by the liberty his position gave him, indulged sometimes in "love tricks." On one occasion when George desired to have a little talk with her, he was annoyed to find her absorbed by a book of whose contents he knew nothing; and taking advantage of a moment when the young lady had turned away her head, he laughingly snatched it from her. Miss Gainsford ran after Zouch to recover her book; but just at that moment she heard her mistress calling her, and she left George, threatening him with her finger.

As she did not return immediately, George withdrew to his room, and opened the volume; it was the *Obedience of a Christian Man*. He glanced over a few lines, then a few pages, and at last read the book through more than once. He seemed to hear the voice of God. "I feel the Spirit of God," he said, "speaking in my heart as he has spoken in the heart of him who wrote the book." The words which had only made a temporary impression on the preoccupied mind of Anne Boleyn, penetrated to the heart of her equerry and converted him. Miss Gainsford, fearing that Anne would ask for her book, entreated George to restore it to her; but he positively refused, and even the young lady's tears failed to make him give up a volume in which he had found the life of his soul. Becoming more serious, he no longer jested as before; and when Miss Gainsford peremptorily demanded the book, he was, says the chronicler, "ready to weep himself."

Zouch, finding in this volume an edification which empty forms and ceremonies could not give, used to carry it with him to the king's chapel. Dr Sampson, the dean, generally officiated; and while the choir chanted the service, George would be absorbed in his book, where he read: "If when thou seest the celebration of the sacrament of the Lord's Supper, thou believest in this promise of Christ: *This is my body that is broken for you*, and if thou have this promise fast in thine heart, thou art saved and justified thereby; thou eatest his body and drinkest his blood. If not, so helpeth it thee not, though thou hearest a thousand masses in a day: no more than it should help thee in a dead thirst to behold a bush at a tavern door, if thou knowest not thereby that there was wine within to be sold." The young man dwelt upon these words: by faith he ate the body and drank the blood of the Son of God. This was what wapassing in the palaces of Henry VIII; there were saints in the household of Cæsar.

Wolsey, desirous of removing from the court everything that might favour the Reformation, had recommended extreme vigilance to Dr Sampson so as to prevent the circulation of the innovating books. Accordingly, one day when George was in the chapel absorbed in his book, the dean, who, even while officiating, had not lost sight of the young man, called him to him after the service and, rudely taking the book from his hands, demanded: "What is your name, and in whose service are you?" Zouch having replied, the dean withdrew with a very angry look, and carried his prey to the cardinal.

When Miss Gainsford heard of this mishap, her grief was extreme; she trembled at the thought that the *Obedience of a Christian Man* was in Wolsey's hands. Not long after this, Anne having asked for her book, the young lady fell on her knees, confessed all, and begged to be forgiven. Anne uttered not a word of reproach; her quick mind saw immediately the advantage she might derive from this affair. "Well," said she, "it shall be the dearest book to them that ever the dean or cardinal took away."

"The noble lady," as the chronicler styles her, immediately demanded an interview of the king, and on reaching his presence she fell at his feet, and begged his assistance. "What is the matter, Anne," said the astonished monarch. She told him what had happened, and Henry promised that the book should not remain in Wolsey's hands.

Anne had scarcely quitted the royal apartments when the cardinal arrived with the famous volume, with the intention of complaining to Henry of certain passages which he knew could not fail to irritate him, and of taking advantage of it even to attack Anne, if the king should be offended. Henry's icy reception closed his mouth; the king confined himself to taking the book, and bowing out the cardinal. This was precisely what Anne had hoped for. She begged the king to read the book, which he promised to do.

And Henry accordingly shut himself up in his chamber, and read the *Obedience of a Christian Man*. There were few works better calculated to enlighten him, and none, after the Bible, that had more influence upon the Reformation in England.

Tyndale treated of *obedience*, "the essential principle," as he terms it, "of every political or religious community." He declaimed against the unlawful power of the popes, who usurped the lawful authority of Christ and of His Word. He professed political doctrines too favourable doubtless to absolute power, but calculated to show that the reformers were not, as had been asserted, instigators of rebellion. Henry read as follows:

"The king is in the room of God in this world. He that resisteth the king, resisteth God; he that judgeth the king, judgeth God. He is the minister of God to defend thee from a thousand inconveniences; though he be the greatest tyrant in the world, yet is he unto thee a great benefit of God; for it is better to pay the tenth than to lose all, and to suffer wrong of one man than of every man. It is better to have a tyrant as king than a shadow . . . for a tyrant, though he do wrong unto the good, yet he punisheth the evil, and makes all men obey, neither suffers any man to exact taxes but himself. A king that is soft as silk is much more grievous unto the realm than a right tyrant. Read the chronicles and thou shalt find it ever so."[1]

These are indeed strange doctrines for *rebels* to hold, thought the king; and he read further:

"Let kings, if they had lever [rather] be Christians in deed than so to be called, give themselves altogether to the wealth [well-being] of their realms after the ensample of Jesus Christ; remembering that the people are God's, and not theirs; yea, are Christ's inheritance, bought with His blood. The most despised person in his realm (if he is a Christian) is equal with him in the kingdom of God and of Christ. Let the king put off all pride, and become a brother to the poorest of his subjects."

We may surmise that these words were less satisfactory to the king. He kept on reading:

"The Emperor and kings are nothing now-a-days, but even hangmen unto the pope and bishops, to kill whomsoever they condemn, as Pilate was unto the scribes and pharisees and high bishops to hang Christ."

This seemed to Henry rather strong language.

"The pope hath received no other authority of Christ than to preach God's Word. Now, this Word should rule only, and

1 *Tyndale's Works*, edited by Russell, vol. i, p. 212.

not bishops' decrees or the pope's pleasure. *In præsentia majoris cessat potestas minoris*, in the presence of the greater, the less hath no power. The pope, against all the doctrine of Christ, which saith, *My kingdom is not of this world*, hath usurped the right of the Emperor. Kings must make account of their doings only to God. No person may be exempt from this ordinance of God; neither can the profession of monks and friars, or anything that the popes or bishops can lay for themselves, except them from the sword of the Emperor or king, if they break the laws. For it is written (Rom. xiii.), Let every soul submit himself unto the authority of the higher powers."

"What excellent reading!" exclaimed Henry, when he had finished; "this is truly a book for all kings to read, and for me particularly."

Captivated by Tyndale's work, the king began to converse with Anne about the church and the pope; and she who had seen Margaret of Valois unassumingly endeavour to instruct Francis I, strove in like manner to enlighten Henry VIII. She did not possess the influence over him she desired; this unhappy prince was, to the very end of his life, opposed to the evangelical reformation; protestants and catholics have been equally mistaken when they have regarded him as being favourable to it. "In a short time," says the annalist quoted by Strype at the end of his narrative, "the king, by the help of this virtuous lady, had his eyes opened to the truth. He learned to seek after that truth, to advance God's religion and glory, to detest the pope's doctrine, his lies, his pomp, and pride, and to deliver his subjects from the Egyptian darkness and Babylonian bonds that the pope had brought him and his subjects under. Despising the rebellions of his subjects and the rage of so many mighty potentates abroad, he set forward a religious reformation, which, beginning with the triple-crowned head, came down to all the members of the hierarchy." History has rarely delivered a more erroneous judgment. Henry's eyes were never opened to the truth, and it was not he who made the Reformation. It was accomplished first of all by Scripture, and then by the ministry of simple and faithful men baptized of the Holy Ghost.

Yet Tyndale's book and the conduct of the legates had given rise in the king's mind to new thoughts which he sought time to mature. He desired also to conceal his anger from Wolsey

and Campeggio, and dissipate his *spleen*, says the historian
Collyer; he therefore gave orders to remove the court to the
palace of Woodstock. The magnificent park attached to this
royal residence, in which was the celebrated bower constructed
(it is said) by Henry II to conceal the fair Rosamond, offered all
the charms of the promenade, the chase, and solitude.[1] From
here he could easily travel to Langley, Grafton, and other
country seats. It was not long before the entertainments,
horse-races, and other rural sports began. The world with its
pleasures and its grandeur, were at the bottom the idols of
Anne Boleyn's heart; but yet she felt a certain attraction for
the new doctrine, which was confounded in her mind with the
great cause of all knowledge, perhaps even with her own.
More enlightened than the generality of women, she was
distinguished by the superiority of her understanding not only
over her own sex, but even over many of the gentlemen of the
court. While Catherine, a member of the third order of St
Francis, indulged in trifling practices, the more intelligent, if
not more pious Anne, cared but little for amulets which the
friars had blessed, for apparitions, or visions of angels. Woodstock furnished her with an opportunity of curing Henry VIII
of the superstitious ideas natural to him. There was a place in
the forest said to be haunted by evil spirits; not a priest or a
courtier dared approach it. A tradition ran that if a king
ventured to cross the boundary, he would fall dead. Anne
resolved to take Henry there. Accordingly, one morning she
led the way in the direction of the place where these mysterious
powers manifested their presence (as it was said) by strange
apparitions; they entered the wood; they arrived at the so
much dreaded spot; all hesitated; but Anne's calmness reassured
her companions; they advanced; they found . . . nothing but
trees and turf, and, laughing at their former terrors, they
explored every corner of this mysterious resort of the evil
spirits. Anne returned to the palace, congratulating herself on
the triumph Henry had gained over his imaginary fears.

[1] The letters from the king's secretaries Gardiner and Tuke to Wolsey,
dated from Woodstock, run from 4th August to 8th September. State
Papers, i, pp. 335–47.

CHAPTER ELEVEN

Wolsey Alone and Facing Ruin

(Summer, 1529)

WHILE the court was thus taking its pleasure at Woodstock, Wolsey remained in London, a prey to the acutest anguish. "This calling of the case to Rome," wrote he to Gregory Da Casale, "will not only completely alienate the king and his realm from the apostolic see, but will ruin me utterly." This message had hardly reached the pope, before the imperial ambassadors handed to him the queen's protest, and added in a very significant tone: "If your holiness does not call this cause before you, the Emperor, who is determined to bring it to an end, will have recourse to *other arguments*." The same perplexity always agitated Clement: Which of the two must be sacrificed, Henry or Charles? Anthony de Leyva, who commanded the imperial forces, having routed the French army, the pope no longer doubted that Charles was the elect of Heaven. It was not Europe alone which acknowledged this prince's authority; a new world had just laid its power and its gold at his feet. The formidable priest-king of the Aztecs had been unable to withstand Cortez; could the priest-king of Rome withstand Charles V? Cortez had returned from Mexico, bringing with him Mexican chiefs in all their barbarous splendour, with thousands of *pesos*, with gold and silver and emeralds of extraordinary size, with magnificent tissues and birds of brilliant plumage. He had accompanied Charles, who was then going to Italy, to the place of embarkation, and had sent to Clement VII costly gifts of the precious metals, valuable jewels, and a troop of Mexican dancers, buffoons, and jugglers, who charmed the pope and the cardinal above all things.

Clement, even while refusing Henry's prayer, had not as yet granted the Emperor's. He thought he could now resist no longer the star of a monarch victorious over two worlds, and hastened to enter into negotiations with him. Sudden terrors still assailed him from time to time: My refusal (he said to himself) may perhaps cause me to lose England. But Charles, holding him in his powerful grasp, compelled him to submit. Henry's antecedents were rather encouraging to the pontiff. How could he imagine that a prince, who alone of all the monarchs of Europe had once contended against the great German reformer, would now separate from the popedom? On the 6th of July Clement declared to the English envoys that he *avoked to Rome* the cause between Henry VIII and Catherine of Aragon. In other words, this was refusing the divorce. "There are twenty-three points in this case," said the courtiers, "and the debate on the first has lasted a year; before the end of the trial, the king will be not only past marrying but past living."

When he learned that the fatal blow had been struck, Dr William Bennett, one of Henry's envoys, in a tone of sadness exclaimed: "Alas! most holy father, by this act the Church in England will be utterly destroyed; the king declared it to me with tears in his eyes."—"Why is it my fortune to live in such evil days?" replied the pope, who, in his turn, began to weep; "but I am encircled by the Emperor's forces, and, if I were to please the king, I should draw a fearful ruin upon myself and upon the church. . . . God will be my judge."

On the 15th of July Da Casale sent the fatal news to the English minister. The king was cited before the pope and, in case of refusal, condemned to a fine of 10,000 ducats. On the 18th of July peace was proclaimed at Rome between the pontiff and the Emperor, and on the next day (these dates are important) Clement, wishing still to make one more attempt to ward off the blow with which the papacy was threatened, wrote to Cardinal Wolsey: "My dear son, how can I describe to you my affliction? Show in this matter the prudence which so distinguishes you, and preserve the king in those kindly feelings which he has ever manifested towards me." A useless attempt! Far from saving the papacy, Wolsey was to be wrecked along with it.

Wolsey was thunderstruck. At the very time he was assuring Henry of the attachment of Clement and Francis, both were deserting him. The "politic handling" failed, which the cardinal had thought so skilful, and which had been so tortuous. Henry now had none but enemies on the continent of Europe, and the Reformation was daily spreading over his kingdom. Wolsey's anguish cannot be described. His power, his pomp, his palaces were all threatened; who could tell whether he would even preserve his liberty and his life.—A just reward for so much duplicity.

But the king's wrath was to be greater than even the minister's alarm. His terrified servants wondered how they should announce the pontiff's decision. Gardiner, who, after his return from Rome, had been named secretary of state, went down to Langley, Northamptonshire, on the 3rd of August to communicate it to him. What news for the proud Tudor! The decision on the divorce was forbidden in England; the cause avoked to Rome, there to be buried and unjustly lost; Francis I treating with the Emperor; Charles and Clement on the point of exchanging at Bologna the most striking signs of their unchangeable alliance; the services rendered by the king to the popedom repaid with the blackest ingratitude; his hope of giving an heir to the crown disgracefully frustrated; and last, but not least, Henry VIII, the proudest monarch of Christendom, summoned to Rome to appear before an ecclesiastical tribunal . . . it was too much for Henry. His wrath, a moment restrained, burst forth like a clap of thunder, and all trembled around him. "Do they presume," he exclaimed, "to try my cause elsewhere than in my own dominions? I, the king of England, summoned before an Italian tribunal! . . . Yes, . . . I will go to Rome, but it shall be with such a mighty army that the pope, and his priests, and all Italy shall be struck with terror.—I forbid the letters of citation to be executed," he continued; "I forbid the commission to consider its functions at an end." Henry would have desired to tear off Campeggio's purple robes, and throw this prince of the Roman church into prison, in order to frighten Clement; but the very magnitude of the insult compelled him to restrain himself. He feared above all things to appear humbled in the eyes of England, and he hoped, by showing moderation, to hide the affront he had received. "Let everything be done," he told Gardiner, "to conceal from my subjects these letters of citation, which are so hurtful to my glory. Write to Wolsey that I have the greatest confidence in his dexterity, and that he ought, by good handling, to win over Campeggio and the queen's counsellors, and, above all, prevail upon them at any price not to serve these citatory letters on me." But Henry had hardly given his instructions when the insult of which he had been the object recurred to his imagination; the thought of Clement haunted him night and day, and he swore to exact a striking vengeance from the pontiff. Rome desires to have no more to do with England. . . . England in her turn will cast off Rome. Henry will sacrifice Wolsey, Clement, and the church; nothing shall stop his fury. The crafty pontiff has concealed his game, the king shall beat him openly; and from age to age the popedom shall shed tears over the imprudent folly of a Medici.

Thus after insupportable delays which had fatigued the nation, a thunderbolt fell upon England. Court, clergy, and people, from whom it was impossible to conceal these great events, were deeply stirred, and the whole kingdom was in commotion. Wolsey, still hoping to ward off the ruin impending over both himself and the papacy, immediately put in play all that dexterity which Henry had spoken of; he so far prevailed that the letters citatorial were not served on the king, but only the brief addressed to Wolsey by Clement VII. The cardinal, gratified by this trivial success, and desirous of profiting by it to raise his credit, resolved to accompany Campeggio, who was going down to Grafton to take leave of the king. When the coming of the two legates was heard of at court, the agitation was very great. The dukes of Norfolk and Suffolk regarded this proceeding as the last effort of their enemy, and entreated Henry not to receive him. "The king will receive him," said some. "The king will not receive him," answered others. At length one Sunday morning it was announced that the prelates were at the gates of the mansion. Wolsey looked round with an anxious eye for the great officers who were accustomed to introduce him. They appeared, and desired Campeggio to follow them. When the legate had been taken to his apartments, Wolsey waited his turn; but great was his consternation on being informed that there was no chamber appointed for him in the palace. Sir Henry Norris, groom of the stole, offered Wolsey the use of his own room, and the cardinal followed him, almost sinking beneath the humiliation he had undergone. He made ready to appear before the king and, summoning up his courage, proceeded to the presence-chamber.

The lords of the council were standing in a row according to their rank; Wolsey, taking off his hat, passed along saluting each of them with affected civility. A great number of courtiers arrived, impatient to see how Henry would receive his old favourite; and most of them were already exulting in the striking disgrace of which they hoped to be witnesses. At last the king was announced.

Henry stood under the cloth of state; and Wolsey advanced and knelt before him. Deep silence prevailed throughout the chamber. . . . To the surprise of all, Henry stooped down and raised him up with both hands. . . . Then, with a pleasing smile, he took Wolsey to the window, desired him to put on his hat, and talked familiarly with him. "Then," says Cavendish, the cardinal's gentleman usher, "it would have made you smile to behold the countenances of those who had laid wagers that the king would not speak with him."

But this was the last ray of evening which then lighted up the darkening fortunes of Wolsey: the star of his favour was about to set for ever. . . . The silence continued, for every one desired to catch a few words of the conversation. The king seemed to be accusing Wolsey, and Wolsey to be justifying himself. On a sudden Henry pulled a letter out of his bosom and, showing it to the cardinal, said in a loud voice: "How can that be? Is not this your hand?" It was no doubt the letter which Bryan had intercepted. Wolsey replied in an undertone, and seemed to have appeased his master. The dinner hour having arrived, the king left the room telling Wolsey that he would not fail to see him again; the courtiers were eager to make their profoundest reverences to the cardinal, but he haughtily traversed the chamber, and the dukes hastened to carry to Anne Boleyn the news of this astonishing reception.

Wolsey, Campeggio, and the lords of the council sat down to dinner. The cardinal, well aware that the terrible letter would be his utter ruin, and that Henry's good graces had no other object than to prepare his fall, began to hint at his retirement. "Truly," said he with a devout air, "the king would do well to send his bishops and chaplains home to their cures and benefices." The company looked at one another with astonishment. "Yea, marry," said the duke of Norfolk somewhat rudely, "and so it were meet for you to do also."—"I should be very well contented therewith," answered Wolsey, "if it were the king's pleasure to license me with leave to go to my cure at Winchester."—"Nay, to your benefice at York, where your greatest honour and charge is," replied Norfolk, who was not willing that Wolsey should be living so near Henry.—"Even as it shall please the king," added Wolsey, and changed the subject of conversation.

Henry had caused himself to be announced to Anne Boleyn, who (says Cavendish) "kept state at Grafton more like a queen than a simple maid." Professing extreme sensibility, and an ardent imagination, Anne, who felt the slightest insult with all the sensibility of her woman's heart, was very dissatisfied with the king after the report of the dukes. Accordingly, heedless of the presence of the attendants, she said to him: "Sir, is it not a marvellous thing to see into what great danger the cardinal hath brought you with all your subjects?"—"How so, sweetheart?" asked Henry. Anne continued; "Are you ignorant of the hatred his exactions have drawn upon you? There is not a man in your whole realm of England worth one hundred pounds, but he hath made you his debtor." Anne here alluded to the loan the king had raised among his subjects. "Well, well," said Henry, who was not pleased with these remarks, "I know that matter better than you."—"If my lord of Norfolk, my lord of Suffolk, my uncle, or my father had done much less than the cardinal hath done," continued Anne, "they would have lost their heads ere this."—"Then I perceive," said Henry, "you are none of his friends."—"No, sir, I have no cause, nor any that love you," she replied. The dinner was ended; the king, without appearing at all touched, proceeded to the presence-chamber where Wolsey expected him.

After a long conversation, carried on in a low tone, the king took Wolsey by the hand and led him into his private chamber. The courtiers awaited impatiently the termination of an interview which might decide the fate of England; they walked up and down the gallery, often passing before the door of the chamber, in the hope of catching from Wolsey's looks, when he opened it, the result of this secret conference; but one quarter of an hour followed another, these became hours, and still the cardinal did not appear. Henry, having resolved that this conversation should be the last, was no doubt collecting from his minister all the information necessary to him. But the courtiers imagined he was returning into his master's favour; Norfolk, Suffolk, Wiltshire, and the other enemies of the prime minister, began to grow alarmed, and hastened off to Anne Boleyn, who was their last hope.

It was night when the king and Wolsey quitted the royal chamber; the former appeared gracious, the latter satisfied; it was always Henry's custom to smile on those he intended to sacrifice. "I shall see you in the morning," he said to the cardinal with a friendly air. Wolsey made a low bow, and, turning round to the courtiers, saw the king's smile reflected on their faces. Wiltshire, Tuke, and even Suffolk, were full of civility. "Well," thought he, "the motion of such weathercocks as these shows me from what quarter the wind of favour is blowing."

But a moment after the wind began to change. Men with torches waited for the cardinal at the gates of the palace to conduct him to the place where he would have to pass the night. Thus he was not to sleep beneath the same roof as Henry. He was to lie at Euston, one of Empson's houses, about three miles off. Wolsey, repressing his vexation, mounted his horse and, after an hour's riding along very bad roads, he reached the lodging assigned him.

He had sat down to supper, to which some of his most intimate friends had been invited, when suddenly Gardiner was announced. Gardiner owed everything to the cardinal, and yet he had not appeared before him since his return from Rome. He comes no doubt to play the hypocrite and the spy, thought Wolsey. But as soon as the secretary entered, Wolsey rose, made him a graceful compliment, and prayed him to take a seat. "Master Secretary," he asked, "where have you been since your return from Rome?"—"I have been following the court from place to place."—"You have been hunting, then? Have you any dogs?" asked the cardinal, who knew very well what Gardiner had been doing in the king's chamber. "A few," replied Gardiner. Wolsey thought that even the secretary was a bloodhound on his track. And yet after supper he took

FF

Gardiner aside, and conversed with him until midnight. He thought it prudent to neglect nothing that might clear up his position; and Wolsey sounded Gardiner, just as he himself had been sounded by Henry not long before.

The same night at Grafton the king gave Campeggio a farewell audience, and treated him very kindly, "by giving him presents and other matters," says Du Bellay. Henry then returned to Anne Boleyn. The dukes had pointed out to her the importance of the present moment; she therefore asked and obtained of Henry, without any great difficulty, his promise never to speak to his minister again. The insults of the papacy had exasperated the king of England, and, as he could not punish Clement, he took his revenge on the cardinal.

The next morning, Wolsey, impatient to have the interview which Henry had promised, rode back early to Grafton. But as he came near, he met a numerous train of servants and pack-horses; and shortly afterwards Henry, with Anne Boleyn and many lords and ladies of the court, came riding up. "What does all this mean?" thought the cardinal in dismay. "My lord," said the king, as he drew near, "I cannot stay with you now. You will return to London with cardinal Campeggio." Then striking the spurs into his horse, Henry galloped off with a friendly salutation. After him came Anne Boleyn, who rode past Wolsey with head erect, and casting on him a proud look. The court proceeded to Hartwell Park, where Anne had determined to keep the king all day. Wolsey was confounded. There was no room for doubt; his disgrace was certain. His head swam, he remained immovable for an instant, and then recovered himself; but the blow he had received had not been unobserved by the courtiers, and the cardinal's fall became the general topic of conversation.

After dinner, the legates departed, and on the second day reached Moor Park, a mansion built by Archbishop Neville, one of Wolsey's predecessors, who for high treason had been first imprisoned at Calais, and afterwards at Ham. These recollections were by no means agreeable to Wolsey. The next morning the two cardinals separated, Campeggio proceeded to Dover and Wolsey to London.

Campeggio was impatient to get out of England, and great was his annoyance, on reaching Dover, to find that the wind was contrary. But a still greater vexation was in reserve. He had hardly lain down to rest himself, before his door was opened, and a band of sergeants entered the room. The cardinal, who knew what scenes of this kind meant in Italy, thought he was a dead man, and fell trembling at his chaplain's feet begging for absolution. Meantime the officers opened his luggage, broke into his chests, scattered his property about the floor, and even shook out his clothes.

Henry's tranquillity had not been of long duration. "Campeggio is the bearer of letters from Wolsey to Rome," whispered some of the courtiers; "who knows but they contain treasonable matter?"—"There is, too, among his papers the famous *decretal* pronouncing the divorce," said one; "if we had but that document it would finish the business." Another affirmed that Campeggio "had large treasure with him of my lord's (Wolsey's) to be conveyed in great tuns to Rome," whither it was surmised the cardinal of York would escape to enjoy the fruits of his treason. "It is certain," added a third, "that Campeggio, assisted by Wolsey, has been able to procure your majesty's correspondence with Anne Boleyn, and is carrying it away with him." Henry, therefore, sent a messenger after the nuncio, with orders that his baggage should be thoroughly searched.

Nothing was found, neither letters, nor bull, nor treasures. The bull had been destroyed; the treasures Wolsey had never thought of entrusting to his colleague; and the letters of Anne and Henry, Campeggio had sent on before by his son Rodolph, and the pope was stretching out his hands to receive them, proud, like his successors, of the robbery committed by two of his legates.

Campeggio being reassured, and seeing that he was neither to be killed nor robbed, made a great noise at this act of violence, and at the insulting remarks which had given rise to it. "I will not leave England," he caused Henry to be informed, "until I have received satisfaction." "My lord forgets that he is legate no longer," replied the king, "since the pope has withdrawn his powers; he forgets, besides, that, as bishop of Salisbury, he is my subject; as for the remarks against him and the cardinal of York, it is a liberty the people of England are accustomed to take, and which I cannot put down." Campeggio, anxious to reach France, was satisfied with these reasons, and soon forgot all his sorrows at the sumptuous table of cardinal Duprat.

Wolsey was not so fortunate. He had seen Campeggio go away, and remained like a wrecked seaman thrown on a desert isle, who has seen depart the only friends capable of giving him any help. His necromancy had forewarned him that this would be a fatal year. The angel of the maid of Kent had said: "Go to the cardinal and announce his fall, because he has not done what you have commanded him to do." Other voices besides hers made themselves heard: the hatred of the nation, the contempt of Europe, and, above all, Henry's anger, told him that his hour was come. It was true the pope said that he would do all in his power to save him; but Clement's good offices would only accelerate his ruin. Du Bellay, whom the people believed to be the cardinal's accomplice, bore witness to the change that had taken place in men's minds. While passing on foot through the streets of the capital, followed by two valets, "his ears were so filled with coarse jests as he went along," he said, "that he knew not which way to turn."—"The cardinal is utterly undone," he wrote, "and I see not how he can escape." The idea occurred to Wolsey, from time to time, to pronounce the divorce himself; but it was too late. He was even told that his life was in danger. Fortune, blind and bald, her foot on the wheel, fled rapidly from him, nor was it in his power to stop her. And this was not all: after him (he thought) there was no one who could uphold the church of the pontiffs in England. The ship of Rome was sailing on a stormy sea among rocks and shoals; Wolsey at the helm looked in vain for a port of refuge; the vessel leaked on every side; it was rapidly sinking, and the cardinal uttered a cry of distress. Alas! he had desired to save Rome, but Rome would not have it so.

CHAPTER TWELVE

To Introduce Thomas Cranmer

(1489–1529)

As Wolsey's star was disappearing in the midst of stormy clouds, another was rising in the sky, to point out the way to save Britain. Men, like stars, appear on the horizon at the command of God.

On his return from Woodstock to Greenwich, Henry stopped full of anxiety at Waltham in Essex. His attendants were lodged in the houses of the neighbourhood. Fox, the almoner, and Secretary Gardiner, were quartered on a gentleman named Cressy, at Waltham Abbey. When supper was announced, Gardiner and Fox were surprised to see an old friend enter the room. It was Thomas Cranmer, a Cambridge doctor of divinity. "What! is it you?" they said, "and how came you here?"—"Our host's wife is my relation," replied Cranmer, "and as the epidemic is raging at Cambridge, I brought home my friend's sons, who are under my care." As this new personage is destined to play an important part in the history of the Reformation, it may be worth our while to interrupt our narrative, and give a particular account of him.

Cranmer was descended from an ancient family, which came into England, as is generally believed, with the Conqueror. He was born at Aslacton in Nottinghamshire on the 2nd July 1489, six years after Luther. His early education had been very much neglected; his tutor, an ignorant and severe priest, had taught him little else than patiently to endure severe chastisement— a knowledge destined to be very useful to him in after-life. His father was an honest country gentleman, who cared for little besides hunting, racing, and military sports. At this school, the son learnt to ride, to handle the bow and the sword, to fish, and to hawk; and he never entirely neglected these exercises, which he thought essential to his health. Thomas Cranmer was fond of walking, of the charms of nature, and of solitary meditations; and a hill, near his father's mansion, used often to be shown where he was wont to sit, gazing on the fertile country at his feet, fixing his eyes on the distant spires, listening with melancholy pleasure to the chime of the bells, and indulging in sweet contemplations. About 1504, he was sent to Cambridge, where "barbarism still prevailed," says an historian. His plain, noble, and modest air conciliated the affections of many, and, in 1510 or 1511, he was elected fellow of Jesus College. Possessing a tender heart, he became attached, at the age of twenty-three, to a young person of good birth (says Foxe) or of inferior rank, as other writers assert. Cranmer was unwilling to imitate the disorderly lives of his fellow-students, and, although marriage would necessarily close the career of honours, he married the young lady, known as "Black Joan," resigned his fellowship (in conformity with the regulations) and took a modest lodging at the Dolphin Inn. He then began to study earnestly the most remarkable writings of the times, polishing, it has been said, his old asperity on the productions of Erasmus, of Lefèvre of Etaples, and other great authors; every day his crude understanding received new brilliancy. He then began to lecture in Buckingham (afterwards Magdalene) College, and thus provided for his wants.

His lessons excited the admiration of enlightened men, and the anger of obscure ones, who disdainfully called him (because of the inn at which he lodged) *the hostler*. "This name became him well," said Fuller, "for in his lessons he roughly rubbed the backs of the friars, and famously curried the hides of the lazy priests." His wife dying a year after his marriage, Cranmer was re-elected fellow of his old college, and the first writing of Luther's having appeared, he said: "I must know on which side the truth lies. There is only one infallible source, the Scriptures; in them I will seek for God's truth." And for three years he constantly studied the holy books, without commentary, without human theology, and hence he gained the name of the *Scripturist*. At last his eyes were opened; he saw the mysterious bond which unites all biblical revelations, and understood the completeness of God's design. Then without forsaking the Scriptures, he studied all kinds of authors. He was a slow reader, but a close observer; he never opened a book without having a pen in his hand. He did not take up with any particular party or age; but possessing a free and philosophic mind, he weighed all opinions in the balance of his judgment, taking the Bible for his standard.

Honours soon came upon him; he was made successively doctor of divinity, professor, university preacher, and examiner. He used to say to the candidates for the ministry: "Christ sendeth his hearers to the Scriptures, and not to the church."— "But," replied the monks, "they are so difficult."—"Explain the obscure passages by those which are clear," rejoined the professor, "Scripture by Scripture. Seek, pray, *and he who has the key of David* will open them to you." The monks, affrighted at this task, withdrew bursting with anger; and ere long Cranmer's name was a name of dread in every monastery. Some, however, submitted to the labour, and one of them, Doctor Barrett, blessed God that the examiner had turned him back; "for," said he, "I found the knowledge of God in the holy book he compelled me to study." Cranmer toiled at the same work as Latimer, Stafford, and Bilney.

Fox and Gardiner having renewed acquaintance with their old friend at Waltham Abbey, they sat down to table, and both the almoner and the secretary asked the doctor what he thought of the divorce. It was the usual topic of conversation, and not long before, Cranmer had been named member of a commission appointed to give their opinion on this affair. "You are not in the right path," said Cranmer to his friends; "you should not cling to the decisions of the church. There is a surer and a shorter way which alone can give peace to the king's conscience." —"What is that?" they both asked.—"The true question is this," replied Cranmer: "*What says the Word of God?* If God has declared a marriage of this nature *bad*, the pope cannot make it *good*. Discontinue these interminable Roman negotiations. When God has spoken man must obey."—"But how shall we know what God has said?"—"Consult the universities; they will discern it more surely than Rome."

This was a new view. The idea of consulting the universities had been acted upon before; but then their own opinions only had been demanded; now, the question was simply to know *what God says in His Word*. "The Word of God is above the church," was the principle laid down by Cranmer, and in that principle consisted the whole of the Reformation. The conversation at the supper-table of Waltham was destined to be one of those secret springs which an invisible Hand sets in motion for the accomplishment of His great designs. The Cambridge doctor, suddenly transported from his study to the foot of the throne, was on the point of becoming one of the principal instruments of Divine wisdom.

The day after this conversation, Fox and Gardiner arrived at Greenwich, and the king summoned them into his presence the same evening. "Well, gentlemen," he said to them, "our holidays are over; what shall we do now? If we still have recourse to Rome, God knows when we shall see the end of this matter."—"It will not be necessary to take so long a journey," said Fox; "we know a shorter and surer way."— "What is it?" asked the king eagerly.—"Doctor Cranmer, whom we met yesterday at Waltham, thinks that the Bible should be the sole judge in your cause." Gardiner, vexed at his colleague's frankness, desired to claim all the honour of this luminous idea for himself; but Henry did not listen to him. "Where is Doctor Cranmer?" said he, much affected. "Send, and fetch him immediately. Mother of God! (this was his customary oath) this man has the right sow by the ear. If this had only been suggested to me two years ago, what expense and trouble I should have been spared."

Cranmer had gone into Nottinghamshire; a messenger followed and brought him back. "Why have you entangled me in this affair?" he said to Fox and Gardiner. "Pray make my excuses to the king." Gardiner, who wished for nothing better, promised to do all he could; but it was of no use. "I will have no excuses," said Henry. The wily courtier was obliged to make up his mind to introduce the ingenuous and upright man, to whom that station, which he himself had so coveted, was one day to belong. Cranmer and Gardiner went down to Greenwich, both alike dissatisfied.

Cranmer was then forty years of age, with pleasing features, and mild and winning eyes, in which the candour of his soul seemed to be reflected. Sensible to the pains as well as to the pleasures of the heart, he was destined to be more exposed than other men to anxieties and falls; a peaceful life in some remote parsonage would have been more to his taste than the court of Henry VIII. Blessed with a generous mind, unhappily he did

not possess the firmness necessary in a public man; a little
stone sufficed to make him stumble. His excellent understanding
showed him the better way; but his great timidity made him
fear the more dangerous. He was rather too fond of relying
upon the power of men, and made them unhappy concessions
with too great facility. If the king had questioned him, he
would never have dared advise so bold a course as that he had
pointed out; the advice had slipped from him at table during
the intimacy of familiar conversation. Yet he was sincere, and
after doing everything to escape from the consequences of his
frankness, he was ready to maintain the opinion he had given.

Henry, perceiving Cranmer's timidity, graciously approached
him. "What is your name?" said the king, endeavouring to
put him at his ease. "Did you not meet my secretary and my
almoner at Waltham?" And then he added: "Did you not
speak to them of my great affair?"—repeating the words
ascribed to Cranmer. The latter could not retreat: "Sir, it is
true, I did say so."—"I see," replied the king with animation,
"that you have found the breach through which we must storm
the fortress. Now, sir doctor, I beg you, and as you are my
subject I command you, to lay aside every other occupation,
and to bring my cause to a conclusion in conformity with the
ideas you have put forth. All that I desire to know is, whether
my marriage is contrary to the laws of God or not. Employ all
your skill in investigating the subject, and thus bring comfort
to my conscience as well as to the queen's."

Cranmer was confounded; he recoiled from the idea of
deciding an affair on which depended, it might be, the destinies
of the nation, and sighed after the lonely fields of Aslacton.
But grasped by the vigorous hand of Henry, he was compelled
to advance. "Sir," said he, "pray intrust this matter to doctors
more learned than I am."—"I am very willing," answered
the king, "but I desire that you will also give me your opinion
in writing." And then summoning the earl of Wiltshire to his
presence, he said to him: "My lord, you will receive Doctor
Cranmer into your house at Durham Place, and let him have
all necessary quiet to compose a report for which I have asked
him." After this precise command, which admitted of no refusal,
Henry withdrew.

In this manner was Cranmer introduced by the king to Anne

Boleyn's father, and not, as some Romanist authors have asserted, by Sir Thomas Boleyn to the king.[1] Wiltshire conducted Cranmer to Durham House (now the Adelphi in the Strand) and the pious doctor on whom Henry had imposed these quarters, soon contracted a close friendship with Anne and her father, and took advantage of it to teach them the value of the Divine Word, as *the pearl of great price*. Henry, while profiting by the skill of a Wolsey and a Gardiner, paid little regard to the men; but he respected Cranmer, even when opposed to him in opinion, and until his death placed the learned doctor above all his courtiers and all his clerks. The pious man often succeeds better, even with the great ones of this world, than the ambitious and the intriguing.

[1] E.g., Lingard, vol. vi, chap. iii. Compare Foxe, vol. viii, p. 8.

CHAPTER THIRTEEN

The Dethronement of Cardinal Wolsey

(October, 1529)

WHILE Cranmer was rising notwithstanding his humility, Wolsey was falling in despite of his stratagems. The cardinal still governed the kingdom, gave instructions to ambassadors, negotiated with princes, and filled his sumptuous palaces with his haughtiness. The king could not make up his mind to turn him off; the force of habit, the need he had of him, the recollection of the services Henry had received from him, pleaded in his favour. Wolsey without the seals appeared almost as inconceivable as the king without his crown. Yet the fall of one of the most powerful favourites recorded in history was inevitably approaching, and we must now describe it.

On the 9th of October, after the Michaelmas vacation, Wolsey, desirous of showing a bold face, went and opened the high court of chancery with his accustomed pomp; but he noticed, with uneasiness, that none of the king's servants walked before him, as they had been accustomed to do. He presided on the bench with an inexpressible depression of spirits, and the various members of the court sat before him with an absent air; there was something gloomy and solemn in this sitting, as if all were taking part in a funeral: it was destined indeed to be the last act of the cardinal's power. Some days before (Foxe says on the 1st of October) the dukes of Norfolk and Suffolk, with other lords of the privy-council, had gone down to Windsor, and denounced to the king Wolsey's unconstitutional relations with the pope, his usurpations, "his robberies, and the discords sown by his means between Christian princes." Such motives would not have sufficed; but Henry had stronger. Wolsey had not kept any of his promises in the matter of the divorce; it would even appear that he had advised the pope to excommunicate the king, and thus raise his people against him. This enormity was not at that time known by the prince; it is even probable that it did not take place until later. But Henry knew enough, and he gave his attorney-general, Sir Christopher Hales, orders to prosecute Wolsey.

Whilst the heart-broken cardinal was displaying his authority for the last time in the court of chancery, the attorney-general was accusing him in the King's Bench for having obtained papal bulls conferring on him a jurisdiction which encroached on the royal power; and calling for the application of the penalties of *præmunire*. The two dukes received orders to demand the seals from Wolsey; and the latter, informed of what had taken place, did not quit his palace on the 10th, expecting every moment the arrival of the messengers of the king's anger; but no one appeared.

The next day the two dukes arrived: "It is the king's good pleasure," said they to the cardinal, who remained seated in his arm-chair, "that you give up the broad seal to us and retire to Esher" (a country-seat near Hampton Court). Wolsey, whose presence of mind never failed him, demanded to see the commission under which they were acting. "We have our orders from his majesty's mouth," said they.—"That may be sufficient for you," replied the cardinal, "but not for me. The great seal of England was delivered to me by the hands of my sovereign; I may not deliver it at the simple word of any lord, unless you can show me your commission." Suffolk broke out into a passion, but Wolsey remained calm, and the two dukes returned to Windsor. This was the cardinal's last triumph.

The rumour of his disgrace created an immense sensation at court, in the city, and among the foreign ambassadors. Du Bellay hastened to York Place (Whitehall) to contemplate this great ruin and console his unhappy friend. He found Wolsey, with dejected countenance and lustreless eyes, "shrunk to half his wonted size," wrote the ambassador to Montmorency, "the greatest example of fortune which was ever beheld." Wolsey desired "to set forth his case" to him; but his thoughts were confused, his language broken, "for heart and tongue both failed him entirely;" he burst into tears. The ambassador regarded him with compassion: "Alas!" thought he, "his enemies cannot but feel pity for him." At last the unhappy cardinal recovered his speech, but only to give way to despair.

"I desire no more authority," he exclaimed, "nor the pope's legation, nor the broad seal of England. . . . I am ready to give up everything, even to my shirt. . . . I can live in a hermitage, provided the king does not hold me in disgrace." The ambassador "did all he could to comfort him," when Wolsey, catching at the plank thrown out to him, exclaimed: "Would that the king of France and Madame might pray the king to moderate his anger against me. But above all," he added in alarm, "take care the king never knows that I have solicited this of you." Du Bellay wrote indeed to France that the king and madame alone could "withdraw their affectionate servant from the gates of hell," and Wolsey being informed of these despatches, his hopes recovered a little. But this bright gleam did not last long.

On Sunday the 17th of October, Norfolk and Suffolk reappeared at Whitehall, accompanied by Fitzwilliam, Taylor, and Gardiner, Wolsey's former dependant. It was six in the evening; they found the cardinal in an upper chamber, near the great gallery, and presented the king's orders to him. Having read them he said: "I am happy to obey his majesty's commands;" then having ordered the great seal to be brought him, he took it out of the white leather case in which he kept it, and handed it to the dukes, who placed it in a box, covered with crimson velvet, and ornamented with the arms of England, ordered Gardiner to seal it up with red wax, and gave it to Taylor to convey to the king.

Wolsey was thunderstruck; he was to drink the bitter cup even to the dregs: he was ordered to leave his palace forthwith, taking with him neither clothes, linen, nor plate; the dukes had feared that he would convey away his treasures. Wolsey comprehended the greatness of his misery; he found strength however to say: "Since it is the king's good pleasure to take my house and all it contains, I am content to retire to Esher." The dukes left him.

Wolsey remained alone. This astonishing man, who had risen from a butcher's shop to the summit of earthly greatness— who, for a word that displeased him, sent his master's most faithful servants (Pace for instance) to the Tower—and who had governed England as if he had been its monarch, and even more, for he had governed without a parliament, was driven out, and thrown, as it were, upon a dunghill. A sudden hope flashed like lightning through his mind; perhaps the magnificence of the spoils would appease Henry. Was not Esau pacified by Jacob's present? Wolsey summoned his officers: "Set tables in the great gallery," he said to them, "and place on them all I have intrusted to your care, in order to render me an account." These orders were executed immediately. The tables were covered with an immense quantity of rich stuffs, silks and velvets of all colours, costly furs, rich copes and other ecclesiastical vestures; the walls were hung with cloth of gold and silver, and webs of a valuable stuff named baudykin, from the looms of Damascus, and with tapestry, representing scriptural subjects or stories from the old romances of chivalry. The gilt chamber and the council chamber, adjoining the gallery, were both filled with plate, in which the gold and silver were set with pearls and precious stones: these articles of luxury were so abundant that basketfuls of costly plate which had fallen out of fashion were stowed away under the tables. On every table was an exact list of the treasures with which it was loaded, for the most perfect order and regularity prevailed in the cardinal's household. Wolsey cast a glance of hope upon this wealth, and ordered his officers to deliver the whole to his majesty.

He then prepared to leave his magnificent palace. That moment of itself so sad, was made sadder still by an act of affectionate indiscretion. "Ah, my lord," said his treasurer, Sir William Gascoigne, moved even to tears, "your grace will be sent to the Tower." This was too much for Wolsey: to go and join his victims! . . . He grew angry, and exclaimed: "Is this the best comfort you can give your master in adversity? I would have you and all such blasphemous reporters know that it is untrue."

It was necessary to depart; he put round his neck a chain of gold, from which hung a pretended relic of the true cross; this was all he took. "Would to God," he exclaimed, as he placed it on, "that I had never had any other." This he said alluding to the legate's cross which used to be carried before him with so much pomp. He descended the back stairs, followed by his servants, some silent and dejected, others weeping bitterly, and proceeded to the river's brink, where a barge awaited him. But, alas! it was not alone. The Thames was covered with innumerable boats full of men and women. The inhabitants of London, expecting to see the cardinal led to the Tower, desired to be present at his humiliation, and prepared to accompany him. Cries of joy hailing his fall were heard from every side; nor were the cruellest sarcasms wanting. "The butcher's dog will bite no more," said some; "look, how he hangs his head." In truth, the unhappy man, distressed by a sight so new to him, lowered those eyes which were once so proud, but now were filled with bitter tears. This man, who had made all England tremble, was then like a withered leaf carried along the stream. All his servants were moved; even his fool, William Patch, sobbed like the rest. "O, wavering and newfangled multitude!" exclaimed Cavendish, his gentleman usher. The hopes of the citizens were disappointed; the barge, instead of descending the river, proceeded upwards in the direction of Hampton Court; gradually the shouts died away, and the flotilla dispersed.

The silence of the river permitted Wolsey to indulge in less bitter thoughts; but it seemed as if invisible furies were pursuing him, now that the people had left him. He left his barge at Putney and, mounting his mule, though with difficulty, proceeded slowly with downcast looks. Shortly after, upon lifting his eyes, he saw a horseman riding rapidly down the hill towards them. "Whom do you think it can be?" he asked of his attendants. "My lord," replied one of them, "I think it is Sir Henry Norris." A flash of joy passed through Wolsey's heart. Was it not Norris, who, of all the king's officers, had shown him the most respect during his visit to Grafton? Norris came up with them, saluted him respectfully, and said: "The king bids me declare that he still entertains the same kindly feelings towards you, and sends you this ring as a token of his confidence." Wolsey received it with a trembling hand: it was that which the king was in the habit of sending on important occasions. The cardinal immediately alighted from his mule and, kneeling down in the road, raised his hands to heaven with an indescribable expression of happiness. The fallen man would have pulled off his velvet under-cap, but unable to undo the strings, he broke them, and threw it on the ground. He remained on his knees bareheaded praying fervently amidst profound silence. God's forgiveness had never caused Wolsey so much pleasure as Henry's.

Having finished his prayer, the cardinal put on his cap, and remounted his mule. "Gentle Norris," said he to the king's messenger, "if I were lord of a kingdom, the half of it would scarcely be enough to reward you for your happy tidings; but I have nothing left except the clothes on my back." Then taking off his gold chain: "Take this," he said, "it contains a piece of the true cross. In my happier days I would not have parted with it for a thousand pounds." The cardinal and Norris separated: but Wolsey soon stopped, and the whole troop halted on the heath. The thought troubled him greatly that he had nothing to send to the king; he called Norris back, and looking round saw mounted on a sorry horse poor William Patch, who had lost all his gaiety since his master's misfortune. "Present this poor jester to the king from me," said Wolsey to Norris; "his buffooneries are a pleasure fit for a prince; he is worth a thousand pounds."

At last they reached Esher. What a residence compared with Whitehall! . . . It was little more than four bare walls. The most urgent necessaries were procured from the neighbouring houses, but Wolsey could not adapt himself to this cruel contrast. Besides, he knew Henry VIII; he knew that he might send Norris one day with a gold ring, and the executioner the next with a rope. Gloomy and dejected, he remained seated in his lonely apartments. On a sudden he would rise from his seat, walk hurriedly up and down, speak aloud to himself and then, falling back in his chair, he would weep like a child. This man who formerly had shaken kingdoms, had been brought into desolation as in a moment, and was now atoning for his perfidies in humiliation and terror—a striking example of God's judgment.

CHAPTER FOURTEEN

New Leaders and a New Policy

(October & November, 1529)

DURING all this time everybody was in commotion at court. Norfolk and Suffolk, at the head of the council, had informed the Star Chamber of the cardinal's disgrace. Henry knew not how to supply his place. Some suggested the archbishop of Canterbury; the king would not hear of him. "Wolsey," says a French writer, "had disgusted the king and all England with those subjects of two masters who, almost always, sold one to the other. They preferred a lay minister."—"I verily believe the priests will never more obtain it," wrote Du Bellay. The name of Sir Thomas More was pronounced. He was a layman, and that quality, which a few years before would, perhaps, have excluded him, was now a recommendation. A breath of Protestantism wafted to the summit of honours one of its greatest enemies. Henry thought that More, placed between the pope and his sovereign, would decide in favour of the interests of the throne, and of the independence of England. His choice was made.

More knew that the cardinal had been thrown aside because he was not a sufficiently docile instrument in the matter of the divorce. The work required of him was contrary to his convictions; but the honour conferred on him was almost unprecedented—seldom indeed had the seals been entrusted to a mere knight.[1] He followed the path of ambition and not of duty; he showed, however, in afterdays that his ambition was of no common sort. It is even probable that, foreseeing the dangers which threatened to destroy the papal power in England, More wished to make an effort to save it. Norfolk installed the new chancellor in the Star Chamber.

[1] It has been often asserted that Sir Thomas More was the first layman to whom the office of chancellor was entrusted. This is incorrect, for several laymen were appointed to the office between 1371 and 1386.

"His majesty," said the duke, "has not cast his eyes upon the nobility of the blood, but on the worth of the person. He desires to show by this choice that there are among the laity and gentlemen of England, men worthy to fill the highest offices in the kingdom, to which, until this hour, bishops and noblemen alone think they have a right."[1] The Reformation which restored religion to the general body of the church, took away at the same time political power from the clergy. The priests had deprived the people of Christian activity, and the governments of power; the gospel restored to both what the priests had usurped. This result could not but be favourable to the interests of religion; the less cause kings and their subjects have to fear the intrusion of clerical power into the affairs of the world, the more will they yield themselves to the vivifying influence of faith.

More lost no time; never had lord-chancellor displayed such activity. He rapidly cleared off the cases which were in arrear, and having been installed on the 26th of October he called on Wolsey's cause on the 28th or 29th. "The crown of England," said the attorney-general, "has never acknowledged any superior but God.[2] Now, the said Thomas Wolsey, legate *a latere*, has obtained from the pope certain bulls, by virtue of which he has exercised since the 28th of August 1523 an authority derogatory to his majesty's power, and to the rights of his courts of justice. The crown of England cannot be put under the pope; and we therefore accuse the said legate of having incurred the penalties of *præmunire*."

There can be no doubt that Henry had other reasons for Wolsey's disgrace than those pointed out by the attorney-general; but England had convictions of a higher nature than her sovereign's. Wolsey was regarded as the pope's accomplice, and this was the cause of the great severity of the public officer and of the people. The cardinal is generally excused by alleging that both king and parliament had ratified the unconstitutional authority with which Rome had invested him; but had not the powers conferred on him by the pope produced unjustifiable

---

[1] *More's Life*, p. 172.

[2] The crown of England, free at all times, has been in no earthly subjection, but immediately subject to God in all things. Herbert of Cherbury, p. 251.

results in a constitutional monarchy? Wolsey, as papal legate, had governed England without a parliament; and, as if the nation had gone back to the reign of John, he had substituted *de facto*, if not in theory, the monstrous system of the famous bull *Unam Sanctam*[1] for the institution of *Magna Charta*. The king, and even the lords and commons, had connived in vain at these illegalities; the rights of the constitution of England remained not the less inviolable, and the best of the people had protested against their infringement. And hence it was that Wolsey, conscious of his crime, "put himself wholly to the mercy and grace of the king," and his counsel declared his ignorance of the statutes he was said to have infringed. We cannot here allege, as some have done, the prostration of Wolsey's moral powers; he could, even after his fall, reply with energy to Henry VIII. When, for instance, the king sent to demand for the crown his palace of Whitehall, which belonged to the see of York, the cardinal answered: "Show his majesty from me that I must desire him to call to his most gracious remembrance that there is both a heaven and a hell;" and when other charges besides those of complicity with the papal aggression were brought against him, he defended himself courageously, as will be afterwards seen. If therefore the cardinal did not attempt to justify himself for infringing the rights of the crown, it was because his conscience bade him be silent. He had committed one of the gravest faults of which a statesman can be guilty. Those who have sought to excuse him have not sufficiently borne in mind that, since the Great Charter, opposition to Romish aggression has always characterized the constitution and government of England. Wolsey perfectly recollected this; and this explanation is more honourable to him than that which ascribes his silence to weakness or to cunning.

The cardinal was pronounced guilty, and the court passed judgment that by the statute of *præmunire* his property was forfeited, and that he might be taken before the king in council. England, by sacrificing a churchman who had placed himself

---

[1] This famous Bull, issued by Pope Boniface VIII in 1302 declared that the "temporal sword" and the "spiritual sword" were alike committed to the church, implying that the pope had supreme power in state as well as in church.

above kings, gave a memorable example of her inflexible opposition to the encroachments of the papacy. Wolsey was confounded, and his troubled imagination conjured up nothing but perils on every side.

While More was lending himself to the condemnation of his predecessor, whose friend he had been, another layman of still humbler origin was preparing to defend the cardinal, and by that very act to become the appointed instrument to throw down the monasteries in England, and to shatter the secular bonds which united this country to the Roman pontiff.

On the 1st of November, two days after Wolsey's condemnation, Thomas Cromwell, one of his officers, with a prayer-book in his hand, was leaning against the window in the great hall, apparently absorbed in his devotions. "Good-morrow," said Cavendish as he passed him, on his way to the cardinal for his usual morning duties. The person thus addressed raised his head, and the gentleman-usher, seeing that his eyes were filled with tears, asked him: "Master Cromwell, is my lord in any danger?"—"I think not," replied Cromwell, "but it is hard to lose in a moment the labour of a life." In his master's fall Cromwell foreboded his own. Cavendish endeavoured to console him. "God willing, this is my resolution," replied Wolsey's ambitious solicitor; "I intend this afternoon, as soon as my lord has dined, to ride to London, and so go to court, where I will either make or mar before I come back again." At this moment Cavendish was summoned, and he entered the cardinal's chamber.

Cromwell, devoured by ambition, had clung to Wolsey's robe in order to attain power. He had served under the cardinal for about nine years, and had conducted most of his legal business. But Wolsey had fallen, and the solicitor, dragged along with him, strove to reach by other means the object of his desires. Cromwell was one of those earnest and vigorous men whom God prepares for critical times. Blessed with a solid judgment and intrepid firmness, he possessed a quality rare in every age, and particularly under Henry VIII—fidelity in misfortune. The ability by which he was distinguished was not at all times without reproach: success seems to have been his first thought.

After dinner Cromwell followed Wolsey into his private

room: "My lord, permit me to go to London, I will endeavour to save you." A gleam passed over the cardinal's saddened features.—"Leave the room," he said to his attendants. He then had a long private conversation with Cromwell, at the end of which the latter mounted his horse and set out for the capital. He did not hide from himself that it would be difficult to procure access to the king, for certain ecclesiastics, jealous of Wolsey, had spoken against his solicitor at the time of the secularization of the monasteries, and Henry could not endure him. But Cromwell knew that fortune favours the bold, and, carried away by his ambitious dreams, he galloped on, saying to himself: "One foot in the stirrup, and my fortune is made!"

It appears to have been through the good offices of Sir Christopher Hales, master of the rolls, that the name of Cromwell was commended to the king. Probably Henry was, at the outset, strongly prejudiced against him. Was he not Wolsey's chief assistant! But other considerations prevailed, and ere long an interview given by the king to Cromwell convinced him that the secretary-lawyer was a man after his own heart.

"Sir," said Cromwell to his majesty, "the pope refuses your divorce. . . . But why do you ask his consent? Every Englishman is master in his own house, and why should not you be so in England? Ought a foreign prelate to share your power with you? It is true, the bishops make oath to your majesty, but they make another to the pope immediately after, which absolves them from the former. Sir, you are but half a king, and we are but half your subjects. This kingdom is a two-headed monster. Will you bear with such an anomaly any longer? What! are you not living in an age when Frederick the Wise and other German princes have thrown off the yoke of Rome? Do likewise; become once more a king; govern your kingdom in concert with your lords and commons. Henceforward let Englishmen alone have anything to say in England; let not your subjects' money be cast any more into the yawning gulf of the Tiber; instead of imposing new taxes on the nation, convert to the general good those treasures which have hitherto only served to fatten proud priests and lazy friars. Now is the moment for action. Rely upon your parliament; proclaim yourself the head of the church in England. Then shall you see an increase of glory to your name, and of prosperity to your people."

Never before had such language been addressed to a king of England. It was not only on account of the divorce that it was necessary to break with Rome; it was, in Cromwell's view, on account of the independence, glory, and prosperity of the monarchy. These considerations appeared more important to Henry than those which had hitherto been laid before him; none of the kings of England had been so well placed as he was to understand them. When a Tudor had succeeded to the Saxon, Norman, and Plantagenet kings, a man of the free race of the Celts had taken on the throne of England the place of princes submissive to the Roman pontiffs. The ancient British church, independent of the papacy, was about to rise again with this new dynasty, and the Celtic race, after eleven centuries of humiliation, to recover its ancient heritage. Undoubtedly, Henry had no recollections of this kind; but he worked in conformity with the peculiar character of his race, without being aware of the instinct which compelled him to act. He felt that a sovereign who submits to the pope becomes, like King John, his vassal; and now, after having been the second in his realm, he desired to be the first.

The king reflected on what Cromwell had said. Astonished and surprised, he sought to understand the new position which his bold adviser had made for him. "Your proposal pleases me much," he said; "but can you prove what you assert?"— "Certainly," replied this able politician; "I have with me a copy of the oath the bishops make to the Roman pontiff." With these words he drew a paper from his pocket, and placed the oath before the king's eyes. Henry, jealous of his authority even to despotism, was filled with indignation, and felt the necessity of bringing down that foreign authority which dared dispute the power with him, even in his own kingdom. He drew off his ring and gave it to Cromwell, declaring that he took him into his service, and soon after made him a member of his privy-council. England, we may say, was now virtually emancipated from the papacy.

Cromwell had laid the first foundations of his greatness. He had observed the path his master had followed, and which had led to his ruin—complicity with the pope; and he hoped to succeed by following the contrary course, namely, by opposing the papacy. He had the king's support, but he wanted more. Possessing a clear and easy style of eloquence, he saw what influence a seat in the great council of the nation would give him. It was somewhat late, for the session began on the next day (3rd November) but to Cromwell nothing was impossible. The son of his friend, Sir Thomas Rush, had been returned to parliament; but the young member vacated his seat, and Cromwell was elected in his place.

Parliament had not met for seven years, the kingdom having been governed by a prince of the Roman church. The reformation of the church, whose regenerating influence began to be felt already, was about to restore to the nation those ancient liberties of which a cardinal had robbed it; and Henry, being on the point of taking very important resolutions, felt the necessity of drawing nearer to his people. Everything betokened that a good feeling would prevail between the parliament and the crown, and that "the priests would have a terrible fright."

While Henry was preparing to attack the Roman church in the papal supremacy, the commons were getting ready to war against the numerous abuses with which it had covered England. "Some even thought," says Tyndale, "that this assembly would reform the church, and that the golden age would come again." But it was not from acts of parliament that the Reformation was destined to proceed, but solely from the Word of God. And yet the commons, without touching upon doctrine, were going to do their duty manfully in things within their province, and the parliament of 1529 may be regarded as the first Protestant parliament of England. "The bishops require excessive fines for the probates of wills," said Tyndale's old friend, Sir Henry Guildford. "As testamentary executor to Sir William Compton I had to pay a thousand marks sterling." —"The spiritual men," said another member, "would rather see the poor orphans die of hunger than give them even the lean cow, the only thing their father left them."—"Priests," said another, "have farms, tanneries, and warehouses, all over the country. In short, the clerks take everything from their flocks, and not only give them nothing, but even deny them the Word of God."

The clergy were in utter consternation. The power of the

nation seemed to awaken in this parliament for the sole purpose of attacking the power of the priest. It was important to ward off these blows. The convocation of the province of Canterbury, assembling at Westminster on the 5th of November, thought it their duty, in self-defence, to reform the most crying abuses. It was therefore decreed, on the 12th of November, that the priests should no longer keep shops or taverns, play at dice or other forbidden games, pass the night in suspected places, be present at disreputable shows, go about with sporting dogs, or with hawks, falcons, or other birds of prey, on their fist; or, finally, hold suspicious intercourse with women. Penalties were denounced against these various disorders; they were doubled in case of adultery; and still further increased in the case of more abominable impurities. Such were the laws rendered necessary by the manners of the clergy.

These measures did not satisfy the commons. Three bills were introduced having reference to the fees on the probate of wills, mortuaries, pluralities, non-residence, and the exercise of secular professions. "The destruction of the church is aimed at," exclaimed Bishop Fisher, when these bills were carried to the lords, "and if the church falls, the glory of the kingdom will perish. Lutheranism is making great progress amongst us, and the savage cry that has already echoed in Bohemia, *Down with the church*, is now uttered by the commons. . . . How does that come about? Solely from want of faith.—My lords, save your country! save the church!" Sir Thomas Audley, the speaker of the commons, with a deputation of thirty members, immediately went to Whitehall. "Sir," they said to the king, "we are accused of being without faith, and of being almost as bad as the *Turks*. We demand an apology for such offensive language." Fisher pretended that he only meant to speak of the *Bohemians;* and the commons, by no means satisfied, zealously went on with their reforms.

These the king was resolved to concede; but he determined to take advantage of them to present a bill making over to him all the money borrowed of his subjects. John Petit, one of the members for the city, boldly opposed this demand. "I do not know other persons' affairs," he said, "and I cannot give what does not belong to me. But as regards myself personally, I give without reserve all that I have lent the king." The royal bill passed, and the satisfied Henry gave his consent to the bills of the commons. Every dispensation coming from Rome, which might be contrary to the statutes, was strictly forbidden. The bishops exclaimed that the commons were becoming schismatical; disturbances were excited by certain priests; but the clerical agitators were punished, and the people, when they heard of it, were delighted beyond measure.

CHAPTER FIFTEEN

"They that Will Live Godly in Christ Jesus . . ."

(1529–31)

THE moment when Henry aimed his first blows at Rome was also that in which he began to shed the blood of the disciples of the gospel. Although ready to throw off the authority of the pope, he would not recognize the authority of Christ: obedience to the Scriptures is, however, the very soul of the Reformation.

The king's contest with Rome had filled the friends of Scripture with hope. The artisans and tradesmen, particularly those who lived near the sea, were almost wholly won over to the gospel. "The king is one of us," they used to boast; "he wishes his subjects to read the New Testament. Our faith, which is the true one, will circulate through the kingdom, and by Michaelmas next those who believe as we do will be more numerous than those of a contrary opinion. We are ready, if needs be, to die in the struggle." This was indeed to be the fate of many.

Language such as this aroused the clergy: "The last hour has come," said John Stokesley, who had been raised to the see of London after Tunstall's translation to Durham; "if we would not have Luther's heresy pervade the whole of England, we must hasten to throw it in the sea." Henry was fully disposed to do so; but, as he was not on very good terms with the clergy, a man was wanted to serve as mediator between him and the bishops. He was soon found.

Sir Thomas More's noble understanding was then passing from ascetic practices to fanaticism, and the humanist turning into an inquisitor. In his opinion, the burning of heretics was just and necessary.[1] He has even been reproached with binding evangelical Christians to a tree in his garden, which he called "the tree of truth," and with having flogged them with his own

[1] More's Works; *A Dialogue concerning Heresies*, p. 274.

456

hand.[1] More has declared that he never gave "stripe nor stroke, nor so much as a fillip on the forehead," to any of his religious adversaries;[2] and we willingly credit his denial. All must be pleased to think that if the author of the *Utopia* was a severe judge, the hand which held one of the most famous pens of the sixteenth century never discharged the duties of an executioner.

The bishops led the attack. "We must clear the Lord's field of the thorns which choke it," said the archbishop of Canterbury to Convocation on the 29th of November 1529; immediately after which the bishop of Bath read to his colleagues the list of books that he desired to have condemned. There were a number of works by Tyndale, Luther, Melanchthon, Zwingli, Œcolampadius, Pomeranus, Brentius, Bucer, Jonas, Francis Lambert, Fryth, and Fish. The Bible in particular was set down. "It is impossible to translate the Scripture into English," said one of the prelates.—"It is not lawful for the laity to read it in their mother tongue," said another.—"If you tolerate the Bible," added a third, "you will make us all heretics."—"By circulating the Scriptures," exclaimed several, "you will raise up the nation against the king." Sir Thomas More laid the bishops' petition before the king, and, some time after, Henry gave orders by proclamation, that "no one should preach, or write any book, or keep any school without his bishop's licence—that no one should keep any heretical book in his house—that the bishops should detain the offenders in prison at their discretion, and then proceed to the punishment of the guilty—and, finally, that the chancellor, the justices of the peace, and other magistrates, should aid and assist the bishops." Such was the cruel proclamation of Henry VIII, "the *father* of the English Reformation."

The clergy were not yet satisfied. The blind and octogenarian bishop of Norwich, being more ardent than the youngest of his priests, recommenced his complaints. "My diocese is *accumbered* with such as read the Bible," said he to the archbishop of Canterbury, "and there is not a clerk from Cambridge but *savoureth of the frying-pan*. If this continues any time, they will undo us all. We must have greater authority to punish them than we have."

[1] Strype's Mem., vol. i, p. 315; Foxe, iv, p. 698.
[2] *Apology*, ch. xxxvi, pp. 901, 902.

Consequently, on the 24th of May 1530, More, Warham, Tunstall, and Gardiner having been admitted into St Edward's chamber at Westminster to make a report to the king concerning heresy, they proposed forbidding, in the most positive manner, the New Testament and certain other books in which the following doctrines were taught: "That Christ has shed his blood for our iniquities, as a sacrifice to the Father.—Faith only doth justify us.—Faith without good works is no little or weak faith, it is no faith.—Labouring in good works to come to heaven, thou dost shame Christ's blood."

Whilst nearly everyone in the audience-chamber supported the prayer of the petition, there were three or four doctors who kept silence. At last one of them, it was Latimer, opposed the proposition. Bilney's friend was more decided than ever to listen to no other voice than God's. "Christ's sheep hear no man's voice but Christ's," he answered Dr Redman, who had called upon him to submit to the church; "trouble me no more from the talking with the Lord my God."[1] The church, in Latimer's opinion, presumed to set up its own voice in the place of Christ's, and the Reformation did the contrary; this was his abridgment of the controversy. Being called upon to preach during Christmas-tide, he had censured his hearers because they celebrated that festival by playing at cards, like mere worldlings, and then proceeded to lay before their eyes Christ's *cards*, that is to say, his laws.[2] Being placed on the Cambridge commission to examine into the question of the king's marriage, he had won the esteem of Henry's deputy, Doctor Butts, the court physician, who had presented him to his master, by whose orders he preached at Windsor.

Henry felt disposed at first to yield something to Latimer. "Many of my subjects," said he to the prelates assembled in St Edward's hall, "think that it is my duty to cause the Scriptures to be translated and given to the people." The discussion immediately began between the two parties; and Latimer concluded by asking "that the Bible should be permitted to circulate freely in English."—"But the most part overcame the better," he tells us.[3] Henry declared that the teaching of the priests was sufficient for the people, and was content to

---

[1] Latimer's *Remains*, p. 297.   [2] Latimer's *Sermons*, p. 8.
[3] Latimer's *Remains*, p. 305.

add, "that he would give the Bible to his subjects when they renounced the arrogant pretension of interpreting it according to their own fancies."—"Shun these books," cried the priests from the pulpit, "detest them, keep them not in your hands, deliver them up to your superiors. Or, if you do not, your prince, who has received from God the sword of justice, will use it to punish you." Rome had every reason to be satisfied with Henry VIII. Tunstall, who still kept under lock and key the Testaments purchased at Antwerp through Packington's assistance, had them carried to St Paul's churchyard, where they were publicly burnt. The spectators retired shaking the head, and saying: "The teaching of the priests and of the Scriptures must be in contradiction to each other, since the priests destroy them." Latimer did more: "You have promised us the Word of God," he wrote courageously to the king, "perform your promise now rather than to-morrow! God will have the faith defended, not by man or man's power, but by His Word only, by the which He hath evermore defended it, and that by a way far above man's power or reason, as all the stories of the Bible make mention. . . . The day is at hand when you shall give an account of your office, and of the blood that hath been shed with your sword."[1] Latimer well knew that by such language he hazarded his life; but that he was ready to sacrifice, as he tells us himself.

Persecution soon came. Just as the sun appeared to be rising on the Reformation, the storm burst forth. "There was not a stone the bishops left unremoved," says the chronicler, "any corner unsearched, for the diligent execution of the king's proclamation; whereupon ensued a grievous persecution and slaughter of the faithful."

Thomas Hitton, a poor and pious minister of Kent, used to go frequently to Antwerp to purchase New Testaments. As he was returning from one of these expeditions, in 1529, Fisher, bishop of Rochester caused him to be arrested at Gravesend, and put him to the most cruel tortures, to make him deny his faith. But the martyr repeated with holy enthusiasm: "Salvation cometh by faith and not by works, and Christ giveth it to whomsoever He willeth." On the 20th of February 1530, in

---

[1] Latimer's *Remains*, pp. 297–309: *A letter written to the King for restoring again the liberty of reading the Holy Scriptures*: 1st Dec. 1530.

Maidstone, he was tied to the stake and there burnt to death.

Scarcely were Hitton's sufferings ended for bringing the Scriptures into England, when a vessel laden with New Testaments arrived at Colchester. The indefatigable Richard Bayfield, who accompanied these books, sold them in London, went back to the continent, and returned to England in November; but this time the Scriptures fell into the hands of Sir Thomas More. Bayfield, undismayed, again visited the Low Countries, and soon reappeared, bringing with him the New Testament and the works of almost all the Reformers. "How cometh it that there are so many New Testaments from abroad?" asked Tunstall of Packington; "you promised me that you would buy them all."—"They have printed more since," replied the wily merchant; "and it will never be better so long as they have letters and stamps [type and dies]. My lord, you had better buy the stamps too, and so you shall be sure."

Instead of the stamps, the priests sought after Bayfield. The bishop of London could not endure this godly man. Having one day asked Bainham (who afterwards suffered martyrdom) whether he knew *a single individual* who, since the days of the apostles, had lived according to the true faith in Jesus Christ, the latter answered: "Yes, I know Bayfield." Being tracked from place to place, he fled from the house of his pious hostess, and hid himself at the binder's, where he was discovered, and thrown into the Lollards' tower.

As he entered the prison, Bayfield noticed a priest named Patmore, pale, weakened by suffering, and ready to sink under the ill-treatment of his jailers. Patmore, won over by Bayfield's piety, soon opened his heart to him. When rector of Much Hadham, in Hertfordshire, he had found the truth in Wycliffe's writings. "They have burnt his bones," he said, "but from his ashes have burst forth a well-spring of life." Delighting in good works, he used to fill his granaries with wheat and, when the markets were high, he would send his corn to them in such abundance as to bring down the prices. "It is contrary to the law of God to burn heretics," he said; and, growing bolder, he added: "I care no more for the pope's curse than for a bundle of hay."

His curate, Simon Smith, unwilling to imitate the disorderly lives of the priests, and finding Joan Bennore, the rector's servant, to be a discreet and pious person, desired to marry her. "God," said Patmore, "has declared marriage lawful for *all men;* and accordingly it is permitted to the priests in foreign parts." The rector alluded to Wittenberg, where he had visited Luther. After his marriage Smith and his wife quitted England for a season, and Patmore accompanied them as far as London.

The news of this marriage of a priest—a fact without precedent in England—made Stokesley throw Patmore into the Lollards' tower, and although he was ill, neither fire, light, nor any other comfort was granted him. The bishop and his vicar-general visited him alone in his prison, and endeavoured by their threats to make him deny his faith.

It was during these circumstances that Bayfield was thrust into the tower. By his Christian words he revived Patmore's languishing faith, and the latter complained to the king that the bishop of London prevented his feeding the flock which God had committed to his charge. Stokesley, comprehending whence Patmore derived his new courage, removed Bayfield from the Lollards' tower and shut him up in the coal-house, where he was fastened upright to the wall by the neck, middle and legs. The unfortunate gospeller passed his time in continual darkness, never lying down, never seated, but nailed as it were to the wall, and never hearing the sound of human voice. We shall see him hereafter issuing from this horrible prison to die on the scaffold. As for Patmore he remained in prison three years before he was released.

Patmore was not the only one in his family who suffered persecution; he had in London a brother named Thomas, a friend of John Tyndale, the younger brother of the celebrated reformer. Thomas had said that the truth of Scripture was at last reappearing in the world, after being hidden for many ages; and John Tyndale had sent five marks to his brother William, and received letters from him. Moreover, the two friends (who were both tradesmen) had distributed a great number of Testaments and other works. But their faith was not deeply rooted, and it was more out of sympathy for their brothers that they had believed; accordingly, Stokesley so completely entangled them that they confessed their "crime." More, acting through the Star Chamber, delighted at the opportunity which offered to cover the name of Tyndale with shame, was not satisfied with condemning the two friends to pay a fine of £100 each; he invented a new disgrace. He fastened to their dress some of the New Testaments which they had circulated, placed the two penitents on horseback with their faces towards the tail, and thus paraded them through the streets of London, exposed to the jeers and laughter of the populace. In this, More succeeded better than in his refutation of the reformer's writings.

From that time the persecution became more violent. Husbandmen, artists, tradespeople, and even noblemen, felt the cruel fangs of the clergy and of Sir Thomas More. They sent to jail a pious musician, Robert Lambe, who used to wander from town to town, singing to his harp a hymn in commendation of Martin Luther. A painter, named Edward Freese, a young man of ready wit, having been engaged to paint some hangings in a house in Colchester, wrote on the borders certain sentences of the Scripture. For this he was seized and taken to the bishop of London's palace at Fulham, and there imprisoned, where his chief nourishment was bread made mostly out of sawdust. His poor wife, who was pregnant, went down to Fulham to see her husband; but the bishop's porter had orders to admit no one, and the brute gave her so violent a kick, as to kill her unborn infant, and cause the mother's death not long after. The unhappy Freese was removed to the Lollards' tower, where he was put into chains, his hands only being left free. With these he took a piece of coal, and wrote some pious sentences on the wall: upon this he was manacled; but his wrists were so severely pinched that the flesh grew up higher than the irons. His intellect became disturbed; his hair in wild disorder soon covered his face, through which his eyes glared fierce and haggard. The want of proper food, bad treatment, his wife's death, and his lengthened imprisonment, entirely undermined his reason. When brought to St Paul's, he was kept three days without food; and when he appeared before the consistory the poor prisoner, silent and scarce able to stand, looked around and gazed upon the spectators, "like a wild man." The examination was begun, but to every question put to him Freese made the same answer: "My Lord is a good man." They could get nothing from him but this affecting reply. Alas! the light shone no more upon his understanding, but the love of Jesus was still in his heart. He did not fully recover his reason to his dying day. His brother, Valentine Freese, and his wife, gave their lives at one stake in York, for the testimony of Jesus Christ.

Terror began to spread far and wide. The most active evangelists had been compelled to flee to a foreign land; some of the most godly were in prison; and among those in high station there were many, and perhaps Latimer was one, who seemed willing to shelter themselves under an exaggerated moderation. But just as the persecution in London had succeeded in silencing the most timid, other voices more courageous were raised in the provinces. The city of Exeter was at that time in great agitation; placards had been discovered on the gates of the cathedral containing some of the principles of "the new doctrine." While the mayor and his officers were seeking after the author of these "blasphemies," the bishop and all his doctors, "as hot as coals," says the chronicler, "and enkindled as though they had been stung with a sort of wasps," were preaching in the most fiery style. On the following Sunday, during the sermon, two men who had been the busiest of all the city in searching for the author of the bills, were struck by the appearance of a person seated near them. "Surely, this fellow is the heretic," they said. But their neighbour's devotion, for he did not take his eyes off his book, quite put them out; they did not perceive that he was reading the New Testament in Latin.

This man, Thomas Bennet, was indeed the offender. Being converted at Cambridge by the preaching of Bilney, whose friend he was, he had gone to Torrington in Devonshire for fear of the persecution, and thence to Exeter and, after marrying to avoid unchastity (as he says) he became schoolmaster. Quiet, humble, courteous to everybody, and somewhat timid, Bennet had lived six years in that city without his faith being discovered. At last his conscience being awakened he resolved to fasten by night to the cathedral gates certain evangelical placards. "Everybody will read the writing," he thought, "and nobody will know the writer." He did as he had proposed.

Not long after the Sunday on which he had been so nearly

HH

discovered, the priests prepared a great pageant, and made ready to pronounce against the unknown heretic the great curse "with book, bell, and candle." The cathedral was crowded, and Bennet himself was among the spectators. In the middle stood a great cross on which lighted tapers were placed, and around it were gathered all the Franciscans and Dominicans of Exeter. One of the priests having delivered a sermon on the words: *There is an accursed thing in the midst of thee, O Israel*, the bishop drew near the cross and pronounced the curse against the offender. He took one of the tapers and said: "Let the soul of the unknown heretic, if he be dead already, be quenched this night in the pains of hell-fire, as this candle is now quenched and put out;" and with that he put out the candle. Then, taking off a second, he continued: "and let us pray to God, if he be yet alive, that his eyes be put out, and that all the senses of his body may fail him, as now the light of this candle is gone," extinguishing the second candle. After this, one of the priests went up to the cross to take it away. It fell, however, and the noise it made in falling re-echoing along the roof so frightened the spectators that they uttered a shriek of terror, and held up their hands to heaven, as if to pray that the divine curse might not fall on them. Bennet, a witness of this comedy, could not forbear smiling. "What are you laughing at?" asked his neighbours; "here is the heretic, here is the heretic, hold him fast." This created great confusion among the crowd, some shouting, some clapping their hands, others running to and fro, but, owing to the tumult, Bennet succeeded in making his escape.

The excommunication did but increase his desire to attack the Romish superstitions; and accordingly, before five o'clock the next morning (it was in the month of October 1530) his servant-boy fastened up again by his orders on the cathedral gates some placards similar to those which had been torn down. It chanced that a citizen going to early mass saw the boy and, running up to him, caught hold of him and pulled down the papers; and then, dragging the boy with one hand and with the placards in the other, he went to the mayor of the city. Bennet's servant was recognized; his master was immediately arrested, and put in the stocks, and in strong irons, "with as much favour as a dog would find," says Foxe.

Exeter seemed determined to make itself the champion of sacerdotalism in England. For a whole week, not only the bishop, but all the priests and friars of the city, visited Bennet night and day. But they tried in vain to prove to him that the Roman church was the true one. "God has given me grace to be of a better church," he said.—"Do you not know that ours is built upon St Peter?"—"The church that is built upon a man," he replied, "is the devil's church and not God's." His cell was continually thronged with visitors; and, in default of arguments, the most ignorant of the friars called the prisoner a heretic, and spat upon him. At length they brought to him a learned doctor of theology, who, they supposed, would infallibly convert him. "Our ways are God's ways," said the doctor gravely. But he soon discovered that theologians can do nothing against the Word of the Lord. "He only is my way," replied Bennet, "who saith, *I am the way, the truth, and the life.* In His *way* will I walk;—His *truth* will I embrace—His everlasting *life* will I seek."

He was condemned to be burnt; and More having transmitted the order *de comburendo* with the utmost speed, the priests placed Bennet in the hands of the sheriff on the 15th of January 1531, by whom he was conducted to the Livery-dole, a field outside the city, where the stake was prepared. When Bennet arrived at the place of execution, he briefly exhorted the people, but with such unction, that the sheriff's clerk, as he heard him, exclaimed: "Truly this is a servant of God." Two persons, however, seemed unmoved: they were Thomas Carew and John Barnehouse, both holding the station of gentlemen. Going up to the martyr, they exclaimed in a threatening voice: "Say, *Precor sanctam Mariam et omnes sanctos Dei.*"[1]—"I know no other advocate but Jesus Christ," replied Bennet. Barnehouse was so enraged at these words, that he took a furze-bush upon a pike and, setting it on fire, thrust it into the martyr's face, exclaiming: "Accursed heretic, pray to our Lady, or I will make you do it."—"Alas!" replied Bennet patiently, "trouble me not;" and then holding up his hands, he prayed: "Father, forgive them!" The executioners immediately set fire to the wood, and the most fanatical of the spectators, both men and women, seized with an indescribable fury, tore up stakes and

[1] Pray to holy Mary and all the saints of God.

bushes, and whatever they could lay their hands on, and flung them all into the flames to increase their violence. Bennet, lifting up his eyes to heaven, exclaimed: "Lord, receive my spirit." Thus died, in the sixteenth century, the disciples of the Reformation sacrificed by Henry VIII.

The priests, thanks to the king's sword, began to count on victory; yet schoolmasters, musicians, tradesmen, and even ecclesiastics, were not enough for them. They wanted nobler victims, and these were to be looked for in London. More himself, accompanied by the lieutenant of the Tower, searched many of the suspected houses. Few citizens were more esteemed in London than John Petit, the same who, in the house of commons, had so nobly resisted the king's demand about the loan. Petit was learned in history and in Latin literature: he spoke with eloquence, and for twenty years had worthily represented the city. Whenever any important affair was debated in parliament, the king, feeling uneasy, was in the habit of inquiring which side he took. This political independence, very rare in Henry's parliaments, gave umbrage to the King and his ministers. Petit, the friend of Bilney, Fryth, and Tyndale, had been one of the first in England to taste the sweetness of God's Word, and had immediately manifested that beautiful characteristic by which the gospel-faith makes itself known, namely, charity. He abounded in almsgiving, supported a great number of poor preachers of the gospel in his own country and beyond the seas; and whenever he noted down these generous aids in his books, he wrote merely the words: "Lent unto Christ." He, moreover, forbade his testamentary executors to call in these debts.

Petit was tranquilly enjoying the sweets of domestic life in his modest home in the society of his wife and two daughters, Blanche and Audrey, when he received an unexpected visit. One day, as he was praying in his chamber, a loud knock was heard at the street door. His wife opened it, but seeing Lord-chancellor More, she returned hurriedly to her husband, and told him that the lord-chancellor wanted him. More, who followed her, entered the chamber, and with inquisitive eye ran over the shelves of the library, but could find nothing suspicious. Presently he made as if he would retire, and Petit accompanied him. The chancellor stopped at the door and said to him: "You assert that you have none of these new books?"—"You have seen my library," replied Petit.—"I am informed, however," replied More, "that you not only read them, but pay for the printing." And then he added in a severe tone: "Follow the lieutenant." In spite of the tears of his wife and daughters this independent member of parliament was conducted to the Tower, and shut up in a damp dungeon where he had nothing but straw to lie upon. His wife went thither each day in vain, asking, with tears, permission to see him, or at least to send him a bed. The jailers refused her everything; and it was only when Petit fell dangerously ill that the latter favour was granted him. This took place in 1530; sentence was passed in 1531; we shall see Petit again in his prison. He left it, indeed, but only to sink under the cruel treatment he had there experienced.

Thus were the witnesses to the truth struck down by the priests, by Sir Thomas More, and by Henry VIII. A new victim was to be the cause of many tears. A meek and humble man, one dear to all the friends of the gospel, and whom we may regard as the spiritual father of the Reformation in England, was on the point of mounting the burning pile raised by his persecutors. Some time prior to Petit's appearance before his judges, which took place in 1531, an unusual noise was heard in the cell above him; it was Thomas Bilney whom they were conducting to the Tower. We left him at the end of 1528, after his fall. Bilney had returned to Cambridge tormented by remorse; his friends in vain crowded round him by night and by day; they could not console him, and even the Scriptures seemed to utter no voice but that of condemnation. Fear made him tremble constantly, and he could scarcely eat or drink. At length a heavenly and unexpected light dawned in the heart of the fallen disciple; a witness whom he had vexed—the Holy Spirit—spoke once more in his heart. Bilney fell at the foot of the cross, shedding floods of tears, and there he found peace. But the more God comforted him, the greater seemed his crime. One only thought possessed him, that of giving his life for the truth. He had shrunk from before the burning pile; its flames must now consume him. Neither the weakness of his body, which his long anguish had much increased, nor the cruelty of his enemies, nor his natural timidity, nothing could stop him: he strove for the martyr's crown. At ten o'clock one night, when every person in Trinity Hall was retiring to rest, Bilney called his friends round him, reminded them of his fall, and added: "You shall see me no more. . . . Do not stay me: my decision is formed, and I shall carry it out. My face is set to go to Jerusalem." Bilney repeated the words used by the evangelist, when he describes Jesus going up to the city where He was to be put to death. Having shaken hands with his brethren, this venerable man, the foremost of the evangelists of England in order of time, left Cambridge under cover of the night, and proceeded to Norfolk, to confirm in the faith those who had believed, and to invite the ignorant multitude to the Saviour. We shall not follow him in this last and solemn ministry; these facts and others of the same kind belong to a later date. Before the year 1531 closed in, Bilney, Bainham, Bayfield, Tewkesbury, and many others, struck by Henry's sword, sealed by their blood the testimony rendered by them to the perfect grace of Christ.

CHAPTER SIXTEEN

Wolsey Falls like Lucifer

(1530)

WHILE many pious Christians were languishing in the prisons of England, the great antagonist of the Reformation was disappearing from the stage of this world. We must return to Wolsey, who was still detained at Esher.

The cardinal, fallen from the summit of honours, was seized with those panic-terrors usually felt after their disgrace by those who have made a whole nation tremble, and he fancied an assassin lay hid behind every door. "This very night," he wrote to Cromwell on one occasion, "I was as one that should have died. If I might, I would not fail to come on foot to you, rather than this my speaking with you shall be put over and delayed. If the displeasure of my Lady Anne be somewhat assuaged, as I pray God the same may be, then I pray you exert all possible means of attaining her favour."

In consequence of this, Cromwell hastened down to Esher two or three days after taking his seat in parliament, and Wolsey, all trembling, recounted his fears to him. "Norfolk, Suffolk, and Lady Anne perhaps, desire my death. Did not Thomas Becket, an archbishop like me, stain the altar with his blood?" . . . Cromwell reassured him, and, moved by the old man's fears, asked and obtained of Henry an order of protection.

Wolsey's enemies most certainly desired his death; but it was from the justice of the three estates, and not by the assassin's dagger that they sought it. The House of Peers authorized Sir Thomas More, the dukes of Norfolk and Suffolk, and fourteen other lords, to prepare a bill of attainder against the cardinal-legate. They forgot nothing: that haughty formula, *Ego et rex meus*, I and my king, which Wolsey had often employed; his infringement of the laws of the kingdom; his monopolizing the church revenues; the crying injustice of which he had been guilty —as, for instance, in the case of Sir John Stanley, who was sent to prison until he gave up a lease to the son of a woman who had borne the cardinal two children; many families ruined to satisfy his avarice; treaties concluded with foreign powers without the king's order; his exactions, which had impoverished England; and the foul diseases and infectious breath with which he had polluted his majesty's presence. These were some of the forty-four grievances presented by the peers to the king, and which Henry sent down to the lower house for their consideration.

It was at first thought that nobody in the commons would undertake Wolsey's defence, and it was generally expected that he would be given up to the vengeance of the law (as the bill of attainder prayed) or, in other words, to the axe of the executioner. But one man stood up and prepared, though alone, to defend the cardinal: this was Cromwell. The members asked of each other who the unknown man was; he soon made himself known. His knowledge of facts, his familiarity with the laws, the force of his eloquence, and the moderation of his language, surprised the house. Wolsey's adversaries had hardly aimed a blow before the defender had already parried it. If any charge was brought forward to which he could not reply, he proposed an adjournment until the next day, departed for Esher at the end of the sitting, conferred with Wolsey, returned during the night, and next morning reappeared in the commons with fresh arms. Cromwell carried the house with him; the attainder failed, and Wolsey's defender took his station among the statesmen of England. This victory, one of the greatest triumphs of parliamentary eloquence at that period, satisfied both the ambition and the gratitude of Cromwell. He was now firmly fixed in the king's favour, esteemed by the commons, and admired by the people: circumstances which furnished him with the means of bringing to a favourable conclusion the emancipation of the church of England.

The ministry, composed of Wolsey's enemies, was annoyed at the decision of the lower house, and appointed a commission to examine into the matter. When the cardinal was informed of this he fell into new terrors. He lost all appetite and desire of sleep, and a fever attacked him at Christmas. "The cardinal will be dead in four days," said his physician to Henry, "if he receives no comfort shortly from you and Lady Anne."—"I would not lose him for twenty thousand pounds," exclaimed the king. He desired to preserve Wolsey in case his old minister's consummate ability should become necessary, which was by no means unlikely. Henry gave the doctor his portrait in a ring, and Anne, at the king's desire, added the tablet of gold that hung at her girdle. The delighted cardinal placed the presents on his bed and, as he gazed on them, he felt his strength return. He was removed from his miserable dwelling at Esher to the royal palace at Richmond; and before long he was able to go into the park, where every night he read his breviary.

Ambition and hope returned with life. If the king desired to destroy the papal power in England, could not the proud cardinal preserve it? Might not Thomas Wolsey do under Henry VIII what Thomas Becket had done under Henry II? His see of York, the ignorance of the priests, the superstition of the people, the discontent of the great—all would be of service to him; and indeed, six years later, 40,000 men were under arms in a moment in Yorkshire to defend the cause of Rome. Wolsey, strong in England by the support of the nation (such at least was his opinion), aided without by the pope and the continental powers, might give the law to Henry and crush the Reformation.

The king having permitted him to go to York, which he had never yet visited although he had been Archbishop of York since 1514, Wolsey prayed for an increase to his archiepiscopal revenues, which amounted, however, to four thousand pounds sterling. Henry granted him a thousand marks, and the cardinal, shortly before Easter, 1530, departed with a train of 160 persons. He thought it was the beginning of his triumph.

Wolsey took up his abode at Cawood Castle, Yorkshire, one of his archiepiscopal residences, and strove to win the affections of the people. This prelate, once "the haughtiest of men," says George Cavendish, the man who knew him and served him best, became quite a pattern of affability. He kept an open table, distributed bounteous alms at his gate, said mass in the village churches, went and dined with the neighbouring gentry, gave splendid entertainments, and wrote to several princes imploring their help. It is even asserted by Edward Hall, a chronicler who was a contemporary of Wolsey, that he requested the pope to excommunicate Henry VIII. All being thus prepared, he thought he might make his solemn entry into York, preparatory to his enthronement, which was fixed for Monday the 7th of November.

Every movement of his was known at court; every action was canvassed, and its importance exaggerated. "We thought we had brought him down," some said, "and here he is rising up again." Henry himself was alarmed. "The cardinal, by his detestable intrigues," he said, "is conspiring against my crown, and plotting both at home and abroad." Wolsey's destruction was resolved upon.

The morning after All Saints' day (Friday, 4th November, 1530) the earl of Northumberland, attended by a numerous escort, arrived at Cawood, where the cardinal was still residing. He was the same Percy whose affection for Anne Boleyn had been thwarted by Wolsey; and there may have been design in Henry's choice. The cardinal eagerly moved forward to meet this unexpected guest, and, impatient to know the object of his mission, took him into his bedchamber, under the pretence of changing his travelling dress. They both remained some time standing at a window without uttering a word; the earl looked confused and agitated, whilst Wolsey endeavoured to repress his emotion. But at last, with a strong effort, Northumberland laid his hand upon the arm of his former master, and with a low voice said: "My lord, I arrest you for high treason." The cardinal remained speechless, as if stunned. He was kept a prisoner in his room.

It is doubtful whether Wolsey was guilty of the crime with which he was charged. We may believe that he entertained the idea of some day bringing about the triumph of the popedom in England, even should it cause Henry's ruin; but perhaps this was all. But an idea is not a conspiracy, although it may rapidly expand into one.

More than three thousand persons (attracted, not by hatred, like the Londoners, when Wolsey departed from Whitehall, but by enthusiasm) collected the next day before the castle to salute the cardinal. "God save your grace!" they shouted on every side, and a numerous crowd escorted him at night; some carried torches in their hands, and all made the air re-echo with their cries. The unhappy prelate was conducted to Sheffield Park, the residence of the earl of Shrewsbury. Some days after his arrival, the faithful Cavendish ran to him, exclaiming: "Good news, my lord! Sir William Kingston and twenty-four of the guard are come to escort you to his majesty."—"Kingston!" exclaimed the cardinal, turning pale, "Kingston!" and then, slapping his hand on his thigh, he heaved a deep sigh. This news had crushed his mind. One day a fortune-teller, whom he consulted, had told him: "*You shall have your end at Kingston;* and from that time the cardinal had carefully avoided the town of Kingston-on-Thames. But now he thought he understood the prophecy. . . . Kingston, constable of the Tower, was about to cause his death. They left Sheffield Park; but fright had given Wolsey his death-blow. Several times he was near falling from his mule, and on the third day, when they reached Leicester Abbey, he said as he entered: "Father abbot, I am come hither to leave my bones among you;" and immediately took to his bed. This was on Saturday the 26th of November.

On Monday morning, tormented by gloomy forebodings, Wolsey asked what was the time of day. "Past eight o'clock," replied Cavendish.—"That cannot be," said the cardinal, "eight o'clock. . . . No! for by eight o'clock you shall lose your master." At six on Tuesday, Kingston having come to inquire about his health, Wolsey said to him: "I shall not live long."— "Be of good cheer," rejoined the governor of the Tower.— "Alas, Master Kingston," exclaimed the cardinal, "if I had served God as diligently as I have served the king, he would not have given me over in my grey hairs!" and then he added with downcast head: "This is my just reward." What a judgment upon his own life!

On the very threshold of eternity (for he had but a few minutes to live) the cardinal summoned up all his hatred against the Reformation, and made a last effort. The persecution was too slow to please him: "Master Kingston," he said, "attend to my last request: tell the king that I conjure him in God's name to destroy this new pernicious sect of Lutherans." And then, with astonishing presence of mind in this his last hour, Wolsey described the misfortunes which the Hussites had, in his opinion, brought upon Bohemia; and then, coming to England, he recalled the times of Wycliffe and Sir John Oldcastle. He grew animated; his dying eyes yet shot forth fiery glances. He trembled lest Henry VIII, unfaithful to the pope, should hold out his hand to the reformers. "Master Kingston," said he, in conclusion, "the king should know that if he tolerates heresy, God will take away his power, and we shall then have mischief upon mischief . . . barrenness, scarcity, and disorder to the utter destruction of this realm."

Wolsey was exhausted by the effort. After a momentary silence, he resumed with a dying voice: "Master Kingston, farewell! My time draweth on fast. Forget not what I have said and charged you withal; for when I am dead ye shall peradventure remember my words better." It was with difficulty he uttered these words; his tongue began to falter, his eyes became fixed, his sight failed him; he breathed his last. At the same minute the clock struck *eight*, and the attendants standing round his bed looked at each other in affright. It was the 29th of November 1530.

Thus died the man once so much feared. Power had been his idol: to obtain it in the state, he had sacrificed the liberties of England; and to win it or to preserve it in the church, he had fought against the Reformation. If he encouraged the nobility in the luxuries and pleasures of life, it was only to render them more supple and more servile; if he supported learning, it was only that he might have a clergy fitted to keep the laity in their leading-strings. Ambitious, intriguing, and impure of life, he had been as zealous for the sacerdotal prerogative as the austere Becket; and by a singular contrast, a shirt of hair was found on the body of this voluptuous man. The aim of his life had been to raise the papal power higher than it had ever been before, at the very moment when the Reformation was attempting to bring it down; and to take his seat on the pontifical throne with more than the authority of a Hildebrand. Wolsey, as pope, would have been the man of his age; and in the political world he would have done for the Roman primacy what the celebrated Loyola did for it soon after by his fanaticism. Obliged to renounce this idea, worthy only of the middle ages, he had desired at least to save the popedom in his own country; but here again he had failed. The pilot who had stood in England at the helm of the Romish church was thrown overboard, and the ship, left to itself, was about to founder. And yet, even in death, he did not lose his courage. The last throbs of his heart had called for victims; the last words from his failing lips, the last message to his master, his last testament had been . . . Persecution! This testament was to be only too faithfully executed.

The epoch of the fall and death of Cardinal Wolsey, which is the point at which we halt, was not only important because it ended the life of a man who had presided over the destinies of England, and had endeavoured to grasp the sceptre of the world, but it is of especial consequence because then three movements were accomplished, from which the great transformation of the sixteenth century was to proceed. Each of these movements has its characteristic result.

The first is represented by Cromwell. The supremacy of the pope in England was about to be wrested from him, as it was in all the reformed churches. But a step further was taken in England. That supremacy was transferred to the person of the king. Wolsey had exercised as vicar-general a power till then unknown. Unable to become pope at the Vatican, he had made himself a pope at Whitehall. Henry had permitted his minister to raise this hierarchical throne by the side of his own. But he had soon discovered that there ought not to be two thrones in England, or at least not two kings. He had dethroned Wolsey; and, resolutely seating himself in his place, he was about to assume at Whitehall that tiara which the ambitious prelate had prepared for himself. Some persons, when they saw this, exclaimed that if the papal supremacy were abolished, that of the Word of God ought alone to be substituted. And, indeed, the true Reformation is not to be found in this first movement.

The second, which was essential to the renewal of the church, was represented by Cranmer, and consisted particularly in re-establishing the authority of holy Scripture. Wolsey did not fall alone, nor did Cranmer rise alone: each of these two men carried with him the system he represented. The fabric of Roman traditions fell with the first; the foundations of the holy Scriptures were laid by the second; and yet, while we render all justice to the sincerity of the Cambridge doctor, we must not be blind to his weaknesses, his subserviency, and even a certain degree of negligence, which, by allowing parasitical plants to shoot up here and there, permitted them to spread over the living rock of God's Word. Not in this movement, then, was found the Reformation with all its energy and all its purity.

The third movement was represented by the martyrs. When the church takes a new life, it is fertilized by the blood of its confessors; and being continually exposed to corruption, it has constant need to be purified by suffering. Not in the palaces of Henry VIII, nor even in the councils where the question of throwing off the papal supremacy was discussed, must we look for the true children of the Reformation; we must go to the Tower of London, to the Lollards' towers of St Paul's and of Lambeth, to the other prisons of England, to the bishops' cellars, to the fetters, the stocks, the rack, and the stake. The godly men who invoked the sole intercession of Christ Jesus, the only Head of His people, who wandered up and down, deprived of everything, gagged, scoffed at, scourged, and tortured, and who, in the midst of all their tribulations, preserved their Christian patience, and turned, like their Master, the eyes of their faith towards Jerusalem—these were the disciples of the Reformation in England. The purest church is the church under the cross.

The father of this church in England was not Henry VIII. When the king cast into prison or gave to the flames men like Hitton, Bennet, Patmore, Petit, Bayfield, Bilney, and many others, he was not "the father of the Reformation of England," as some have so falsely asserted; he was its executioner.

The church of England was foredoomed to be in its renovation a church of martyrs; and the true father of this church is our Father which is in heaven.

[*An Index will be found at the end of Volume Two*]